Youth in Contemporary India

Parul Bansal

Youth in Contemporary India

Images of Identity and Social Change

Springer

Parul Bansal
Psychology
Lady Shri Ram College for Women
New Delhi, India

ISBN 978-81-322-0714-6 ISBN 978-81-322-0715-3 (eBook)
DOI 10.1007/978-81-322-0715-3
Springer New Delhi Heidelberg New York Dordrecht London

Library of Congress Control Number: 2012946204

Printed on acid-free paper

Springer is part of Springer Science+Business Media (www.springer.com)

To

My Parents, who made me who I am

and

Nitin, who believed I could be more!

To develop a sense of identity and fidelity in youth is a joint task of the consistency of individual life history and the ethical potency of the historical process. . . . . .Diversity and fidelity are polarized: they make each other significant and keep each other alive. Fidelity without a sense of diversity can become an obsession and a bore; diversity without a sense of fidelity, an empty relativism.

Erik H. Erikson
Identity: Youth and Crisis

Foreword

This book is a research text about youth in India. It explores their choices, roles, commitments, values, goals, motivations, emotions, desires and fantasies. It attempts to formulate and represent their life stories by delving in their inner worlds.

My Personal Journey

The idea of this book was born out of a coalescing of disparate perceptions, emotions and memories amassed over my lifetime (albeit not too long) that emerged in the form of an acute consciousness in my youth (somewhat protracted and still ongoing…). Struggles with myself were sustained in this stage by a permissive family environment and stimulating educational context. After having lived much of my life in an unselfconscious manner, feeling quite comfortable in my own skin, the moment of making a career decision at the end of college posed a challenge to my selfhood. Faced with a decisive choice for the future, I stood transfixed to the ground. There was ambivalence towards following a popular path which neither offered passion nor surprise, but at the same time I felt fright about being 'too out of place'. This was the time when I began to realise that growing up in a middle-class family had afforded me freedoms and opportunities but at the same time had a structuring effect on my aspirations and imagination. While I was too sensitive to follow a modish trend which didn't appeal to me personally, I was also not rebellious enough to break the mould. In the years that followed the decision that I took then of pursuing higher education which kept me in a sort of 'protracted youth', I have often returned back to that crisis experience to understand: Why was there a crisis in the first place? What did that crisis precipitate for me? What all led me to make the choice that I made then and the ones that I made before that event and in the subsequent years? Why do certain options remain psychologically unavailable to me? Many semi-deliberate strenuous moments of introspection (in individual and collective spaces) led me to revisit my past, come to memories of growing up, probe the influences of parental figures and family culture and compare them with the countervailing and/or reinforcing influences from extrafamilial influences. This was a bid to identify signs of certain evolving themes of feeling and mental life and also anticipate the future likelihood of continuing/changing 'how one has been and what one is doing'. This form of self-knowledge has been often experienced by me as quite tragicomic. For while it helped me make an interesting (at least to my own self) story of my life lived so far, which can be told and retold with some variations (depending upon the mood, viewpoint and audience setting), it also made me recognise my place in the world. It tells me at least for the foreseeable future 'where I belong', 'where I can belong' and 'where I don't belong'.

As one characteristically begins to become aware of the deep effects upon one's personality of one's family, society and culture, one is motivated to look at others to see how their lives are shaping up. As I looked around, observed and talked with my contemporaries, I was struck with the aspirational value of corporate world amidst parents and children alike. Having made the choice of pursuing social sciences over the professional fields of science and commerce in school itself and later deciding to make a living through academics, I often felt anomalous in the peer culture beset by frenetic competition for admission to the engineering and management institutes, especially the Indian Institutes of Technology and the Indian Institutes of Management, the lure of multi-lakh salaries, the glamour of jet-setting and globe-trotting lifestyle and ambitions of expedient vertical mobility. As a young lecturer in a Delhi University college, I have been questioned by successive batches of students younger to me by only a couple of years—'So. . .what do you want to do in life?'—and when I would respond that I would like to teach and research and basically have time for my own self and family, many of them would appear baffled, and few would even feel amused at what appeared to them as an 'uncool' choice of life. Over the years, I found that for a majority of students, their own aspirations are of meeting their 'tryst with destiny' with the corporate world in the diverse fields of management, law, media, advertising, marketing etc. and they are driven by the dream of making mega bucks. Thus, a part of my research trail was derived by a need to have a closer look at the lives of such young people whose primary concerns appeared to be ensuring high academic performance, securing admissions in the best of professional institutes and getting plush jobs —to understand their struggles and motivations. Such youth has been termed as the corporate youth in the research because of their interests in the business world of private profit. On the other end, I have been intrigued by young people who have been making credible appeal to social change and are sociopolitically active and been inquisitive about finding out what 'activated' them and what got 'activated' in them? In my mind, they appeared as idealised images that were rebelling against the pervasive middle-class apathetic attitude to dehumanising social reality that surrounds us. They have been questioning and moving beyond the self-centred vision of elite living. Coming from a middle-class background with its conflicts of convention and liberalism, ambitions and ideals and wants and limitations, my own non-participation (or non-possibility of participation) in the fantasised rebellion must have created its own dynamic. This heterogeneous group of participants is referred to as humanist youth in the research because of their involvement in the cause of welfare of humanity.

About the Book

Youth, identity and social change are interrelated phenomena. The self-definitional process of identity formation utilises the resource of strong identifications made in one's personal past and relies on new possibilities of workable roles (vocation, relationships) offered in young adulthood. Societal changes affect the process of identity formation. Identity confusion is exacerbated and embraces a much larger population of young people in a historical period of rapid change when traditional values and roles break down, adult support for youth's search for an identity lacks and the guidelines of acceptable and desirable behaviour during youth phase become blurred and contradictory. Just as social change affects the lives of youth, the young also drive social change. Societies need the energy, imagination and dynamism of youth to create new forms of social order either based on repudiation of old world view or renewal of traditional values.

This book is intended to provide few illustrations of nature of social change taking place in present-day urban Indian society through in-depth study of identity process in youth and their psychosocial contexts. Family is seen as the social group where the impact of social change can be understood in great depth. In a collectivist culture like India, family is considered as the central institution of socialisation and a psychological locus in the lives of a vast majority of people. Research provides evidence that in collectivist cultural groups, individuals are more compliant and other directed. There is high commitment to family values and subordination of individual needs to family needs. An attempt is made here to examine how intergenerational relationships within Indian urban middle-class families are structured in contemporary times of social change. Are Indian families changing in response to exposure to market forces, globalising influences and increased pressures for achievement and competition? Are they allowing for greater expression of assertiveness and self-direction amongst children? What is the nature of feminine self of mother and masculine authority of father with which youth are identifying as well as seeking freedom from? Through a narrative study of lives, an effort has been made to trace the multivariate expressions of individuality vis-à-vis parental traditions amongst the Indian youth. The search is to find how the psychological tendencies of autonomy and relatedness are finding their balance within their life space. Such an investigation allows for verification of claims that cultures across the world are increasingly converging in outlook under the forces of globalisation and social change.

A simultaneous focus of this book is to understand whether youth are engineering social change through an exploration of the kinds of social values and roles, goals and aspirations and dreams and desires that they have. The young position themselves in various discourses offering resistance or conformity to the dominant social establishment. In this work, an endeavour has been made to examine how different sections of urban youth relate and engage with the liberalisation-privatisation-globalisation (LPG) model of growth based on ever increasing cycles of production and consumption. What are the educational-vocational-ideological choices they are making? What social ideals and meanings are they reproducing? What are the kinds of stresses, tensions and splits they experience?

Study of identity in times of continuous and rapid social change also puts to question the definition and understanding of the term 'identity'. One is compelled to ask what are the more appropriate metaphors to describe the experience of identity—sameness or transformation, continuity or disjuncture, coherence or diversity, essential core or performance? In the present work, attempt has been made to work with an as-well-as approach rather than either-or approach. While engaging with the many-sided, fluid and contingent nature of identity process, what self-elements cohere and what endures in the lives of people is also reflected upon. Erik H. Erikson, whose seminal work on identity straddles the conceptual fence between the intrapsychic and the contextual, states that identity in youth is experienced as 'I am what I care to do, be and become – even in changing roles' (1950). He elucidates that even an actor is convincing in many roles only if and when there is in him an actor's core identity and craftsmanship (1974). Robert Jay Lifton, a psychohistorical thinker, also emphasises change and flux rather than stability. However, he separates himself from those observers, postmodern or otherwise, who equate this plurality with disappearance of self. Rather, he sees self as an integrative experiential reality, an agency and guide of our ethical action. He seeks to make the claim that the self strives to be both fluid and grounded, however tenuous that combination (1993).

Acknowledgements

After having crafted this book, a process which fructified painstakingly yet excitingly, as I look back to acknowledge all those who have been co-travellers, supporters and guides, I am overwhelmed with memories, impressions and emotions. So many people have contributed to my thought process, facilitated my expressions and articulations, made me into who I am and shaped the work as it eventually turned out to be.

I, first and foremost, wish to acknowledge that the seed of this work was planted and nurtured by the writings of thinkers like Erik H. Erikson and D. W. Winnicott. Speaking through their work, they have become luminous presences and enabling teachers for me. Their musings on self and identity have made me sensitive to the delicate relation between insight in work and insight into the self.

With a deep sense of gratitude, I wish to recognise and thank all the research participants who made the research work (on which this book is based) possible. By sharing their lives and including me in their life worlds, by helping me build network of contacts and by making relevant suggestions and recommendations about the directions the work can take—they involved themselves with the research process validating it as a meaningful activity for all of us. By listening to their stories, I learnt much about different shades of life, till now unknown, and could critically engage with our theories and their relation with 'living'. Without doubt, I grew immensely, both emotionally and intellectually, through my association with each one of them.

Turning to my teachers, I would like to thank my first 'real' teacher of psychology, Dr. Rachana Johri, who has effectively introduced generations of students including me to the realm of 'psychosocial' thinking in psychology. Over my years of association with her, I found in her an evolving teacher and supportive colleague who preserves in herself the tensions of keeping alive theoretical and methodological pluralism in the discipline. A very special teacher, Dr. Honey Oberoi Vahali or Honey Ma'am, as she is affectionately referred to by all her students, has been a constant source of knowledge, inspiration and emotional comfort for me. For me, she embodies the values of excellence, commitment to work, honesty, a sense of balance and humanism, and these are the qualities that I strive to bring to my work and being. With fond regard, I remember my teacher Dr. Ashok Nagpal, a person of remarkably creative mind and astute clinical sensitivities. It is to an internalised image of him that I gratefully attribute my emerging capacity to work through flux and chaos which experiential inquiries like this bring with them. His impassioned search for truth and deep understanding into life processes is an exciting endeavour which holds my curiosity and engages my playful spirit. I am especially grateful to Prof. Mishra for his mentoring and guidance. He has always encouraged and helped me challenge my boundaries. I look forward to a continuing mutually fulfilling work companionship with my teachers and guides.

With the deepest gratitude, I recognise the unbounded support, love and care of my parents and sister without which this work would not have been possible. My parents created a highly conducive physical and psychological ambiance for me that enabled me to be devoted to the work. Always felt as non-demanding, both of you have patiently and graciously borne my failures in attending to your needs. My mother's hopeful spirit of persistence towards a goal and my father's sensitive psychological mindedness have been immensely formative influences on me. Nitin, my husband, has been instrumental in prodding, pushing and encouraging me to write this book. Thank you is a small word for the great strength I derive out of the feeling that you share my dreams. My second set of parents, my in-laws, has been most supportive of my efforts. Along with them, my two dear friends, Rakhi and Indu, helped me see through some of the most difficult phases of this work. Friends, big thanks to both of you for I could always partake in your positive spirits. The collective belief of my family and friends in me and my capabilities are my internal sources of strength and hope. Besides, I always felt the blessings of my grandparents around me keeping my morale high. Bade Papa, you have been an inspiration behind my academic endeavours. I hope I am able to do all of you proud.

My sincere thanks to Prof. Meenakshi Gopinath, the principal of my college, Lady Shri Ram College for Women, for the consideration she has shown towards me. She has in her own ways mentored and shaped many of my ideas and sensibilities that framed this work. Also to my students whose youthfulness kept me engaged with the area of work. Finally, I am truly grateful to the editorial team at Springer Publications, especially Sagarika, for understanding the spirit of this work, allowing me the creative freedom to shape this text and providing useful inputs.

And finally, to God who keeps me in his grace; this is because of You!

Contents

Part I
Foundations

Introduction

What Are the Aims of the Book?

India is witnessing what the demographers call a 'youth bulge'. The youth bulge consists of large number of adolescents and young adults who are born when fertility is high followed by declining number of children born after fertility declines. Some scholars have described youth bulge as a situation in which 20% or more of the population is in the age group 15–24 years. In the case of India, approximately 19.1% of the total population falls in this age bracket. The median age of Indian population is 26.2 years. Such an age structure of population has made Indian youth target of special attention. There is increasing requirement to understand the special identity needs of adolescents and young adults in liberalising and globalising India and to comprehend the assets and liabilities of having such a large young population. Media regularly covers varied aspects of lives of the young, be it the salary packages that the IIM graduates get, their attitudes on issues of personal and political relevance, the leisure time activities they pursue and so on. From these depictions comes alive a phenomenon of youth which is multifaceted; they are seen as sources of hope as well as signs of moral decay, heralded as involved in the spirit of the era and also defiled for being alienated and confused. *So then questions like – What is urban youth? What are the preoccupations and concerns of this generation growing in liberalising–globalising India? How are they living their lives and participating in the social reality around them?—are raised everywhere.*

Adolescence and its extension into youth is a developmental phase between childhood and adulthood. It is a stage in which young persons are likely to be simultaneously confronted with multiple and diverse tasks, all of which are instrumental to the 'way of life' that they develop as they mature as adults. The young grapple with developmental tasks such as coping with pubertal changes in the body and the resulting strong sexual drive; choosing a vocation that is consistent with one's favoured capacities on one hand and with available opportunities on the other; finding a meaning in life by choosing from a variety of ideologies, beliefs and values to which one has been exposed; and developing a personal style of love and care amenable to a particular mode of intimacy and parenthood. Negotiations with these facets of growth move a young individual towards a differentiated and integrated sense of individuality experienced as identity. In an affirmative sense, identity is felt as having a sense of direction and an inner assuredness of recognition of those who are important. Identity formation is a self-definitional process which involves an assimilation of native temperament, trained capacities and significant identifications into a configuration that provides a semblance of internal coherence and meaningful relatedness to the outside world. *This book is concerned with understanding the psychological dynamics of conformity, rebellion, individuation, initiative, relatedness, directionality and ideological values which pervade youthhood and has attempted to describe them as emerging out of the interplay between universal processes of human development and the Indian cultural milieu, specifically the Indian family. By virtue of having a psychosocial perspective, the work explores how the interlinked growth contexts of family, education and work in neoliberal high-tech global economy shape and organise the experiential reality and developmental potential of young men and women in contemporary India.*

In the process of growth, one of the key issues young persons have to confront and resolve in some fashion deals with their strivings towards increased autonomy and a rearrangement of their previous relationship of dependence upon parental figures. In the context of a collectivist culture like India where family is the primary unit of socialisation, the text is interested in addressing the following questions: Are the young in India moving towards more individuated and autonomous positions vis-à-vis the parental authority? How much do they feel themselves to be defined by 'internalised parent'? Are Indian families providing opportunities for making new beginnings to this generation or are they insisting on continuation of culture, lifestyle and choices of the previous generation? Is the youth able to take chances with oneself and explore possibilities within themselves? How their life trajectories may be similar/different from their parents?

The need for a coherent worldview intensifies during youth and is usually met through the solidarity of fellow mates in domains of inspired activity. The youth try out various role possibilities and worldviews available in one's historical times to etch out a vision of future inclusive of the remnants of one's past. They want a sense of purpose, meaning and orderliness in their existence. As a work endeavouring to be a study of youth in its historical context, the book also reflects on the ideological elements that lend coherence to the diverse youth identities in India. Through an exploration of their orientations towards competition, materialism, dissent, democracy, social responsibility and power, it attempts to respond to the popular perception that Indian youth are conformist, alienated from social realities and living for immediate returns on traditional goals of status and power to the exclusion of the pursuit of knowledge and creativity. The questions raised in this work are: Is the neo-liberal capitalist ideology characterising the business world being internalised by the young people? How are the concepts of money, drive for achievement, competitive individualism and consumption woven into their emerging selfhood? Are there young men and women who are involved in serious, constructive appraisal of values, attitudes and current realities? What are the images of intervention in the social world found in their thought frameworks and work activities? What are the key concepts/principles/intellectual and ideological perspectives that animate their debates, conversations and imagination regarding social change?

In its essence, this book attempts to explore how the sense of individuality in contemporary Indian youth is seeking its own balance of relationality with parental figures and cohesion with social order? *At one level, it endeavours to understand whether and how a sense of psychological individuation is being negotiated by the young Indians from within familial embeddedness.* The text tries to refresh the cultural understandings of psychic potentials by presenting young India's expressions of individuality. *At another level, it tries to comprehend the nature and process of engagement of youth with different definitions, goals and values of social system through which they come to evolve their own self-definitions and relationship with the neo-liberal sociopolitical order—challenging, resistive, conforming and ingratiating.* It attempts to understand how are social realities such as competition, individualism, materialism and democracy intrapsychically represented. *At a broader level, the work reflects on the nature of intergenerational continuity and change due to social change in Indian society.* In this endeavour, the theoretical and methodological precepts of psychoanalysis have been the bedrock. Psychoanalytic thinking underscores the inherent affectivity of social life. It provides an axis between ebb and flow of psychical life and society. The Eriksonian framework is particularly instructive in this regard as it keeps alive the mutuality of psyche and culture, that is, how within a given sociocultural order particular psychological tendencies develop and which later influence the culture's institutions and social forms. An individual's identity conflicts and crisis are reflective of the delicate interplay between the 'old' and 'new' elements in the social world. His/her solutions to such crises are then the driver of social change.

What Is the Methodological Approach of the Book?

This book is based on a qualitative research inquiry about the lives of young men and women in urban middle class India today. *Methodologically, the research work was a psychoanalytically informed, process-oriented, context-sensitive work using in-depth, exploratory interview method.* Research is a form of human curiosity. It is an invitation to revisit phenomenon of interest, renew observations and impressions about it, re-examine perspectives, reinterpret the emergent meanings and re-present them in imaginative ways. Research is, thus, an exciting journey to refresh our visions and articulations of diverse aspects of the world. As a qualitative inquiry, the research process here involved striving to feel and understand the life of participants by empathically entering their subjective worlds as they begin to narrate their experiences in the interview space. The researcher engaged with the memories, experiential segments and significant incidents in the participant's life so as to discern some patterns and create a narrative. Using the psychoanalytic method of listening, the researcher was attentive to the feeling states of the participants as well as of one's own. This is integral to discerning the meaning of the communication. Disciplined exploration of one's own feelings, reactions and emotional states by the researcher during the interaction gave clues about the emotional world of the participants. The interest in a research like the present one is not in finding the 'historical' or factual truth. Spence (1982) holds that historical truth is impossible to access after the fact, as it is subject to numerous revisions and interpretations. What is important is how the self reconstructs a particular happening, a metaphorical elaboration of what was 'fact'. It is the way the self constructs meaning or organises associations to create narratives that is of significance here. This narrative of the self is the 'narrative truth' which provides access to subjective realities of participants. It is the act of telling which turns inarticulate experience into a more tangible sense of reality. As Sartre says in *Nausea*, 'Nothing happens while you live... But everything starts to change when you tell about a life' (1965, pp. 56–57). Such phenomenological, research reworks notions of generalisability, validity and reliability. Generalisability is often established at the level of abstract explanations for a class of participants rather than necessarily at the level of concrete behaviours. Also, the attempt in such works is to appreciate and retain the typicality and uniqueness of life, at the same time, gathering observations and lived processes which are shared amongst participants. The meaning of validity goes beyond the traditional meaning of correlation of results with an independent criterion. Instead, it hinges on what do objects, events and behaviours mean to people engaged in and with them. Such research in understanding contextual behaviour tries to establish interpretive validity. Reliability does not mean replicability. Rather, it means internal logic and adequacy of explanatory formulations.

What is the relevance of this book?

This inquiry has contemporary relevance in trying to understand the psychological condition of urban middle class Indian youth and the directions they are taking in their lives that have an impact on the nation. The thinking and behavioural patterns of large middle classes shaped by being at the frontiers of the project of modernisation have a trickle-down effect on the masses below them. Most susceptible to the pressure of social change, the identity conflicts and resolutions of members of this class are indicative of direction of social change in India.

Such a work also provides insights into the process of internalisation of cultural aspects by the growing individual through the mediating environments of family, peers, education and work. How the personal and social become intertwined? It tries to bridge psychological development and cultural–historical change—the reciprocal relationship between social, technological and cultural changes and human development. It is through such inquiries that we can perhaps move towards a better understanding of the psychology of cultural change.

The depth of psychological work of this nature is rather sparse in the Indian context. The rich and depth-oriented narratives of sections of Indian youths' lives offer multilayered understanding of challenges and conflicts endemic to their developmental stage and psychic condition. It, thus, has the potential of making theoretical and methodological contributions to the specialties of developmental, clinical and cultural psychology as well as to educational policy for youth.

In the field of qualitative research in psychology, there is a great lack of research texts which can exemplify the application of psychoanalytic theory and technique in research contexts. Its psychoanalytically informed methodology hopes to provide a novel understanding of how the psychoanalytic technique of listening and interpreting can be used beyond the clinical encounter.

The work is unique in the sense of looking at two divergent groups of young people who are engaged in different kinds of vocational and ideological pursuits. Examining the lives of young men and women who constitute the ideological polarity characterising the current historical moment in the liberalising–globalising India allows us to generate possible understandings of how engagement with different kinds of definitions and visions of social change affect the evolving self-process of youth. Such inquiry chips away the monolithic notion of new-age youth as conformist. It may also enable us to reflect on the relation between socio-historic times and youth dynamics.

How Is This Book Organised?

The book has four sections. The first part lays down the foundation of the research text. It has the introduction and an overview of the conceptual and methodological precepts underlying the text. The overview, firstly, endeavours to provide definitional understanding of the stage of youth. Then, it tries to sketch phenomenological realities of the inner world of young persons. It traces the multiple possibilities of identity (student, soldier, rebel, delinquent, patient) with which the young experiment. The third subpart brings forth the definitional aspects of identity that underlie the conceptualisation of research text. It examines the theoretical formulations of thinkers whose writings and ideas form the bedrock of this work. The research has consulted frameworks of Erik H. Erikson, Robert J. Lifton, Adam Phillips, Margaret Mahler, Donald W. Winnicott, Heinz Kohut and Ruthellen Josselson. The conceptual underpinning is that, especially in youth, the self-delineating process is marked by contingency, multiplicity and polyvocality. Relatively freer to take chances with themselves and their environment, paths of the young are strewn with twists and turns, experiments and possibilities. Their search for meaning and authenticity may lead them to unexpected forays, unknown explorations and untried jobs. Need for cohesiveness of self, however, does not preclude the tendencies towards multiplicity of involvements with varied kinds of people, ideas and activities. Rather, it strives for a balancing act between responsive shape-shifting, on the one hand, and efforts to consolidate and cohere, on the other. An adept self-process can maintain a certain equilibrium that allows for flexible adaptation. The fourth subpart explains the dynamics of autonomy and relationality as critical to identity formation. In the fifth section, a psychoanalytic statement on self–other relationship is presented which serve as useful guide in our search for forms and spaces of individualised self-expression in Indian youth's lives, both self-created and culturally given. This sets the stage for review of culturally contextualised formulations of Sudhir Kakar and Allan Roland on Indian identity in the sixth section. Relevant research works on themes of development of ideological concepts in stage of youth and process of identity formation amongst women have been presented in the next two segments. They have been found to be useful in providing methodological directions as well as descriptions of human subjective experience. In the next two subparts, a framework of research methodology has been formulated. This book has argued in favour of the qualitative research paradigm that opens new vistas to explore the unique human subjective experience shaped by its historically specific culture, which is lost in the positivist paradigm amidst distantiated numbers and statistical figures. Making a case for narratives and life stories as insightful data sources of human and cultural behaviour, a note on the methodological process of research inquiry is presented. It fleshes out the psychoanalytic method of listening and interpreting. The context, aims and presentation of data are discussed thereafter.

Part II and III present the life stories of the participants. *Part II* consists of eight life stories of the corporate youth followed by a discussion of a few relevant identity-related themes. In *Part III*, eight life stories of the humanist youth are presented, the shared themes of which are discussed in the end.

Part IV concludes with few insights and reflections on experiential reality and developmental potential of youth in India. It also comments on psychosocial contexts of urban middle class young Indians that mould and organise their developmental experiences in contemporary times.

Identity in Youth: Conceptual and Methodological Underpinnings

An IIM graduate is offered the highest pay package of Rs.18 lakhs per annum by a U.S.-based M.N.C. He tells a reporter, 'Coming from a modest small town background, this is truly a dream come true for me and my family'.

The candidates contesting university elections manhandle the election officer and peer down smilingly from their posters that have been smeared on the flyovers all over the city. The elections witness a poor turnout of voters.

Thousands of aspirants queue up at the venue of audition for the talent hunt, few having given their exams a miss, trying to give themselves a chance to make a mark in the glamour world. 'I want to be the next Shahrukh Khan', declares an aspirant.

A theatre group of young persons present an eye-opening play on the political situation in a northeastern state. They struggle for 'justice' for the people in the state.

A young woman drifts from job to job, from one failed relationship to another, and is given to smoking and drinking and spending her life in a somewhat dissociated state. A general sense of confusion and purposelessness pervades her being.

A corporate employee gives up the lucrative job to work with underprivileged children, a vocation after his heart. 'Corporate culture alienated me from the true purpose of my life. I had to come back to this for myself'.

Two 18-year-old boys were held by police for hacking the websites and email passwords. They confessed to be doing it because they were 'bored of life and needed some thrill and excitement'.

The snippets above introduce us to the kaleidoscope of youth. Young men and women are most vigorously driven to respond to the diversity of roles, activities and values offered by societies in a bid to explore and create/take their place in the world. They are differentiated with regard to their experiences, their perspectives and their hopes for the future. They may respond to their social landscapes with enthusiasm, passion, idealism, indignation, protest, silence or apathy. They also evoke a rich variety of intense reactions from the others in the social order. On one hand, the youth are represented as reckless, irresponsible and uncommitted; on the other hand, as dedicated, deferential and conformist. Youth is lauded as a symbol of hope for the future while scorned as a threat to the existing society. While pushed to the margins of political power within established order, they attract serious attention as a site of commodification and a profitable market.

P. Bansal, *Youth in Contemporary India: Images of Identity and Social Change*,
DOI 10.1007/978-81-322-0715-3_1, © Springer India 2013

I

Definitional Aspects of Youth

Youth is one of the most interesting and keenly observed phenomena the world over. Many sociologists (Keniston 1971; Doughlas 1970; Moller 1968) have noted that prolongation of education due to the requirements of economic life in modern age has opened up opportunities for an extension of psychological development, which in turn is creating a new stage of life called youth. This is not to suggest that youth is in an absolute sense a new developmental stage and unique to the modern era. But what is 'new' is that this extended stage of life is being entered not by tiny minorities of young men and women but by large number of people.

Youth[1] as a biographical life stage is located between adolescence and adulthood. It is conceptualised as beginning with the end of secondary education, usually age 18 in American society, and ending in mid- to late 20s for most people as the experimentation of the period is succeeded by more enduring life choices (Arnett 1998). *It is distinct demographically and subjectively from adolescence (roughly from ages 10–17) and adulthood (beginning roughly since 30). Demographically speaking, it is a phase characterised by exceptionally high level of change and diversity.* For example, 20s are the years of frequent changes and transitions in occupation, educational status and personal relationships (Rindfuss 1991). The majority of adolescents do not believe that they have reached adulthood, and majority of people over 30 and older believe they have, but most people in their 20s see themselves as somewhere in between adolescence and adulthood: the majority answer 'in some respects yes and in some respects no' when asked whether they feel they have reached adulthood (Arnett 1997, 2001).

The definitional aspects of youth cannot, however, be easily settled with reference to age group and concepts of adolescence and adulthood. *Firstly*, the meaning of adulthood is under siege. More and more people at later stages of their lives want to feel, behave and appear as young (Cote and Allahar 1994). Increasingly, adult lifestyles have come to be characterised as pseudo-youth subcultures. Virtues of maturity and rationality compete with excitement and hedonism in the lives of contemporary adults. The musical tastes of parents and children are often the same. Their peership extends further to sometimes children bringing their parents up because in the altered historical conditions, parents can no longer serve as complete role models for their children. Hence, they are often more hesitant in their guidance to their children. Being a student is no longer unambiguously associated with a certain age as necessities of professional sphere impel adults

[1] This phase was originally termed youth by Keniston (1971). The more recent term for this phase of development is called emerging adulthood (Arnett and Taber 1994).

to return to school and act as students. In the knowledge society, skills and expertise become obsolete so rapidly that adult experience weighs light in front of youths' updated knowledge and proficiencies. In contemporary knowledge societies, the mantra is to be a 'learner' always.

Secondly, the transition to adulthood is becoming more individualised and diversified. In the traditional societies of the past and present, the constant developmental emphasis for adolescent persons is to learn and become competent to share the burden of family maintenance as soon as possible. The various rites of passage and ceremonies of initiation in primitive tribes and in ancient civilizations guarantee that everyone grows up, transition to adulthood is clearly marked and there is no backsliding to childish ways. However, in those societies, cultures and nations that are affected by urbanisation and industrialization, there are age-free criteria of professional skills, political power and economic status which means the young are no longer confident of 'inheriting' power in their adulthood. Rising industrial productivity allows teenagers to remain outside the labour force, and there is little productive role or community participation that they are involved in. There is a weakening and sometimes a breakdown of traditional institutions like family and kinship units thus making them progressively less capable of determining individuals' orientations and behaviours by their history and tradition. In a complex world, influences outside the family such as peers and mass media inundate the reality of the young with various images.

Thirdly, the ideology of cultural individualism reinforces the norm of individual independence and notions of lifelong self-exploration. The spread of individualistic culture amongst youth has led to more young people claiming the right to define their own lifestyles and legitimising their ideas, plans and actions on the basis of their own needs, motives and interests. Hence, a 'graduation farewell' is no longer a guarantee for a sizeable section of young to go over from the world of explorative learning to the world of committed work. The work trajectories of many young people are fractured with phases of 'returning to school' or 'taking time off' interspersed between periods of paid work. In the domain of personal relationships, the institution of marriage is witnessing many changes with late marriages gaining currency, cohabitation emerging as a viable alternative and sexuality being given expression within the context of any form of intimate relationship. In the contemporary historical era, the possibilities of lifestyles and action potentials are flexible, diverse and numerous. No longer is it essential, viable or possible for a person to settle on a lifestyle that will be satisfactory for the rest of one's life or to find a community in which one could live for the remainder of one's life.

Thus, there is a prolongation, diversification and individualization of the transition patterns to adulthood. For a young person, the self-definitional attempts to delineate his or her place in the society, to choose from competing options of 'way of life' and to develop a life plan to lend order and meaning to one's existence are becoming individualistic and fluid because of the waning of the power of the imagery of cultural groups like family.

II

Youth and Its Relation to Social-Historical Times

The young stand between alternate ways of life. Their growth processes take various forms. There are few who choose to experiment freely with a variety of roles and others who cling tightly to a certain organising theme in response to multiplicity of choices. Many young persons are gifted enough and have adequate training to land on new roles offered by the dominant consolidation of the historical era. Such youth can accept the ideological outlook implicit in the roles offered by society and therefore need not go through the often painful process of examining and choosing alternative ideologies. There are others who feel estranged since they are eager for but are unable to find access to the dominant techniques of society. They may turn against the society with a vengeance that can be exploited by the propagandists of ideological systems which promise a new world order at the price of total and cruel repudiation of an old one (Erikson 1968, p. 309). Few creative young persons feel too out of place in the prevailing ideological trend and strive to disestablish a sector of this world's outworn fundamentals and make a place for a new one. They suffer, court misery, sickness and failure to see and say, to dream and plan, to design and construct in new ways. Thus, the measuring yards for youth should not be only inner balance, consistency and proficiency but must also encompass confusion, dare devilry, extremism and fragmentation. *Youth, thereby, represent multiple possibilities from delinquency to creative deviancy, rebellion to conformity, alienation to vigorous involvement in the spirit of the era.*

Deviants and rebels have always evoked ambivalent fascination in the public with their transgression of the social mores. In India, the Naxal Movement[2] has been a landmark struggle in the history of left wing extremism. The Naxalites found ardent support amongst the educated elite. The 1970s was undoubtedly a time of idealism amongst intellectual youth of that time. Ajoy Bose (2009), a Delhi-based political columnist and author, recalled in *Mail Today* his own journey of getting drawn to the political philosophy of engineering drastic social change through violence to his withdrawal from the armed struggle following the realisation that 'violence was a horrendous brutish thing in reality'. He shared that there was "the romance and thrill of the revolutionary path as opposed to the tedium of

[2] The Naxal Movement traces its origin to 1967 in a village called Naxalbari in West Bengal in India from where a rebellion emerged amongst the peasants who retaliated against their oppression and started forcefully capturing their lands from the feudal lords. Within a short span, it acquired great visibility and support from cross sections of communist revolutionaries in different states. The dominant faction of Naxalites believed in 'annihilation of the class enemy' and adopted 'allegiance to the armed struggle and non participation in the elections' as their cardinal principles to secure justice to poorest of peasants and tribals. Since its inception, the Naxal Movement has witnessed internal divisions along the ideological basis and forms of struggle, but its presence is still strong amongst few of the poorest districts of the country.

studying Shelly and Keats in the English honours course I increasingly detested. But I still believe the most important factor that drew me away from the comfort and security of mainstream was a burning sense of injustice and an impatience with conventional democratic politics to redress many facets of socio- economic exploitation. Simultaneously, there was this urge to bring about meaningful social transformation. On a gigantic scale, that seemed impossible to achieve through electoral acrobatics or NGO tinkering. For us comrades at St. Stephen's it was also important to distinguish ourselves from the armchair revolutionaries who remained content in spreading their message in university coffee houses".

A large majority of youth is, however, politically acquiescent, who makes use of the socially sanctioned moratorium to play along with apprenticeships and adventures that are in line with the society's values. They are the beneficiaries and guardians of tradition and practitioners and inventors of technology of one's cultural milieu. The success stories of Indian techies in America's Silicon Valley are a case in point. It is estimated that there are about one million Indians in the technology capital of the world. They are not only serving as skilled employees but are also climbing the ladder to reach leadership positions as CEOs. Their entrepreneurial potentials are also receiving a fillip in the conducive technology-business environment of the Silicon Valley. Closer home, the software revolution has spread across the country which is contributing immensely to the wealth as well as the reputation of the nation in the global world. *The energies of the vast majority of youth are absorbed in the efforts to acquire the skills and attitudes to negotiate the opportunity structure within modern economy for which they receive encouragement and appreciation from their parents and teachers.*

A growing minority of young men and women are using the available spaces within the system to respond to the needs for innovation and development in the society as well as to their social concern and stirrings to 'bring a change', 'take a challenge', 'be different'. On the 60th anniversary of India's Independence in 2007, a leading national newspaper group, *Times of India*, started a Lead India campaign to find new-generation leaders for the country. It threw a challenge that if India Inc. can produce so many strong, highly motivated and transformational leaders, why can't Indian politics? Satyam Darmora, 27, and Aseem Puri, 28, were just two of the many young candidates who decided to use this opportunity to realise their visions of social change. Satyam, born and brought up in a small village in Uttarakhand, took the IIT-IIM route to a cushy corporate job with a leading multinational bank. But he had not forgotten his roots and believed that his empathy with the disadvantaged was his USP. Coming from a background with minimal employment opportunities and poor infrastructure, he strongly felt the need to create a platform which would provide opportunities, create employment in rural areas and develop self-sustaining source of livelihood for them. His agenda in the campaign was to set up vocational training centres and to launch microfinance schemes as an empowerment tool for women. Aseem was a brand manager of a leading FMCG managing a global team across 15 countries. He nominated himself because he felt hollow everytime he faced rural India's stark reality. In Bihar or when asked if he had the grassroot level experience to be a leader, he said, "I have the ideas and I'm sufficiently motivated towards delivering solutions. There is enough space in the national landscape for me to do my own thing." He was working on an ambitious project to develop inexpensive filters to provide clean water to Indian villages.[3]

On the other hand are those who are eager for, yet unable to find access to, the ideological trend associated with a new technical and economic expansion because of either being systematically excluded on the basis of their birth circumstances (ethnic, caste, class considerations) or because they are ungifted. They are likely to feel not only estranged from society but 'also upset in sexuality, and most of all unable to apply aggression constructively' (Erikson 1968, p. 309). An instance of this phenomenon is Bajrang Dal, the violent youth wing of a Hindu Nationalist organisation called Vishwa Hindu Parishad (VHP).[4] Nandy et al. (1997) provided a brief analysis of the activities of this volatile group. The youth power of Dal is drawn mainly from the ranks of the poor, upper caste population of the smaller cities and semiurban areas. They are partly educated and socialised to enter the burgeoning modern sector of India but are often jobless. The VHP helps them to cope with their economic and social anxieties by handing them a cause to fight for and by persuading them that on their young shoulders lies the responsibility of restoring to the Hindus their lost honour and pride. As if out to prove their worth to society and themselves, the Bajrang Dal youth have expressed their restlessness and frustrations through some of the more violent incidents that have taken place as part of the Ramjanmabhumi agitation. In more recent times, Bajrang Dal has shot to prominence for opposing the Valentine's Day celebrations in the Hindi hinterland on the ground that it is a Western concept and it spoils the Indian culture because it promotes indecent expression of love. The outfit has vandalised restaurants, shops and hotels celebrating the day and also beaten couples who frequented these places and parks.

---

[3] Why India needs a Second October? (2007, October 2). *The Times of India, New Delhi*, p. 2.

[4] The core idea of VHP is to create a self-conscious Hindu identity and make it coterminous with Indian nationalism. Thus, the Ramjanmabhumi issue, one of the most vital issues for the outfit, is 'not a quarrel about a small piece of land. It is a question of national integrity'. The Rama temple, then, is a response to the mourning of Hindu society: a mourning for lost honour, lost civilization, lost Hinduness. The name of the Dal invokes the imagery of the army of monkey warriors in the Ramayana, led by their king Hanuman, also known as Bajrang. No efforts are spared by the functionaries of the Dal to reiterate that Hanuman was the most devoted and obedient of all disciples of Lord Ram and fought on the side of the lord against the demon king Ravana to ensure the triumph of good over evil.

III

Understanding Identity

Identity is an experience that lends a sense of self-sameness and continuity to a person across time and space (Erikson 1968). This highlights the fundamental paradox that identity plays into, that is, preserving sameness in the midst of inner and outer changes. Identity serves the function of providing the structure for understanding who one is; providing meaning and direction through commitments, values and goals; providing a sense of personal control and free will; striving for consistency, coherence and harmony between values, beliefs and commitments; and enabling the recognition of potential through a sense of future, possibilities and alternative choices (Adams and Marshall 1996). A need for the sense of identity emerges in the face of incongruities and incompatibilities amongst the various elements of the self and/or the ways in which one is positioned by particular social discourses of gender, class, race, religion and one's own self-understandings. It is these moments of disjuncture that heighten self-awareness and reflection and create an identity crisis. It impels a person to question—'who am I?' 'what can I make of myself?' 'what are the worthwhile goals of my life?' 'can I reconfigure the meanings of the ascribed social roles?' 'do I have the space and the freedom to be myself?' The answers to these questions mark out the contours of the self-identity.

Erik H. Erikson

Erik H. Erikson, a psychoanalyst, has been a salient thinker of the concept of identity. Identity is a core concern in Eriksonian thought, and in his work, he exemplifies the developmental processes that underlie the formation of a workable identity in the stage of youth and which is open for revision all through one's life course. His explorations and descriptions of identity are multifaceted and multidimensional. Rather than offering a definitive explanation, he conceptualises identity by providing illustrations of it in various contexts: the biographic excerpts from the youth of George Bernard Shaw,[5] William James[6] and Hitler,[7] the quandary of Shakespearean character Hamlet,[8] the pathology of Freud's patient Dora,[9] the plight of a young Negro child,[10] survey of life and character of Thomas Jefferson[11] and a range of

---

[5] See Erikson (1968).

[6] Ibid.

[7] See Erikson (1950).

[8] See Erikson (1968).

[9] Ibid.

[10] See Erikson (1964).

[11] See Erikson (1974).

clinical material and everyday observations. In his writings, one senses and picks up nuances of unconscious motivation, experience and expression of identity conflicts and resolution, its positive and negative elements, its developmental path and its social-historical backdrop.

One of the biggest contributions of Erikson is his psychosocial theory of development in contrast to Freudian theory of psychosexual stages. *'Psychosocial' here means specifically that the stages of a person's life from birth to death are affected by social influences interacting with a physically and psychologically maturing individual.* A basic assumption of his theory is mutuality which implies a dynamic relationship between the growing person's readiness to interact with a widening social radius in predetermined steps and the readiness of society to welcome, invite and influence this interaction. The individual's life is seen as operating within a shared/communal space, wherein he or she is introduced to a particular cultural style. Following is one illustration from Erikson's work on this interplay between the individual and the social: 'A child who has just found himself able to walk, for example, seems not only driven to repeat and perfect the act of walking by the promise of libidinal pleasure in the sense of Freud's locomotor eroticism, or by the need for mastery in the sense of Ivan Hendrick's work principle: he also becomes aware of the new status and stature of "one who can walk", with whatever connotations this happens to have in the coordinates of his culture's life plan—be it "one who will swiftly run after fleeing prey", "one who will go far", "one who will be upright", or "one who might go too far" ' (Erikson 1968, p. 49). Contact and engagement with new facets of one's milieu (from 'maternal' to 'mankind') and expanding biopsychological capacities to negotiate with them set up a turning point, a basic crisis representative of each stage of development. *Crisis, in this theory, does not signify a catastrophe or problem; rather, it suggests a critical moment normative of that stage that has the potential of setting forth the emergence of psychic capabilities and strengths as well as leading to specific vulnerabilities and pathological tendencies.* Erikson posits eight stages of psychosocial development, each with its crises, basic strengths, core pathologies, relevant principle/aspect of social order, binding ritualization (culturally patterned way of doing or experiencing something in the daily interplay of individuals) and ritualism (forced, rigid, repetitive and formalised communication). The life cycle of an individual coexists with the life cycle of the social institutions, and the specific psychosocial strength is the individual's heritage from and contribution to the succession of generations and to society's establishment. *According to his psychosocial theory of development, as a person enters adolescence, he or she is confronted with the crisis of identity.* Equipped with physiological maturation and intellectual maturation, a young person faces impending adulthood, that is, one has to find one's place in society through useful work, meaningful cause and practical life plan. Making use of the psychosocial moratorium, a time span and permissive space granted to the young by the society to playfully experiment and try out the various roles offered by the cultural milieu, a young person comes to invest fidelity in a niche which is firmly defined and yet uniquely suited to his or her talents, temperament and liking. In finding the match between inner needs, aptitudes, potentials, aspirations and ideals with the opportunities and constraints of the environment, the young strive to glimpse a meaningful resemblance between what they have come to see in themselves and what the significant others judge and expect them to be. The process of identity synthesis is continuously threatened by identity confusion exhibited in the intense self-consciousness experienced by adolescents and a bewildering flux of orientations towards roles, values and lifestyles. *In Erikson's deliberations on identity in youth, the following aspects are salient for the present work*:

1. Identity synthesis represents a sense of 'a present with an anticipated future'. This implies that past, present and future are not separate and distinct, rather they coexist together. The present carries impressions of the past, and in that sense, the past is an actual alive portion of the living present. It also counterpoints the future possibilities and prospective potentials. *According to Erikson, one's self-identity is made of various elements such as self-images fashioned after parents and other significant adults, strong feelings of identifications with images and roles recognised and crudely imitated in childhood play, defences employed and lived affects accumulated throughout the pre-adolescent period.* In the light of contemporary situation (such as successes and failures, new information, novel growth settings, unique experiences, available opportunities), the youth appraises the self-elements, selectively abandoning those that are no longer serviceable or appealing and dynamically integrating the old and the contemporaneous ones, acquired through new identifications with age-mates and leader figures outside one's family, into a renewed vision of selfhood. This permits a sense of internal continuity across time and space.
2. Identity serves to integrate numerous and possibly conflicting identifications that have been amassed over one's childhood and adolescence. Unorganised multiple self-conceptions do not allow for a psychologically required sense of sameness and continuity. Erikson conceives of an intrapsychic process whereby multiple identifications are transformed into a unified structure. In order to explain this transformation, Erikson introduces the concept of 'configuration'. A configuration implies a set of relations amongst many components. Identity formation is, thus, the evolving process of the ego configuring the relation amongst diverse identifications. *He states, 'Identity formation arises from the selective repudiation and mutual assimilation of childhood identifications and their absorption in a new configuration' (Erikson 1968, p. 159).* Here, he describes three different processes as being involved in the creation of a configuration: '*selective repudiation*' refers to a process whereby certain identifications are rejected and/or suppressed; '*mutual assimilation*' suggests synthesising process whereby two or more identifications somehow are merged into one, without rejecting either; '*absorbing identifications in a configuration*' implies a process where different identifications are still seen as separate, none are rejected and they continue to exist separately side by side in some sort of dynamic balance.
3. Identity is meant to convey the process of meaningful relation between inner life and outer social reality. In explicating the identity confusion of young George

Bernard Shaw, Erikson provides a description of his crisis in the man's own words: 'I made good in spite of myself, and found to my dismay, that Business, instead of expelling me as the worthless imposter I was, was fastening upon me with no intention of letting me go'; ... in the meantime, he (Shaw) seemed to avoid opportunities, sensing that 'behind the conviction that they could lead to nothing that I wanted, lay the unspoken fear that they might lead to something I did not want' (1968, p. 143). In youth, a person searches for a right match between inner needs and environmental opportunities and constraints, need recognition of one's potential and worth. Emotional and social development of youth onto adulthood requires adult support and recognition of the emerging style of individuality of the young.

4. Gaining a sense of identity, a step towards maturity, requires devotion to a workable and practical life plan guided by a perspective. *By investing themselves into some kind of work roles and activities, the young develop an ideology—a worldview, cosmic mood, pervasive outlook.* Ideology provides a coherent perspective on life, of the world around and of one's place within it. It allows for a sense of belonging with such group(s) of people (e.g. immediate family, a religious cult, an organisation of political activists, a professional body, a group of rock music lovers) whose typical characteristics of language, behaviour and customs are felt as worth sharing intimately, whose tales of past glory induce pride and current problems evoke pangs and with whom one can collectively weave aspirations for a utopian future. *Need for commitment is also balanced by a need for repudiation.* In cases where there isn't a positive cause to invest one's fidelity in, the negative one, that is, repudiation, becomes predominant. What is negated is the lifestyle of the parental generation which is subdued most rigorously both within and without.
5. *Identity is located in the interplay of change and continuity, at both individual and collective levels.* As forerunners of social change, youth's experiences and expressions of conformity and deviancy, rebellion and rededication provide an insight in their attempts to test the strength of the system and then decide whether it needs to be 'confirmed' by them or 'reformed' by them. Wherever the generational values are very different and at odds with each other, parental authority is apt to be violently resisted.
6. Erikson posits a range of identity processes from identity synthesis on one end to identity confusion to another; positive identity, on one hand, to negative identity, on the other; deviant, delinquent, pathological, totalitarian to conforming, creative, conservative, well-adjusted youth; humanist and technological young persons. The dominance of specific kind of identity process will depend upon the reciprocal interaction between inner resources and communal milieu of the person. He points, 'The historical era in which (a person) lives offers only a limited number of socially meaningful models for workable combination of identification fragments. Their usefulness depends on the way in which they simultaneously meet the requirements of the organism's maturational stage, the ego's style of synthesis, and the demands of the culture' (1968, pp. 53–54).

Beyond Erikson: Lifton's Protean Man and Phillips' Flirt

Robert Jay Lifton

Of specific interest to this work is Lifton's view of the 'protean self' that is based on a variety of observations made by him in Asia, Europe and the United States during the 1950s, 1960s and 1970s. Research with activist youth in Japan, Europe and the United States on their experience of self and culture in their contemporary setting; survivors of Hiroshima; Chinese and Westerners who had been subject to thought reform programs; returning American prisoners of war of Vietnam; observations of widespread phenomenon of current historical period and analysis of wide range of literary and artistic forms are some of the sources which he uses to tease out and describe specific characteristics of protean self. In his analysis, Lifton provides images of fatherlessness, survivorhood, free-floating emotions and communities, fragmented ideological struggle for form—all in a bid to renew notions of coherence, consistency, predictability and stability associated with identity.

Derived from the Greek mythology, Proteus is able to change his shape with relative ease—from wild boar to lion to dragon to fire and flood. But what he finds difficult and will not do unless seized and chained is to commit himself to a single form, a form which is his own and in which he can carry out his function of prophecy. *Lifton views proteanism as a biographical adaptation to the changing historical conditions wherein there is a break in the sense of connection which men/women feel with vital and nourishing symbols of their cultural tradition (family, ideologies, religion), flooding of imagery, ideas and cultural influences over mass communication networks and an awareness of the threat of extinction made possible by our technological capacity.* As a response to these universal historical forces, proteanism enables the individual(s) who embody it to seek meaning and authenticity through interminable explorations and experiments (Lifton 1993). In a world where uncertainty reigns, possibilities abound and variety flourishes, self is not likely to do anything in a completely linear, straightforward fashion. Rather, it is prone to juggle multiple and varied involvements with people, ideas and activities. Self-images can be disparate and in continuous transformations, and commitments can be more transitory. Fatherlessness and homelessness associated with shifts in authority and mentorship are cultivated. Absurdity expresses the lack of fit between the way the world presents itself and the way one actually feels about it. *The struggle of life in the contemporary world is to open oneself to many possibilities but at the same time also to hold onto certain experiences, principles and relations that can provide a degree of form, grounding and cohesion.* Thus, expressions of proteanism depend upon the existence of relatively established corners of self.

Adam Phillips

Flirtation is the saboteur of fidelity. In terms of youth phenomenology, it can be seen as equivalent to experimentation which is the mandate of socially sanctioned moratorium granted to youth. For after all, youthful explorations and rebellions involve an infidelity to one's origins and, like flirtation, indulge in a game of taking chances, of plotting illicit possibilities. *Flirtation allows for refusal, deferring or even a denial of the known end and allows for falling more into one's own subjectivity to make us wonder which ways of knowing, being known, sustain our interest and our excitement in other people.* In flirting with ourselves, we can have many versions of ourselves; we grant ourselves the freedom to proliferate selves.

As a healthy state of being, flirtation eroticizes the contingency of our lives and makes a pleasure out of instability which is an inherent condition of life. Rather than encapsulating time or wallowing in doubt, it keeps the future open, cultivates wishes, exploits the idea of surprise and turns doubt into suspense. Phillips says that flirtation is 'what all children can do sexually with their parents, assuming that parents maintain the Oedipal prohibition' (1994, p. xxiii). By setting the limits of permissible, they nurture the child's sense of possible future selves. The child discovers the incest taboo by trying to sabotage it. In the oedipal flirtations of childhood, there is a fundamental asymmetry between the adult who is certain that nothing will happen and the child who urgently wants something to happen but cannot be sure what it is and is also not equipped to deal with it. This inevitably unstable relationship then becomes internalised as one of the primary relationships one has with oneself. The adult part can be playfully sceptic of its own authority, and doubts can unsettle its convictions. In doing so, uncertainty is tolerated, one's omniscience is repudiated and waiting emerges. It chips away at our notions of self-sufficiency and invincibility and confronts us with own desire, dependence, vulnerability and loss.

IV

Individuation and Relatedness: Dynamics of Identity

Individuation, autonomy and identity formation are interlinked. From a phase of absolute dependence on the care of the mothering other, identity development proceeds towards independence, self-care and the potential to take care of others. Identity formation in adolescence expands on the early developmental process to effect separation from the maternal matrix. Mahler et al.'s (1975) theory of separation–individuation traces the earliest emergence of the sense of identity. *They propose that the process of separation–individuation proceeds along two tracks: separation refers to the infant's movement away from fusion with the mother, and individuation consists of those steps that lead to the development of an individual's own personal and unique characteristics.* Individuation refers to the development of infant's ego, sense of identity and cognitive abilities. In the beginning of psychological life, there is no self. The newborn infant, as best as we can understand it, experiences pleasure and pain but has no sense of an 'I' that is doing that experiencing. Neither is the infant aware that there is a separate and distinct mother who is or not gratifying. By the age of 3 years, the young child has developed a firm sense of self-boundaries and knows clearly that he or she is a person separate from other people with unique thoughts and inner experiences. The aspects of the object world, like the parental characteristics, love and their demands, are also gradually internalised by the child. This helps the child to individuate and display attitudes of mastery and autonomous functioning without undue tension or need for clinginess. The child develops a sense of individuality, a core of selfhood, on which all later identity formation is based.

Blos (1962) posits a second separation–individuation phase at adolescence. A similar, yet far more complex individuation experience occurs during adolescence in which the adolescent oppositional, rebellious and resistive strivings, the stages of experimentation and the testing of the self by going to excess—all these have a positive usefulness in the process of self-definition. The resurgence of instinctual impulses along with the psychosocial demands of the environment to make choices that will count towards the future identity heralds this phase. Arriving at an intuitive sense of self-definition is preceded by a developmental journey that is arduous or straightforward, conflicted or smooth, in different proportions. Young persons experience a developmental crisis, normative of their stage, wherein they may suffer from a paralysis of choice and action, confused and pointless experimentation, fear of engulfment/isolation in close relationships, pathos of dependence and obedience, the oppression of prescribed role and/or the fright of being in self-created role and absence of personally relevant philosophy of life, to sketch out a few phenomenological realities of the inner world of young persons. One experiences conflicting need to submit to ready-made role or create a self-role, urge to test one's self against contemporaries and in multifarious roles, contradictory impulses to discard the 'oft-beaten, normal, mundane path' and alternatively, to submerge oneself in the crowd. Conflicted youth may lead bored, static, fragmented or violent lives. They are often given to a sense of despair and individual futurelessness. From this internal battleground, many emerge stronger and with greater potential to use their constructive energies to propel themselves in a functional manner, while few may continue brittle and inauthentic ways of living. *The identity struggles of youth are aimed towards moving closer to increased autonomy, self-direction, feelings of self-worth and confidence, augmented sense of responsibility and commitment to one's choices in the purview of work, sexuality, relationships and guiding principle(s).*

The watershed issues of identity around which an adolescent tests his or her sameness and difference from the parental images can be many: vocational plans, leisure and pastimes, religious beliefs, political values, caste/class orientation, sexuality-related attitudes, friendship, dating, marriage, parenting, gender roles and work/life balance. Impacted by a social world far larger than the home environment and aided by enhanced physical maturity and cognitive powers, the adolescents are faced with the developmental challenge of reconciling the diverse and potentially conflicting identifications with parents and those acquired with age-mates and leader figures outside one's family into a renewed vision of selfhood. *They often judge their distance from their families by how much they carry on parents' expectations of achievement and success, whether they follow the family's religious traditions, whom they choose as friends, to date and to marry, what sexual values they adopt, what are their attitudes towards saving vs. spending, what is appropriate feminine/masculine behaviour, how do they relate to the larger world. These become the negotiation points for separation–individuation during adolescence and youth which lead towards a sense of adult identity.* At the close of youth, the first decisive choices are made. With its end, the young person carves out a place in the world, and society identifies the person as responsible for choices made.

Much of the early theory conceptualised adolescence as a period in which psychological independence was won by detachment and replacement of parents as important objects (Freud 1958; Fountain 1961; Blos 1962). Therefore, autonomy or individuation is viewed as the opposite of, or a move away from, connectedness or relatedness to parents. Mounting research evidence, however, led to a revision in that theory as it became clear that adolescents do not abandon or disown their parents as a necessary condition for growth (Douvan and Adelson 1966; Offer et al. 1981). *Separation–individuation in adolescence requires a revision of relationships with parents, a revision that nevertheless preserves connection.* What is critical is that aspects of the self become reworked during adolescence so that the young person has some choice in the creation of a self, a self that will function autonomously but in relation to the parents.[12] In fact, the paradoxical needs for individuation and intimacy, with their accompanying fears of isolation and fusion, continue throughout the life cycle.

When a new element of self is formed, it tends to be tested, at least in fantasy, in the context of the parents from whom the young person is individuating (Josselson 1980). A young college woman who gets involved with a man with a religion very different from her family's or a young man who decides to drop out of college is quite likely to imagine what their parents will think of this. Should they tell them about their activities? How will they handle parental disapproval? This is an internal debate, a discussion with parents who are inside the self, who seem to be insisting that one may not change, may not be different. While many times it is the fear of loss of love or the guilt of disappointing parents which keeps the youth away from possible transgressions, on other occasions, it is the feeling of vulnerability of leaving the safety of parental positions. Becoming like parents, remaining within the predictability and certainty of family closeness and excluding exploration of alternative models and relationships help them feel right and secure. The challenge of this developmental phase is to gain a feeling of individuality in the context of an ongoing relationship to parents.

---

[12] A view on autonomy that differs from the perspective of 'autonomy as separation' is 'autonomy as agency'. Adherents of this view (Kagitcibasi 1996; Ryan 1993; Ryan and Deci 2000) use notions like internal locus of control, self-determination, strong sense of confidence, ability to function independently and competence to describe autonomy.

V

Psychoanalysis on Self–Other Interface

A cardinal element of modern consciousness is the idea of individualism. As the name suggests, modern Western individualism takes individual as the basic social unit. The individual is considered inviolate, the supreme value in and of himself or herself, having his or her rights and obligations, with each equal to the other. Society is considered to be essentially subordinate to the needs of individuals, who are all governed by their own self-interest in mutually consenting contractual relationships in their political and economic strivings. Rather than being rooted in hierarchical social, collective and cosmic order, the individual is set on one's own. Enlightenment notions of individualism view the rational, thinking person as most real and valued, with analytic deductive modes of thought that explore causal, logical relationships as primary. Rationality is considered intrinsically superior to emotions. This rational, thinking mind is viewed as autonomous in each individual. Views of the world become primarily secular and scientific, the latter in particular becoming supremely valued. The imagery of the autonomous and purposive individual, free from the constraints from without and capable of acting on his or her behalf and responsible for his or her actions, incipient in cultural individualism, has been carried to the realm of the psychological. The ideology of Western individualism incorporates a conception of individual development as a gradual unfolding of the inherent potential to engage in purposive, responsible action. Different theoretical traditions in psychology have engaged with the assumptions and images of 'individual' thrown up by cultural individualism.

Psychoanalysis, from Freud onwards, has been in a continuous dialogue with the culture of individualism. *All of psychoanalysis has undermined the assumption of self-contained individual by showing that in the individual's mental life, someone else is invariably involved as a model, as an object, as helper, as an opponent—what is called the 'other'*. From the very beginning, individual psychology is at the same time social psychology. The psychoanalytic man/woman is always in the midst of dynamics of relating and separating from significant figures in one's social surround.

Freud severely and successfully critiqued the enlightenment's idea of man's inherent rationality through his formulation of the unconscious and primary process thinking. Freudian model of human development was conflict-oriented, and he saw the maturing ego, the sign of emergent individuality, as constantly buffeted by the forces of desires, instincts and drives, on one hand, and norms, traditions and values of one's culture, on the other hand. Thus, he acknowledged that the rationality of an individual is at the peril of being subdued by the irrational contents of one's fantasy and instinctual life as well as the time-resisting traditions and judgments of value. Culture, in Freud's view, was an edifice built upon a foundation of coercion and renunciation of instincts, and the question which engaged his attention in many of his writings was 'whether and to what extent it is possible to lessen the burden of instinctual sacrifices imposed on man, to reconcile men to those which must necessarily remain and to provide a compensation for them' (Freud 1927, p. 7). Thus, personal autonomy lies in the formulation of psychic mechanisms that allows for expression of instincts and drives in and gratification from social order, though not without guilt and strife. The paradigm of psychoanalysis doesn't ever see the individual as 'fully socialised'. *The primacy of inner mental life with its contents of fantasies of bodily life and idiosyncratic representations of familial and cultural aspects keeps the individuality alive in the midst of collective pressures to conform. It's a refuge as well as also the wellspring of our ingenious apperception.* The dream and fantasy conveys a particular culture's versions of the impossible and forbidden; it reflects what seeps out of the crevices in the cultural floor.

Patienthood is seen as an emergent condition whenever inner complexity and expression are inhibited or violated by external reality. The individual's symptom is thus revelatory of what the environment has failed to hold or handle of his or her personal subjectivity. Therapeutic interventions, experientially oriented or behaviourally oriented, attempt to make good of this failure. It is instructive to note that Erikson, a Jewish immigrant to America, a wanderer and artist in one's youth, writing in revolutionary decades of 1960s and 1970s, made search for identity in adolescents, youth radicals, immigrants, ethnic minorities and war veterans as his central concern. In times of dislocation and disruption, it is an internal sense of continuity and coherence, the experience of identity which becomes conflicted. While writing on youth revolt against establishment, he saw patienthood also as an opposition to conformism. He perceptively remarks, 'We must begin by recognizing our patients as the inverted dissenters, too sick for the modish malaise of their time, too isolated for joint dissent, and yet too sensitive for simple adjustment' (Erikson 1975, p. 196).

Winnicott (1971) in his thesis on *transitional phenomena, playing and cultural experience* provides a creative illustration of the interplay between separateness and union of individual and society. Between the inner world of dream and the outer world of fact is the playground of human beings (baby, child, adolescent, adult) where imaginative living is possible. In this potential space, where we are when we are neither simply thinking nor simply behaving, the person is creatively experiencing. The original gesture of a baby who reaches out for the mother's mouth, feels her teeth, looks into her eyes, seeing her anew; a child lost in play with its toys; an adolescent boy's flirtations; and an adult's enjoyment of listening to music are variabilities belonging to day-to-day living, in which the shared reality is renewed with one's own unique content and the inner life is enriched by cultural elements. In this realm, perception is creation; doing is not ritual but playful. Granting oneself the formlessness that comes in states of relaxation, one gets in touch with one's creative impulse that lies at the core of self. Inventiveness, thus, lies in the interplay between originality and acceptance of tradition.

Amongst the ego psychoanalysts, Erikson is viewed as formulating the central psychological dimension of individualism: the *self creation of one's identity* in a Western society where autonomy and options are granted to the growing individual in areas of vocation, love, recreation, etc. Erikson, however, saw the individual as an integral part of the social, cultural and historical milieu whose roles, values, ideals and norms profoundly shape and are part of a personal identity. He saw identity formation as the normative crisis of the adolescent and young adult to make adult commitments in domains of vocation, intimacy and ideology by integrating the salient identifications with parents, peers and leaders and self-images developed throughout growing up with the role opportunities offered in the present stage. Identity synthesis can be created around positive potentials affirmed by peers, confirmed by significant adults and in line with worthwhile 'ways of life'. It can also be based on negative elements, that is, identifications and roles that are presented as most undesirable or dangerous and yet also as most real by one's milieu. In his theoretical framework, he points to spaces in different cultures for the compensations that are built in for the members to have a measure of individual autonomy and creativity. In response to Thorat's reminiscences of his childhood in an untouchable setting permitting the development of a 'stigmatised identity',[13] he stresses on cultural relativity in the form and the focus of disapproval (in this case, awakening a sense of impurity such as being polluted and polluting someone else). At the same time, he suggests that locomotion- and cognition-wise advanced child, anywhere, while exploring the leeway of possible and permissible (in this case, the implications of an untouchable boy's ball's proximity to the village well), develops an inner division and demarcation of the world into fateful contrasts of good and bad, clean and dirty, beautiful and ugly. He poses the question that how in the absence of some compensations for every boundary designating what zones of the body are considered polluted or polluting, what thoughts are thinkable or must be repressed even in fantasy and what areas of the environment are permissible or out of the bounds, can a much restricted life be rendered liveable and some creative re-ritualizing like Ambedkar's endeavours can be thought of. Thus, cultural 'designs for living' can make demands on personal adaptation but only within limits which guard a manageable degree of anxiety and conflicts and assures vitality and health to its members.

The object relational school stresses on the internalisation and internal representation of the relationship between the self and objects (primarily the mothering person and then significant others). The gradual separation of 'self-' and 'other' images as well as self- and object constancy is essential for autonomous functioning of the individual. Self-constancy represents a beginning sense of the self as separate from others, continuous in time and space and possessed of an ongoing sense of sameness despite fluctuations in emotions and bodily feelings or external surroundings. Object constancy is the genesis of the ability to retain a stable internal representation by integrating the affectionate and persecutory images of 'important others' that makes it possible for the child to maintain a connection in the mind with significant others whether they are present or absent or frustrating or gratifying. The Kleinian notion of 'depressive position' makes it clear that the separation of self- and object images is accompanied by a greater awareness of one's own individual subjectivity as well as recognition of the other as a mind of one's own. *Separateness and individuation, however, require a responsive dyadic relationship in which each level of autonomy and independence occurs in parallel with new levels of reciprocity and mutuality.*

[13] See Erikson (1979).

Kohut (1971) stresses the *interrelationship of subjectivities* in all human relationships. He emphasised the needs for mirroring, idealising and twinship fulfilled through self–object relationships throughout life for maintaining self-esteem and self-cohesion. *Mirroring* is the self–object need for self-affirmation and approval from significant others. It is instrumental to the formation of healthy assertiveness and ambition. *Idealising* is the self–object need for feeling caretakers as perfect and powerful. It is central to the formation of positive goals and ideals. *Twinship* self–object experiences are necessary for feeling genuinely a part of human race and one's gender and for the development of talents and skills. Thus, the nuclear self is a creative, cohesive self striving with ambitions and ideals towards a full realisation of a person's skills and talents.

VI

Identity Development in Indian Settings

Cross-cultural perspective has questioned the universal and unitary conception of evolutionary schemas amongst human beings in different societies and cultures. Research in psychoanalytic anthropology as well as clinical work with patients in non-Western societies has revealed that the kinds of potentialities persons actually develop, how they function and communicate in society, what their mode of being and experience is in the world and within themselves and what their ideals and actualities of individuation depend on the given culture and society to which they belong. In this light, few relevant ideas of Roland and Kakar are reviewed below. The attempt is to understand how the cultural ideals and symbol systems give meaning and form to the social patterns and child-rearing and thus ultimately shape the development of potentiality and range of individuation in Indian society.

Roland and the Indian Familial Self

Drawing from psychoanalytic case material of well-educated, urban, middle to upper middle-class Indian patients in India and America and extensive discussions with Indian psychoanalytic therapists and social scientists, Roland has drawn out the contours of Indian self and he refers to it as 'familial self' (1988, 1996). He sees the Indian person as growing and functioning within the Indian extended family and the richly complex hierarchical relationships that constitute it and other group relationships (caste and professional groupings). The inner landscape of the familial self enables the person to function well within the psychosocial dimensions of the familial hierarchical relationships that are characterised by an intense emotional connectedness and interdependence with a constant flow of responsiveness between persons, by a strong mutual caring and responsibility with full expectations for reciprocity and by highly empathic sensitivity to one another's feelings and needs without explicit expression.

Roland (1988) spells out *four major suborganisations of the familial self:* (i) *symbiosis–reciprocity* or the affective and experiential dimension of 'we self' which stems from strong identification on the part of both men and women with their families and communities as well as orientation to a multiplicity of hierarchical relationships, (ii) *narcissistic dimension* of we self regard in which feelings of self-esteem are experienced not only around oneself and one's body image but equally around the reputation and status of 'we' of the extended family and communities one belongs to, (iii) *the Indian conscience* which is oriented around the conscious containment and often unconscious repression or dissociation of angry feelings and to a lesser degree, sexuality along with a socially contextual ego ideal which allows to pick cues for appropriate behaviour in different situations and act accordingly, and (iv) *cognitive aspects of ego functioning* in which contextualising and metonymic thinking are central.

Roland (1988) states that process of identity formation that grants the person autonomy to create himself or herself through the child-rearing practices emphasising separation–individuation, independence and initiative and ego orientation towards mastery, assertiveness, ambition and competitiveness is typical of Western individualistic societies defined by choice, competitive individualism and egalitarian-contractual relationships. In contrast, child-rearing in India fosters capacities for intense dependence and interdependence, an ego orientation towards receptivity and sensitivity to others and rather than an I self, a we self with permeable outer boundaries and a highly private self. The central cultural ideals of individuation revolve around the gradual realisation of the spiritual self, wherein subtle differences and nuances in inner make-up, temperament and inclinations are all utilised in the spiritual quest. However, Roland acknowledges that the traditional familial-spiritual Indian self has to contend with strong individualising changes occurring with modernization, especially in urban areas, leading to a variety of conflicts as well as expansion of self. He exemplifies it in his detailed case studies. One of which is of Ashis who internalised strong Western cultural norms and values through his identification with his father as well as education abroad. As a representative of an increasing number of such Indians who are placed in the intermediary space of indigenous and Western cultural norms and values, he was used to a much more individualised way of working. Hence, on his return back, he felt stifled as a junior member of his organisation where an Indian hierarchical order traditionally gives little recognition or scope to the junior member, in contrast to many American organisations which value autonomy, initiative and self-actualization. Another example comes from the life of Shakuntala belonging to a highly educated, middle- or upper-middle-class urban elite family which allowed her to receive college and then postgraduate education and then to have a veto over their choice of groom. The high degree of individualization in her life and an intense relationship with a much married man which could be managed in the anonymous environment of the modern, cosmopolitan city like Bombay led her to reject arranged marriage as too limited, thus putting her in conflict with her mother. In other cases, he noted the conflict over individualization emerging between the woman and her in-laws and/or spouse. Such conflicts have the potential of expanding Indian self to incorporate increased individualization and individuation in its functioning.

Kakar and Indian Identity

Kakar has systematically drawn upon anthropological evidence, life historical and clinical data, mythology and folklore and literary and cinematic narratives to understand the developmental processes of intrapsychic structures of Indian identity. Using an Eriksonian framework, he has endeavoured to keep alive in his thought and writings the mutuality of psyche and culture, that is, how within a given social-cultural order particular psychological tendencies are developed and potentials are idiosyncratically elaborated in the individual psyche, later to influence the culture's institutions and social forms and thus, perpetuated from generation to generation. He has also provided glimpses of the possible directions of transformation of identity of Indian men and women in response to the press of social change. In his psychosocial explorations of inner worlds of Indians on matters as diverse as infancy and childhood, spirituality and mysticism, religious violence, gendered subjectivities and sexuality and traditional healing practices, he has entered the shadowy realms of collective fantasy as well as daily worlds of people. His 'ambivalence in being an Indian and a psychoanalyst and the experience of living at the margins of both Indian and western cultures' (Kakar 1982, p. 10) has been constructively used by him to get into the interstitial space between cultural relativity and psychological universalism. In understanding particular cultural phenomenon through an elaboration of its context as well as also locating it in a wider framework of understanding provided by psychoanalytic knowledge, Kakar has striven to show the realities of East and West as similar and, in the times of unprecedented social change and intercultural exchanges, as coexisting actualities. In this search for universals, the conceptual categories of psychoanalytic models and cultural views are stretched and/or reformed to render a compelling psychological idiom. Kakar's presentation of a triad of images of women (in contrast to the Freudian mother/whore dichotomy) populating the inner world of Hindu males, consisting of the mother, the wife as a partner in ritual and the sexual woman, is an adept illustration of expanding the psychoanalytic categories. His delineation of hidden images of individuality incorporated in traditional cultures (mystic being one) is one such creative example of renewing the cultural understandings of psychic potentials. Broadly speaking, Kakar through his writings highlights the cultural emphasis on the emotional and spiritual qualities of life, on the primacy of primary group relationships (family and jati) in the inner world of the individuals and on the celebration of dyadic intimacy (with the mother, guru) and the struggle for individuation in his portrait of Indianness.

VII

Youth, Identity and Ideology

The need for a coherent worldview becomes intensified during youth and is usually met through the solidarity of fellow mates in domains of inspired activity. Drawn into certain kinds of educational-vocational set-ups, the young individual's energies are harnessed in the service of an ideology—a worldview, a cosmic mood, a practical life plan characterising the communal domain, which helps to stamp, as it completes, the individual's identity. *Erikson (1968) says, 'Identity and ideology are two aspects of the same process. Both provide the necessary condition for further individual maturation, and with it, for the next higher form of identification, namely, the solidarity linking common identities in joint living, acting and creating' (p. 189).* Psychoanalysis provides us with conceptual and methodological means to trace the motivational roots of affinity to and/or creation of ideological elements amongst human beings in different cultures.

Erikson in *Childhood and Society* (1950) while discussing the American identity sees a configurational analogy between American family life and national mores. He uses it to answer the question 'How does his home train this [American] boy for democracy?'(p. 274). Similarly, in tracing the origins of the ideological force of 'militant nonviolence' in Gandhi's life, he puts together various elements of Gandhi's life together—from his big ears to his nonviolent teasing of animals in his childhood, to his special status with his father and mother, to his sexual appetites, to the role of the vow to abstain from meat, women and wine, etc. (1969). Following Erikson, Kakar (1981) too has attempted to find and understand aspects of Swami Vivekananda's life in order to weave a pattern of meaning about his historic attempts to integrate the rational, scientific model of inquiry and the aims of technological modernization with the essentials of the traditional Hindu world image. The search led to the internal psychic territory of the introspective yogi and activist monk which was the battleground of integration of divergent strivings for individuation as a man with the yearning for fusion with some ultimate divine matrix. Yet another important text is *Alternative Sciences: Creativity and Authenticity in Two Indian Scientists* (1995) by Ashis Nandy. He has, amongst other things, presented the personal contexts of scientific creativity of two Indian scientists—Srinivasa Ramanujan and Jagadish Chandra Bose. In here, he has traced their science to early socialisation, the traditions of their society, poverty and colony status and the needs of the modern science at that time. Focusing on the exchanges between individual creativity and social realities, the intellectual effort in this text has been to understand how these scientists developed their concepts of science, that is, their world views. Keniston (1968) also provided interesting leads on the psychological development of young activists—the New Leftists. With them, he explored the connections between family life and tradition, growing up experiences and the later political views and activities.

The effort in the present book is to understand what in the inner world of certain sections of youth has become ideological. It seeks to trace in the lives of the youth participants the decisive influences of their psychosocial contexts on development and the internalisation of ideological values pertaining to aspects of social world such as competition, money, power, democracy etc.

VIII

Woman Youth

Women youth often appear as a paradoxical phrase. This is so because the anticipated 'adult roles' of homemaking and motherhood are made clear to the growing girl rather early in her life and she is socialised for the same. In that sense, the future appears more foreclosed for her. Ruthellen Josselson is one of the pioneering researchers in the gender-sensitive and narrative genre of qualitative research. Her research and theorizations have their origins in her dissatisfaction with the established theories of human development which have a distinct andro-centric bias that either ignore dynamics of female development or tack them as an addendum. *There is an increasing acceptance of the view that the concepts of autonomy, independence and separation do not describe the central issues of women development (Josselson 1988).* Connection to others which is the primary theme of women's identity is de-emphasised in these developmental models. However, comparison between men's and women's developmental models often leads to a simplistic and naive dichotomy between agency and affiliation: men's identity is egocentric and women's identity is interdependent; men are concerned with separation in defining the self and women are concerned with relating to the human community; individuation is more important for men and relationships are more important for women. It is in this respect that Josselson as a theorist stands out with her nuanced understanding of women's identity. *Her model of female development includes connection as a core construct but also adds competence as a second core (Josselson 1996). She redefines competence and connection as neither rigidly dichotomous nor specifically gender identified.* Competence refers to the feeling of being effective and doing things of value; connection refers to having ties with others. Competence and connection, as used by Josselson, are broader than Freud's view of work and love. Competence goes beyond employment, and connection goes beyond relationships with partner and children. 'Women bring relatedness to the workplace [and] they bring working to relationships' (Josselson 1987, p. 184). For instance, for women with children, their children are an integral part of their identities. However, identity as a mother is more than the title itself but is also rooted in being successful in this role—being a 'particular sort of mother with carefully etched values and goals: a good mother, a loving mother' (Josselson 1996, p. 219). Thus, the element of competence gets intertwined with connection in the role of mother. Josselson found that women without children also rooted their identities in connection, often through other people's children as an aunt, godmother or close friend and through being a daughter, a sister, even in spirituality. Even at the place of work, women seek a sense of communion and togetherness.

Josselson began her research in an effort to 'view identity in women in women's own terms' (Josselson 1987, p. 27). She built her research on Marcia's work (1966) to develop a theory on the 'internal and developmental roots of identity formation in women' (p. 33). By interviewing women during their last year in college and again at ages 33 and 43, she collected evidence of the ways that women form and transform themselves and their identities. Josselson asked 'how women go about the task of consolidating identity?' 'what are the psychodynamic and developmental roots of their differing modes of identity resolution or nonresolution?' 'what are the different pathways they take?' She sought to understand the developmental processes that seek to synthesise the parts together in some meaningful whole and to sketch out the varying and complex identity trajectories that these women created through the negotiations with the developmental issues within their particular sociocultural milieus. By following women's lives from adolescence through adulthood (at age 33 and 43 years) in the subsequent studies, she was able to illustrate the impact that late adolescent identity resolution had on the adult women. Josselson followed Marcia's protocol to assess the identity status of women at the end of their college life. She chose a cross-sectional representative sample of college women in their senior year because prior theory had predicted that identity status would be more stable at this point. The women had the opportunity to explore choices within college and were now poised at the brink of adulthood with many important life decisions ahead. Josselson stressed that the women in the study were in many ways, ordinary women, women who didn't have any special achievements nor were known for any deviance and thus were often not studied or understood. Questions about the women's experience with crisis and commitment were asked in four areas—occupation, politics, religion and sexual standards. From these semi-structured interviews that followed the concerns of the participants, they were placed in one of the four identity statuses: foreclosure, achievement, moratorium or diffusion. She later renamed these types as 'guardians' (foreclosures), 'pathmakers' (achievers), 'searchers' (moratorium) and 'drifters' (diffusions) to reflect language that is more accessible and descriptive than the previous terms (Josselson 1996). In subsequent interviews, questions about life history (familial, educational, professional changes and the motivations surrounding them), general circumstances (e.g. health and financial status) and issues of personal growth were added.

In Josselson's work, the categories served to frame themes of development and the ways that development differs amongst the four groups. The descriptions related to the process of development, not necessarily to an end state. Josselson's case narratives are rich in detail and close to the lived experience of the women participants. For the present inquiry, it also helps to frame insights in the identity experiences of female youth and the question—What are the consequences of the modernising process for the emergent dynamics of individuation–relatedness in a young woman? She employs her 'clinical' sense to unravel the latent meanings of the participants' verbalizations. She makes use of their dreams, fantasies and her impressions/experiences of relating with them during interview sessions to understand their ambivalent desires, conflicts, defensive motivations and crucial themes of life. Her narratives capture the experience of the present stage in the participants' lives that is then woven with strands of the past and projections in the future. For the present work, this research work demonstrated a way of doing psychoanalytically informed, gender-sensitive, process-oriented research.

IX

A Note on Methodological Process of Research

The qualitative research study forming the base of the book has as its foundation the psychoanalytic ideas on identity and self, and it makes use of the psychoanalytic method of listening and interpreting.

Since the research work is a qualitative work having a process orientation, the in-depth, semi-structured and exploratory interviews were the tools used for generating experiential data with the participants. The interviewing technique was rooted in the clinical tradition of seeking a prolonged and sustained dialogue between the researcher and research participants. In order to reach insight and deepen meanings in the lives of the participants, multiple meetings were held with them over a period of time, as per mutual convenience.

The researcher would usually have few areas of interest and questions to pursue for every interview. The exploratory, semi-structured interview technique gave her the flexibility to take her research concerns as far as possible with the participant by following the flow of the communication. After the initial question, no fixed sequence of questions was followed; rather, the questions followed a logic and sequence inherent in the communication flow while ensuring that issues and themes relevant to one's research are addressed. The research questions were also revisited and revised over the course of the research in order to accommodate the newer and more refined queries and directions which emerged through the interactions.

Following the psychoanalytic method, the researcher attempted to attune herself to the emotional worlds of the participants by picking up their nuances of language; noting the facial expressions and gaze; registering the tone, pitch, pressure and speed of speech, body tone, posture and movements, energy levels and reactivity to the environment. *It was imperative to attend to the discrete and fluctuating feeling states of the participants that occurred during particular segments of interview material which were useful in guiding one's senses to what was important and understanding the intrapsychic meanings of their expressions—verbal and nonverbal.* The feeling states and associated perceptions evoked in the researcher during the actual interview and during the listening of the recorded interview, when the interview is relived in the mind of the researcher, aided in intuitively sensing his or her affective-motivational dynamics and giving shape to the emergent narrative of the participant.

In such inquiries, the participant, to some extent, interrupts his or her life history as lived in the unselfconscious balances of private and public life in order to, for a while, favour and observe part aspect of his or her self. *The researcher plays a key role here in introducing him- or herself and method and theory in other's life. In agreeing to be a participant, the individual is inclined to and encouraged to historicize his or her own position, to think back of one's past and to ponder about the continuities and changes in oneself over one's growth.* This work trying to understand the identity development of youth is committed to the idea of developmental probability stated by Erikson (1969). According to this idea, what a man adds up to develops in stages. Typical traits are at work early in life in a form commensurable with the condition of being a child or an adolescent or a young man/woman and have a certain pervasive quality which matures throughout life. These developmental trends in the realms of strivings, capacities and temperament were deciphered and represented in the life stories of the participants in order to show their process of identity formation. The congruence of affirmative strivings, native temperament and trained capacities is seen as the sign of a man having come to himself—having found a sense of identity through vocational and ideological choices. Also, the Eriksonian theory of psychosocial development was central to the understanding and conceptualization of lives of the participants. *While listening to the participant, the researcher was required to keep an inner contact with her conceptual models of understanding the experiential data. It is only when she related the data to psychoanalytic theory that insights about the intrapsychic dynamics of the participant's lives could be grasped.* Thus, the process of generating meaning and insight involves shifting between psychic closeness that allows the researcher to engage with and relive in one's mind, the lived experience of the other and become aware of the thoughts, emotions, ideas and images generated in one's mind as well as intellectual distance that enables the researcher to reflect, interpret and develop relevant thematic configurations. This forms the crux of 'analytically disciplined' empathic engagement between the researcher and research participants (Erikson 1964).

In the psychoanalytic technique of listening, the researcher/clinician listens with free-floating attention to the free associations of the participant/patient. It means that rather than focusing on any one item too intentionally, the researcher/clinician waits to be impressed by recurring themes. These themes will first faintly and then ever more insistently signal the nature of the participant's/patient's message and its meaning (Erikson 1964). *She listened for what might be learnt from the participant and how it linked up with other feelings and observations that had been made of him or her. It is important to note that listening was done within a framework of participant-specific range of ideas consciously and preconsciously available to the researcher through the history of their working together.* In this context, the methodological aspect of repeated interactions with the participants, to explore new themes and deepen certain dynamics, gains importance. Sensitive probing and clarification seeking, sharing preliminary understandings and responding to the material brought forth by the participant helped in keeping the communication moving leading to clarity as well as complexity and sometimes, new and surprising insights for both researcher and participants. Access to certain personal combination of available emotion and responsive thought was found to be useful by the researcher in enabling the participant to summon more associations.

For analysis, the researcher had to balance the demands of the research questions with preservation of the authentic coherence of the life under study. Thus, the interview transcripts were read with double focus: one, to seek answers to the research questions through the experiential data obtained and, two, to formulate life stories in a manner that preserves the complexity and authenticity of lives. The transcripts pertaining to each participant were engaged with in totality, allowing all aspects of what is spoken, thought and felt vis-à-vis him or her to influence the analysis at each stage—data generation to final writing of the life story. Since, the work is psychosocial in nature, the researcher also developed her perspectives on the relevant social contexts of the participants, which included various things like reading about the caste culture of a participant, the brand of IIT and state of technical education in India, the philosophy of an organisation of a participant, the state of social movements, etc. The researcher in this psychoanalytic tradition is not only sensitive to the phenomenology of the individual but, in locating individuals in the midst of a flux of social realities, also realises the possible influence of these realities in shaping individual sense of identity.

When certain intrapsychic dynamics began to impress upon the researcher with their recurrence, they were abstracted and conceptualised. The assumption is that repetitive themes represent more significant and stable intrapsychic aspects or organising functions of the individual.[14] Analysis is a cyclical process. One had to reread the material, constantly trying to see the nature and scope of the story being told. The pre-understandings were to be perpetually corrected and refined so that interpretation could move towards greater accuracy and complexity (Cartwright 2004).

As far as possible, the participant's story is told in his or her own voice, represented through a mix of conversations and narrations. For want of space, however, narrations have been majorly edited, and selections of interview data have been presented. At some places, session-wise interview data has been presented, while in some instances, data gathered across different interview sessions and time periods has been woven together to provide a narrativized flow of communication. In terms of presentation of lives, in most spaces, the participant's voice is first given its due representation and is then followed by

[14] Kakar (1990) refers to certain conventions of 'psychoanalytic competence' formulated by Donald Spence (1982) that affect the analyst's overall understanding of the material and his sense of the important units of meaning. First, thematic coherence, namely, that there is underlying commonality among separate, discrete details. Second, thematic continuity which means in spite of the narrative's detours and discontinuities, the original theme recurs. Third, thematic significance, which holds that significant issues are always under discussion, no matter how trivial the details.

analysis on the psychological themes of individuation and ideology which were relevant to the research. In few instances, even as the narrative is being delineated, a simultaneous focus discusses it. Thus, not following any uniform order, the presentation of lives is guided by an aim to best justify their richness, to be aesthetic in its appeal and provide adequate evidence for the interpretation, informed by theory.

X

Context and Presentation of Study

The present research work is a study of youth as a developmental stage in the life cycle of an individual and in the life cycle of a generation of Indian middle-class young men and women rooted in the contemporary historical moment. The present generation of youth residing in urban Indian towns and cities has been raised amidst information revolution, connectivity boom, lifestyle brands, coalition politics and open economy. In mid-1991, a series of economic reform were announced which dismantled the state controls on the Indian economy and facilitated its greater integration with the world economy. The liberalisation process opened the vast Indian markets to the economies of the world. The World Wide Web and satellite television brought cultural artefacts and information from all over the world right into the drawing rooms of people's homes. The trunk call communication metamorphosed to instantaneous email communication. Internet, mobile services and satellite television are penetrating deep into the interiors of the country. The increase in the purchasing power of the Indians is being readily exploited by the international lifestyle brands. India has emerged as a huge market for high-end gadgets, gizmos and automobiles, luxurious travel holidays, fashion apparel and the list can go on. The new economic dispensation has ensured that its beneficiaries, the expanding middle classes, have many more opportunities to make money and even more avenues to spend it on global brands and lifestyle choices. A new atmosphere of optimism has been generated by the economic reforms. In 1996, a columnist wrote in a leading newspaper: 'New technologies, new ventures, new jobs are being introduced as never before. Foreign exchange coffers are filled as never before. Industry is booming as never before. Most of all, there is palpable hope in the air. People are doing lucrative deals, getting well paid jobs, travelling and vacationing, convinced that India is at last over the hump.'

The contemporary Indian youth in the age range of 18–28 years spent their growing up years feeling the palpable hope in the air and witnessing the world-wide perception that India is an emerging global giant. It has come of age as India moved from the shadows of the socialist past into the strobe lights of hedonist consumerism. As the first nonsocialist market economy generation, it has access to opportunities their parents' generation could never have dreamt of. This is also a generation that has grown up when multiculturalism is in fashion and thus may never experience in their interactions with the outside world that they are second best. The Indian diaspora and the large NRI populations in the UK and US have actually had an influence on mainstream preferences in those countries. Indian food and fashion is as much of our export to the west as the brands of our premier educational institutions like 'Indian Institute of Technology' and 'Indian Institute of Management'. Bollywood icons like Amitabh Bachchan and Aishwarya Rai now rub shoulders with Pierce Brosnan at Madame Tussauds. Besides the Indian entrepreneurs, techies and executives who head international organisations, Indian names like Arundhati Roy to Amartya Sen and Kalpana Chawla to A.R. Rahman have captured the imagination of international establishments in fields as diverse as academia, public policy, science and technology, entertainment, literature and culture, etc. This goes to make a young generation feel integrated in the world in a way that was not possible before. The new economic dispensation of liberalisation and globalisation unveiled in 1991 brought more sections of Indian people closer to the modern ethos of choice, initiative, interdependency, innovation, consumption and competitiveness through increasing interlinkages with diverse world cultures, polity and economies.

The process of liberalisation and globalisation is, however, not without its criticism. It has, over two decades, created a glaring gap between the two Indias, one aspiring to be globalised and the other hopelessly, despairingly marginalised. At the height of the euphoria about the dynamic possibilities unleashed by the reform process, a leading weekly in the country carried a cover story of people living on the brink of starvation in the poorest villages of India in Rayagada, Orissa. The fruits of economic liberalisation are yet to reach the masses in any significant way. Many neo-liberal economic policies like unthoughtful privatisation of public sector, forceful acquisition of agricultural land and forest areas for 'development' purposes, dismantling labour protection and raising foreign investment in sensitive areas like insurance and pension funds have raised critical questions of 'whose development is it?' and 'what is the direction and consequence of this kind of highway to progress?' The rural poor, tribals, women and children are amongst the most marginalised and adversely affected groups by such 'developmentality'. There is an emergence of people's movements and non-governmental organisations which are resisting this form of development and carving out developmental alternatives so that universal healthcare, employment to the poor, free primary education, safe drinking water, affordable housing and social security are guaranteed to all to help people across strata develop their human potential. There are different ways in which the broader development enterprise is thought about and engaged in. At one end are the reformist, intervention-specific notions of alternatives and on the other end are the radical, systemic alternatives which seek broader transformations in political structure and social relations.

The primary objective of the research work is to explore the psychological development of Indian youth (men and women) belonging to urban middle classes in the context of their communal culture, understand their psychological condition in the stage of youth and capture psychological and historical themes in their struggles of defining an identity for themselves located as they are in the contemporary historical moment. The work proceeds via narrations, conversations and life stories of young men and women. They provide dynamic descriptions of the growth processes as well as of the lived experience of the youth stage of the participants. In most cases, taking a biographical perspective, the work develops in-depth life stories representing the self-definitional process of integrating self-elements, identifications, roles and skills cultivated in one's personal history with the ideal prototypes of the day. While taking a stock of what the youth is 'doing' in vocational and avocational domains, each individual life story moves with his or her experiences of conformity, dissent, rebellion, initiative, directionality and dedication, trying to capture the disjunctures as well as continuities in his or her inner world between the personal and social and between previous experience and new demands.

The research questions are addressed to two groups of young men and women in the age group of 20–29 years.[15] The ones that have been chosen to present in the thesis are illuminating the youthful engagement with the questions of vocation, social role, lifestyle and relationship to the existing social order. *They belong to the urban middle classes of India which are most susceptible to the pressures of social change and are at the frontier of making psychological adjustments to them.* As D.R. Nagaraj notes in his introduction to Nandy's book *Exiled at Home*: 'It was the cultural will of the westernized middle classes to build India in a certain way, a way which has become the vehicle of the civilizational forces of western modernity. The success of these classes lies in the ability to impose their will on an entire society by transforming and presenting it as an inevitable and desirable logic of historical change. The cultural will becomes a terribly attractive, "undeniable" reason' (1998, p. xi).

The two groups which have been identified constitute the ideological polarity characterising the current historical moment in the liberalising–globalising India. One group is finding its niche within the liberalisation–privatisation–globalisation (LPG) regime of ever more technological progress and economic advancement. The other is offering a resistance to the strident march of such ideals and instead is insisting on introspection, appropriate brakes and corrections and new ethics that will balance progress with inner freedom and dignity for all. *Thus, while one worldview has private profit as its symbol, the other has humanity as its insignia. In this research, the former group is called the corporate youth, and the latter is called the humanist youth.*[16] The corporate youth are selected from

[15] Emerging adulthood, a term that in recent times have replaced the term 'youth', is conceptualised as beginning with the end of secondary education, usually age 18, and ending in mid- to late 20s for most people as the experimentation of the period is succeeded by more enduring life choices (Arnett 1998).

[16] Erikson refers to these two groups, in his time, as the technological and neo-humanist youth. He asks, 'For does not an interplay between a new dominant class of *specialists*—those who "know what they are doing"–and an intense new group of *universalists*—those who "mean what they are saying"—always determine the identity possibilities of an age?' (1968, p. 36).

professional educational institutions as well as from commercial work set-ups. The humanist youth are drawn from diverse non-profit set-ups like awareness- and advocacy-oriented social organisations, human rights' organisations, action groups, social movements and community living arrangements. The reason for selecting these two groups defined by their vocational–ideological orientation is an understanding gleaned from the Eriksonian framework that the questions of 'What do I want to do in life? What do I make of my life?' are the primary preoccupations of the youth stage. These preoccupations lead the young towards making vocational–ideological choices which allow them the scope to apply their intelligence, skill and energy to some undertaking. The inspired communal activity of work is crucial in its function of 'making a living', a phrase that includes not only the economic dimension but also the coherence of life.

In presentation, the life stories are divided into two major groups—the corporate youth and the humanist youth. Out of a total of 35 lives related to, 16 lives have been represented to reflect on the social psychological worlds of Indian middle-class young men and women. Eight have been presented in the section on corporate youth. The segment on humanist youth has descriptions of eight lives. There are ten life stories and conversations depicting the lived experience of the youth stage of men, while six narrations represent young women. *The selection of the lives has been made on the basis of the particular emphases that they bring with themselves. Attempt has been made to cover a panorama of identity dynamics of individuation and ideological convictions within the professional domains of business and non-profit sectors.* Many of the participants are given more representation as they covered enough common ground and reflected not only their own but also the experiences of many others who shared their circumstances. Few others in being unusual have helped to open up novel directions for analysis and discussion. A few lives have been presented in brief because of shorter interactions with them. They, nonetheless, added dimensions to the overall objective of the work. In all cases, the analysis centres around and follows individual voices. Then, shared themes have been abstracted and explicated in the discussions. There are two sectional discussions, each placed after the presentation of narratives and life stories of corporate and humanist youth. The emphasis in these segments of the thesis is to understand how youth through engagement with different goals and values of social order come to evolve their own self-definitions, belief systems and roles. Such analysis provides clues about the diverse directions in which young Indians are moving. Then, there is a final discussion tying up the themes of research placed at the end of the work. The pivotal focus here is on understanding the process of social change through the theme of autonomy and relatedness between youth and parental generation which is responsible for intergenerational continuity and change in any society.

Part II
Narratives, Conversations and Life Stories of Corporate Youth

Introductory Note

'India Shining', 'India as the global economic superpower' and 'Brand India—these are the few epithets which one often comes across in media reflecting the general spirit of optimism and confidence surrounding the economic progress in the liberalised–globalised India. The rapidly expanding and globalising private sector has lifted the hopes of successive generations post-1991 to 'make it big'. The corporate sector has emerged as the 'ultimate destination', the promise of all good things in life. We are living in a media culture which promotes hedonism, indulgence and freedom and presents the business world as the ideal route of making money, having fun and making an impact.

A total of 20 young persons (men and women) were spoken with for the purpose of research in this section. In the age range of 21–27 years, all were either pursuing professional education or were working in corporate sector. They were drawn from the business fields of IT consultancy, banking, software services, marketing, law, media and advertising. Most of them belonged to elite educational institutions where they had faced stiff competition and high standards of performance. In a bid to explore a range of identity dynamics charted in traditional and non-traditional maps, a cross section of people covering employees, entrepreneurs, and freelancers were interviewed for the research.

For the purpose of presentation, an attempt was made to select those participants who had some work experience (at least 1–2 years) in their field. This was done because in the course of research, it was felt that they had more formulated and realistic opinions, values and understandings of their work lives than those who were still preparing for them. A total of eight lives are represented (six of men and two of women), six in more detail in the form of life stories, narrations and conversations while two in a briefer manner. The more detailed life stories provide deeper insights into the intrapsychic dynamics of individuation and ideology of youth. In spite of their brevity, two shorter cases have been presented as they bring to light certain novel aspects of psychic functioning amongst the young.

Krishna

Krishna, 24 years, was a final year student of a business management program. He was tall and towered over me and had a gentle voice. In the brief contact meeting, he introduced himself formally as H. Krishna, a Tamilian residing in Hyderabad for over a decade now. I came to know that he was the general secretary of the student's union and thus a 'very busy' person. He agreed to talk, somewhat reluctantly, but since some campus activities were coming up in the days ahead, we decided to begin the research interactions after that. The next time, I began by giving him a brief overview of the research concerns in a halting, somewhat faltering, manner, unsure of his participation. At the end of it, he smiled and said, 'Let's start'. The first interview turned out to be an unravelling of his self. It became an interaction in which Krishna felt safe enough to make few 'personal disclosures'. Below are salient fragments of the first interview:

- *We can begin by you telling something about yourself and your family.*
  Fine! My name is Krishna. H. Krishna, I call it. I was born in Chennai. Most of my life, I have stayed in Hyderabad. I have done my high school there. Later went on to do my engineering studies there. My work experience was in Hyderabad before I came to Delhi for management studies. Before Hyderabad, I have lived all across India. I have lived in places right from Assam to Jammu to Vishakhapatnam. My dad was in a transferable job, so we used to stay in each city for not more than 2–3 years. So ... that helped me learn Hindi in the first place. It also helped me to become more adaptive to change. Now it's OK when I move out of a city. I don't feel threatened. That way, my dad and his job helped me. I have a.... Ok! My mom is a homemaker. She was born and brought up in Chennai. My dad was born and brought up in Bihar. He is a Tamilian, but he was born and brought up in Bihar. He has an M.Phil. so far, and he wants to pursue PhD. He is 57 years of age. *I have a younger brother. He is also an engineer. He is in Hyderabad and is currently working in IT company. He is again an MBA aspirant. Trying to follow my footsteps.* That's about my family.
- *What does your father do?*

Names and other identificatory information of all participants have been changed to ensure confidentiality.

DOI 10.1007/978-81-322-0715-3_2,

My father works in XXX (a public sector undertaking in power sector). He is GM of human resources of that company in Hyderabad.

- *Is your father also an engineer?*
  No. He is basically into law and human resources and labour studies.
- *So . . . he has stayed with this job since the beginning?*
  No. He has been in this job since the past 15 years now. But he started his career as a cleaner in another government undertaking way back in 1975–1976. But he has graduated over time and across various companies. He joined the current company in 1991, if I am not wrong, and has stayed on in it ever since.
- *Had a modest beginning.*
  Yes. We are a . . . were a modest . . . we were a lower income. . .middle class family. My father started as a cleaner at the age of 17. You can imagine, he used to clean the machines. From there he graduated to supervisor level, clerk level, this and that level and currently is a general manager of human resources.
- *Hmmm . . . That's quite a life. Must have worked his way up.*
  He did. It's a success story! Planning to write a book about it one day!
- [*Smile*] *Yeah . . . I am sure, it will be very inspirational.* [*After a pause*] *What were your paternal grandparents doing in Bihar?*
  My grandfather used to work in the same company from where my father started as a cleaner.
- *Your father studied alongside working?*
  Yes! That's right. He has 2 M.A.s, an M.Phil., an LLB degree and he is trying to pursue his PhD.
- *Does he share his experiences, his days, his past?*
  He used to while I was growing up. He used to tell me tales of how he used to do this and used to do that and how easy it is for us. He was kind of motivating me and my brother. He used to tell me his day schedule, how he used to wake up at 4o'clock, milk the cows, sell milk across the town he was staying and then catch a train, go to work, come down. Catch the evening class—his degree class. And at that time, he was married. My mom shares all the stories in fact. My mom shares all these stories of my dad. He also shares them. He has no hesitation in sharing them, but it's my mom from whom I have heard a lot of stories.
- *She must have been an observer of his life.*
  Yes! Also a supporter. My mom when she married my dad, she hadn't moved out of Chennai. She belonged to a typical orthodox Brahmin family—a girl who was never supposed to go out of home alone. She was sent to Bihar and she was all alone at home. For her my dad was the only person. She used to narrate all the tales—the good tales, the bad tales, and the interesting tales. It's a good story.
- *What were few of the good tales like?*
  Ummm . . . Like how he used to work very hard. And we should also follow his example . . . etc., etc. Basically the stories of the kind of dedication he had and the place he had been able to create for himself.
- *And the bad tales?*
  Not bad, in that sense. But his struggles and challenges. We have it easy comparatively.
- *How was your educational journey?*
  Pretty smooth actually if I look back now. Ummm . . . OK . . . I should tell you this, till class 9th, I was a horrible student. Believe me. I still remember the day when at the end of the 9th class exams, my principal called me aside and told my dad to get me out of the school. *He said, 'He has just got 41 marks in maths. I don't think he can go past. We can't take the risk of taking such students and risk our 100% results in class 10th exams. I don't think we can afford him.* He might fail and that will reflect badly on the reputation of institution which is proud of sending 100% students to next class'. *Oh! That was a shocking moment.* That was probably the only shocking moment for me in my life. Of course! My dad argued, convinced and ensured that I was there. And that

kind of opened my eyes and changed my whole perception towards studies. *That's when I realised that I have to study hard and I have to be a good student.* I studied very hard and *topped my school in mathematics* in class 10th. Then I went on to do my +2. I took engineering coaching during those years. Then I wrote my engineering entrance exam for colleges in Andhra Pradesh. There are more than two to two and a half lakh people who appear for this exam. I *was there in top 1000 amongst them*, so I got through the best engineering college in A.P. in electronics and communications field. After engineering, I got a job in a multinational consultancy company through campus placement. It is supposed to be *one of the best consultancy company* in the whole world. If you have heard of Accenture, Mckinsey [I nodded in agreement.] ... yeah! So this company falls into the same league. Was there for 2 years. Then came to do my MBA. Journey so far had been smooth. *Of course, at each stage, I had to work hard. All the hard work that I had put in, at least, showed results.*

- *What have been your parents' aspirations for you?*
  My dad wants me to do PhD as soon as possible. He wants me to do away with the placement process next year and make sure that I finish my PhD before I actually settle down in life. *He always wanted me to study well, do well academically.* For him, he says that he is never interested in me topping the exam. I have never been a topper, though I have always done well. I have not been a gold medallist or someone who used to top. But I used to do okay—60–70% types. He was pretty satisfied with that. He always said—do your best. For him, if I get a first division, he is happy ... I am surprised. He wasn't interested in seeing me working also for 2 years. He always used to tell me that this is not the time for working right now. Please go and study. Finish your studies and then work. That's the best way to go forward. Basically, he wants me to add more to my profile. Probably, in his own career, he has seen that qualifications matter to be successful. That's what he is trying to reinforce in me. Ensure that *I am loaded with degrees*, appropriate degrees and a doctorate if it's possible before actually doing a job. *So, he has always encouraged me to study, study, study* [speaks with a tired expression]. *My mom, till engineering, was like—make sure you make the family name proud.* Make sure you do this, make sure you do that. Now that I have done that, she is happy. She knows that my kids, wherever they would go, they wouldn't let me down. She is pretty silent right now. Just do whatever you want. My dad is still ... last week when I went back home, he said—so what are your PhD plans? Have you discussed it with your professor? I said—Not yet [in meek voice.]. So he always wants me to study, study, study ... It's nice.
- *Education seems to hold importance for him. He wants to do a PhD at the age of 57 years. He wants you to acquire qualifications.*
  He is currently enrolled for a degree in law—LLB. He wants to practice law after he retires in 3–4 years. To practice law, he needs to get his LLB degree from a recognised institute. Those days in 1960s, he got a diploma from an institute in Bihar which is currently not recognised. He attends the class with all the 20-year-olds in the morning. He goes every day in morning and attends the classes, even now. He probably feels that he missed out on academic work when he was young because of economic conditions. He had to begin work at the age of 16–17. Last month when I went back home, my father asked me to take him to the bookshop from where I bought my books. I took him to the second hand books' store because he wanted to buy his books. So we went to buy books for my dad [laughs]. I don't know how many children will do that for their dads. But I did that.
- *It's quite a reversal of roles ... How does he manage his work and studies?*
  He is a very dynamic person. He spends very less time at home. He attends his class in the morning. Goes to office at 9–9.15 and doesn't come home before 9.30–10. He has loads of work, but somehow he also manages to study. He is a high energy person.
- *He must have been very busy. Was he available for you people at home?*

Yes. Yes. He always kept a tab on us. That was never an issue. Always kept a tab on our results, what's happening at home? *Sometimes, we used to feel that he is pestering too much. Ya! Too much.* But as a dad, probably, I'll also do the same.

- *Did you also try for IIT-JEE?*
  Yes, I did, but I couldn't make it. I asked my dad should I try for it again. My dad said no! Don't waste a year. That's what my dad said. Actually for me, it was IIT or one of the other top institutes of Andhra Pradesh. I had to take a call in class XI because preparations for both these exams are very different and tough in their own way. I wrote a few entrance exams for the coaching centres that prepare you for IIT. If you get through them, you get through to IIT. So, I wrote a few entrance exams for these coaching institutes. There are coaching institutes that prepare students to get into these IIT coaching institutes. [To my shocked look] Yeah, there are. There are students from class VII, VIII, IX that go into these coaching institutes. You should see the craze there. It's maddening. I tried to get into IIT coaching centres. I couldn't. I decided there and then that IIT is not happening. Definitely, I will try and target the best engineering institute in Andhra. I focused my energies there and was able to make it. Though, it would have been nice had I made it to IIT. But . . . sometimes when you don't get to the best place, you are motivated to work hard. No regrets!
- *What was your job profile?*
  Shall I tell you the technicalities? Ok let me simplify it for you! My company used to do projects across Europe and US. So . . . the clients used to tell the company—listen! I want to install SAP and Oracle in our organisation. Help us do that. The company would say—fine! And tell my team that it's your responsibility to make sure that Oracle and SAP are installed in this company's system. So I'll get back to the client and ask what is it that they require? I will ask for problem documents. The person on the client side will document all the problems that they have and give to me. I have a manager who coordinates the entire operation with another manager on the client side. Both of them discuss and decide what needs to be done and in what time frame. So I have to finish the work within time. Problem A can be that some database somewhere is not working properly. Or some business function has to be added which is currently not there. So, I just log into the client's system from here in India and I use my technical skills to work on it and make it as close to what the client desires. Sometimes, you have to go to the client location as well to fix the problem. I do the first initial implementation and tell the client that hey! I have done something—why don't you have a look at it? He will have a look at it from whichever country he is in and say—it's looking fine. But also do something in here, here, here. I do that. Give it back. That's it. One problem is solved. Then another and so on. Basically my work there in the initial year was highly technical. I used to get a problem, solve it and give it back. The main concentration is that whatever technical output we give, there is no flaw in that. It works as per requirement. It was during the second half of second year of my job that apart from all of this, I also took the managerial responsibility of deciding who does what, interacting with the client side to decide what should be the time schedule, duration. Had I stayed on with the company, I would have become highly technical Oracle/SAP consultant. I had to take a call whether I want to do that or jump onto a managerial post. I wanted the latter for which I needed an MBA.
- *What is the lure of management degree?*
  It's like—*if I am a technical guy i.e. an engineer and I work on a tech job, my average salary will be 3–4 lakhs per annum. Now, I see a manager who is from FMS, IIM-A, ISB Hyderabad and that person has been recruited in the same company as the manager. He is given salary of 11 lakhs, 15 lakhs, 17 lakhs. I would wonder—what is the difference between that person and me? The only difference is that he is a graduate from a top business school.*The reason why a company pays so handsomely to a management graduate from a top B-school is

that they are supposedly the top of the cream of 3–4 lakh students who write the competitive exams. They have the basic skills and are smart. So it's like if you want this talent, pay them and get it. That's the reason why FMS or IIMs students get paid more. The moment you jump from this to the second level of B-schools, the salary plummets. That's the biggest reason why technical employees shun their jobs and prepare for CAT and other MBA exams.

Besides, the tech jobs are repetitive. It gets very boring beyond a point. Also, I think the engineering education system is very poor. To be honest, it's pathetic. The faculty is not good. It doesn't inspire love, curiosity, interest in technology. People like Abdul Kalam were inspired by their teachers. Most colleges don't have such teachers. *People join engineering colleges for a degree.* There are textbooks, there are guides. You read them, pass the exams. *For 4 years, I had no curiosity to learn more or to dig deeper into what is electronics. Do some research on it? No way!* The students are good . . .they are the best in analytics, mathematics. But you don't have teachers who can shape this talent. *So the tendency of appreciating technology, innovating with it is not prevalent with 99% of the engineers and that includes me. You know that there is a TCS, Infosys waiting for you to give a job. Now, the job you get is a technical job because you are an engineer.* The first 2 years are great. You will feel good working with TCS, Infosys, Deloitte. I know that my mom is sharing proudly that my son is working here. In all the parties, all the ladies are talking—where is your son working? Infosys, Satyam . . . The craze is too much. Everyone is earning handsome amount of money. But soon you realise that the job that you are doing never interested you because you never had an interest or inclination towards that. *During engineering, you didn't have a vision or dream about how you can work with technology.* When you are touching 2 years, you realise that this is not what you wanted to do with your life. Then you see your manager who earns crazy money by just ordering a few people around, and you wonder how I can reach that stage. That's a commonsensical question I ask. I don't want to be here. I want to be there. How can I do that? Write a CAT exam, write other management entrance exams. Do an MBA. When you look around, you see that all the top guys are MBAs. I saw with my own eyes, the guy who led my Oracle-SAP vertical was an MBA. All the group leads were MBA. My country head, my deputy country head was an MBA. What chance do I have of being in these places without an MBA? None whatsoever. Ideally, even if I am a tech guy and I work well, I should reach the high posts in my vertical, at least. But that doesn't happen. *All the seniors at the top level are just MBAs and that's what scares you sometimes.*

There are some people who say 'To hell with it'. I don't want to be a top guy. I don't want to do an MBA. I am happy with the way I am, what I have right now. I am happy doing the same job till I retire. Ok! Good luck! But for most people when they see only MBAs upstairs, they panic and they don't see any scope of reaching the top level.

- *How much were you being paid in your first job?*

  When I joined in 2004, I was being paid 2.9 lakhs. In the first year, I was given an increment and I was around for 2 years. So by the end of 2 years, my salary had reached around 4.5 lakhs. I am living off that money now. I am paying for my education and living expenses. Money is not so much of an issue. You have a continuous amount of money supply coming to you in such companies. You have your own AC room. It's a life of its own. For people who don't have aspirations in life, who don't want to grow big, there is nothing like TCS, Deloitte, Infosys. *It was interesting when my last salary was more than my dad's salary. I am talking about basic pay* [*smirks*]. *And I was what then?? 22, 23 years old.*
- *You discussed it with your father?*

  Yeah! My dad was like 'Ok! Money will come. First study. Money will come.' [Curt tone] He always did that. *He never used to encourage me, or showed any enthusiasm towards it* . . . Probably because he never wanted me to get blinded by what I was earning. I was earning almost 40 K per month when I was 22. It was easy money for me. My dad, now I realise why he was so concerned. He wanted me to keep preparing for the exams and not get blinded or lose my focus. It's very easy to get blinded. Money is coming. So much of it is coming. What is the problem? Enjoy! *But my dad used to continuously let me know that I had to study, otherwise, I'll have some tough time!* [laughs]

- *So how was life when you were working, besides the work? You were earning well, so you could now splurge.*
  Interesting [far away look]. Very interesting ... Actually not so interesting. I used to work 14 hours a day. Come home, prepare for CAT for 3–4 hours, sleep. Again work for 14 hours a day, come back, prepare ... I had little expenses. I was staying in my own home. My mom used to cook for me. I used to get a cab to take me from home to office. There were no other expenses. Everything was going in my savings account.
- *Good boy lifestyle?*
  Yes!
- *No party scene, no holidaying, no shopping?*
  Not me. No! [After a pause] OK ... For that I need to reveal something more. *There are two phases of my life.* Till I landed the job, I was very quiet. Forget girls, I never used to even speak with the boys. *Ultra, ultra, ultra traditional* ... Something to do with my attire and the way things were at home. *My father had this big personality and I was always this subdued kind of guy.* I used to just go and do my work and come back. I was obese. I was 140 kilos. You probably will not understand what it means [Silent for a while with a grim expression]. Things were ... I don't know ... things were crazy. *I was a good student and I was doing my work well and all that was great. But I never used to shop for anything because I never used to fit into one. So till then, I was like absolutely zero, nothing, zilch. Then something happened. I fell in love with a girl.* I had to lose weight for that. I lost 40 kilos of weight in 3 months. It was then that I bought my first jeans. I am still wearing that. I bought T-shirts, my first pair of Reebok shoes.

At this point, he felt overwhelmed with emotions and became a bit remote. I too was moved by his disclosure. After a brief silence, I remarked how love brings about an expansion of self to which he agreed and added that he felt good and free with her. Since, we had almost run out of time, we decided to meet again and fixed up the date and time of the next meeting.

I

In the next 2 meetings, I tried to explore more deeply Krishna's relationship with his father, where I sensed an intense ambivalence, concerns about his obesity and his growing up years in order to understand his disparate self-elements—a subdued son under the patronage of a dominating father and a confident general secretary of students' union who bragged that everything revolved around him; the under-performing student before class 9th and an achieving student since then; an obese child and a well-built young man.

From his sharing in subsequent interviews, Krishna's father emerged as a dominating figure, someone who was 'always at the back of you'. He felt happier being at school because it meant freedom from his father's nagging. He recalled thinking that he had to go back home and there was a dad there and he would quiz him on this or that . . . what happened in school, what did the teacher do, what did he do, did he speak up in the class, when was the next test, how was the performance in the last test, was he studying, had he done his homework? He felt dominated and suffocated in his presence. He could not speak freely to him. He would speak to his father when spoken to. He described his father as a big personality who was involved in every aspect of the home. According to him:

> My father is a hands-on person. So, whatever happens to mom, to me, to my brother, he wants to ensure that he is involved in it. For eg. Suppose—if both of us are at home and an MBA admission notification comes out. He would tell me to study and would go out to buy the form. Even if I would protest and tell him that I can get it myself but he would insist. Of course, he is trying to help but sometimes, it can become suffocating, frustrating. *If I was a dad, when I have a son, I'll do it differently.* I'll say Son! Go and get the forms. I will not spoon feed him. My dad's intents are very clear—he wants his son to succeed and do well. But probably, the means may not be the best. Again, if I have a son, I'll say studies are fine but how many friends do you have? Why don't you call all your friends home? He will feel happy. Instead, if I keep telling him OK! Studies, exams, studies, exams. That's not the end of the world. *Of course! I understand that he was trying to do the best but I will understand that there are multiple personalities/angles to a person and you have to help develop all of them.*

Talking of his childhood, Krishna recalled having stayed in different parts of India because of which he regretted not having long-standing friendships of 10–15 years like the way he saw other people had. He also faced difficulties in adjusting to the language and culture of each city. His general sense was of being uprooted every now and then. *One lasting and pleasant impression of his childhood was that he used to play a lot of cricket and football with his friends. Playing sports for 3–4 hours in the evening was an integral part of his life.* During interval in school, he used to make strategies, form his team, and that took a lot of his energies. He spoke with passion about the excitement of matches between this road and that road, this apartment building and that apartment building. Regarding studies, he said that before 9th, he was an average student. *He never cared much about studies.* He wouldn't sit in front of the books for more than 1–2 hours. He would study only for exams and would get 60–70 % marks which were considered OK by his parents. While they always prodded him to study, they were fine with the marks that he was getting. *For him, the priority was his cricket team and winning matches. The class 9th episode was a "shocker" for his parents and him. He saw the incident as 'a humiliation as well as a challenge to my ego'. It became a turning point for him after which he began to sit in front of books for hours and hours together.* Solve maths problems, read science book. He would wake up at 3.30 in the morning, used to go for a maths coaching class, come back at 5.30 and read science on his own and then go to school. After coming back from school, he would do his homework and solve more maths problems. He remembered his mother sitting next to him and helping him study. *He set targets for himself that he had to be in top 5 in school, get into a good engineering college and get a good job. All of that led to him remaining more and more indoors. He left playing and concentrated completely on his studies. Academics* began to dominate his life. In his words:

> The moment academics took over in class 10th, 11th, 12th and engineering, it was just books, books, books. And it didn't help that I got my first specs, and my father ensured that I wore this big specs. *I used to look like a 'padaku'* [nerdy], *not bothered about anything*

> *else apart from books.* Not wanting to develop friendship with anybody. Zero time for playing. Because of that I had become obese. People used to say [in a derisive tone] 'Oh! He is studying. What else he can do? Nothing! He will study, then go back home.' During those years, I didn't have friends with whom I could speak freely. In that sense, I was completely disregarded as if I was a nobody. I never used to go to people's homes for parties. I wouldn't go for freshers' party, farewell party. *I used to think that people will make fun of me. I am obese. I had this very very deep inferiority complex . . . that I didn't count for much, people don't like to speak with me, I am not considered worthy of anything.* I had very few friends . . . I was very unsocial.

Though, he attributed his current 'successful' station in his life to all the hard work and focus he showed during those years, he was disappointed that he couldn't combine it with fun in the way his other peers were able to. He used to console himself like this:

> When my friends were partying, I used to think let them party. *I'm going to get more marks than them or I'll get a better rank than them in the engineering entrance exam. Ultimately, I'll be the winner.* Let them play their cricket. Instead of wasting 3 hours there I will spend 3 hours in solving more maths problems. That's the attitude I developed. And that helped. None of my school/college mates have reached the level where I have reached now. But they are all together. They have their own camaraderie. They don't call me. I miss that. I'll be honest about it. But I console myself by saying—fine! I am here, they are there.

Another phase of Krishna's life began when he fell in love with a girl who worked in his office and travelled with him in the office cab. She was an extroverted, talkative, carefree person with whom he 'felt free and relaxed'. He could talk spontaneously to her about his stresses, work, family and past. According to him:

> It was fun to speak to someone. It was the first time, I was speaking about these things to someone else. She used to understand my brand of humour and reply in the same way. Usually, these things you do with friends. You can speak anything and they will retort back. They will make fun of you. That's the first time, I did it to somebody. It felt nice.

But when he proposed to her, she rejected him, asking him to look at his face in the mirror. It was again an incident where he felt humiliated and hurt. But he took it to be the much needed 'kick on my backside'. He got down to jogging, exercising and dieting, and within 3 months, he got his weight in double digits from 140 kg. Then he bought for himself branded clothes and shoes and presented himself to her and won her approval. He had wanted to marry her, but the affair lasted for a year. The reasons of the break-up were not shared by Krishna because he was uncomfortable doing so. The break-up was a very painful experience for him—one which took away someone who was very precious for him. Soon after it happened, he came to Delhi for his management studies.

Many observations of and conversations with Krishna revealed a *simmering rage and rivalry against father and fatherlike 'authority' figures* along with his need to be affirmed and identify with them. The father, as the above description showed, was experienced as 'big' and 'powerful' in his deeds and in his sphere of control. The father's success story of rags to riches was shared with intent to impress the listener with the father's unbridled ambition, undiminished zest and infinite ability to work hard which by virtue of him being his son, was hoped to be transmitted to him as well. *The tales of struggle of his father shared by both the parents were not only grave reminders of how terrible their fate would have been had the father not 'sweated it out', and thus an instruction in hard work and discipline so as to extend the good fortune, but also more effectively, instruments of guilt inducement in sons if they took the privileges for granted and went off on other trails.* The father's big persona casts a long shadow over the household and family members from which no one and nothing could escape. The mother was also experienced as someone who was dependent on him and was also his supporter. Such an imposing father was experienced as always 'being on one's back'. *The grandiose, nagging over presence of the father had led him to continuously feel small and be restrained and meekly compliant in front of him. The insistent 'spoon feeding' curtailed the space of autonomy of a son who wished to grow up and beyond the parental domain and required the encouragement and affirmation of the father for the same.* The right to wield initiative of imagination and action is often accompanied with *anti-authoritarian stance* in the youth in which the authority figures are held guilty for their shortcomings and for limiting their area of exercise of enterprise. In Krishna's narrative, one came across it in his damnation of teaching faculty in engineering institutes. It also came up in his rather cheeky remark during a casual conversation about his teachers at the management institute (who complained about the current crop of students being very money minded). He remarked with a relish that he wondered how the wives of professors would rate their worth, considering they earn even less than their students. *I noticed that while Krishna took great pleasure in having outdone the father figures in terms of money, a culmination of secret hope of the child that one day he would be big enough to defeat the father, he took on the same schoolmaster tone while chiding his juniors for letting the money go into their heads.*

The class 9th incident marked a discontinuity in Krishna's existence. Being named as someone who could bring discredit to the school and family name was experienced as *shame* in which one feels exposed and being looked at in a way one is not ready. It was also a jolt to the confidence that he had in his academic competency. In order to counter these painful emotions and re-establish one's worth, he *gave himself up to academics with a vengeance. He wanted to 'prove a point' to all those who had berated him and this time, wanted to 'show them what he can do'*. The incident created a powerful estrangement within him because it led him so completely away from his enjoyable way of organising social experience through planning, sharing and experimenting in play. The sportive competition provided an arena for cooperative play with peers, exuberant self-expression and a sense of mastery. Krishna noted with disappointment that he couldn't combine the two worlds of play and work. *So when he applied himself to the school life of concrete pursuits and approved goals, he did it in an uncompromising fashion.* The internalised voice of self-guidance and self-punishment in him, perhaps, exacted obedience more literal than the one even the parent wished to exact. The self-constriction was overcompensated in a great show of tireless initiative, in a quality of '*go-at-itiveness*' at any cost. It was fuelled first and foremost by aggressive ideals of defeating the contemporaries and proving the world wrong which once doubted his worth. It was energised by *dreams of 'making big' that were fostered by his avid interest in reading about the lives of corporate honchos.* The glorious achievements of the likes of Ambanis and Tatas and other CEOs animated his fantasies of conquest and linked his initiative to a sense of ambition and purpose. *The strain of being 'on the go always' had an effect on his body resulting in obesity and premature greying of hair.*

His industriousness and the outward success that it offered him gave him relative satisfaction, but it didn't resolve his sense of inferiority. His latent sense of being 'not good' persisted. Nothing that he had achieved seemed to count with his contemporaries and help him gain their company. *His appearance, his unsociable behaviour and his conventional lifestyle made him a misfit in the social circles and precluded him from the youthful exuberance in friendship and competition, in argument and gossip and in joint inspiration.* This exclusion only deepened his sense of isolation and sharpened his rageful competitiveness. *His sense of inferiority may also be because, in comparison with his father, he still measured much 'smaller'*. His father was a much more handsome man, in commanding position, and someone whose achievements were projected as almost insurmountable. *A wanting companionship between father and son and a hopeless rivalry in which the father's non-affirming stance towards the son's monetary status (which was the most concrete index of success for Krishna) was countered by even more loud proclamations of his ambitions behind his father's back.* It didn't allow for an experience of essential equality in worth to develop between the son and the father.

He saw the love relationship as a positive event in his life which got him out of his staid living. Improvement in his appearance, fun and the affectionate responsiveness of a loved one helped him expand his sense of self. *Love often serves as psychic loosener, jarring the soul out of the narcissistic sheath of normal, everyday, self limiting routines. He hatched out of the constrictive, conservative parental culture and joined the exciting, materialist trend—visiting coffee joints, watching movies, shopping.* Having gained acceptance in the peer culture, his introversion lessened and he became more confident. He discovered himself afresh—physically and emotionally. He felt that he could do much greater things than he was doing for the past few years. Fantasies and desires of togetherness were released: they wove dreams of living in Switzerland, he setting his own enterprise in which she would be the head of human resource, buying a car. *The love relationship helped him psychologically distance himself from the home by providing access to a tender and affectionate feminine presence that could thus, supplant the mother who till then was the only comforting figure in his life.* He had a fantasy of coming back home from office and lying down with his head in his wife's lap, like he did with his mother, and she would place her hand on his head and soothe him. Another flight of his imagination had him wishing his girlfriend to come to his home and handle his father with her chatter and opinions, something that he couldn't manage to do. Interestingly, they both were HR professionals, and Krishna had high opinion of her abilities. Incipient in this fantasy was the desire of seeing his father finally finding his match who could cut his big personality to size.

The break-up of the relationship was painful, but his admission in an MBA course provided the change in the environment which helped him in his recovery.

The academic life, away from home, laid open the horizon of possibilities which linked long-standing dreams to tangible opportunities. One of his long-standing secret wishes was to stand on stage in front of 10,000 people and address them, influence them and get applauded by them. Till he came to the B-school, it remained a fantasy—an alternative world in the recesses of one's mind from where we continue our long-standing quarrel with reality. Here, he saw the opportunity to actualize his dreams. However, it presented the dilemma of continuing to be an academically oriented student the way his parents wished him to be or develop his personality which would make him a good manager/leader in the corporate world—the heroes who always exploited his enthusiasm. The power of his childhood fantasy led him to decide in the favour of the latter without irrational guilt at crossing the boundary. *Hostel life offered him many avenues for youthful escapades, and the post of general secretary absorbed his fantasies of leadership.* All the fervent desires and wishes he had of having a lot of friends, going for parties and on trips outside the city which were stuck inside of him and couldn't find an expression were released. He spoke of his life in B-school as 'living my dream'. *He confessed to his academic performance not matching the standards that he had earlier, but it was a trade-off that he was happy making.*

II

The last interview with Krishna was held close to the final placement season, and the focus was to map his aspirations and attitudes towards work career. *Over a period of time, one had sensed the importance that he attached to money as an index of one's success.* Many of his jokes were about economics of love. Hence, an attempt was made to understand what 'money' meant for him. Krishna began the conversation by sharing about a company that had come to the campus for presenting its profile to the job aspirants. The company was offering an extremely lucrative salary package of Rs.30 lakhs per annum. He shared laughingly: 'Everyone is salivating! After all it is 1/3 of a crore. Few of them have already decided which car to purchase with their first salary'.

- *What is the fantasy associated with fat pay cheques?*
  It's got to do with ego and the sense of achievement. *A feeling of winning.* It's like 10 years back, my parents were scolding me for not studying but now I have become successful. *And also proving the detractors wrong.* Everyone has had altercations with somebody in their batch or seniors or teachers. *Just getting back to them and showing them they were wrong!* See what I am getting and you made fun of me ... *Secondly, it gives people bragging rights in their circle and everywhere else. I had once heard a quote—money can't buy love, but it improves your bargaining position.* Also, the *pride that the family feels* when the person who gets 30 lakhs calls back home and says—it's done! The parents feel great. They would call the neighbours and relatives and tell them—look, what has my son done? *Considering the kind of family backgrounds we come from, 1/3 of a million is a dream.* The actual salary figure doesn't matter. It could be 28, 30, 35 lakhs. As long as it's huge and is removed from the average figure, it's

great. It's about satisfying people back home. *Again this arises out of the expectations that people back home carry.* There are few parents who would be easygoing and let the child be. Got a job, ok! Others will be—be a topper! Do this, do that . . . He will do it for one's folks. They would love it. *Kids are programmed to satisfy the parents.*

- *Which sector and what job profiles are hot propositions right now?*
  Finance! Finance is where the moolah lies right now. Those who want to make lots of money and want to go very far in life want to go to finance sector. So that's where I am going. The finance profiles offered are in investment banking, treasury, corporate finance, private equity. That's where big money is. Most people want to join big brands like HSBC, Standard Chartered, McKinsey & Co., Accenture, KPMG, JP Morgan Chase and Lehman Brothers. The newer trend is that people are considering joining smaller companies which are offering excellent money and good experience and exposure. Like this company which is offering 30 lakhs is a little known investment banking firm. But still people are queuing up for it. You work there for 3 years and then skyrocket to another company from there.
- *People also keep changing their jobs a lot.*
  Yes! Do you know the percentage of people who would leave their jobs after the 1st year? Close to 96%. Why? Because they are jumping. If they are managers in one company, getting a senior manager profile in a competitor company, they jump. From there, to someplace else . . . jump. Jump, jump, jump. *The designation matters. Senior manager, vice president, I am heading marketing in India, in SE Asia, I am heading corporate finance. All of this is a big ego boost. What matters to people is what goes out in public. How are they known to the outside world . . . and designations are big things.*
- *So big money, brands, designations are the elements of corporate dream!*
  Yes. That's what we aspire for to become successful. Success will mean promotion almost every year, max every 2 years; reaching the C-level job in next 10–15 years. Ideally retire at 45 and then enjoy with family. After that you wouldn't have to work. You can always do consulting. Or you become such an expert that you are called for all the talks and make money out of that.
- *But everyone is dreaming of the same thing, so there is a lot of competition. How do you retain the hope that it will be fulfilled?*
  Confidence! Everyone has the basic level of confidence. *The moment you come to an IIM or XLRI or FMS, you know that you are top 1% or top .01% of your peers.* If at all anyone can dream and convert the dream into success, it is very probably you. Start dreaming! They know that they have the training, the qualifications and the networks. They are inherently there. It's also about 'globing'. MBAs specialise in it. You know what it is? [I nodded in negative.] *Ok! Globing means talking about everything and anything with so much confidence, even if you don't know anything about what you are talking, that people in front are blown away.* [laughs] *We are different from the normal MBAs.* If I want to meet a CEO of a company, I go to the secretary and give my visiting card. By having the word MBA from top B-school, he will call me in. Talk to me for at least 5 minutes. He will think there would be something in me.
- *You have a visiting card as a student as well?*
  Yes! [He gave it to me—it carried the name of his B-school.] When, I will go out from here, I'll write my educational qualifications and the institutions I belong to. [laughs mischievously] *You have a brand associated with you. Sell it!*
- *So this is a dream! What's the reality? I mean, you don't really retire at 45.*
  Yessss! The reality is, well . . . different, very different [sarcastic tone]. To begin with, you often end up not getting your dream job. *I have seen people of the same batch sitting in the same auditorium . . . some ecstatic, some smiling, some crying.* It's a strange sight! The company you want to get into may not come on the first day. And by the time, it comes, you might have already got placed. There is a very cool song which is heard in all B-school campuses. The best part about the song is when the main character gets low marks in his exams and has to wait till day 2 to get himself placed. He eventually gets a sales job, the most fucking job possible, where he would have to sell soaps in rural

> districts [laughs out aloud]. We actually used to feel a sense of déjà vu while listening to this one in campus. Beside, you don't retire at 45, of course! You retire at 55–60. The salaries, yes! By the way, never get carried by the salaries. They are the cost-to-company (CTC) figures. They are bloated. The actual salary is much less. Like, a bank will say, we are offering 15 lakhs, which means that you may not probably get more than 10–11 lakhs because a large part of it will be variable incentive based on performance. [pauses] ... I must also tell you this—the company that I was talking about which is offering 30 lakhs ... the person who had come to do the presentation said that if you join the company, you should be prepared to work 24X7, 365 days a year. No Sundays, no holidays. He said that he hadn't slept for the last 3 days because he was working on a deal where he had to be on call from Australia, UK, US and the boss in Bombay. He is loving it. If interested, do apply. *So, the company pays you, but it squeezes the life out of you. You won't survive! By 30 you are gone ... You will be suffering from BP, diabetes. But still, we all aspire for such money! It's crazy !!!!* What else ... Yeah! Did I tell you this that my friend is an AVP in HSBC and all what he does is selling cards! So this designation thing is also very dicey ... Many times it's just a heavy word to add to the aura. One should be beware of it! People don't talk about the dissatisfactions of their jobs because it opens them to ridicule from peers. I know of a guy who is doing really boring job but he says it's cool! Another friend of mine in MBA, he wants to be a musician. But I know that he wouldn't pursue a full-fledged musical career. He will get a job, earn his bucks. Money corrupts! It makes us lazy. People forget their dreams. *There are times when I think ... the current generation is mad after jobs, competition, money. Why? Because of the way we have grown up, the way we have been trained by our parents. 90% come from middle, lower middle class backgrounds. When we were growing up, the focus was on education. Do well! Do well! Otherwise nothing would happen. By the time our kids will grow up, they will be rich! Super rich! I don't know what I would be saying to my children?* I would not be forcing them—study, study! Otherwise it will be disastrous [simulating anxious/threatening voice]. That doesn't make sense. *I know the value of education, but they wouldn't have the pressure.* How will they grow up?

In the above discussion, Krishna articulated work-related stances of his own as well as his contemporaries. In him, one sensed a rageful readiness to 'make it big', to outdo all rivals. While in the past, he had been seen as unworthy and inferior, now he willed to be visible as admirable and grand. *His attitudes towards work—the space where the initiative is directed—reflect his generation's somewhat narcissistic clamour for attention and exhibitionism.* Money and status were, therefore, cultural objects which could mean for many of them the insignia of victory in a contest over favoured position with a parent, loved partner or peer; a gift from a son to the parents in which they can take delight in an unmasked fashion. While higher education sanctions genteel boasting and sportive competition, in Krishna's case, *competition over money and status* took on a hostile and wilful turn in which they were used as aggressive ammunition to blow away the punishers and competitors. The intensely competitive and free market work environment makes it imperative for every player to have *open-ended vision of opportunities, to gloat more on the future possibilities rather than impediments, to be the first mover and indulge in 'narcissism of small difference' with respect to peers in domains of skill sets, tastes and opinions. The ideology of capitalist individualism promised an imaginative, bordering on illusory, scope to his aspirations of 'changing the world through the route of acquiring companies, hiring/firing people'. The attitude learnt from the sphere of consumption was also applied to one's own self—advertising oneself, to package oneself erotically with the right kind of sociability, eloquence and sophistication. All of this was perceived as essential for success not only in work but also in love.* However, these tendencies lie in an uneasy tension with the inner dynamics of his personality shaped by a long history of socialisation in an environment that was conservative and parochial. He often shared how shocked he was to see the behaviour of few of the students in terms of their abusive lingoes, aggressive self presentation and buttering skills. His clothing, musical and food preferences still remained provincial. The feelings of inferiority kept surging and destabilising his sense of certainty. *The corporate dream while being the lasting basis of his wish and will to learn and work was also seen capable of becoming embittered and embattled by the reality.* He not only privileged it but also subtly mocked it. Though wanting to be a spectacle to beheld, he couldn't help feeling self-conscious and exposed in his weaknesses. This was dramatically displayed during an event he was compeering in which he lured me to 'see him there'. On the stage, he faltered many times, overcome as he might have been by the fright of turning into reality one of his most fervent wishes. But it was also noteworthy that he persevered through the ceremony with silent resoluteness, something which was a typical trait of him, and carried him through the challenges of his life.

Aanchal

I met Aanchal at the home of one of my other research participants. On getting to know that I am a psychologist 'basically trying to understand what all young people are doing and why' (that's the way her friend phrased the research concerns for her), she laughed excitedly and said that in response to this she would say, *'Twenty six, lawyer, having a party every day of her life'*. She struck me as a cheerful, gregarious person. All through the period that I saw her with her friend, she brought a certain positive charge to the interaction. I came to know that she was a corporate lawyer who had done her double bachelors' degree in law and was working in a law firm. In between smoking a cigarette and chopping vegetables, she listened, responded thoughtfully, cut jokes and sang to herself. She volunteered to talk about herself, and we exchanged phone numbers. I contacted her a couple of weeks later. She was holidaying in Goa at that time.

We met a week after her return in her flat where she lived with a flatmate. A two-bedroom flat with a living room and kitchen in a posh colony was simply furnished. It gave an appearance of a makeshift house which had all the necessary household articles and provisions stacked around somewhat carelessly. Her bedroom was considerably more settled and aesthetically done up with colourful curtains, cushions and an all floor seating arrangement. One of the walls was adorned by a beautifully embroidered panel from Kutch which her boyfriend had presented to her. The other had a big blown-up family photograph, featuring her parents, her elder brother and herself, radiating togetherness and happiness. There was music piled at one end of the room and few legal books at the other end. A small temple with a couple of idols was mounted on one of the walls. She was spilling with stories of her trip with her boyfriend and other common friends. I vicariously enjoyed her fun and romantic moments following which she checked herself and asked me smilingly to get on with my work. Since I was interested in knowing about her family, I pointed to the photograph and commented that that they all looked like one happy family to which she enthusiastically agreed. She added after a moment's silence that the happiness was sometimes overshadowed by disagreements and differences between the parents' and the children's lifestyle. On being

P. Bansal, *Youth in Contemporary India: Images of Identity and Social Change*,
DOI 10.1007/978-81-322-0715-3_3, © Springer India 2013

asked to elaborate further on this, she said that probably it would be better for her to start from the beginning. She shared:

> My father is an engineer working with a PSU and my mother is a political science teacher in a school. My elder brother is a doctor, and he is working in England. I have done all my education from one school in Delhi and well! It was kind of both good and bad. It was good because it gives you the stability—same friends, same teachers. It was not so good because it constrains your world. You interact only with one kind of people who have been with you throughout and you feel that that's what the world is all about. *So school was a lot about studies. It was always very competitive ... in everything—be it studies, extracurricular or sports.* Academics was very important for me ... also because it was expected out of me that I should do well. *Both my parents, more so my father, have been very particular about our grades and so on. There weren't any punishments, but there was disappointment when either I or my brother was not in the top 3 of the class.* So in school, both of us ended up studying really hard. And I used to actually quite like studies also, especially the social sciences and languages. My brother was more into studies than I was. He was always the quiet, very sincere, studious type ... till the time he was in school. Many things changed when he went to the medical college [winks]. I was active in debating and sports in school. I used to play football with boys, I remember! It was great fun. My parents used to always worry about my safety, you know, because it can get rather rough. But I guess with me around the boys used to go a little slow [laughs]. Then interschool debating competitions used to be always great fun. *I still remember how my dad used to help me write my debate. He took a lot of interest in that and he was very good in it.* Because he is so well read and informed ... he reads minimum of 2 newspapers a day and magazines. Besides, he is always hooked onto news channel and stuff. But he was great ... I mean I knew that I have to just sit with him when he would be back from office and we would be able to work out the debate. So school was good. It helped me build solid foundation, but it was always very ... umm ... [after reflection] tied up! *You know, what I mean ... It was like OK! Exams ... study! OK ... I have to come first. Debate competition ... I have to win it. So whatever I did, I wanted to come tops! And it was very satisfying.* I mean who wouldn't want to do well after putting in all of one's efforts. And it was always appreciated back home. I have a rack full of books that I have received as prizes for standing 1st or 2nd in school and prizes from winning competitions. Frankly speaking, I still feel quite proud of all of that*! Then, I went to law school and it was a whole new world.* For the first time I was staying away from my family in a different city. The 5 years there were complete blast. Had the best time there! [excitedly] Studies were, of course, there and still were important but they weren't all important, you know, the way it was in school. In college, I had a really 'bindaas' group. So almost every weekend, we would go out. Hang out at discos. Went for the first time to a pub. Before that, my parents allowed me for night outs sometimes at my friends' homes but I hadn't gone to a disco or a pub before. So it was a different kind of experience. *Also, there were people drawn from all over India so the cultural exchanges were very interesting.* I think the biggest contribution of that phase was that it taught me time management. I could study, attend an interesting workshop or colloquia and hang out with friends. *So, life was a big party! And then I think I got used to party [laughs loud]. My father firmly believes that it spoilt me because now I find it tough to stay at home. I have a large friend circle and an active social life.* So he doesn't approve of it. He doesn't like it when I tell him that I returned back home at 1 in the night. Part of it is safety, which I understand but part of it is also that girls shouldn't do all of this and all. So that's the conflict I was talking about. My parents would like me to live with them but since my workplace is so far from my home, I decided to live here. *It's a good*

arrangement because I have my independence and at the same time I am in the same city as my parents. So they come over or I go back home sometimes. It's usually the latter because my mom is always like Oh God! How are you living? You don't have this, that ... I keep telling them, I am fine. It's OK! Chill! [irritated].

- *How did he take to your recent trip to Goa?*
[Smiles] He didn't like the idea at all. He doesn't especially when it's a mixed group thing. He freaks out on it! My point is that I am not going with strangers. These are people I know. *And most importantly, I can take care of myself.* I give them all the details of the travel so that they know where I am and also keep messaging and talking to them. *You know, parents will always worry about you because they don't want any harm to fall on you. But you can't let yourself be bogged down by that and not have your fun.* My point is that I know what I am doing and I am responsible towards myself and towards you but *I cannot live within the limits set by you* [firm tone].
- *He doesn't want you to mingle with men? Does he know about your boyfriend?*
Well! Both my parents are quite cool with my interactions with men. I have always studied in a co-educational school and I have always had guys as friends and they phoning me up. I never had a boyfriend in school, though. Not because of anything else but I guess, *I was just too busy with studies and other activities to have a boyfriend.* In fact, some of my school friends tell me now that they felt that I was too focused and driven and they are surprised that I now socialise so much more. Even in law school and after that in workplace, you are always with men. So as such, that's not an issue. But yes! They have issues with close proximity with guys. *I had a brief relationship with a guy in college. I told my mom about it. She was worried about me and my performance.* I told her I shall take care. But it didn't last long—about 6 months or so because he was just too possessive. He would want me to be with him all the time. He was a nice, introverted kind of a guy but he was sort of becoming dependent on me and wanted me to just be with him. I could not take that kind of demand and we broke off. I am with my present boyfriend for the past 2 years now and touch wood! It's going on smooth. I told my mom about it. She made her usual enquiries—what does he do, parents, family etc. Then she was like ok. My father has recently got to know from my mom. I only told her to tell him. I feel more settled in the relationship so I thought it was ok to bring him in. He was initially quite upset more so because he wasn't told before [laughs merrily]. So I spoke with him and told him that I was also not so sure of it so I didn't want to tell him. It would have unnecessarily become an issue. Then I also reminded him that my brother also has a girlfriend and guys can be nice and all the sound logic you can give to your parents to make them feel at ease with you and your life decisions. So now he is fine with it ... accepted it. He has met my friend once or twice and I guess he finds him OK.
- *You feel more comfortable sharing about your life with your mother?*
Yes! She is more open minded than my father. She is a teacher and she deals with adolescents all the time, so she knows what young people want and how we think. For eg., in law school after the college farewell, the entire batch went to a discotheque to party. When I was showing the photos to my parents, my dad was like why do you have to go to a disco? You had already partied. Now he didn't understand that there is a big difference between official farewell and partying on your own. My mom understood because she sees it happening in her school as well with class 12 students. So that's the thing! *Basically my father is simple.* He has worked in the government sector all his life. He is a very family man—going to work, coming back home, involved with children. He has his own small set of friends with whom he socialises, drinks and all. *So he finds it difficult to understand the lifestyle of young people.* I tell her because I have nothing to hide. My conscience is clear. I am having fun and they

should know about it. Like from the photos they knew that I was wearing a knee-length dress. They could see me dancing, drinking. I know they aren't very comfortable with it but I am doing things within my limits.

- *And your limits may not be the ones that they may like to set for you ...*
  Exactly! They cannot be in many domains. *My work culture is very different. I am not likely to be back home by 3–4 in the afternoon like my mother.* I am in a very competitive environment where I have to perform well as well as also network, manage relationships with clients. When I go for clients' parties, I always wear formals—Western or Indian. I am a thorough professional there. I take a drink sometimes ... many times I just stick to juice or soft drinks. You got to maintain your professional dignity at the same time being friendly and approachable. But I don't stay beyond 12 in such parties. I excuse myself on the pretext that I don't want to drive back home too late in the night. So in these ways, you create your boundaries. When I am with my friends, then I am more relaxed. I smoke once in a while with them. I can afford to get drunk with them [laughs]. If I am getting late, then either I stay over at someone's place or ask my friends to drop me home. So I take the necessary precautions for my safety. I am not addicted to smoking or drinking. I do it to have fun, to relax, to be with my friends. In fact, there are many times when we decide to go "pure" as we call it! It means that we drink lemonade and tea and generally chat or watch a film. That's also a lot of fun! *The good thing is that most of my close friends are balanced. We all have worked very hard on our careers and we still are working hard to progress well in them and for us our social lives are a relief from the tensions of work. We meet up, we bitch about our bosses and colleagues, let off steam. We look out for opportunities for each other, counsel each other when we are down, so friends are also like a big support network.*
- *Your parents know your friends?*
  My mom knows most of my close friends with whom I generally hang out. They drop at home. Few of my friends are from school. A couple of them are from law school. A few from the previous firm that I was in. The rest are my boyfriend's friends. So actually the close group has about 15–20 people. Then of course, there are other casual friends with whom one meets up once in a while. Actually, when my parents look at my Facebook friend list which has over 400 contacts or my mobile phone address book which has about 250 numbers, they think that I am crazy and half the world is my friend [laughs merrily]. So I tell them that all these contacts are not like friends. Most of them are professional contacts or random acquaintances.
- *How did you meet your boyfriend?*
  We had few common friends. So we sort of knew each other. Used to meet up for films, picnics etc. But at that time, he was dating someone else and I was too busy setting up my career. Actually, it was mischief of our friends. When he was single and I had been single, they set us up for a date and we decided to give it a try and it clicked [smiles].
- *What does he do?*
  He is an entrepreneur. He has his own biotech start-up. He is an engineer by training. He is also ... quite a guy! He took such a big risk. He had no industry experience and still he went ahead and formed his own company because he wanted to be his own boss. Most people at his age would settle for a stable job. It's very tough to run a company but he and his team did it. Now they are doing reasonably well, as in making profits and all. They are now planning to scaleup operations.
- *Are both of you considering marriage?*
  I think a lot of people around us are considering marriage for us! [bursts out laughing] I am not sure. [pauses] See, it's not as if we haven't talked about it at all but we are not actively taking it up. It's just been 2 years. See, it's like, it's like ... we like each other a lot, I like to be with him and similarly for him. Both of us are very busy with our careers as well. I think we would like to give ourselves some more time, a year or two more. At the moment, neither of us is sure....

- *Hmmm ... you are not sure of timing, each other or the institution of marriage?* [Looks surprised] That just hits the nail on the head. [Speaks slowly] I think timing wise, it's not good. I have joined this new firm about 9 months back and *I am very ambitious.* I want to do really well in my career and this is a workplace which I was eyeing for a very long time. It's a place where I can grow professionally. I worked very hard to reach here and *I don't want to give it up for marriage* [Firm tone]. For him also, this is a very crucial phase. His team is planning to expand their operations which require a lot of efforts. They are also working on some technology so running around for funds, patents etc. is really taking the life out of him. *In fact, we sometimes don't get to meet each other for long because we are working the weekends, he is touring. So we talk over phone almost every day, we chat, and message....* As far as the person is concerned, one of the major factors that keep us together is that we have a lot in common to talk. We gel well ... you know! Like your wavelengths meet! *But I can say for myself that marriage does psych me out! I can't picture myself in marriage at least for now.* I think I am having too much of fun right now in work, with him, with friends. I don't want to lose out on it because of marriage. Though my parents have begun to now ask me. Till now they had left me alone because they have also been ambitious for me. *They have always wanted me to get into best of institutions, get best of work assignments and currently I am doing all of it.* It took me 3–4 years to reach here but I am happy and they are happy with the way my career has shaped up. Now marriage means that I would not be able to give that much of time to it, the way I am doing till now. So it doesn't fit into my picture. But then everyone says that you need to look at the big picture and not just work.

Towards the end of time, she informed that she had been selected to go to UK by the company for a training program with a London-based law firm. I congratulated her, and we arranged to meet again in the coming week.

As I gathered impressions about Aanchal, I found her to be a self-focused person making good use of her identity resources of early locomotor vigour, social and intellectual initiative and intrusiveness to join the domains of work and sociability in a way that is usually exploited by men. *Her competitive ambitions and tireless endeavours in the realm of work drew upon her intellectual habits perfected by a long academic regimen, drivenness and activity honed by involvement in vigorous sports. She had a sense of confidence that she could be safe yet successful even in 'rough' situations which was perhaps derived from competently encountering aggressive masculine prowess in sporting or social occasions. Her exciting leisure time was supported by the availability of a large friend circle which concurs on the definition of 'fun', ease of mobility and money.* Having remained under parentally supervised sociability all through her school life, she was able to get a release from it as she moved away from home for higher education and work. Her parents who had been supportive of and encouraged her professional ambitions were anxious of her active social life which put her in close proximity—physical and emotional—with men. For them, more so for the father, it spurred fears about the safety and sanctity of female body, of her becoming somewhat unfeminine in her language and behaviour and thus rendered 'unmarriageable', of diverting her mind from the concrete work goals and getting emotionally hurt. *One could see that Aanchal made sincere attempts to manage the anxieties of her parents by informing them of her movements and generally behaving in a responsible fashion which allowed her to redefine the boundaries of her autonomous functioning.*

During the next interview, in keeping with the research objectives, I tried to explore her career-related attitudes as well as her ambivalences about conjugality and the reasons for perceiving career and conjugality as incompatible. In spite of it being a weekend, she had gone to office and spent half the day there. She looked tired but happily informed that the company had recently got a big merger and acquisition (M&A) deal in which she was involved. In between the conversations, she was texting on her Blackberry for some office work. Below are the significant excerpts of the interview:

- *What made you choose law as your profession?*
  Oh! I was always good with arguing my case so I guess I was naturally suited for this job. [Smiles mischievously] No! But that's the truth!! I usually think logically about any issue and then decide on a side and argue for it. At home, my mom is a political science teacher and I read the constitution . . . some parts of it. I enjoyed it! The social sciences . . . history, politics and all! When I was younger I used to be very impressed with one of my cousin brothers who was a lawyer . . . much older than me, but he was like a hero for me! He influenced me. He used to tell me stories of courts and I was very impressed by the fact that both Gandhi and Nehru, our great leaders, were lawyers. *I think . . . somewhere I thought that the way to do something big is through this route.* You know, when you are a child you think like this. But in class 12th itself, I had told my parents that my first preference is going to be law. They were surprised and also worried I think, because they thought that I was entering into a professional field too early. A lot of people think like that. But since, I knew I will like it, I didn't want to do other things. So I took the exam immediately after I finished school and cleared it and got admission in the best law college. So I was set for life!!
- *You chose to become a corporate lawyer. Were you not interested in litigation?*
  [Begins sarcastically] *Litigation is a very slow career path.* You have to work with senior lawyers and there is very less money in the initial years. People begin for as low as 5,000 rupees a month. It's peanuts and it's a pity. Since, I am a first-generation lawyer, I thought it wise to be a corporate lawyer. Though, when one enters law, one has these romantic notions of wearing the black robe and arguing your case in front of the judges . . . the way you see it in Hindi movies . . . but then you realise you would feel so hot wearing it in Indian summers!! [chuckles]. So I decided, I am not going that way. In fact, a part of my work is to ensure that my client never gets into the situation where he may have to wade through our court process. *Besides, for corporate lawyers, the current economic scenario in India promises to be a gold mine and the way in which our economy has taken off in the past couple of years has made the lives of most corporate law firms.* Given that every dollar of inbound investment translates into work of some sort for corporate lawyers, the opening up of our economy coupled with the forces of globalisation means that the amount of work will increase exponentially over the next few years, especially in areas such as IPRs, BPOs and insurance. So it's a very exciting field to be in. The money is very good and the work is challenging. Like a litigating lawyer has to work in supportive role for the first 3–5 years of their career. But corporate lawyers are thrown at the deep end right from the word go. We get to interact with clients directly, writing opinions, attending conferences etc. Of course, we are supervised initially because you only learn law in those 5 years in law school, you know the practice of it only when you begin work. I love my work. *I keep crazy hours, work sometimes on weekends but it's all worth it because I get a kick out of it!*
- *What are your career plans for future?*
  This firm I am working with is a relatively new law firm but its *work environment is very chilled out. It's a young place.* I am working on this big M&A transaction deal which is a *big learning opportunity.* Then I will be going for this training program in one of the

best UK law firms with which our firm has recently tied up with for referrals, trainings, etc. So I am currently learning and growing. *It would be great to move into a bigger law firm with bigger accounts, bigger money.*[Excitedly] Probably one day our firm will be covered in media for a big acquisition deal . . . that will feel great!! Or I can move into a company as a counsel. Hey! Tata, Birla, Reliance . . . I am available [makes a mock gesture of waving her hand]. It's a cool job! You earn much more and also lead a more relaxed life. Work over by 5, play golf after that.

- *Yeah! Relaxation is what seems to be missing from your life. Lots of work!! What do you do to relax?*

  Yeah! There is a lot of work pressure. But there are also phases when one works 5 days a week or have shorter work days. So no complaints! Ummm . . . How do I relax?? I like to meet up with friends as much as possible, share a cigarette with them, watch a film, have a drink or chat over coffee! I love to hang out with Rohit (her boyfriend) and I drive him crazy while shopping!! [bursts out laughing] I am a very finicky shopper . . . so he gets completely pissed off with me. Then I make him eat chocolate and he is fine again . . . he is such a sweetheart! [smiles fondly] Yes! *Going back home is hugely relaxing for me. It's nice and cosy with mom–dad around.* I cook my dad's favourite dishes, gossip with my mom. That really recharges my batteries . . . I like to cook. It makes me feel peaceful and listen to music—gazals and all . . . no dinchak pop/rock for me please! It's ok for discos when you are in a mood to party. Otherwise listening to gazals while cooking takes the stress out of you immediately.

- *You like cooking . . . [smile in disbelief]*

  Yeah! I like cooking. You don't believe me, no!! Nobody believes that. [Gets agitated] I don't look like someone who would like cooking. Just because I live alone, smoke and drink and party, people think I am spoilt and unmarriageable. *In fact, I think I am responsible. I have made my choices, taken charge of my life and I take full responsibility for my actions. I take care of all my things from finances, to health to travel. I am not dependent on anyone.*

- *You are right! Such impressions are formed because we look at only the behaviour and not understand the motivations behind them. Also, people usually have different sides to them.*

  Absolutely! [Continuing in somewhat agitated tone] Like I don't believe in being fuck buddies . . . at least I will never be one. I can't unless I feel emotionally connected to the person. But this whole 'preserving yourself for marriage' business is nonsense. *I don't endorse promiscuity. But I have allowed myself the freedom that since I am in a committed relationship with Rohit and we do feel strongly for each other, we can have physical relations.* A lot of my other friends are also sexually active before marriage. This in no way makes us loose women. It's consensual and it's based on love and trust. I think this matters more than an institution which just legitimises sex. [After a brief pause she begins slowly.] *I don't know whether we will marry each other but I guess that's not the issue. It's about living fully what you have right now.* There are times when I feel so protective about him. I fuss over him when he is unwell. He is happy about my trip to London, though I am not very thrilled because I don't like to live so far from home and him for so long. He is very headstrong but he also keeps doing sweet things [smiles] . . . so we are happy together. So then why not? We didn't rush into it . . . I took my own time . . . *For me it was a tough thing to overcome . . . you know! All the moral preaching and fears and it's not as if I don't have them now or they are gone. They are times I feel very anxious, very very anxious . . . what if this relationship doesn't materialise, what if it ends? I feel very guilty when I think of my parents because they don't know about this . . . my brother knows . . . I told him.* He understands. . . . But then I feel and actually many of my friends go through these same cycles, so then I feel that I know what I am doing. It feels right to me because he is the right guy and it's happening in the right conditions—it's not casual.

- *Why does casual sex rattle you?*
  It rattles me because ... I feel there is little feeling in it. There is little commitment towards the person and practically a non-existent bond. I mean, my idea of relationships is not this. I can have casual friends but I will not have physical relations in a casual fashion.
- *[Smilingly] Since you privilege commitment and also value emotional bonds and relationships, I assume that you are not averse to conjugality?*
  You talk like my mom [smiles broadly]. No I am not, truly. I have no reason to. I have seen my parents. They have a solid relationship. They have given us stability and security. I will also marry ... most probably. Also because I want to have a home of my own, a companion to share my life with and a child. You know, I tell you what ... I think I am getting to what's the issue. [Silence] *I have always thought myself to be this very individualistic person, career oriented. I am not sure of whether I have a need to love someone, whether I can care for someone. I think these questions are what have been at the core.* But, with Rohit, I have felt these feelings. I like to cook for him. Recently he was running high fever, so he was over here and I had taken 2–3 days leave, not because he had asked or anything like that but because I wanted to be around him. His parents don't live here. Yeah, so basically I played his mom and he quite liked it and was asking me to become his mom and I was telling him that it's very exhausting! [smiles happily].
- *He seems like a nice guy...*
  Yeah! He is nice. Stable, responsible type. Can be inflexible at times, then you need to know how to tackle him. The best thing about him is that he is very honest. Good or bad, he will tell you clearly what he is feeling and thinking. So then you know where you stand vis-à-vis him. I personally find that very comfortable. We both can communicate well with each other.

We ended our conversation on this note. I wished her all the best for her trip to London. She good-naturedly wished me luck with my research, and we hoped to remain in touch.

Interaction with Aanchal excited me. Her good girl demeanour coupled with her verve was attractive for me. She was attempting to make the most of her personality potentials within the leeway provided by the social structures and roles surrounding her. *Having learnt to work well, she was also learning to loaf as was evident by her enlivening activities outside work in which sexuality also came alive.* She was battling guilt and anxiety over her sexual activity outside the sanctioned space of matrimony; a suffering that is fated whenever the moral laws of one's social world are transgressed. The parental imagoes don't leave us when we leave home. *But Aanchal was experimenting with a midway space, between her natal home and matrimonial home, the physical site of which was her own flat.* She was developing her personal codes of feminine conduct to negotiate this space which wouldn't lead her too far from either home, i.e. not to lose out on parental trust and love or rendered 'unmarriageable'. At the same time it gave her the freedom to deal with both of them as per her autonomous good will. *Her stance of responsible fun and sexual expression is a telling example of strivings of young men and women to move beyond inhibition and prohibition to enjoy life more fully.* Sexual expression within the context of meaningful human relationships, of intimacy and of mutuality when chosen by people with minimum of denial and guilt and maximum of insight and conviction, 'feels right'.

One also glimpsed in her the inner reserves of repose and care and a resourcefulness to relate with others. She could be her father's daughter while cooking his favourite dishes. Having been mothered well, she could recover her own 'motherliness' while tending to the needs of her boyfriend. She, however, found it exhausting probably because she had to delve deep into her being to assess those parts which had been relegated to that space in a bid to enter the productive world of work privileging masculine initiative and competitiveness as was expressed by her: 'I have always thought myself to be this very individualistic person, career oriented. I am not sure of whether I have a need to love someone, whether I can care for someone. I think these questions are what have been at the core'. *In the inner economy of an individual woman, certain potentials are overdeveloped at the cost of certain others in trying to become 'one of the boys' and to play the game at seemingly equal footing.* This is aided by both parents and teachers who are her guides in her growing up years. While this bargain reaps fruit in the role of the worker, it creates conflicts when it comes to the life tasks of intimacy and parenthood. One, and this is true for both men and women, is never only a worker, and with a divided self-image, one has little chance to embrace these other life tasks with enthusiasm and ease. *For Aanchal, the challenge was to reconcile freedom and responsibility, agency and care within her feminine self.* For a woman to do so willingly and with ease, the inner economy of male partner also has to be considered since he lives with as much of inner divisions. An emotional ecology in which there is freer inter-identification between sexes in everyday life, conjugality and parenting will lose at least some of its unnecessary forbidding aspects for both sexes.

Disha

Disha, 25 years, was working as a marketing manager in a telecom company. She came across as an attentive and enthusiastic person. Curious about the research, she asked various questions and made few suggestions. Over the 3 interactions, she impressed upon me as a thoughtful, aware and a well-managed young woman. Disha was clear in her communications, choosing her words, often taking her own time to pause and reflect before replying. She had an air of someone who knew her mind and would ensure that she got her way.

Following are excerpts of interviews sketching her *family milieu and growth experiences* which help to gain an insight in her individualised functioning. She described her family as: 'I belong to Allahabad so we live in a joint family. There are about 15 people who live in the same house. My father has 3 brothers and 1 sister. All my uncles and their families stay there. We are together 5–6 children. I have an elder sister. She is married. My father is a businessman. He deals in building material. My mother is a homemaker'.

- *The business is also jointly owned by your father and uncles?*
  Yes. The area where we live is a market for building materials. So, on the ground floor there is a shop which is jointly run by my father and uncles. Even our neighbours are our distant cousins. They are in slightly different businesses. *So in the older generation everyone is business oriented. But this generation is trying to come into services.*
- *What do your cousins do?*
  Actually my father is the eldest. My sister did her graduation in commerce and then MBA. But she is not working. She went abroad after her marriage. Now she has come back to India and is helping my brother-in-law in his business. I have done engineering and now I am pursuing a degree in management. I have 3 cousins. One of them is in 3rd year of engineering. One has dropped a year this time to prepare for engineering. The last one is in 7th standard. *Everybody is the same … engineering and MBA sorts.*
- *If the younger generation enters service industry, then who will run the business?*
  First the younger generation wants to get professional degree and be independent. For next 15–20 years, the business can be run by my father and his brothers. So it's a distant thing. Also, the nature of the business is such that it can always be wrapped up. There isn't much investment involved in it. Also, it doesn't require much of manpower. So … it is not necessary for my cousins to enter business. Anyways, they haven't thought about it. At the moment they are planning to get their professional degrees and be self-sufficient.

P. Bansal, *Youth in Contemporary India: Images of Identity and Social Change*,
DOI 10.1007/978-81-322-0715-3_4, © Springer India 2013

- *How is the experience of living in a joint family?*
  I think one important thing is being considerate to other people's requirements. To take a very small example—we didn't have cable television because we were studying—me and my sister. So my mother said that there will not be any cable TV connection at home. Other people had to compromise. Also like since all the children in the family are in different age groups, you can mentor the younger ones. Like my youngest cousin is 13 years old. He and the others come to me and ask me what academic streams they should take and about other studies/career-related issues. I also feel joint family gives a lot of liberty to parents. Like my mother could go out while most of my friends' mothers were at home because they couldn't leave their kids alone. We had our uncle and aunty to take care of us. When there were marriages in the family, my mother would go for 15–20 days even when we had our school. This was possible because we had our aunts to take care of us. But this also meant that we never shouldered any family responsibilities. Like when parents go out, children have all the responsibilities. But we always had someone with us so we never had to cook or take care of closing the doors and all.
- *Who are the primary caretakers for you, authority figures?*
  Like food was common. We have a common kitchen. But other things like—buying things for ourselves—we used to shop with our parents. The responsibilities at home are distributed. In terms of authority . . . [thinks], my uncle and aunt never tried to be authoritative in the first place. *And as far as me and my sister is concerned, I don't remember when we went against everyone and did something.* So in that sense, my mother and father were the primary people for us. But even with them, I had a lot of negotiations. *It was not like if I had to go somewhere and my father said No!, I would be like O.K. I would argue and come to a conclusion.* At the same time, I don't remember an incident where they asked me to do something and I didn't listen to them. But in most cases, I feel, they didn't exert their authority. Another important thing is that though my uncles and aunts didn't have much of an influence on me, my parents' advice is sought for my younger cousins. So when my cousin was deciding whether he should drop a year or take up a particular branch in engineering, he asked my parents for advice. So my mother said that Disha did this and Rupali [her sister] did this. When we were taking such decisions, we didn't ask because they hadn't been through it, but they now have our example to learn from.
- *How was your childhood?*
  Umm . . . nothing very striking. *I remember lot of attention to academics.* We used to study everyday after school. The schedule was to revise whatever was being taught in the class everyday. *Somehow, academics got an upper hand but I had fun whenever I had to.* Parents never said don't go out with friends. I had a very good friend circle at school. My birthdays were celebrated. My whole album is full of photographs of birthday parties only [smiles]. Used to go to Lucknow to my maternal grandparents' house every year for a month.
- *Were you always a bright student academically?*
  [Hesitatingly] Till class IVth, I don't know but I really managed to fail . . . and I don't know how. Somehow, everything changed in class 5th. Actually the first 4 years of my life . . . it's not very significant, but I used to be ill a lot. Every year, I would get jaundice. *So first 4 years, it was really bad but then I picked up. After that I was always in top 5.*
- *How was your engagement with academics? Did you like studying?*
  It was a general culture that you had to study everyday for 2–3 hours. It was cultivated by my mother. She used to take a lot of care that there is no distraction in terms of TV, someone talking outside my room. That's how she showed that it was an important thing. Never took it lightly. Even if there was no electricity, she used to make sure that it didn't suffer. *Also, I had a friend circle which used to talk a lot about academics.* I went to the best girls' school in the city. It always held an important position though no one

likes studying as such. But yeah! I used to read a lot in the library, a lot of books. I never used to crib about studies. I used to enjoy studying. Even in classes, I would listen and be attentive. Since everyone in my peer group was sincere about academics, it came naturally to me. *Also, if you do very well in academics, you get a lot of leeway with parents. Like no one can say that this time your party is cancelled because you didn't get good marks.* Or you can't do this because your performance was not up to the mark. So the best is to study hard and get marks and get your way. Then the parents are always ready [laughs out aloud].

- *As parents, what were their expectations from you?*
  I think they never expected me to do an MBA or engineering. *Actually my career goals were never directed by them. They didn't have much knowledge about career options and all because they aren't professionally qualified and they aren't into service sector.* When I was in class 10th, my mother and father used to say that we are not forcing you to study or do professional courses. But till wherever you study, you should study well. Whatever you study, your concepts should be clear. That's why I took my academics seriously. They wanted me to be academically sound, be a good student. My sister was also a very good student. So the most they would say is OK! She got this much marks. But as such there was no pressure on me to perform or any standards for me to achieve. *But how I thought my career should look like was shaped by my friends a lot.* I had a very close friend who was very focused. Her father was an IAS officer. Her sister had already gone into engineering. So this is how my focus also built up that engineering is a very good option. *And when everyone around you are discussing about career and engineering, joining coaching classes, I also began to think that engineering is a good option and I should try for it.* I don't remember even a single sentence from my parents that you should do engineering. It was driven entirely by my friends. *But the best thing is that my parents always supported me in whatever decision I have taken.*
- *So it was at +2 stage that you decided to go for engineering?*
  Yes! But I came to it very differently from the way my friends did. My friends had decided their career focus in class 10th only. I was quite clueless. My sister had found it difficult to cope with science, so she advised me to take commerce. So I took commerce. But my class 10th results were very good. So then everyone said that I should take science. I should use my capability. Then my friend's mother also advised me that I should take maths because it would help me in entrance examinations. So this is how without much thought, I took science. Even the focus for engineering came slowly for me. I didn't know many things. Like I didn't know that there is an NTSE examination. I came to know about it only 1–2 months earlier. I used to see my friends preparing for engineering entrances, applying for colleges. Even for engineering, I decided very late in class 12th. So I just wrote one exam and was put on the waiting list. By the time I decided to try engineering as a career option, the IIT form date had already expired. So I dropped a year and next year appeared for 5–6 entrance exams. That year I got 6th rank in the entrance examination for regional engineering colleges in U.P. I was offered computer science stream in the best college in U.P. located in Allahabad. My mother was also very happy that I would get to study in Allahabad only.
- *How did you and your parents take to your going to Bangalore to work?*
  All these changes took place slowly. When I joined engineering, I never thought that I would go so far alone to work. But then I used to see seniors go and then the whole concept dawned on me and my parents that OK! I would have to go to metros because there is no work in Allahabad. I used to tell them that she has gone to Delhi, he has gone to Bombay. So by the time my turn came, they had got used to the idea. But in the first year, I remembered thinking how will I go so far. Also, many of my friends were going to Bangalore from Allahabad. So then I was really looking forward to it because it was the first time I was going out of Allahabad. People used to say Oh! All the time, you have been in Allahabad only.

I

As the above conversation revealed, *Disha grew up in a traditional form of family organisation in India: the extended family.* There was a common residence in which each brother's family occupied a separate floor, common kitchen and common economic, social and ritual activities. The householding responsibilities were shared as a single family unit. Her father being the eldest brother held an especially powerful position. It was he who had started the business in which the younger brothers later joined. He enjoyed the allegiance and obedience of his younger brothers and their families [wives and children]. Her mother, by virtue of being the eldest sister-in-law, exercised considerable domestic power, not only amongst the other women of the household, but with her husband, and she often made many of the vital decisions affecting the family's interests. Disha thought very highly of her mother. A science graduate from an elite college of Lucknow, she was characterised by her as 'very intelligent and an efficient planner'. Disha recounted fondly:

> She used to make all these Vikas Patras [investment bonds] because at that time interest rates were very high and getting these deposits was very profitable. She has a file in which she maintains all the financial records of the investments made. Also, when Big Bazaar opened, there was this 3-day sale. She went early and got a great deal. My other aunts are not very comfortable with technology but she is very curious and wants to learn. She was very interested in learning computer and sends me messages on cell phone. She also looks after the accounts of the shop. Every day, she spends about 2–3 hours checking the accounts. She is very smart, I would say.

In Disha's narration, one found a *psychological nuclearisation* within the framework of extended family. As the daughter of the eldest brother, her obligations of obedience rested with her parents. She had to negotiate her decisions and choices with her parents alone and not had to take into consideration the wishes and judgments of other elders in the family. *She saw herself as wrestling for her independent space whenever required—whether it was demanding that her birthdays be celebrated with style, bargaining to go for friends' parties or setting aside comparisons with her sister's genteel behaviour with a firm 'I am like this only' stance.* Also, as the first professionally qualified girl working in the corporate sector, she was a role model for other children in the family. *She was seen as a benchmark of excellence worthy of emulation.* Because of her success in educational and career endeavours, her parents were also looked upon as guides for the younger children by the families of the younger brothers.

Disha's individualised functioning could be attributed to multiple factors: *Nurturant identification with a clear-headed, determined woman like her mother who had influence and autonomy helped her build her own identity resources of assertion, independence and initiative.* Her mother represented in her style of being and child-rearing almost a deep conviction that there is a meaning in what she is doing which forms the very basis in the growing girl a sense of being 'all right', of being oneself and of becoming what other significant people trust one will become. She credited her mother as playing a very big role in her life—someone who always defended her. With her around, she felt protected and assured that if something happened she would be there for her. It was her mother who ensured that her daughters get the best of education. She decided that her daughter would go to the best girls' convent school in town even though none of the relatives' daughters had studied there and it was also quite far off from home. Though not ambitious about her career, she was highly appreciative of the direction that Disha had chosen for herself. The lenient affection and attention bestowed on her by the mother had generated in turn self-esteem and strength of will. *In addition to her mother's empathic connection with her, she also received support and encouragement from her father for pursuit of her educational and career endeavours.* He also took interest in her personal grooming—recommending hairstyles to her, correcting her walk, wanting her to be mannered. In deference to her wish to do engineering, her parents supported her decision to take a year off after school to prepare for entrance examinations. Her mother even gave her the option of going to Delhi to enrol herself in a reputed coaching institution. Internalisation of strong maternal expectations for intellectual mastery and achievement led her to value academics and invest herself in it with zest. *She used her academic accomplishments to gain the family's love and approval as well as to leverage increased consideration for her specific wishes, abilities and inclinations.* As she said with a relish, 'If you perform well in studies, no one can point a finger at you. You can then demand what you want'. She also enjoyed a kind of admiration and sense of being singled out as special by the family elders as well as younger cousins because of her good academic track record and the subsequent career enhancement initiatives. Though there had not been a precedent of working women in her extended family, her uncles asked her to join an MBA immediately after engineering. Surprised, when she asked them the reason for the same, they replied that they wanted her to become the very best so that they could also tell people with pride that their niece was an engineer and an MBA. Hence, her education and her work capacity were also seen as enhancing the reputation of her natal family.

The modernising family environment and the much more unstructured, free environment of engineering college also contributed to her increasing individualisation. In spite of being the second daughter of her parents, she did not experience any gender discrimination or cultural devaluation as a girl. *Disha had not been subjected to any deliberate training in how to be a good woman or to the conscious inculcation of culturally designated feminine roles.* In fact, she had been exempted from domestic sphere of feminine activity including the mandatory tasks of house-holding, cooking and childcare because of the presence of other female adults who would take care of such responsibilities. *As she stayed away from home after school, she enjoyed considerable freedom from the routinised discipline of home. In hostels and subsequently when she lived independently in Bangalore where she held a job, she lived by her own initiative.* She shared:

> My habit of studying daily just vanished when I went to live in hostel. It was a lot of fun—hanging out with friends, watching a lot of movies, sitting in canteen and studying just before examinations. Even in Bangalore, we used to go out for ice cream at 10 in night. It was great fun.

Mostly educated in all-girls convent school, the engineering college was the first co-educational milieu for her. Staying away in hostel gave her various kinds of liberties and in general the college environment was much more unstructured, heterogeneous and liberal where there was much more choice of courses and activities. It was here that she met her boyfriend, but the relationship blossomed only when they both moved to Bangalore for their jobs. The affair could be managed far more easily in the modern, cosmopolitan atmosphere of Bangalore which afforded anonymity and privacy of relationship. In Allahabad, which was her home town, the dating culture was not prevalent and was frowned upon. When questioned about parental attitudes towards dress, behaviour and being with boys, she did not perceive her parents as being unduly critical or restrictive. What did emerge, however, were remarks which conveyed indirectly that she should be careful of her step. If she wore cargo pants, her father made a disapproving comment. Her father and uncles did not like her talking to boys or their coming over to their house. She remembered laughingly that her father would try to put off the boys by asking them, somewhat harshly, their names every time they visited. *She assimilated these messages of acting with circumspection but that did not interfere with her more open, individualised expression at home as well as outside.* She admitted to being more loud and outgoing than her elder sister which coincided with my observations made during the interactions with her. In her dressing too, she was far from being traditional; often coming for the interviews in figure hugging jeans and tops, complementing her lean frame.

Peers played an important part in her life. A fragment of memory dramatically illustrated how she used her friendships to shake loose dependence on her parents and imagine differentiated spaces of existence. In her own words:

> I remember, once we visited Kumbh Mela. I was very young, probably class I or II. I was being very adamant about something and my father said angrily OK! Just leave her here. Everyone else just got into the car and I was like—Let them go. I'll beg, do whatever but I will not go with these people [excitably]. I still remember what I was thinking at that time. I was thinking my friend is there. I will go to her place and her father would definitely take me. I was in a panic but I was thinking all what I could do.

Through them, she became aware of diverse paths of life in spheres of occupation and intimacy, understood that she had the choice to move towards the various opening frontiers which were different from the ones determined by her parentage and social origins and prepared herself to face and meet situations that were novel. *Hence, it helped her reduce reliance on her family for guidance and direction and also eased the pressure to follow traditions.* This trend was also observed in her decision to marry her boyfriend who was a South Indian. She confessed to be very apprehensive about the workability of their relationship since she was a North Indian. She said:

> Actually like everything else, this has also not happened in my family—love marriage and that too with a South Indian. So I wondered whether it would work out. But when I looked around at friends, I saw that such things do work out. People don't bother much about caste and regional differences even in arranged marriages. On being asked how she thought her parents would respond to the arrangement, she replied, 'I had told my mother about him.

> She was not really thrilled about it. I know. But she was like o.o..o..k, ya! If I have taken a decision then it must be correct. Something of that sort. I haven't had any direct communication with my father on this issue. My mother had told him. This time when I had gone back home, I had thought that he would bring up the issue but he didn't . . . so I also didn't. My mother told me that it is ok with him'. On further prodding, she said softly, 'I am sure that he is not very happy with my decision. But there isn't much to talk. In November, they are going to meet his parents. So it's ok. There wasn't even one heated discussions regarding this. I was ready that there might be few, but when I took the decision, I was sure that they would agree in the end'. Then I asked her—What gave you that confidence? She replied, 'Well! One of my mother's very close friend's daughter had an arranged marriage with a South Indian boy. That's when it occurred to me that they were open to such marriages. Probably, they also expected me to go for love marriage. Because, all through my engineering days, all my relatives used to tell my parents that OK! Now you don't have to worry for her marriage, she will find someone for herself. Once, I also conducted a survey at home on my elder cousins, brothers-in-law and my mother and asked them—Now that all of you are married, what do you think is better—love marriages or arranged marriages? Everyone said that love marriages are slightly better. So now I tell them that you people voted for love marriage, that's why I am going for it [laughs heartily]. Also a lot of my friends were opting for love marriages. This generation is not going for arranged marriages. I used to tell them that this friend of mine got married to a senior in college.... So they must have got used to the idea'.

What was evident from Disha's life was that she was continuing to bring herself up in order to adjust and adapt to the extra familial environments: material, social and intellectual. In the process, she also 'brought up' her parents. She was their window to the changing social–economic mores. They relied on her judgment, confident in their parenting that she would be watchful of her conduct and not go 'too far'. Less self assured, they didn't hold themselves up as exemplars—when the child knew better. She used the opportunities of modern education, independent living and being around peers to gain the wider ground available to her outside the home. It wasn't the rupture but the stretching of traditional values that became a means for her to realise her dreams and desires for life.

II

Another important focus of the research was to understand the significance of work and how it influenced the personalised versions of lifestyle and worldview of the participant. As can be gleaned from the selection of interview conversations above, Disha had steadfastly worked on her academic career. Guided by her friends and supported by her parents, she decided to pursue professional education and career in service industry. She had done an early assessment of suitability of IT jobs for girls since it didn't involve any physical labour or shop floor work. She did her engineering in computer science, one of the top-ranking branches of engineering. Following which she worked for two years in an IT company and thereafter completed her management degree. Below are excerpts of interviews detailing her work-related attitudes and motivations.

- *You have been a diligent, disciplined student. What gratifications did you derive from your work habits?*
I used to study regularly in school. Though in college the habit disappeared. But I still used to study well whenever required. I don't like not knowing anything. When you go for an exam, it feels nice if you know everything. Even when there is no pressure, it feels so nice if you know everything. The teacher asks you a question in a class and you know the answer, it feels good. Otherwise there is so much tension.... Also, if you get good marks and do well, no one bothers you much.
- *How well do you take to competition?*
I never feel that confident ... never feel that I would beat this person. I just want to perform well. Maybe because my parents never said that you have to top or come first. They always said that you put in your best efforts. Whenever you study, study well. *So I believe in doing my best.* If it lands you somewhere, good enough. If it doesn't land you somewhere, it's OK. Also, there was no peer pressure that she has scored this much so I should score more than her. Somehow I have been satisfied with whatever rank I have got. I have topped sometimes, sometimes I have come 5th in a class of 90. So I am fine with whatever....
- *After engineering, you took up a job?*
Yes. Through campus placements, I joined an IT company. I was placed in Bangalore. But in the first week itself, they asked me to shift to Pune where I didn't want to go. I had no idea that I would have to go to Pune. So I had rented a good accommodation in Bangalore. There were four of us from college who were living together. So I changed the job. I joined another software company.
- *How was your placement rated in the whole placement scenario?*
It was considered good but not the best because pay structure was not attractive. It was about 1.96 lakhs per annum. General was 3 lakhs per annum. But I was happy.
- *How has been your work appraised? What kind of a worker are you?*
In my appraisals, there were three ratings—above expectation, meets expectations, totally average. I have always been rated as—'Meets expectations'—one below the best. *That is why I am very sure that given any situation, I can do an average job. I will meet expectation. I might not over perform, but whatever is required of me, I can do.* And one thing with me is that I can work on anything. Some people say that I can only do this sort of work. I don't have passion that I can do this work brilliantly and can't do that work at all. Give me any work and I will do it ... a decent job. It can be an asset or a liability. Even the company where I did the summer job during MBA had offered me a job with them. So I had a job even before the placement season began. That again gave me confidence. Though it was not the kind of work that I particularly liked but I did it decently well. *I thought this work has been given to me and I am responsible for it, so I will do it with sincerity.*
- *How was your experience of doing the job?*
Actually it depends on the project. The project I was involved in was very big. We were making a performance monitoring system which was to be deployed across Europe. So it gives a lot of boost that it is being deployed across Europe. *I was handling the whole module ... as such a very small part of the whole thing but the very thought that it would be deployed across Europe was exciting ... it was a pleasure.* So that was it! But I am not very emotional about my work. I find some people are. I am not very attached to my work. Probably because in the first year, I wasn't given much work. In the 2nd year, I worked very seriously for 5–6 months, but in the later part, my MBA preparations took priority. In those 5–6 months, I worked very hard because a lot of work was given to the new recruits. There was a resource crunch and I had no guidance, no help, only deadlines to meet. It was tough!
- *So how did you deal with the work pressure?*
I would say it was a very difficult phase. Too much work was given to me. There was no one in the company to whom I could turn to for technical help. You browse web, get

information … just do it anyhow! That's the time when I couldn't sleep. I am telling you, I couldn't sleep! I had to finish something by Friday and that was the first deadline that was given to me. It was already Monday and I had no clue how to do it. I just couldn't sleep, I remember. I used to call my mother and almost cry that how I will finish my work … I can't figure out anything.… I have so much work … don't know what to do. I used to crib in front of my boyfriend. But then I used to stay late, work on weekends. Finally I finished it on time! But it was a struggle. Thankfully, there are technical books which one can rely on. Then I used online forums where you can ask questions and get answers. Then the client was there. It was a sort of outsourced software development. So the client also knew what needed to be done to some extent. So I got some information from there as well. At that point of time, even though I was new on the job, I could directly write a mail to the client and ask for help/clarification. So I was given a lot of autonomy … not because of design but because of default. Because there was a resource crunch. But the best part was that I got a lot of appreciation from the client for the work I did. The work was found up to the mark. I was very happy. That boosted my confidence a lot … whatever said and done I'll be able to do the work. I don't know how but I will be able to do it.

- *Since you were doing well in your job, what prompted you to do an MBA?*
  MBA is essential nowadays. It actually changes the point from where you start your career. An engineer starts from a lower level than an MBA grad. Another reason is that any level just being a graduate might be limiting because you are just a graduate. *MBA is the criteria for being at top level in most companies.*
- *You aspire for being at the top … What level do you want to reach in your career?*
  I think … some CXO level. Not at the top! *Ah … I am not very ambitious that I have to head a company or something. Even a level lower is fine by me.*
- *CXO is?*
  CXO is CEO [chief executive officer], CMO [chief marketing officer], CFO [chief financial officer], CSO [chief sales officer] of any vertical in a country of that company.
- *So that's the level you want to reach?*
  That's the best! [Excitedly] That's the best thing that I can have … can happen to me. It can even be less. Actually, I don't really think that much as to what level I want to reach. I will go and see what happens. I have actually not planned my life that much. I never planned to do engineering, MBA.
- *What is the significance of career for you?*
  Firstly, career is an identity. Just being somebody's wife isn't bad, but it limits your influence. This is the only way you can do something big, contribute to the larger.… Having a career is a channel by which you can do something. If you have a career, you can go beyond family and friends. You can go across. You can go across nations. There is no limit to it. The company and career gives you a platform to grow across boundaries. *Like you can contribute to the mobile networks, build a brand or this performance monitoring software that we devised which was deployed across Europe. That's the thrill!* When the company is doing something good, you can do something big through it and affect a large audience. And I think you feel more gratified when your work is known across nations. *Second, is the economic independence which is a big incentive of a career. Besides, career means that you have something to do.* If I don't have a full time job, I would have a lot of spare time and what would I do in that time? *I don't know how will I fill my time? I'll feel very bored …* [smiles].
- *Do you think your professional education and career experience influence other domains of your life? You are able to carry forward your learning into other domains of your life?*
  Yes … it does. More so when you talk of MBA. Because what you learn in MBA has to do with everyday things. When you are doing engineering or when you are in an engineering-oriented job, you talk technical stuff and that too of your vertical and

your industry—IT/Telecom. But here, what we are learning has applications across industries and across economies. I have seen that the kind of conversations I have with my brother-in-law have changed ever since I joined MBA. We discuss market trends, Indian economy and all—knowledge that I have gained through MBA. In fact, so much so that recently when I was watching a film with my MBA friends, I was like OK! That's the way they have placed their brand. They are advertising like this … using such a marketing strategy. It has changed my outlook.

- *How are you foreseeing your future in terms of a married working woman and later as a working mother? How do you propose to manage work with householding responsibilities?*
  I don't know … *I think husbands are supportive of woman's work nowadays. Also, paid help comes to our rescue. These days many companies also offer many kinds of services such as helping employees to pay up their bills and other small chores of home so that employees are not bogged down by these hassles. Another thing is that I am looking forward to my mother to take care of my family* [bursts out laughing]. I have already told—See! I can't handle it. I am going to do a job also. You handle the kids whenever they come and she was like—Yes! Yes! No problems … don't take any tensions. But I think I will definitely take a break because I think 3–4 years are crucial when you need to invest in your family. After that you can actually go back to your career and take it forward. It's not like you are out of industry. A woman's career graph usually has a break. If there are any career sacrifices to be made for the children, it's always made by the woman. It also makes sense to me that at least 1 person should be there with the child. And if sometimes I take a break, sometimes the man takes a break, none of the careers would go high.

Through the long years of education and preparation for job or career as well as on the job, Disha had proved to be perseverant, disciplined and competent. *In her industriousness, one noticed a mix of enjoyment of learning, pleasure of applying one's intelligence to the completion of tasks as well as a sense of duty in doing well what one was expected to do.* The actual work situation provided her ethos of action where she could freely exercise her dexterity and intelligence to the tasks assigned to her, thereby inducting her in the productive adult life of cooperative work. *She felt her working status to be an inalienable part of her individuality, offering her the delight of establishing a wider, almost unlimited radius of influence and reach as well as a sense of invigorating purpose that counteracts boredom and promises a fulfilment of one's range of capacities.*

In her sharing, one also heard a halting admission of not being very ambitious. She acknowledged to being content with a level lesser than the top post, of desiring average salary. *These modest aspirations can be understood as the signs of feminine initiative which has to coordinate the concrete pursuits and approved goals of work life with the cultural expectations from a young woman to keep up the traditional manners, attitudes, values and responsibilities within the family relationships.* Young women like her are well aware that their working status and earnings are usually subordinate to their husbands' in terms of prestige and monetary value. Aggressive competitiveness and tireless initiative can disturb the marital relationship and also invite disapproval and loss of love even from the natal family, especially the mother—a condition that a girl can ill afford. Hence, a woman's sense of initiative and industry is prey to conflict and guilt especially when it threatens to transcend the culturally sanctioned domain of womanhood, an integral part of her ego ideal. *While Disha's environment did not place her in a situation where she had to deny or inhibit her strivings to live up to her imagination and feeling, she had learnt to moderate these drives by hearing the inner voice of self-observation and self guidance trained by the surrounding cultural mores.* So, she could 'go across nations' only if the 'husband accompanied her'. The supportive image of the mother who could be relied upon to mother her own children also allowed her to imagine a career. Also, she had had a fluid life course as compared to the other participants of the group which allowed her the freedom to be and had internal standards of satisfaction that protected her from relentless comparison and competition with peers. Her inner sense of worth was not contingent on her career success. Rather, she looked forward to balance the multiple dimensions of her life.

Aasheesh

I met Aasheesh when he was pursuing his management degree from a premier institution. Aged 27 years, he was a civil engineer from a reputed engineering college following which he worked for 3 years before he joined MBA. He helped coordinate a group of students for me to talk about my research work and enlist their participation in it. A shy and self-conscious person, he was initially hesitant to become a participant of the work, but later agreed with a request that he would need my inputs to improve upon himself. His request surprised me because it was the first of the kind made to me. I responded that I shall be happy to share my understandings and observations about his life and self as would emerge when we converse. However, the work was not evaluative in terms of judging someone's strengths and limitations from a certain vantage point. But we could always discuss his concerns about the 'grey areas' of his life where he found the need of improvement and build understandings and solutions from there. He was fine with the arrangement, but over the four interactions, he never explicitly brought up the areas of his concerns. Even when I reminded him of it, he replied that he did not have much clue of where all he should get better, but he was looking forward to my help to develop himself. Thus, during one of the interactions, I asked him what he thought were his limitations. To that, he replied 'I feel that I am not devoting that much of time which is required to excel in a field. I want the same result that others are getting but I am not putting the effort that is required to get that output. I am not studying as hard as I should. I am wasting my time listening to music, sleeping, going out, chatting. As far as analytical skills and communication skills are concerned, they can just be fine-tuned now. They can't be improved to a great extent'. He described himself as '*I am not completely useless but I can be set as a bad example.*' These self-evaluations were found to be central in understanding his identity dynamics. Via the interactions, his growth contexts of family and education as well as his work life were explored.

P. Bansal, *Youth in Contemporary India: Images of Identity and Social Change*,
DOI 10.1007/978-81-322-0715-3_5,

I

Aasheesh described his family as very close knit and his greatest asset. His father was a judge and his mother a homemaker. His sister had completed her law degree and had started working. *He emphasised that he shared each and every thing with his family, especially with his mother, whom he was very close to.* She knew everything that he did and where he was during every part of the day. She knew that he smoked cigarettes and also took non-vegetarian food—habits that were frowned upon by her. She would often cite examples of successful elders in the family who had become 'big' without having to resort to them. He spoke of his grandparents and relatives in the same vein as his immediate family. His grandfather was a lawyer and he practised for 57 years. His father was also earlier practising law in district court in a city in U.P. When he got inducted into the judiciary services of U.P. state, his grandfather left his practice and travelled around with his son. He attributed his grandfather's decision to quit his legal practice to his failing health as well as to his father's need to keep him with himself. He said that he had always seen his father following his grandfather's footsteps, actively consulting him for the legal matters and also for other household issues and also agreeing to his advice always. Since his father was in a transferable job and was posted to small townships, he was sent to Delhi to his Tauji's (father's elder brother) house so that his studies did not suffer. So 8th class onwards, he had stayed with his Tauji's family. Since, they also had only one daughter, he was like a son to them as well. *In fact, he considered himself as having two sets of parents and always bought identical gifts for them.* Good-humoredly, he acknowledged that he had been 'almost' spoilt by the affection and indulgence he received from his Taiji (father's elder brother's wife) and grandfather. *He said that he was very close to them as well as other members of his extended family.* He visited them regularly and represented his family in their functions and weddings. His younger cousins recognised his parents because of him and referred to them as 'Aasheesh bhaiyya's parents'.

An interesting story tumbled out when I inquired about the unusual spelling of his name. He was named by his grandfather (he was the eldest grand child), and the spelling was carefully crafted by him. He wanted him to have a name beginning with alphabet 'A' so that he would always be the 'first one' in any list and doubly ensured it by putting a double 'A'. *He was a highly respected lawyer in the area and also a commanding figure in the larger family.* He had taken care of the education of members in the extended family. Besides, he was always looked upon as someone whose judgment about family matters could be trusted. Thus, people consulted him when they had to buy property or take a marriage decision etc. His parents always took his consent for all the decisions that they made when he was alive.

Speaking of his educational career, Aasheesh rated himself as a slightly above average student. Surprised at his admission because he had studied in the premier institutions in which he gained entry via intense competition, I asked him whether it was modesty speaking. To which he replied smilingly:

> It is the truth. Till class 5th, I was either 1st or 2nd ranker. In class 6th and 7th, I dropped down to rank 3rd–4th because of my interest in sports. I got admission in Delhi school

because of my marks and admission test. Here I continued to do well but not managing to top. I could not get through a good engineering college in the first instance. I dropped a year after 12th and prepared again. I could not get through IIT even the second time around. But I made it to another decent college in the civil engineering branch. So I was okay with it (smiles). The good thing with me is that I don't brood over these things. If I am demotivated because of something that hasn't happened according to my wish, the feeling doesn't stay with me for a long time. After a good night sleep, a movie, meeting with friends, the mood comes back to normal. Though it can't be said to be a major strength. Also, the double Is (implying IIT and IIM) have their own aura and charm. It does pinch that I was not able to make it to either. Sometimes you do feel that had I cleared that exam, I would have been much better placed today. But still ... you can't do anything about it. Probably that's the way it is planned.

The conversation thereafter went as below:

- *How did you fare in engineering?*
  Top 15.
- *Which is good enough? Very Good?*
  Out of a batch of 70 people, I was 14–15. But academically, you see a difference. The person who is topping is the one who gets most noticed. Once, you are not in the first 5, you are not considered academically very strong. *I never wanted to be an academically oriented person. I wanted to be an all rounder.* Academics ... you can always develop. You can go into hibernation for 6–8 months and study what you want to. You can do well there. *But college time is one where you can really build yourself.* You can develop things that you cannot develop later. *Because you can't take time off to develop your personality like communication skills or networking skills. And eventually, these are skills that also help in job market. That's what took me away from studies* (smiles). I knew that I have to ensure that I get a certain percentage of marks so that I get shortlisted for interviews by companies. So, I used to attend my classes and do my practicals. After that you are free. Just used to study 15 days before exams. So I was into all kinds of things—sports, going for interactions with the companies, getting companies into campuses for all kinds of activities—lectures, case study analysis. That was a thing we used to do a lot in engineering. Not everyone used to do that. We were a focal group who did that a lot. It was actually a very good learning experience. (Energetically) To get sponsorships from company. To convince them to shell out some money without a proper return of investment is a very difficult task. So if you are managing to do that without any contacts, you are learning something. We used to tap each and every company in Connaught Place, NOIDA, Gurgaon. Used to visit them, call them hundreds of time without any fear. So the fear of talking to a person or company was gone right in the 2nd/3rd year. Then bringing them on the campus, treating them well so that they don't feel that they haven't been treated well on the campus. We used to take special care that whatever companies and dignitaries that we have on our campus are treated very well. We used to have one person escorting every guest when people used to come on campus. We used to escort them from gate and drop them off at the gate. I value my engineering days a lot. (Continues energetically) *We used to feel that we are a part of everything, right from cultural events to sports.* Whatever was happening in the campus, we used to just ... just land up there. Talk to people, collect visiting cards and then call them up and say 'Sir, we met you at the alumni dinner. We are doing this kind of event on campus, and we need your participation'. We never used to say that we only wanted money. Because we also wanted speakers who can come and tell us what they had done in the industry. How the industry is growing? What are the opportunities for us? We needed judges for our events like case study analysis events. And we had given them flexibility. If they wanted to conduct some event on campus, we said 'We are ready. We will provide you with the entire infrastructure and the operational facilities you

want. You just come and conduct that event'. I had got 6–8 free memberships from British Council for one year and gave them as prizes for our events. I was also coordinating with Swatch sponsorships in college in the 2nd and 3rd year. So that was a big catch I had at that point of time. I also went to IIT Kanpur as a member of sports contingent to play. Because we were so involved in so many activities, the faculty members also knew us. We were given a room right next to the HOD room on the campus. There was a phone, A.C. in there. We used to spend hours in that room just planning out our strategy and working towards our goals. We used to work there till 2–3 o' clock at night, sleep there and just rushed before the HOD arrived (laughs). It was really fun! I knew people who were 2 years my juniors and 2 years my seniors. It involved team building as well. Knowing who is good at what and assigning tasks accordingly. We used to have dinner together late at night. It is the bonding that you remember. I am still very close to my engineering friends.

- *Sounds fun! So you balanced academics with extracurricular activities.*
  Yes! I managed to reach that minimum level—65% marks—which was required to get your CV shortlisted by most companies that come for recruitment on the campus. I had got marks in late 60s. Once, you are at the interview stage, then it's on you . . . how you guide your interview.
- *Academic achievement had been always expected of you by your parents?*
  Yes. Always! *Basically, the thing they say is that you should be amongst the best and top. If you want to pursue a course, do it from the best institutes and do it well. In the end, you should be successful and happy.* And that has been a constant complaint also. My mom has been after my life. *Why don't you study?* Everything is a priority for you, except studies. You don't devote time to studies. Otherwise, you can give us good results. And I agree with it. *Even during my training days in company, my mother used to say—study, study, study.* I was like—Mom! Who studies during training? I now tell her that you have been fooling me right since class 10th. Study for boards and you will get a year off in class 11th. But when in 11th, you begin preparing for competitive exams. You are told, study now . . . later your life will be smooth. Once, in engineering college, you have to study to get good marks for getting shortlisted for jobs by the companies. *So, basically, the pressure is never off you. You have to continuously perform. It's a vicious cycle . . . never-ending cycle.* Now, I tell her, I am not going to fall for it. But now with the final placements around the corner, the pressure to study is building again. I tell my mom—you have great patience. You can see that it is not having any effect on me but still keeps saying it (smiles mischievously).
- *So, you are not studying?*
  I am doing the bare minimum. I am not doing full justice to the studies. *I know that I should devote 3–5 hours of work, but I am not doing that. I am not able to manage my time.* Earlier, I was busy with placements for the junior batch. But now I have time but I am wasting it. Doing all kinds of recreational activities, but not studying. *Just don't feel like.* Sometimes, I think that I will work after coming back from an outing. But, then you are tired or many times, there isn't much time left to do quality work. So there isn't much satisfaction there and that's what my parents also say that you should feel satisfied with what you are doing. You should do justice to what you are learning. I agree with them but can't help it. I am not able to prioritise properly nowadays. But I know this should not continue for very long because otherwise it will create problem in job.
- *What does an engineering degree equip its student with? What skills are imparted and honed by it?*
  (After a long pause) Frankly, I can't think of any as such. (Laughs out aloud). It just makes you a little more analytical. You are doing numbers. You are also working in laboratory so you also have some hands on experience. Plus, it definitely gives you a more stable platform than graduation. It leads to a job. Also, for MBA, it helps. It is

much easier for engineers to crack the entrance exams for management courses. Once in it, the number crunching skills help in the course work.

- *Have you worked as a civil engineer?*
That's an interesting question. No! I never wanted to work as a civil engineer. I did two of my trainings—summer and winter—during college in this field. But I didn't like the work that was done or even the way it was done. People used to cheat, do all kinds of petty things for as low as Rs. 500–1000. That's one reason why I decided not to enter this field. The other reason was that I wanted to do an MBA immediately after that but couldn't get admission. So I decided to continue with my job and come back to do an MBA after work experience. I started with a marketing job in an insurance company. I thought that it would help me with communications skills and development of personality as a whole. Also in my preparation for group discussion and interview for MBA exams. Because in marketing, you tend to become more aggressive. Then I took the exams again. Couldn't clear it that time also. Then I shifted fields and went to Infosys. I needed a foothold in IT industry and Infosys was giving me that. Worked there for almost 2 years and then took all the management entrance exams. For me, it was the last chance. I got through this institute. *So, I have worked as a marketing person. I have worked in IT. Finance is an area in which I don't have any experience. So I have picked up finance as an optional this semester. Let me see what's in there? I can always go back to IT and marketing. I am also doing a course in intellectual property rights. Law is my family profession.*
- *That's quite a diverse portfolio. How rewarding is this kind of diversification?*
Yes . . . it is. I would say there is diversity but I am not able to do justice to all the things. I haven't worked as a civil engineer. Let's see how I make use of these 2–3 fields of law, MBA finance, marketing. *I still don't know where I am progressing! I am just keeping all my options open.* That was one of the main reasons for me to opt for finance. You need to have backup plan. *I was telling a friend today that I don't want a similar thing happening to me after MBA, what happened after engineering. The year we passed out of engineering, the IT bubble had just burst. None of the mass recruiters came for campus placements. There were hardly any jobs available in the market.* Most people in my batch were preparing for MBA. So the competition for MBA entrances was fierce. I hope nothing of this sort happens this time! Thankfully, the economy is on a big time upswing. Hopefully the job scenario would be good for us.
Besides, if you want to be a consultant then you need to have knowledge of as many fields as possible. You can't restrict yourself to only one field. *Probably with such varied exposure, I'll be able to do justice to consultancy! I don't know!! Also, in today's time everyone needs to be a jack of all trades. The competition is so much that you don't know what you would need at what point of time.* If you are too specialised, you are not too good. In order to survive in today's time, you should be known for a particular thing but you should have minimum level of expertise and command on different fronts. *I am still looking for a field where I can gain mastery.* Because, it is essential to have an area where you have command. But you should try and get information and knowledge in as many different fields as possible. Plus, even in society, you are meeting people and there are so many topics to discuss. If you know only two topics, then you would be sitting idle for the other 8 topics. That's what I feel you should be able to discuss anything with anyone, whichever field that person is from. At least for 10 minutes . . . then you can change the topic! Otherwise the person would not be interested in talking with you.
Another thing is that there are so many MBAs, you need to differentiate yourself. Earlier, engineers had to differentiate by doing an MBA. Now, as an MBA, you need to differentiate. Two years down the line, you need to differentiate on something else. Everyone is studying. Everyone is doing well. Everyone is taking so many degrees . . . international CFA, CA and some other banking courses. *I don't know how long you can do this thing. . . . keep differentiating!*

As I listened to Aasheesh, I realised that his experienced sense of self was that of *familial self which was felt to be highly relational in different social contexts.* The social pattern of family was traditional which emphasised strong family ties and jointness in matters of life cycle rites, vacations and property amongst members of the extended family. It also remained the major social circle for him; peers formed a close second. *The grandfather–father relationship was a prototype of the hierarchical intimacy relationship between father and son in relationship centred cultures like India.* There was an intensely emotional intimate relationship between the two. Within the emotional structuring of the relationship, the father was an authority figure who was responsibly concerned about the son and actively supported and involved himself in his son's life and work. The son in turn showed proper deference and subordination to his father and relatively little effort at any autonomous self-assertion all through life. He strongly idealised his father and intensely needed him as an important self-object to his self-regard. In strong identification with his father, he followed the legal profession and surpassed him by entering the judiciary service. However, he continued to carefully observe reciprocal responsibilities and obligations towards the father and also needed him for approval and guidance throughout. *This pattern of hierarchical relationships was also the inner psychological organisation for Aasheesh.* He spoke of his grandfather in an affectionate idealising manner. His father came across as someone who was overtly distant and aloof, a disciplinarian towards the son as well as being responsibly concerned. He was sponsoring his management education and bearing his living expenses. *Aasheesh looked up to his father, respected his high status and integrity as a judge and spoke with admiration about his calm and efficient way of being.* Being around many elders, he had developed a public self which followed the social etiquette in varying interpersonal contexts and situations. In my observations of his interactions with superiors (teachers/guests), I found him to be deferential and obedient.

As the only son in a modernising traditional family, he had been allowed considerable freedom in the domain of educational and vocational choices. Though his father would have liked him to try for civil services because of the status and prestige that its officials enjoyed, he decided to join the expanding private sector. While his father took after his own father by joining the legal profession, Aasheesh saw himself as standing apart from his family; his sister having taken the family trade ahead. He, aided by the presence of his Tauji who had in his own life taken a different path by pursuing engineering and management and then entering the public sector, could take on a different course of life and do engineering and later management. Hence, the familial relationships were accommodative of his specific wishes, abilities and inclinations with a greater recognition that he might function in a somewhat more independent way. But he was also pursuing a course in intellectual rights and patents and was contemplating doing a course in company law. *This need to maintain connection with law was driven by an emotional need to remain identified with the family profession. It was also legitimised by him as a move which would help him in his career progression.* Also, certain forms of behavioural conformity were still expected. For instance, he confessed that since his parents would live with him, he would not throw parties at home in which liquor would be served.

During the two months of interaction with Aasheesh, I found him diffused. *His general appearance was that of being tired and lethargic, someone who was going through the motions of life without much of interest, direction and anticipation. This was also borne out by his inability to manage time well, his difficulty in investing himself in studies and to forge a definite course of his life in terms of which industry would he want to go. All of this was causing anxiety in him and more so in his parents who continuously urged him to get focused in life to get best results.* He was keeping himself afloat by putting in the minimum amount of effort required to make satisfactory academic grades, socialising and maintaining the hope that he would get a reasonable job. During one of our meetings, I found him looking particularly distressed and worn out. On inquiring about the reason for it, he spoke dejectedly about how he had done really badly in a class presentation. All his other classmates were much better prepared with more incisive analysis, but he had started work on the presentation at the last moment after watching the cricket match till late night with his friends. He was upset not only at his poor performance vis-à-vis his classmates which was a reflection on his abilities (according to him) but also at his low motivation to apply himself energetically at the academic tasks at hand.

Unsure and worried about what the future holds for him, he appeared to be caught in a state of doubt about what he can be and shame over what he might have already become. In terms of identity dynamics, the self-conscious doubt might have its roots in too early initiation in *the competitive ethos of 'being first' and 'being successful'* defined in terms of bettering one's status relative to peers. This precluded him from engaging in that experimental play and work through which he had the chance of learning to find and insist on his own kind of achievement and his work identity. Assimilation into the dominant trend of the kind of workmanship in demand, however, had provided him the optimum combination of free choice, peer solidarity and compliance till the time he was pursuing his engineering. *He spoke of his college time with vigour and energy which is experienced by that section of youth which finds itself in the wave of a technological, economic or ideological trend seemingly promising all that youthful vitality could ask for. Getting through a reputed engineering college also helped him to reflect well on family and paternal reputation, enhancing his self-regard, as well as gaining the love and respect of family elders.* This psychological element derived from his familial selfhood coexisted with his more individualised strivings for individual fulfilment and competitive success which was sponsored in him from an early age.

The affirmatively exciting time during engineering college ended on a debilitating note when he experienced a job scarcity and a failure to get admission in a management institute of choice. He suddenly found himself at the mercy of luck and chance, which the language of 100% placement in college campuses and the rhetoric of ever-expanding job market tend to decry. This created a chink in the trustworthiness of time as a sufficient guarantor of satisfaction which makes wanting and working worthwhile. The marketing job that he took up post engineering was initially experienced as easy. But when he was given independent charge of meeting the sales targets, he found it very difficult to manage the targets. In the IT company he joined subsequently, he was initially reprimanded for his college like sociable behaviour which led him to be an isolate which again was disapproved of by the superiors. He was bypassed for promotion in spite of his faultless performance because of his lack of innovative and creative inputs as per the performance appraisal. He shared sadly that because of work pressure there were times when he had dinner at 1.30 in the night all alone. Such not so positive experiences and evaluations of one's identity have the potential of creating painful self-consciousness because Aasheesh had great stake in it and it was hard earned. *In the work environment, he was exposed to comparisons with age-mates and judgements by superiors—all of which gives rise to a sense of shame over one's inadequacies and failures.* They create a discrepancy between one's self-esteem, the aggrandised self-images as an autonomous person and one's appearance in the eyes of others. His potent statement 'I am not completely useless but I can be set as a bad example' is a reflection of this. While retaining some modicum of positive self-worth, he was also beset with occasional obliteration of self-esteem and self-conscious doubt. The loneliness and self beating would get to him so much that he used to tell his 'mothers' (his real mother and his Taiji who was also like a mother to him) that he wanted to come home ... if he failed, he would come back home and asked them—Would they take him back? And much to his comfort, they always stood by him and boosted his morale.

In Aasheesh's case, his sense of accomplishment was also contingent upon gaining evidence of father's respect and recognition, as well as reflect well on him. He perceived his father to be very focused, very dedicated in his work. Unlike him, his father did not have the attitude of just completing the task. He would do full justice to each and every case. According to Aasheesh, whatever judgments he had given had been appreciated by senior judges. And that was a quality that he wanted to imbibe from his father—his quality of work should be appreciated by his seniors. *However, his inner core of heightened self-regard originally derived from early maternal environment was kept vulnerable by the frequent digs made by his father, which were made light by him by perceiving them as jokes.* His father's statements that his money was getting wasted on him; as parents, they did not expect any returns from him; he had to only take care of himself and not worry about them because they had no expectations from him—only served to reinforce that he was failing them in some way. Thus, he found himself playing with elements of negative identity, making him believe that he could be 'set as a bad example'. Erikson (1968) noted that the negative identity is dictated by the necessity of finding and defending a niche of one's own against the excessive ideals either demanded by morbidly ambiious parents or indeed actualised by superior ones. *Here, his refusal to apply himself to studies, to continue with his kind of social life which included indulging in smoking, drinking and eating non-vegetarian food—all of which were highly disapproved by the family—were forms of unconscious resistive behaviour that mocked subtly the expected role of a 'son' who would always bring referred success to his family* via *his work and conduct. This experimentation also allowed him some freedom from the excessive ideals set by his grandfather and father.*

II

An attempt was also made to understand the corporate world view and his opinions about it. The following are excerpts of interviews underlining the prevailing attitudes in the corporate world of work:

- *Why is there so much of a craze to do an MBA? What is the advantage of this degree?*
  It has become important, no doubt! Basically, MBA opens a new line of growth. You enter into middle management straight away after doing this degree. If you are an engineer then it will take you 5–6 years just to reach a middle management level. Also your growth path is slightly different from a person who has done his MBA. *So if you want a faster growth, you need to have additional degrees.* Say in the marketing field, people who have done sales, people who have gone to the shops and sold, they become unit managers, channel managers and only then they reach the level of area sales manager. It has taken them 10–12 years. And a fresh graduate from a B-school directly joins at the level of area sales manager. It is an ego clash. Just getting a 2-year additional qualification, someone joins at the same level where you have struggled to be after so many years and he would move up the ladder in a much faster way. In India, degrees are valued besides a person's capabilities. I can be a better manager, marketing person than a person passing out of B-school, but since he has a degree, he will be valued more and obviously will be inducted at a higher level. Unfortunate but this is what is happening across industry.
  In fact once in job also, people are doing certifications, extra studies in the field they are working. That helps them to grow faster. Sometimes they want to diversify. Say a person who has worked in IT field and wants to come in a banking domain, he takes domain-related certifications to enhance his knowledge of banking and financial services. He moves on from doing a simple IT job to do a job which means more responsibility and more money.
- *How is the work environment in the corporate jobs?*
  It is very challenging ... very very competitive in terms of peers. If you are doing your job properly, it is OK with them. Everyone around is doing their work properly. *If you have to stand out or if you have to grow faster, then you have to be innovative. That's the first word they use.* You have to come out with solutions and ideas which help the company improve. I was told this in the IT company I was working with. Managers told me that they wanted people who can develop model practices, best practices that can be used by the company to grow and save money and time. That's the pressure. They say directly that out of four people working at the same position, at the time of promotion all of them cannot be given the same rating. They cannot be satisfied at the same go. Probably two people who have worked with me and who have shown initiative and innovation, they are given a higher rating. It is up to the other two to react. Lots of people quit, few go for higher education, few develop a nonchalant attitude. Besides, interactions with clients, meeting deadlines, dealing with your superiors ... are the pressures that one has.
- *But in this continuous competition, necessity to project oneself as innovative, exacting standards of performance, what does it do to the self-esteem and confidence levels of the employee?*
  Sometimes, it helps. It's a challenge all the time. *Every 2–3 months, you have to prove yourself. You obviously keep improving or passing the benchmarks that you have set for yourself.* But if you are an easy going person, then it is a problem. Otherwise, competition is a good thing. It gets the best out of you. *I don't know how long a person can keep doing that—probably 6–8 months, 3–4 years, but I don't think he can always keep improving his benchmarks.* That's the time frustration creeps in. It takes a toll on your family life, health everything. One of my friends is 25 years old and he had been admitted once for high BP. I have never heard it happening to someone of my age group.

It is totally because of work pressure and stress. He is travelling, working in the office Monday to Saturday. He is being paid well but the other side is that you are burnt out by 40–45 years. Then what? But I think that if you can work right now, work. If you avoid work right now, you are going to struggle for a longer time. You can dedicate more time now. Otherwise you wouldn't to be reaching that position in another 15 years. So I think that if one has the capacity, then he should put in his best efforts at this particular point rather than doing it at 40 when it is too late. Most people want to take it easy once they have passed 35–40 years.

- *Everyone is marketing oneself, everyone is bettering oneself . . . is there an end to this? No! It's a rat race. People have substance, confidence and lots of marketing skills.* The younger generation is even more competitive and better at marketing itself. This kind of confidence is being brought in right from childhood by school and parents. People are doing self checks. They are figuring out where are they lacking and how can they improve. *People are continuously bettering themselves, all around. There is no limit for that. There is no one who is really satisfied with what one is getting. There are very few who are. And it should be the case. If one is satisfied, then obviously growth will be affected.* Somebody who is satisfied at the age of 30, what is he going to achieve for the next 30 years of his life and with what pace is he going to attain that is also important.
- *Why this expediency—the great hurry to reach faster, to get more, at a quicker pace?*
I have no justifications for it. But it comes automatically. You see people around, doing well and getting ahead so there is definitely a need to be competitive or at least stay along. *Many times, one is not very disappointed by one's own failure but more with other people's success or achievement if one is not able to match with other people.* I don't think someone would be complaining if his best of best friend's bonus is also delayed. You just don't want to be left behind. That's the primary reason why everyone is driven crazy for money or success. Maybe the other reason is—too much, too soon! That's the mantra of the younger generation. They have whatever is given to them by the families. *Now they want to have everything that their parents' had at the age of 50–55 right at the age of 20.* That can be a reason for speeding up. And also more lavish, bigger.
- *How important it is to have a keen sense of opportunity?*
Very important. You have to keep your eyes and ears open. It's not that you can sit on your seat and jobs will come your way. *You have to take an initiative.* You have to see magazines, newspaper, be online. *You have to network, be connected.* First evaluate yourself whether you can do justice and take up this new thing. I think you should take challenges—new opportunities, new initiatives. Otherwise if you are just banking upon your existing things, even though, it is giving you good returns but no risk, no return!
- *What difference do you see between private sector and government jobs in India?*
Somehow, the kind of status and prestige an IAS officer, judicial officer or a judge enjoys, you can never imagine that kind of respect even if you are a managing director in any company. You will be known only in that company or among other CEOs. I will be known only in the team/vertical that I am working in. Even if you are driving a Mercedes, a police constable can shoo you away. That kind of social recognition is not there. An IAS officer is more respected than any B-school graduate from even the best universities like Harvard, Carnegie Mellon. Even I feel that the kind of input that is required to clear IAS, allied examination is much more than say clearing IIT-JEE or CAT. The control at the age of 30 years a District Magistrate enjoys is enviable. *My dad's choice of service was based on this. He chose status over money.* In the last district, he got a glorious farewell. (Speaks with pride) After farewell, the staff pushed his car for 1–1/2 km right from court to our residence and everybody was travelling with him in 6–7 cars.
- *What is your vision for your professional future?*
Say 5 years down the line, I don't know which industry will I be working in or which position I will be working at. But the main aim is commanding responsibility and respect of people around me and seniors. Money is not that important for me. In the sense that

> money will not be the only driving force. Because, materialistic requirements are there till the age of 35–40 years. After that, you don't have a craze for all these cars and gadgets. *It is recognition, status and respect for your work, your skill and talent that is more important for me.*

The above conversation clarified that Aasheesh was experiencing a confusing mix of new age values of enterprise culture and traditional familial ideals. His inner interdependency oriented psychological needs of personalised, nurturing relationships with superiors and shouldering greater responsibility and earning recognition at work were at variance with the prevailing individualistic practices that embody contractually oriented relationships, egalitarian values and organisational impersonalness. The disapproval of his personalised sociable behaviour at his workplace was an example of the same. Also, a long history of honouring prescriptive hierarchies and obedience made it difficult for him to show innovative thinking at work because of which he was overlooked for promotion. He was advised by his superiors to be assertive with them and say 'no' to work when he was overburdened. He spouted the normative messages of enterprise culture which demand ever-increasing performance, competitiveness and efficiency through a constant stream of fads and initiatives. In order to function and be a success in such environment, he was playing by its rules of valuing competitiveness, the constant display of energy and initiative and the setting of material goals. However, he also understood ruefully that in this world, life became a perpetual endeavour where stress, fear of failure and guilt loomed large; where the workaholic ethic-threatened familial and personal relationships, health and leisure pursuits; where companionship in the workplace was constantly threatened by rivalry and suspicion; where emphasis on accountability and performance exacted its toll.

His individuality lay in forging a path between the ethos of reciprocal emotional interdependencies nurtured by familial environment and competitive individualism fostered by modern education and work contexts. The balance, of course, is elusive and reconciliation at times impossible. *While the direction of his life was implanted early in life by the elders, he also had learnt to respond to signals from a far wider circle than is constituted by the closely knit unit of family.* Much like radar, he had to be able to receive signals from far and near, from multiple sources and deal with rapid changes in order to make himself at home in the outer world. The new age value of 'networking' embodied this skill. Aasheesh prided himself at being good at networking, a skill he developed during his college days. He shared that his mobile phone did not have the memory to save the phone numbers of his ever-expanding list of contacts. He joked that his parents worried that they would have to host his wedding reception in a cricket ground because of the large number of people he knew. By networking, he meant connecting in virtual as well as real world with diverse people from various walks of life and engaging in superficial intimate responses to them like greetings on festivals, birthdays and anniversaries in order to gain help in terms of information, contacts etc. This was in contrast to his father's social life which was restricted and was much guided by concerns of status and occupational sector. Though, networking is guided by the age old value of developing patronage which can come to one's aid in times of need, in today's times it also serves an all important purpose of remaining connected and informed about the opportunities and developments in the larger world. *He knew that unlike his father he would need to be somewhat of a generalist rather than identifying too closely with a domain of knowledge, skill and expertise. He would also need to be a leader who can work with people because he was placed in work situations where he would be heading teams of people rather than working alone as in the case of his father's legal profession.* Also in terms of lifestyle, he saw himself pitched differently than his parents—more embroiled in the ethos of competition, consumption, unpredictability and initiative. *Hence, in Aasheesh, one saw a way of preserving more traditional lifestyle in the familial sphere and the more contemporary lifestyle in the work sphere by carrying into both groups an internalised ego ideal that is oriented towards identifying with the group's norms, customs and attitudes, with a strong deference and respect for hierarchical authority.* By choosing a work context (he ultimately went in the IT sector which is known to be more stable, expertise oriented rather than marketing oriented, and moderately remunerative by the existing standards), he showed assimilative tendencies.

Deepak

Deepak, 23 years old, was an M.Sc. Physics student. One of the first research participants, I met him initially as a part of the group of students to whom I presented my research idea in order to enlist their participation. He was a curious and active part of the discussion and struck me as someone earnest, with a serious look and reflective mind. I contacted him after a week and we decided to meet. During the research relationship that spawned over five interactions, he shared his life journey with eagerness. He startled me by telling me at the start that before the first meeting, he had locked himself in his room for a day to ruminate over his life and to discover the reasons of his personality. He added that for him, life was a quest to know the truths of the world and its people. *He was given to a habit of indulging in deliberate strenuous introspection about his own self and observation of others' lives.* The empathic and non-judgmental interpersonal communication space was used by him to express his understandings of his life's events and experiences that had influenced him and shaped his personality. The first two interactions were depressive outbursts in which there was a palpable emotional distress and need to release it. In the latter two interactions, the pressure of his emotion was less, but *life themes of inferiority and isolation* kept recurring through the conversations. *He spoke with sadness and bitterness about how he was caught in the matrix of parental control and obedience because of which he could not take the decisions and make choices for himself and felt suppressed and divided within himself.* His two 'failure' experiences—one of not getting through IIT for engineering and second of not winning the love of a girl—and the frustrations that he felt in the last 4–5 years were his standpoint from where he wove his life story.

Deepak belonged to Bokaro Steel City from where he had completed his schooling. His father was a non-executive employee in the steel plant. He had an elder sister who was working in Pune. His mother was a housewife. As a science student, he prepared for IIT-JEE during classes XI and XII. But he could not clear the exam, a big 'failure' for him. Rather than dropping a year for preparation of IIT-JEE, his father thought that it would be better for him to take admission in a Delhi university college

P. Bansal, *Youth in Contemporary India: Images of Identity and Social Change*,
DOI 10.1007/978-81-322-0715-3_6, © Springer India 2013

and prepare for the entrance exam simultaneously. He got admission in B.Sc. (Hons.) Physics but did not attend his classes because he was concentrating on preparing for IIT. He narrated:

> During that time, I was really very much crazy about IIT. I kept thinking and fantasising about it as if it was a girl. Actually, throughout my life, I never performed really well in studies. Suddenly, I realised that it is my last opportunity to prove whether I am good or not. *Back home in Bokaro, it is a closed society. People there aspire that their children become either engineers or doctors. There is no other option that is entertained. If you are preparing for engineering and don't get into IIT, then you are useless.* I remember when I didn't qualify for IIT, my father returned back from his office with a sad face. Later, I found out from my mother that he had a bad day because everyone was asking him about my result and one of his colleague's sons had got through. It was a kind of emotional blackmail. Also my parents were spending a lot of money on my education and stay in Delhi. So I was under a lot of stress. *For me it was a situation of 'Perform or Perish'. The FIIT-JEE classes that I joined just exposed me to the kind of competition I was up against. It worsened my condition.* I felt that everyone else knew everything. I felt very homesick and lonely. There were no friends with whom one could share. Whenever I would perform well, my expectations would rise ... from just being in IIT to better ranks in IIT-JEE. There was no one to check me. I would calculate time in terms of numbers of hours remaining. In this phase, for the first time, I had a suicidal notion that if I am not able to complete a portion of my work by a particular time, then I am dead. Ultimately, my health began to deteriorate. Because of which I couldn't study much. A week before the exam, I consulted a doctor who diagnosed me with jaundice. The exam went off OK. I had a hope but I didn't make it. *Ultimately, I had nothing ... I had wasted a year and ended up with physics and depression.*

For Deepak, that year was a watershed year of his life. Away from home for the first time, wanting to prove himself in a highly competitive scenario took a toll on him. A feeling of failure took a vice-like grip over him. He consoled himself by saying that he had done his best. He rejoined graduation. *In the second year of graduation, he began to think of doing MBA. This decision was guided by his need to outshine his peers who cleared IIT-JEE. It was also a way of winning the praise of his parents and shut the mouths of the detractors.* But he had to prepare himself for the field of management that required social skills and extraverted personality which he felt he did not have because he had never participated in any extracurricular activities in school. So during graduation, he tried to come out of his shell, gave less emphasis to studies and started to open up and make friends with people. He prepared for both JAM [Joint Admission Exam for M.Sc.] and CAT [entrance examination for Indian Institutes of Management-IIM]. He did not make into IIMs but got selected in IIT for M.Sc. Physics. He was very happy about it and so were his parents because finally their dream to see him in IIT was fulfilled. But after one semester, he began to feel that he was a second-grade citizen. There was a big divide between the B.Tech. students and the postgraduate students like him. The job placements and remuneration were just not attractive enough. Also, the highly competitive and individualistic environment of the place unsettled him. In the first year itself, he realised that he had landed in the wrong boat. He did not want to make his career in physics. He became quite miserable and his performance suffered. He again began to think of MBA and began to prepare for it. Around the time we were meeting, he had got a job with a company with a package of 2.56 lakhs/annum, much less than what he had desired but it had at least given him some security and confidence.

Deepak experienced his second failure in love. His affections for a college classmate were not reciprocated by her. In the beginning, he was not sure what he felt for her because he knew few emotions and categories of relationship—friends, parents, sisters and teachers. His interactions with girls had been limited. He recalled an incident as a child, in which a girl made fun of him asking others not to play with him because he was fat. That remark hurt him a lot. After that day, he decided not to interact with girls. What drew him close to his classmate was her radiant smile and carefree attitude, both of which were counter to his personality. Her cheerful persona would brighten his mood. *While strongly attracted to her, he struggled to accept his feelings for her because they threatened to distract him from his studies and career. He believed that such feelings ruined one's career.* His articulation of his feelings towards her was hence always cautious and hesitant. Also, a part of him believed that he was not a good match for her because of his aged looks (he had a serious expression on his face and was balding) and an average future in which he was not sure whether he would be able to take her to dine at Park Hotel, as was her wish. But he still harboured a faint hope of getting back to her when he would settle down in a job.

The initial interactions with him left me quite depressed. I felt a great sense of sympathy for him. He spoke sadly and often resentfully of incidents after incidents of how parental overcontrol and insistence on conformity to standards of behaviour and achievement led to thwarting of his self and created feelings of shame and guilt in him. *Gradually, his sense of victimhood began to rankle me. It began to impress upon me, due to the sheer tenacity with which he held on to it, as a rigid sheath which enabled him to minimise the role of choice and agency in his life and experience himself as a 'good son'.* Whenever I questioned him about the possibility of reaching some balance between individuality and relatedness, he consistently evoked ideal of duty towards parents and privileged a way of living life according to the expectations of significant others rather than by one's own initiative which he thought to be selfish. *I wondered why he was not ready to acknowledge or carve any space for autonomous functioning which he so yearned for.* Much after I completed my work with him that I began to understand the subtleties and complexities of his inner psychological make-up and the soil and climate in which it grew and functioned. *I recognised that his self was far more rooted (in comparison with few other participants) in the traditional familial ethos of deference to the wishes of the elders, observance of proper behaviour as per the expectation in a specific context, upholding the reputation and honour of the family, empathic awareness of others' feelings and moods and fulfilment of duty and obligation towards the significant others.* In this kind of Indian family relationships, the considerations of separate or individualised self are transcended by more enmeshed relating mode of giving and asking, of caring for and depending on, of influencing and being influenced, of close, warm emotional connectedness and interdependence. Although, the pervasive, cultural value system was continuing to influence his self, there were also considerable strains and conflicts that existed because of it. *The attempt of research was to understand the nature of conflicts that Deepak experienced in his negotiations with the parental matrix in an effort to understand the psychodynamics that emerge when the individualised functioning of a growing individual is sabotaged and constricted by sociocultural patterns.* Deepak had a self-narrative in which he saw an inherent trade-off between self-assertion and obligation towards parents. He tilted towards the latter so as to minimise the conflict between his personal strivings for individuation and the cultural pull against separation and individuality. His individualised functioning was much restricted than the usual as witnessed in the modernising urban Indian familial setups where relationships stretch to allow for increasing consideration of the child's and particularly the adolescent's specific wishes, abilities and inclinations in the social, educational, occupational and marital sphere, with a greater recognition that a person may function in a somewhat more independent way.

What was evident from Deepak's personal history was an especially high familial pressure to achieve and strong parental emphasis on academic performance as an indicator of not only intellectual competence but of human worth. Deepak complained:

> All my life, I have been under constant pressure to perform in studies. *For my parents, it was a priority. They always asked me to study. I don't remember they ever asked me to play.* But when you are a child, you want to play, you want to watch movies, you want to go shopping. Later even when my father used to ask me to come with him to the market or film, I would refuse. I would think I can spend that much time studying. But because I used to only study, my performance also plateaued.

His success, academic as well as professional, was instrumental to enhancing the position, honour and material well-being of his family. Identified with the family's striving to protect and enhance its reputation and rank within its own community, he perceived any of his failure as a 'black mark' on the family resulting in a 'loss of face'. Recalling a turning point in his life, he narrated an incident in which during a family marriage he along with his cousin deflated cycle tyres. On coming to know about this, his uncle gently reprimanded his son, while his father scolded him a lot in front of everyone. Exposed as he was to the eyes of everyone, he felt extremely ashamed and small and vowed not to do anything which would displease his parents. *He came to feel that his 'naughtiness was evil' and brought bad name to his parents.* He became circumspect around his elders, enjoying their praise and appreciation about his good conduct. But away from them, he was expressive in his feelings if he felt that no one would learn about it. *Thus, how he would be regarded by others became a central inner dynamic.*

As a sensitive child, rather than moderating these values of academic achievement, he overidentified with them, hence, developing a precocious conscience, using it as weapon against him when his performance slumped. Unable to achieve mutual regulation with the parents in this large area of his life, he conformed to their will and compromised his ability for self-assertion. This resulted in *studies becoming a matter of repetitive ritual. Lack of social play with peers that provides the space for sportive competition, experimentation and imagination (also because of a leg bone ailment) aggravated his isolation and fostered tendencies of obsessiveness and procrastination.* The exacting standards of performance that his parents had for him expressed in not appreciating him even when he got good marks in maths and comparing him with his cousin who was more achieving than him, created an excessive awareness of as well as abhorrence of competitiveness and a lasting sense of doubt about one's ability to come out top.

He wanted to be seen as a 'good son'. No other self-image could compete with the tyrannical moralistic imperative that backed this self-image. He was guilt stricken by any endeavour that could 'break the heart of [his] parents'. The inflexible moralism was fuelled by tales of struggles which characterised the lives of parents and the hardships they endured to provide comforts to the children. *Hence, he imposed pedantic limitations on the horizons of his imagination.* He wouldn't want to go abroad for his doctoral work nor would he want to get too busy with his work—future scenarios that held out the possibility of him not being there for them when needed. In order to maintain the highly valued emotional relatedness and connectedness between family members, he needed to contain the anger and ambivalence generated by slights, disappointed expectations and lack of reciprocity. An incident highlighted how the son's aggressive behaviour was immediately cut off by father. *During one of the family trips, his father asked him to go and board the plane while he stayed behind to do something. The official caught him and shoved him aside since he didn't have the ticket. Embarrassed by this, he went and spoke with suppressed anger to his father that since tickets were with him, why did he send him in? After being seated, his father reprimanded him for his rudeness towards him, stating in a hurt tone that he had already begun to be disrespectful to his parents, something which was fearfully anticipated in the future.* This incident highlighted certain cultural ideals: the intense expectations for deference and social etiquette that was expected of him in hierarchical relationships; a requirement of a superego profoundly oriented towards the conscious containment and often dissociation of angry feelings, through a number of defence mechanisms; and instant criticism and shaming for what is forbidden (Roland 1988). *To be achieving and dutiful were the ideal prototypical images held up to him by his immediate social milieu.*

The negative elements were summarily banished from one's consciousness. However, they lurked close by as represented in his fantasies and unconscious manoeuvres to slough off standards of behaviours. Often, he used to just keep his books open in front of him and daydream of fun and adventure, of things that were denied to him. The painstaking detailing with which Deepak spoke of his illnesses before the two crucial entrance exams, almost in a bid to rationalise his failures in the outcomes, left a question in the mind of the researcher about the psychological significance of illness. Is it possible that the bouts of jaundice that he suffered from were protests against the pressure to perform and provided a respectable excuse for his likely failures? There have been instances where he confessed to having 'played' with his career. Just before a crucial exam, he sat down to write a mail to the girl he loved, confessing his feelings for her, thereby messing up his exam paper.

He himself admitted to feeling exhausted by the burden of being responsible and mature which for him meant subduing his wishes and needs. It felt even more hurtful when his sister who was always a rebel of sorts went against the parents' wishes to marry the boy of her choice. It was a painful reminder to how he could have also stretched the boundaries laid out by his parents and lived his life more on his own terms. Besides, his image of the 'successful man' also stood reformed because his sister's choice was a man who was neither handsome nor too educated and rich and belonged to a different caste. As a child, he had suffered the *ignominy of being fat* and the sexual self-images that surround such embarrassing physical appearance. The feelings had continued in his youth and only served to intensify his self-consciousness about his appearance and, thus, lowered his confidence. The wedge between duty and desire, the acceptable and unacceptable, was intuitively captured by him in his *description of two sides of his personality*. One face was the *frivolous, footloose, carefree side* which did not follow any set rules. The one that *wanted to be naughty and have fun, to seek pleasure for itself* by consuming objects like gizmos and bike, much like his contemporaries. It was also *aggressive in its pursuit of goals, not letting any emotion come in its way*. When in that phase of mind, he felt more interactive and creative. That part '*can take risks, more daring, wants to become an entrepreneur*'. The second was the *moral police* which exerted a strong control even over the other self-element. *It was quiet and submissive, scared of society and underconfident*. It was the storehouse of his painful memories which he used to understand life. This part was *philosophical and spiritual* which would get affected by the sufferings of people and wanted to help spread happiness around. Terming it as the mature and sensitive part, he felt that if he were to delete it, he would become self-centred and apathetic to his people.

Deepak could not get away with either side of these divisions in thought, fantasy, and feeling nor could they get integrated to provide a consistent sense of direction; hence, they coexisted in uneasy relationship with each other. His IIT dream was nurtured through childhood. *IIT loomed large in his consciousness as a mighty institution which makes its members invincible, unbeatable*. The 'utter craze' that he had for it and the 'deep despair' that he felt at his failure to get into the institution and become an IITian—the most fancied identity for him, merited understanding of what the institution represented to him. IIT is undoubtedly India's biggest and most powerful brand and export to the world. *The brand IIT, with its delectable mix of fact and fiction, has a seductive appeal for scores of Indians dreaming of global opportunities and high status*. Those who make through to the precincts of this hallowed institution through an intensely competitive procedure are stamped as super achievers and are believed to be destined to become leaders in their chosen fields. As a boy, belonging to a lower middle class family, growing up in a small steel town of India, it was not unusual for Deepak to fall prey to the seduction of this institution. *He fantasised about it 'much like one's girlfriend' who offers the much-needed affirmation of one's masculinity—the modality which intrusively and vigorously enters spaces unknown with an excitement that is unaware of one's limitations. In his fantasies, IIT perhaps held out the promise of giving him an identity of being a 'successful son', that is, a man who while fulfilling the parental expectations had also gone beyond the paternal provincialism; who has not only absorbed the moral sense of the permissible but who can also set off in the direction towards the possible*. In essence, it offered the exciting challenge of a new reality of choice and initiative and new chance of being reborn as someone with guiltless ambition and competence.

While he nurtured the dream of conquest inherent in the fantasy of IIT, becoming an entrepreneur and taking his girlfriend to an expensive hotel, his native temperament as well as the social growth contexts did not quite provide the necessary nutriments to 'go for a killing'. In his words:

> I didn't like competition. I believed in harmony and hence never had the kind of competitive attitude. *For me, competing with others never made sense but I knew that if I get good marks, my parents will feel good. I wanted to keep them happy.* I wanted to become a good boy. But often I got compared to others who were performing better than me in studies. It hurt my ego. It forced me to compete with others. Why can't people leave me alone with my day dreams?... I could never understand. I wanted to be a scientist. I loved experimenting with things and numbers. I loved spirituality and philosophy. I wanted to see and keep everyone happy. I want to open old age homes and orphanages. I have seen the way old people are mistreated in their families. I want to help the poor and needy. In IIT, I was volunteering with an NGO and teaching slum children. I wanted to do M.B.A. after my B.Sc. only because it was the way of earning comfort for my parents and to shut others' mouth. But deep down in my heart, I wanted to be in research.

Competition which can often be disruptive of relationships was not liked by him. He cherished the values of cooperation, affection and understanding. The ideal goal for him was to live in harmony with the multiple relationships of family and society. *His philosophical and non-materialist mental disposition along with an emotional nature set him apart from his peers who were perceived by him as carefree and consumerist.* Deepak could not participate in the sportive competition, peer politics and experimentation with roles because of the isolation demanded by exclusive focus on academics. *The necessary aggression required in self-insistence, in consumption of objects of desire and building ambitions was inhibited in him.* Reminders that forced him to think of himself and his needs as evil and dirty led him to minimise his needs. After being scolded severely by his father for buying a toy and cartoon book as a young child, he decided against asking his parents to buy him anything. In class 12th, he told his father not to get him clothes as he would like to buy new ones only when he got into IIT. Because he thought it improper to watch TV, he would not switch on the TV himself but would wait for his sister to do that and then would sneak in. If he had to ask his father for permission to go for a school picnic, he would indirectly mention what was his wish. The only acceptable form of initiative was in the form of denial of ambition as a possible way of totally avoiding guilt. *His inner world of ideals and evils did not correspond to the social world with its goal and dangers—a necessary prerequisite to join the ideological trend with enthusiasm and vigour.* His naughtiness was wickedness according to him but what escaped him was that the shrewdness and playfulness incipient in it is an essential quality for survival in the real world. *The ideal of understanding life in its spiritual dimension ran counter to the credo of amassing and enjoying the sensual pleasures of materialistic life.* He was oriented more towards the development of relational, familial self and also towards self-transformation through the growth of more subtle qualities and enhanced inner powers in order to become a 'better person'. Hence, he found himself somewhat of an outsider to the dominant world view of material prosperity, competition and individualism that offers the solidarity linking common identities in joint living, acting and creating in the present era.

At the same time, he felt that there was not much of an appreciation amongst his parents and friends for his empathic, affectionate and responsible being to which he was subsuming many of his more individualised needs. Though he saw his parents as nurturant and considerate, he was easily hurt and disappointed when his expectations for reciprocity and fulfilment were not met. He used to remember with pain how he was never praised openly by them for his behaviour and performance. The mother too doubted his good intentions to take care of the parents as was reflected in her caustic remark: 'At the moment, your father is earning and you are at the receiving end. Things will be different when you will earn and we will be at the receiving end'. All of this depressed his inner world because his sense of self-esteem was dependent on familial recognition and appreciation of his efforts to live up to certain ideals and idealised images of oneself. His friends also made fun of his sensitivity and called him an impractical, emotional fool. *He longed for an affirmation of his emotional, dutiful, responsible self. He likened himself to a lamp that burn but which also sometimes require that its wick is supported so that it continues to glow and give light to others.*

Deepak's life was an example of how parental overcontrol and insistence on conformity to standards of behaviour and achievement could inhibit the growing child's sphere of free choice, grossly limit the exercise of free will and constrict his initiative and sense of purpose leading to an acute sense of incompetence and thus precluding him from the promising affirmation of the prevalent technological, economic or ideological trend. It also highlighted the painful affects and conflicts that get generated in a young person when traditional Indian cultural ideals of receptivity, sensitivity and responsibility towards others clash with Western modes of assertiveness, ambition and competitiveness; being contrast with doing, familial and group interdependence opposes personal autonomy for self-creation.

His last research communication just after he joined his job was an email he wrote to me. On the threshold of a new beginning, he summed up defeats, small victories and unfulfilled wishes of a pivotal phase of his life which was apparently coming to an end. Something of it still continued in his memories and longings, while he readied himself to face the world with optimism and fresh vision:

> I vividly remember the night previous to my leaving IIT. It was when I was packing my belongings, a gust of warm breeze came in through the open window and filled my room giving me a nostalgic fit that reminded me of the two great years that I had spent in that mighty institution. How I chose to stand apart from my classmates, the decision to leave physics and go for a job, the journey from depression to that state of faith and the way I didn't let my career get ruined because of my feelings. *At last, I was at least an average chap with a tag of a great institution.* Although I never counted myself as an IITian, because I thought I was not, but at that point of time I took the opportunity of counting myself in that class. For me IITians were those whom nobody can defeat [I know it's not true and boastful but it's my school day's notion]. Since I carried myself steadily through all the difficult situations, I think I did justice to me by calling myself IITian. *Everything was perfect except for her* [*referring to the girl he loved*] *absence from my life. Was I a coward or was it because of lack of faith in myself that I lost her? I don't know. Before leaving I wrote to her that she is far better than me but also asked if she will marry me. Once again I wished for 'NO' as a reply. But I didn't get a reply.* A new journey thus began . . . a journey towards unknown, both in physical and metaphysical world.

I decided to forget that there is anything called past or future. In the time between leaving IIT and joining a job, I decided to take complete rest. It meant that I would neither spend my time studying nor thinking about future. I wanted to just live in the present. I had the best time during the training period for the job as there was nothing to fear and no one to care about. This was the time which was only about me with myself which I used to rejuvenate and cure myself. *I didn't bother myself with studies and did every adventurous thing that I could think of. There I made a lot of friends. The adventurous things and carefree mind helped both my sides to become friends. Now I am one. The extrovert part always thought of the introvert one as a coward and the introvert one being shy and timid thought that everyone will laugh at extrovert one. But after so much of self assessment, there is no more ambiguity.* I feel younger and more expressive. I am now juggling between my dreams, family and my job. It really needs a lot of courage to leave a secure job [which ensures mental peace for my parents] and go on a wild goose chase after my entrepreneurial dream. I am following the golden rule called patience. *I am spending my days in understanding business models, dreaming about my dreams and being with my family, understanding my role in new job and career prospects, contributions that I can make to this company and social initiatives that can be started. Apart from all these, needless to say but, I am still waiting for 'her' to come back in my life.* She has left for Italy to do her Ph.D. Although there are too many complications in our relationship but hope has not died yet.

Kapil

Inspite of the brevity of interactions, Kapil's life stood out for a different emphasis it brought with itself in the realm of identity dynamics amongst youth. The major concern in his life had been love. *In a certain sense, his was a voice that de-emphasised the apprenticeship life of youth stressing upon perseverance for concrete pursuits and approved goals. Instead, he searched for life's pleasure in loving relationships.* When I introduced myself as a researcher also teaching in a college (which happens to be a girl's college), he got super excited and squealed that he would really like to take a tour of the college and have a look at the girls. A 25-year-old MCA (Masters in Computer Application) working in a BPO (business process outsourcing) company, Kapil spoke in an easy-going manner mixing Hindi and English together. Engaged to be married to his girlfriend shortly, he described academics and work part of his life as 'All cool!' His mischievous opening remarks to the request of sharing something about his life were 'Academics have always been very very not happening. The only happening thing in my life has been my love life'. He added:

> I don't know... I have been performing very consistently. I don't know how. *In school also, whole time, studies wise, it was all cool. I never bothered much about what will happen after 12th. I didn't have this craze for IIT and all.* I used to go to coaching classes just to keep my routine going, being conscious that at least I am going. But I used to wait when it will finish. I used to leave difficult questions during the preparations for engineering. Beyond me!! *My parents also never pressurised me. I think that's the reason why I didn't take pressure for my studies. About career and all, I know that I have to keep working hard and I am naturally sincere about my work. I put in time and effort. But it's not a priority.* I work for my satisfaction. I work as much as I like. I haven't taken much tension for it. College also I performed average. After graduation, I failed three times in job interviews. Felt really bad but my father would just cool me down by saying that it doesn't matter! If nothing happens then you can always join me in my business. He runs a lady suits' shop. That took off whatever little pressure I had. I wanted to do postgraduation. Couldn't clear it in the last year of my graduation. Gave it again a year later very coolly. Got through very coolly. In the end everything happened very coolly. *Actually, my situations have always been 'nothing to lose' types.* I took a chance with MBA also. In one of the mock interviews during coaching, an IIM guy asked me few questions. I tried replying but whatever I would say, he would laugh, an insulting laugh. It was a very bad interview. I was about to cry. But

P. Bansal, *Youth in Contemporary India: Images of Identity and Social Change*,
DOI 10.1007/978-81-322-0715-3_7, © Springer India 2013

I count it as an important day in my life. I realised that you have to be artificial in MBA. You have to show more than you are. The cut throat competition and all. I wouldn't be happy with such a job. In technical job, you can be yourself. Then I figured out that this is my line. In software and all, you can laze around. You can do work according to your time. I didn't want to do a job that requires a lot of running around or pressure. I don't have much of a preference for any particular kind of work. In MCA, we were supposed to do a project. I couldn't decide what topic should I work on. I asked my seniors to suggest so they asked me what am I interested in? I said ... nothing in particular! I am like this. I can't take a decision. Bad at making choices. Keep thinking of the other choice that I couldn't have.

In school, I used to be very shy till about class 8th. I used to feel very shy, conscious talking to girls. When I would see other guys talking to girls, I would be like – Wow! How smart! They can talk to girls. Girls would also talk to them. *Then I also got into the company of boys who were in touch with girls, so I also got in touch with them and slowly became free with them. Now, I am more comfortable with females.* In school, I had this crush on a girl in class 11th. She was going around with someone else. Somehow, I hooked up with her. She left her boyfriend. Then we went around for about a month. *I was very excited. She was my first. I was like Oh! My God!! Something great! I have a girlfriend... But... I don't know what... I was not able to impress her or she didn't like me ... she went back to her old boyfriend.* This happened 2–3 days before my exams were to begin but still I sailed through. There was another girl who used to like me all along 11th and 12th class. I became friends with her. I have this problem that any female friend that I get along well with, I tend to develop special feelings towards her. Initially it's like a cool friendship, sharing, talking and then suddenly I began to have feelings. So I fell for her. After we passed out of school, she didn't get admission in a course of her choice here. So she went to US. She came back again ... not because of me but some other reason but then finally decided to go back to US. Then we broke up in communication. *Then in college, I met a girl with whom I only got very spontaneous with, I used to open out to her. You know, there is something about some people which makes you open out to them.* She didn't have any very good friend which I became. I almost forced myself as a good friend on her which was a very different feeling for her. So as it happened, I don't know whether I really felt for her or not but I just kissed her once. We went along even though I was not very sure of my feelings. It kept going up and down. Sometimes, I felt that I have gone really far with her so I shouldn't go back now. But then I also thought that it wouldn't be honest if I don't love her. I was very very confused. So it got really bad. Really really bad! Once she slapped me in the lab. I slapped her back outside the college. She was also a very intense type of person, very dramatic. So things became bad in college. Our group in college got divided. People were supporting her and not me, so I used to be really lonely in class. There was another girl in the college whom I liked because I was good friends with her also. So I told her about my feelings for her and this was in between I was going around with the other girl. So obviously, she was like he doesn't know what he wants. This was true also. In college because of my girlfriend, I had become very conscious. It was a difficult phase. But after college, when I joined work, I was free of all my worries. *Somehow, I don't know whether I keep looking or what. I fall for people very easily. I met another girl in office. She is the one I am marrying now.* This time I waited for a lot of time. The first time I had a thought that I liked her, I didn't speak of it for the next 2–3 months. I just kept making her feeling special a bit. *That happens with me. When I like someone, I spontaneously express it ... it just comes out.* She also felt it. So she asked me whether I had a crush on someone. I said yes and honestly it's you. She also made me wait for another 2 months and then we finally got together.... *I don't know whether it is a clash of sun signs or what... I am usually calm and composed, a bit more open with females which she doesn't like. She is very very like you should be exclusive to me. At times, I feel free with her, at times bound. But then I also think that maybe I need that bondage otherwise my mind can flow anywhere.* At times, I feel secured within myself that I need that boundary, never mind if it can't be created internally and she is doing it for me. So that fits us well. Rest! We have our fights. I am not able to understand her much because of the kind of person she is. She is a Scorpion... Scorpion girls are powerful. She also gets sick of my analysis. I analyse a lot. I read a lot in magazines, etc., about relationships, parenting and all. So she gets bored of all of it. Recently, we had a big fight. She said you take me for granted. I have a tendency to grow cold. *Because life has been so faithful to me, I tend to take things for granted. So I am scared that what if I grow so cold ... and she is a permanent kind of person ... she always remains the same. So, I am always very scared of what if she also becomes cold and then she wouldn't change for the rest of her life.* Such thinking disturbs me.

I get scared about things I take for granted. *I take my parents for granted.* So I have weird thoughts at times. *What if my father is not there? I have never seen adversity in life.* I can have mental solutions for them but I don't know how will I react in real life. I am very dependent on him. I need his support in all my decisions. Till my MCA, I took pocket money from my father. I never withdrew money from my salary account. *I am a very much a kid still. I have had a very pampered, protective upbringing. Now I am trying to be more responsible.* I try to help in getting things done, running jobs.

My father is like my idol, one whom I look up to and learn from. He is like an umbrella on me so that there is no hard sunshine on me. He sets me free but also keeps an eye on me from behind. If he sees me going wrong, he will say things indirectly, probably share his own experience. *I used to keep porn magazines in my bag, in school. I know that he must have seen it. He would talk about issues indirectly, and then I began to talk directly about it. My mother is someone who gives me food, takes care of my needs.* While rushing for my office, she would push food in my mouth. Once, in a while, when I am very upset, I would go and lie on her lap. I have an early memory of coming back from school and not finding my mother home. This was when she used to work in an office, close to home. She used to be home by the time, we would return, but that day she got late. I cried all the way to her office. After that she didn't go to office. My parents must have discussed ... that's what they have always done. Done things for our good without our knowing, so that we have best of everything.

What I really look forward to in my life is never in terms of career, money, but in terms of family. In terms of how I want to love my wife a lot. Since the college phase, I have this in my mind. I hated myself so much in college. I can't cause harm to anyone. But because I couldn't decide, my confusion, I hurt a girl badly. Somehow that regret is still there. It doesn't go. Perhaps, because of that ... sometimes I think it's because of that... I have a very deep urge that I get along very well with one person all my life and I really love her a lot. *My life ambition is to keep my wife happy, keep my parents happy. That's how my life is. Probably because I have been loved and cared so much that I look at brighter side of life.* Now I feel more responsible about my parents and all. I want to love them all. Also because there is no tension of the future. Everything has been smooth, so will it be in future.

His narrations help to develop few understandings about the growth processes during youth. An *affectionate, approving family environment* which had not been expectant of academic achievement or professional success of high standards and protected him from a damning sense of failure whenever he encountered them helped him maintain narcissistic reserves of self-esteem. He felt himself 'much a kid still' dependent on and *enmeshed with the parental matrix for satisfaction of his emotional as well as material needs*. He had been protected from experiencing the lack, precariousness and contingency of life by the security and authority offered to him by his parents, especially his father. While being much loved and cared for led him to feel whole, safe, powerful and active, he also *experienced an acute sense of anticipatory anxiety about the possibility of losing this life-sustaining framework.* Given his almost-merged existence and lack of independent responsibility, separation from or absence of the stable, affirming ground on which he stood could activate devitalising feelings of powerlessness, emptiness and annihilation in him. An ego process was glimpsed which was aiding him to recognise his age-inappropriate dependence, contain such threatening affects and become more agentic and responsible for his own life and those around him.

His academic and work life had been described as 'cool', an expression that is contrasted with the 'happening' love life. A consistent and sincere worker, his performance had been average. In comparison to other participants, he had studied in ordinary institutions of higher education where the standards of competition and performance were lower. He did not pine for admission in the elite courses like engineering and management and had a modest job. *Overall impression he conveyed was of a smooth cruise along the transitions from school to work which did not engage much of his efforts and enthusiasm. Relatively free from parental and self-imposed careerist demands, his youthful excitement and exuberance were channelised towards heterosexual love.* It was in serial relationships with girls that he sought intense feeling, passion and pleasure. Close awareness of one's position within the web of nurturing interrelationships, as in the case of Kapil, often creates a potential for love.

A shy and self-conscious young boy, he used to envy his peers who could approach and evoke response from girls. Getting into their company, he slowly changed into a confident adolescent who felt free with girls. Adolescence is accompanied by genital maturation and heightened sexual excitement amongst both boys and girls. In this phase, sex play takes on various forms in which reading porn magazines and masturbation are common. The competitive spirit of adolescent boys in their conquest of girls and their noisy and predatory approaches to gain girls' attention and evoke their response was glimpsed in *Kapil's exhilaration in winning over a girl whom he fancied.* She left her boyfriend to be with him which was a shot in the arm for him. Besides, the narcissistic boost of finally getting a girlfriend greatly excited him. *However, it was a short-lived affair which left him with a niggling feeling of 'I was not able to impress her or she didn't like me'—a blow which didn't disturb him that much that he would mess up his impending exams.* Sailing through the examination, soon enough, he became friends with another girl who fancied him for 2 years. His feelings went from *'cool friendship'* to *'special feelings'*. Because of brevity of our interactions, deeper explorations of nature and depth of his feelings during these two states could not be made. From stray references, one can conjecture that while the previous state was more casual, consisting more of conversations and getting to know each other, the latter stage was more about wanting to be with the person, deeper liking and needs of forging deeper intimacy, both physical and emotional. After school, the girl went to the USA because of which they broke up in communication. Alone again, he met another girl in college whom he used to open out to and urged her to become friendly with him. *He had a moment of physical intimacy with her, but the relationship did not have the emotional clarity that is needed to give the sexual act its meaning.* As an intense person, probably the girl saw it as a movement towards deepening of relationship, while his own stance was more explorative.

This mismatch of commitment levels made the relationship go sour, and it ended on a bad note. His sense of shame over inability to decide about his feelings and guilt over hurting a girl remained with him. It probably nudged him in the direction of becoming more mature in his feelings and actions towards his love objects as is reflected in his statement 'I have a very deep urge that I get along very well with one person all my life and I really love her a lot'. In the workplace, he met another girl who was now his fiancé. This time, *rather than rushing into expressing his feelings, he chose to give it time.* He confessed to not understanding her much and felt that she was a powerful, controlling lover. Probably insecure because of his tendency to develop feelings for any girl he gets along well with, she demanded exclusive commitment from him. *He felt a mix of feelings of being contained and restricted by her.* In terms of heterosexual coupling, he felt a sense of completion with her. *Probably as an active figure, she joined the group of nurturant and guiding caretakers in his laid-back life.*

Though not much data about his feeling world with respect to his affairs with girls is available, certain tentative understandings can still be generated. As he shared about his love life, one felt an urge and an attempt on his part to make sense of this most important aspect of his life. What emerged rather clearly was that *he had a proactive approach in seeking the opposite sex and in getting them to be with him.* He needed, liked and felt comfortable in the company of girls whom he could open out to. Gaining their acceptance and trust affirmed his narcissistic worth as an attractive male. He must have also experienced narcissistic injuries in this regard, but he seemed to take them in his stride. In order to feel whole, he needed to possess with self-evident certainty the love and warmth of those he loved which included his family and his fiancé. *Few questions regarding the development of heterosexuality in him lingered in my mind—Did his sentiments towards the girls involve a fusion of tenderness and sexual love? Was his heterosexual strivings more of an expression of seeking self-gratifications and enhancement or was he also able to extend nurturing care and protective love to the partner? What did the feeling that 'his mind can flow anywhere' mean? Did it imply labile emotions which could find their anchor with many but were not ready or ripe for finding the final home in that exclusive belongingness to each other? Was he, in experiencing his fiancé as controlling and powerful, feeling the threat of a new dependency, emotional surrender and submissiveness that such attachment arouses? Was his 'kiddishness' on its way to develop into mature masculinity in which sexuality is tied with an attitude of active concern and preservation of love object?*

Prashant

A young man of 25 years, Prashant was a mechanical engineer by training. Around the time when I met him, he had left his job in an automobile company and had joined a start-up in the field of clean technology. I contacted him for research purpose on the recommendation of a friend when he was in Delhi. When I explained to him the research objective of understanding the directions in which young people are taking their lives, their motivations, challenges and conflicts and scope of choice and freedom in taking life decisions, he exclaimed that this is what most young people are always thinking and talking about. He expressed his willingness to help, and we met up once. Since he was on a work trip to Delhi, we had a short but informative and engaging conversation. In that interaction, I found Prashant genteel in his manners, reflective and enthusiastic.

Speaking about himself, Prashant quipped—'*Well! I am basically a regular guy with some irregular ideas and interests*'. He elaborated:

> Like, I went on to do my M.Tech which not many people do [smiles]. Then I left my job and am getting into a start-up of my friends. *While in college, I did different things—entering business plan contests, social work, reading up on latest trends in designing which is my area of interest. I generally liked to be informed about what's happening in technology, at business front. I followed the 'Lead India' contest very closely.* I think it is a very healthy sign of things to come that educated, city people are using their skills and energy to work with the masses.

Excited by his multifarious interests in the field of technology as well as humanitarian concerns, I asked him about his *family and educational environment*:

> My father was in Defence Services. So I have pretty much travelled all over India with him. Though cantonment life is secluded but there is also a substantial amount of interaction that takes place with the outside world. *It's a part of army life . . . charity, welfare activities etc. So I have seen my mother taking a very active part in organising charity like food distribution, giving out clothes and also other things like awareness-building campaigns, teaching children etc. My father has been a big influence on me. He always stressed on all round development of personality.* He himself is also a sportsperson and is very interested in gardening. We always used to get a lot of compliments from our neighbours, friends and relatives on our well-manicured garden [speaks with pride]. Since I was more introverted and liked studying and all, he used to keep asking me to go out with friends and enjoy.

P. Bansal, *Youth in Contemporary India: Images of Identity and Social Change*,
DOI 10.1007/978-81-322-0715-3_8, © Springer India 2013

My brother works with UN. He went abroad and studied Social Policy and Development. Now he goes travelling around the world monitoring development programs etc. He has a cool job! He loves it.... I love it too [smiles broadly]. Wouldn't mind trading places!! ... Yeah! So I took up engineering. While in college, I realised that I like designing. So I used to do designing assignments for my batchmates. College was good fun. *My friends were very versatile.* Two of them had always wanted to start a company. So they used to go for different competitions like business plan or the new tech ideas and products contests. I also used to work with them on drawing up ideas, technological challenges and business models. It was a huge learning experience. Besides, there is so much to do in engineering college and so much of time! *I used to also volunteer for a lot of things like SPIC MACAY events, social campaigns etc.*

I enquired further:

- *What kind of social campaigns?*
  Like I have been to Jantar Mantar couple of times. Once I went with a friend to participate in *people's parliament on the issue of relief and rehabilitation of displaced people* because of development projects. Another time, I went in *solidarity for Indo–Naga Peace Process.* I had a friend who was from Nagaland and he used to describe the sad state of affairs there. *Around the time when Godhra happened, few of us were quite active and we screened documentaries, participated in peace marches, invited speakers.* The incident was outrageous.
- *How did you decide to join this start-up? You had a decent job.*
  Hmmm ... Everyone is asking me the same question. [Silence] *Actually, after my B.Tech, I joined M.Tech because I was interested in research. I had few areas of interest and I wanted to gain in-depth knowledge and practical problem solving skills.* Those two friends that I was talking about dropped out of placements and decided to start their own company. They wanted to do something in clean technology. *Undoubtedly, the future belongs to clean technology and it will be a major driver of sustainable economic growth in times to come.* After much struggle, they managed to get a seed funding and they launched their start-up. They are trying to build a technology which will help enhance fuel efficiency while limiting exhaust emissions in cars. After I completed my M.Tech, they asked me to join them because I have always been interested in this field. It is very much needed. The world economy is facing lots of challenges from energy price spikes, resource shortages, global environmental problems like climate change and security threats. So use of renewable sources of energy like solar power, wind power and biofuels, waste treatment and recycling, green buildings and green transport are all leading trends in clean technology. Also use of CNG is one step closer to more environmentally clean fuel alternative to petrol or diesel. It is also cheaper and much safer than other fuels in case of a spill. However, it is still a fossil fuel. So we need biofuels like biodiesel, bioalcohol etc. I wasn't sure whether I wanted to work in a start-up. *After M.Tech, I joined an automobile company. I didn't quite like the work because there wasn't much to learn there. There were no challenges—technologically, which is what I am primary interested in. Not much scope of to think of innovative applications of knowledge, to design solutions for a specific practical problem.* This time my friends asked me to join a R&D job so I jumped at it. I am feeling quite enthusiastic about the work. Looking forward to exercise my grey cells now and cracking some problems [smiles happily].
- *How did your family respond to this decision of yours because it does imply a risk?*
  That's right! My mom was not happy. My dad was ok. I told him I want to try out and learn. So he doesn't think that it's that much of a risk. I also don't think so. *I am still young and I want to try out few things. I want to grow and this is a perfect opportunity for me. It's a growing industry worldwide. All three of us in the company are young, optimistic and confident and willing to work hard.* My brother was very supportive. He told me to go for it!

- *Do you think India is on its way to become technological innovation hotspot? What role do start-ups play in that, and is the supporting infrastructure in place?*
  Well! There is definitely a lot of talk around innovation and invention. Besides fundamental research, there are many ideas that are being incubated in R&D labs and at the shop floors of companies. The world's major growth industries—biotechnology, microelectronics, telecommunications etc.—are knowledge industry, that is, they are research based. They require continuous improvement and upgradation. *So it actually pays to be innovative.* India is definitely supporting innovation. The CSIR-led New Millennium Indian Technology Leadership Initiative has created a huge public–private partnership with private sector companies and laboratories and academic institutions. The aim is to create things that work and to create wealth through scientific research. *Start-ups are also playing a big role in this regard. Technopreneurs have entrepreneurial minds and technology in their hearts. They are also trying to work on different tech ideas.* I think there is growing awareness about the importance of filing patents, that intellectual property equals competitive and commercial advantage. In the knowledge market, the new weapons are information and usable knowledge.
  But scientific innovation takes time. A start-up requires someone who stands by the idea. You require patience and tenacity to go the distance. Then funding is a major challenge. Investments increase sharply as one moves from idea incubation to prototyping to manufacturing. There are many technology incubators that are supporting tech start-ups. But a lot more venture capitalists are required. Finding customers is another big challenge. *But the upside is that there is a lot of buzz about entrepreneurship in general in India.* A lot of first generation people are getting into it. *You get to meet people who are trying to do something different, exchange ideas, and it does feel good to be part of something big. There isn't much money to begin with in a start-up but the challenge, the thrill, the enjoyment of having something of your own and to shape it according to your own beliefs is awesome!* My idol is Narayana Murthy, and his philosophy of Compassionate Capitalism completely inspires me....
- *That's interesting! Can you elaborate on Compassionate Capitalism?*
  It is what Narayana Murthy believes in. *I think it is a much better way of combining profit making with larger good than socialism. I remember having a lot of debates with my father who is a big time supporter of socialist values.* Being a part of government establishment all his life, he strongly believes in governmental regulation and all. The profit-driven private sector doesn't quite agree with his public service orientation. *I never quite agreed with him, but when I read about what Narayana Murthy had to say on this, I was thrilled. It gave me a direction.* There is a very interesting story about how he came to this. Do you know it?
- *No!*
  [Excitedly] Ok! It goes like this—He was hitchhiking from Paris back to Mysore. He was dropped off at the railway station of a town called Nis, a border town in former Yugoslavia. It had got late, so he had to sleep on the railway station. When the train came, he got into it. The only passengers in the compartment were a young girl and a boy. He began a conversation with the girl who talked about the difficulties of the living in an Iron Curtain country—its regimentation, lack of freedom etc. Suddenly, a bunch of policemen came and got hold of both of them—Narayana Murthy and the girl. Later, he understood that they were called by the boy who thought that they were criticising the communist rule of the country. He was dragged on the platform into a small cubicle. He was kept in it in inhuman conditions for almost 2–3 days. His backpack and other belongings were confiscated. He had thought that he would die in that cell. After a couple of days, he was dragged out of the cell and put on the goods' train and told that he would be released after 20 hours when the train would reach Istanbul. The last words of the guard were 'You are from a friendly country called India. That's why we are letting you go!' In that lonely, starving, cold journey, Murthy thought of what does communism mean? If this is what it means, then he had lost all faith in it. It's a chilling story!! [Silence] I have also read many interviews of him. He says from his

experience that in the West even the socialists understand that wealth has to be first created before it can be distributed. And the job of the government is to create an environment where it's possible for people to create wealth. *He says that responsible capitalism is one that creates wealth and allows it to percolate down to the lesser fortunate. In fact, he was the one who in line with the socialist vision had 100% stock option coverage amongst all Infoscions. I also believe that people need opportunities, incentives and competition to better themselves. That's what capitalism achieves. But, yes! This capitalism should have the spirit of fairness, transparency and honesty. There should be private participation in different sectors of society, and private sector should contribute towards the betterment of society because no company can prosper on a sustainable basis if it doesn't make a difference to the context in which it exists.* There is an Infosys Foundation which has made various donations towards charitable causes and community development projects.

Also, Infosys, I have learnt, is an ethical company. Murthy is a champion of work/life balance. Its top bosses have a clean record, they lead by example, are honest, and it favours meritocracy.

- *Hmm ... The Indian IT sector is often under attack from its detractors who say that it doesn't do anything for an average village Indian. Do you think IT can help provide a better life for the rural India? Also, is IT really the hotbed of innovation, or are we only creating software coolies?*

  [Thinks for a while] As far as your second question is concerned, I do agree that we are largely doing back end work which is not technologically challenging. Yes! Indian IT majors are not creating IT products like Google, Microsoft etc. but they have consistently improved IT processes in many global sectors. They have delivered well on their core proposition and that is the reason why their customers have always kept coming back to them and their market position has strengthened.

  For your first question, the example that comes to me is that of e-choupal, a venture of ITC. What it did is quite revolutionary. It has set up an alternative distribution system for agricultural commodities. Through Internet, the farmers can get information on best practices in farming, weather trends, market price, and it can also serve as alternative trading platform. So, the middlemen have been rendered obsolete. The farmers are in direct touch with the buyers and their incomes have gone up.
- *You are rather well informed.*

  All thanks to my father [speaks smilingly]. It is from him that I picked up the habit of reading newspapers and following current events...

On this note, I thanked him for sharing his views and life and took leave. On my journey back home, I thought over all what Prashant had spoken and could not help but feel impressed by how *he was integrating the usually conflicting objectives of private profit and common good.* The guiding philosophy of Compassionate Capitalism had provided him an ethical framework wherein wealth creation had less reason to be divorced from welfare measures. *In Narayana Murthy, entrepreneur and Chairman of the Board and Chief Mentor of one of India's foremost and most respected IT company, Infosys Technologies, he found a role model representing a meaningful combination of the oldest and the newest ideals.* Murthy is often spoken of as someone who has a 'Capitalist Mind and Socialist Heart'. Through idealisation of him, Prashant could align his socially responsible orientation imbibed from his mother's involvement in various social work activities and father's socialist values with capitalist principles of free competition, profit making and private enterprise that characterise the economic ethos of the day. Having found a mentor whose exemplary creativity, entrepreneurial spirit, ethicality and sincere asceticism made him not only a global success story in the world of business but also a highly respected Indian internationally, Prashant could look beyond the narrower identification offered by the father in this regard. *This attractive wholesome direction allowed him to be more conflict free in utilising the possibilities and opportunities on offer during one's own times and renewing the means and meanings of social responsibility and personal success. It could simultaneously meet the ideological requirement of his maturational stage, the ego's style of synthesis and the demands of the culture in which socialism in its pure form has become a bygone option.* Prashant's and his friends' ingenious endeavours in the field of clean tech—an emerging field that while providing solutions to the global challenge of ecological damage and depletion also offers competitive returns for producers and customers—are an example of how each age offers exciting options of human teamwork in which the newest of techniques can be used in the service of ever-relevant humane aims.

Another important psychological facet of Prashant's identity was *his closeness to his father* who stressed on all-round personality development and general education. Emphasis on professionalism and specialisation has made the idea of general education outdated in current times and has deprived work and knowledge of their earlier connotations of being conducive to the production of rounded personality. His father was an army personnel, and defence training is known to cultivate different personality aspects of its recruits. It prides itself on developing 'Gentleman Cadets'. He was also a sportsperson with an abiding interest in gardening, current affairs and had a public service orientation. Given the range of roles, interests and talents, one can speculate that his identity repertoire would have diverse elements: discipline, respect for hierarchy, courage, singularity of purpose, war patriotism, risk taking, energetic, mental and physical alertness, seeker of information, concern for humanity, and love for nature, to name a few. Loving identification with such a father contributed to his wholesome development and nurtured various aspects of his personality adding up to a uniquely integrative pattern of self.

Samrat

Samrat, 27 years old, was a technological entrepreneur in the field of wireless and communications technology. He started his own technology company when he was 23 years old. As a fresh graduate in electrical engineering, he preferred to set up his own company than to choose the other mainstream options of taking up a job, or an MBA degree or pursuing higher education. I was led to him through my search for forums that support young entrepreneurs. In my first interaction with him over the phone when I told him that I would be interested in studying what factors could have encouraged him to take this risk, he promptly responded that he did not think that it was a risky decision to have a start-up. He wanted to do it, and if it had not materialised, he would have gone on to take up a job. His self-assurance set the tone for our interactions, and in the subsequent meetings, I explored his motivations, attitudes, approach towards work life along with his growth process and life contexts.

The initial few meetings took place in the Technology Business Incubator of an engineering institute where the company was housed since its inception in 2003. The atmosphere of the incubator used to be abuzz with activity of many young men and a couple of women bustling around. It represented a heady mixture of work and fun. Thereafter, they were conducted in his new office premises. *Samrat emerged as an eager participant of the research interested in 'an experience'*. He was generous with his time and provided an easy access to himself. *He brought a certain quality of freedom of spirit and inner aliveness to the interactions.* A chuckle would often animate his features and induce me to smile and savour his playfulness. Below is a selection of excerpts from the interviews providing an understanding of Samrat's motivations and attitudes responsible for his foray into entrepreneurship.

I

- *Why did you choose to start a company after you completed your studies in engineering?* Till the middle of my fourth year, I never thought I will do a start-up. If someone would have asked me, what you would do after B. Tech, I would have not said that I will do a

P. Bansal, *Youth in Contemporary India: Images of Identity and Social Change*,
DOI 10.1007/978-81-322-0715-3_9, © Springer India 2013

start up. I was kind of thinking of pursuing higher education in US—M.S. and all. It would have been an extension of my life in college—comfortable … and once in a while solving some problems. But, I wasn't so keen on going abroad and being there for long period of time. I had been to Switzerland on an internship while in college. It is fine to go there, see around. It is a neater, cleaner, greener place, that's all. But one doesn't have friends, people to talk to over there. I wasn't interested in taking up a job in the companies that were coming for campus placements. I didn't want to become a software engineer and do low end, boring work. So I was not applying for jobs. And I wasn't interested in doing MBA. *In November, I had started to think of making some kind of electronic product.* Since there was no company that was offering me this kind of work, I wanted to become a project associate in college itself and do it myself. Then I worked very hard on my research project and for the first time I got an A grade [smiles]. It was a bit unexpected. *In engineering, I had never tried to work towards marks.* The only reason I worked hard this time was so that I could ask my professor to take me on as a project associate. When I spoke with him, he told me that in the 6 months time that I was aiming at, I would probably not be able to achieve much. *The product that I was trying to make required a lot of effort and a much bigger team. So he told me about the Technology Business Incubator facility in the institute. By that time one student-led company had already started. I went to talk to the people behind that company and immediately liked the challenge. After that there was no looking back.* I mailed to my class that I am starting a company and whosoever is interested can join. Many people showed interest but eventually, only three of us got together and launched it.

- *So, you came upon this idea through a method of elimination?*

  Yeah. Nothing else interested me. [After a pause] I had seen the way I was in college. *I did reasonably well in the 1st semester. I was among the first ten students. After that, I just didn't find academics interesting and exciting enough, so I just let that part be. By the time I graduated, I was in the bottom half of my class.* It took me some time to reach there [chuckles]. I used to like programming. So, courses and assignments that required me to do programming, I would do them well. Otherwise, I would be roaming around, not attending many classes. I got more involved in the extracurricular activities…. So, by the fourth year, I had begun to feel that I had not been… I had been enjoying life, so to speak, doing things, but I would want to do something that would be lot more productive. *I really, really knew that if I had taken up a job, I would continue in the same way … unmotivated. I will at the most do the assigned task but would not be focused on anything.* I would have managed reasonably well but would not have put in as much effort as I am putting today.
- *Hmm … you were drifting?*

  In college, if someone wanted to go somewhere, I would go with him. If somebody wanted help with something, I'll do that. I was pretty comfortable watching a movie a day [laughs]. *My grades didn't matter to me. But, I also didn't come to a stage where I would fail a subject.* Had I failed, it would have been a shock. I would have probably done something then. Otherwise I just didn't care much. I knew I would complete my degree.
- *How were you sure of that?*

  I had many friends who helped me out with studies. They were better than me academically. They would wake me up for exams, arranged notes for me. I would always get someone to teach me for a couple of hours before the exam. I managed like this.
- *Why was there a loss of interest in academics, considering that you always did well at school and getting into engineering itself is a big academic achievement?*

  In school also, I was not a diligent student. I was never first in class. My teachers would typically say that I could perform better. For class 12th boards, I began studying 2–3 days before exams. I didn't have regular study habits. But, college was different because here classes were held till the last moment before the exams. So one would not have time just before exams to prepare. One would have to study regularly, attend classes.

This I was not doing. *It would be too much of a pain for me, boring to go and sit in the lecture theatre. I would rather take up a book and read it up on my own, at my own pace. I could always study on my own.* So whenever I would bunk classes, I would find someone to chat with over coffee or play something. Nothing really productive but more interesting. *Besides, I was in hostel for the first time. There were more distractions.* At home, there is only so much that you can do. You are more regulated. After a point, you will pick up books. In college, I would sleep at 4 in night, get up at 12 noon. There are friends. I had a huge friend circle consisting of seniors, juniors and batchmates. I also got very involved in the extracurricular activities. I would be an active part of dramatics, music, painting competitions. In 3rd year, I was organising security for the annual festival. Over 200 students were working under me. *All of this was more exciting for me.*

- *What do you mean by 'productive'? What would have been productive for you? Did you search for something productive?*
  Well, productive meaning something that would be challenging, which would make me work hard. In college, I wasn't searching for anything. I wasn't planning anything. *I never thought I needed to go anywhere. I had enough to do, friends and extracurricular.*
- *What kind of extracurricular activities were you involved in?*
  See, extracurricular activities are competitive. I was involved in the interhostel competitions. So, if there is a play competition, one would have to search for a script which would stand out because all the others would also be good. Once, we had a play in which there was a conversation with the audience. Similarly, in the instrumental music competition, we got pots to play with. That was different. The late night meetings to discuss who would be the best person for a job, what should be our strategy, what would be others' strategy, brainstorming all of this was fun. I used to put people together, give suggestions about how to go about doing things. Random things....
- *Did you participate in inter-college level activities?*
  No. I didn't want to invest that much in anything.
- *Were you not worried about future?*
  I knew something or the other would happen. I will do something or the other. I will not get the best of jobs. Grades are important for that. But I will get some job. I wasn't getting anxious about my grades because I wasn't putting in effort so I couldn't have expected any outcomes.
- *Now how do you look back at that period of your life?*
  Well! I think I could have done much better. I didn't do any work for four years in engineering. You realise that at the end, you didn't feel much of satisfaction. Probably by putting in more effort I would have been more satisfied. It was all of that which motivated me to get out of that inertia. *If I had not gone down that low, I would have remained in the middle for very long. But because I hit the bottom, I managed to come out.*
- *What was the process of setting up a company like?*
  The three of us got together and made a business plan. We spent months writing it. Then it was approved by the incubator. We set up an office there and got an initial seed funding from it, about 8 lakhs. We finished it off in nine months. We didn't have an output at that time. The market was still down. For around a year, we spent a lot of time meeting people, our potential customers, making a lot of sales pitch to get projects. That one year we were learning the basics, how to make a business plan, how do you get costumers, how do you plan a project, how do you make the product. I would go and take part in seminars and conferences on entrepreneurship, talk to people who had done start-ups. I read up a lot of technology books, biographies of people who started companies. The initial days were bad. We would go and ask people to give us a project for our company. They would tell us to come and work for them. One of them said three people do not constitute a company. Sometimes we were treated as kids, given advice. A couple of months later, one of the persons left. By the end of one year, we were down

to two people, had no money and no business. At that point, we considered shutting it down and move on. But then we decided to stick around. Finally we got a project. We were quite bad because we didn't know how exactly to execute it. We managed to pull it off. After that the company had enough to pay salaries and stay afloat.

- *It would have been very difficult?*
  It was challenging. We started the company, but that didn't mean that we knew how to start and run a company. We started a technological company and we didn't have much technical know-how because we were in the bottom half of the class [smiles mischievously]. We hadn't ever worked before and industry experience helps. There is not a single person in the industry who would tell you how to get money, customer, execute a project. *But we stuck around stubbornly. I was very determined and ready to work very hard. We were also smart enough to know that we didn't know anything and we had to learn a lot on the way.* We picked knowledge, suggestions, ideas, tried them and retained what worked. I worked very hard during the initial couple of years. My day would have 16–18 hours of work.
- *But challenges can be very intimidating.*
  [After a long silence] See, I never think of a task as too big, difficult. *For me a task is doable and achievable. For me it is like if there is a way of doing things, then I will do it. One needs an imagination to figure it out.* If I want to do something, I will keep working at it till I figure it out. Something will come out of it. We tell people during recruitment that people who fail lack in imagination. When someone tells me that something is not working, then I tell that person that it will work, if you believe that it will work then it will work. I am confident about this philosophy. *I am very optimistic, sometimes over optimistic* [smiles]. My professor tells me that. So I need people to tone me down.
- *You don't come from a business family. So it was not a natural step for you. Also, engineering education doesn't prepare students for entrepreneurship. Besides, one doesn't really see many young people having a start-up. In the face of such reality, how did you decide to take this risky step?*
  [Grins] Yeah, so everybody told me that I shouldn't do it. Seniors told me not to do it. Most of my friends told me to take up a job. My professor also later told me to think about it again. When I started approaching the idea with my parents, they shot down the idea so quickly that we could never have a discussion about it. But I wanted to do it because nothing else was as interesting as this. Also because I knew if I work here, I will apply myself here. In any other situation, I will just . . . not give my 100%. *For me, how unconventional this step was or how difficult or risky it was, were never barriers or hurdles. I knew that it would require a lot of work and a lot of learning and I was prepared for that. Beyond it nothing mattered. For me it is like painting a landscape, something that I want to paint on my own. Other people may have painted the same landscape or they may not have. That is immaterial for me. For me it is my own, something I liked doing having my own touch.*
  As far as education is concerned, I think it is more about environment than education. The college provides opportunities to know about the developments in the field. There are conferences, seminars that are held. I attended them and knew that it is doable. *There is an active incubator that makes life simpler for people like us. It gives you office space, initial money, also helps you build contacts. It is a safe zone.* You see some of your seniors have done it so that encourages you.
- *You were taking chances with yourself. There was always the risk of failure. Didn't that bother you?*
  I was taking a decision for myself. It didn't affect anyone else, neither my parents nor my friends. *So it was just about me.* A lot of people told me that I would fail. Whether I would fail or succeed, or the chances of success or failure are not what I take into consideration while doing something. *The outcome is typically not important for me.* Like, once, I took part in a race in college even though I am not an athlete and I was

completely out of form. *I knew I would not win but I felt that I should run the race because no one from our hostel was agreeing to participate. What was important was that I ran the race.* Similarly, in this case, my interest in the work, my belief that I would work very hard, kept me on it stubbornly. [Forcefully] I don't get a self doubt that I would not be able to do it. *Even now, there are many risks we are taking.* We are getting into chip designing for new age mobile phones. It is a huge technological challenge that we are taking. This kind of work requires 10–15 years of experience in industry. It requires money to the tune of 2–3 million dollars. We don't have either. It is not the kind of work that is done in India before. I have got a friend to help us out with it. He left his job because he felt that he was stagnating there. He trusts me. I told him you just focus on technicals, rest I will take care of. We have contacted people in US who have the technical know-how of this kind. We can't afford them for a year but we will get them for 3 months. Rest of our team will learn from them. We recently got a funding for a million dollar. We will try to have patents. People ask me, how will you recover the money? *I don't think that I will not be able to work around it. I feel like a climber who is climbing a mountain. The guy enjoys the process, does his best but is not sure whether he would reach the top. But the climber is not panicking. I am also not panicking. If I panic, if I doubt myself then I would not be able to manage it.* Anyone trying to do something more than what they are capable of, if begin to doubt themselves would never start. It is important to begin, to work on it. You will achieve something. The worst thing will be that I will lose money. But I will still survive. [After a pause] The first year when we ran out of money, I borrowed it from home. I had set up a deadline for myself. After that we would have taken up jobs. I knew I could take up a job and repay money back. I could come back to it later. I was not panicking. I knew that it wouldn't be a sure shot success. It has never been a do or die situation for me.

- *How is the company doing now?*
  Quite fine, I would say. It is making money, making profit. We have now shifted out of the incubator and set up our office here. It is a kind of psychological break from incubator which is a safe environment. If you manage to move out and stabilise yourself, it is an indication that you can stand on your feet. There are always challenges that keep coming up in this work. *I know that I can start a company and keep it running. Now, I have to see whether we can increase its scale, which means diversifying and managing more people.* At the moment, we are a company of 30 people. I know I can manage teams of 10 people. I need to evaluate whether I can manage more. We are all product engineers. We don't consider ourselves as hardware or software people. Since, we develop entire product and not a part, which is our differentiating factor from other companies in the field, we need to have different skill sets and know different technologies. Also in our field, technology gets outdated fast. So, if you want to compete and stand out, you need to be someone who can update new technology and be comfortable with it. *One has to continuously update oneself.* At the moment we are working as a design house for manufacturers. We design the entire circuit and software of a product as per the requirements of the manufacturer, get it fabricated and then test the fabricated product. *We would gradually move towards developing our own product, developing technology like designing a chip.* All of this requires finance and also we need to know how to manage big teams. We have also learnt from our experience that we should try and build technology that the customer needs rather than accepting that this is the technology available and we should build the solution based on it.
- *What is your aspiration for the company?*
  People tell me that it is my company and I should try to make it grow big. [Pauses] What I want it to become is like the largest global dominating company in our field, like Microsoft. Make it that large. Have a kind of work environment that Google has. It is a fun place, lots of facilities for its employees. They have a vibrant, dynamic work culture. It promotes new ideas.

- *What are your personal goals which are being fulfilled by this enterprise?*
  My personal goals are mostly about learning a lot, doing the kind of work that I want to do. So for 3 years, I was doing marketing, business development. I have got customers, given presentations, talked to a lot of people. For 3 years, this work gave me a sense of accomplishment that I can present, speak spontaneously. Now I am shifting back to technological work because I want to learn it. This is a difficult shift for anyone in a job but I can do it because it is my company. *After 5 years when the company is big, I might not do the usual work.* There will be enough people to work. Then I can easily take some money from the company and set up an NGO or something. That will be very different from the goals of the company. Just because it is my company, I can do it. If I want to visit New Zealand, I can just find a customer there and go [grins]. [Pauses and speaks reflectively] *Basically, what I want to do is to be able to help a lot of people do what they want to do, persuading people to find out what they want to do and then help them do it. The company is a small step in building credibility to start work in that direction....*
- *What is this direction that you are thinking of?*
  It's still an idea. *But I would really like to promote entrepreneurship in India. Help people begin their start-ups, pursue their dreams.* [Energetically] I feel that every company wants to become a Goliath in its field. But the world doesn't belong to one Goliath. *It belongs to all the Davids who will bring down the Goliath.* One Microsoft cannot match the innovations that can be brought about by thousands of companies changing the world for the better. So I want to help people bootstrap their own start-ups and social ventures—to empower that army of Davids who will make a bigger impact and change the world for the better.
- *That's interesting! How did you come upon this idea?*
  [Grins] I ... thought and thought and thought and couldn't think of anything bigger to aim for. *I am seeing how much can I stretch. There is fascination of challenge. I need to do new things ... challenging ones.* Something which has lot of creativity and which keeps the fun factor high. I need to enjoy what I do. And this is what I enjoy ... helping people do what they want to do, help them dream and fulfil their dreams. Help put smiles on their face [Smiles inducing me to smile with him].
- *Where does your company figure in all of this?*
  [Thinks...] I don't know. I started this company when I couldn't think of anything better than this to do at that time. I worked hard at it and it taught me many things. But it's not the end of the world for me. *It is a company that I started and I can start so many others.* I feel good if the canvas looks good once I am done with it and I tell everyone that this is my painting and feel more good. But I am not afraid of losing the canvas. I can give up the canvas. I want to see how far I can reach. I just want to see... [his eyes shone bright with a smile playing on his lips]. *I can choose not to play the game ... and then I will never win. But I am going to play the game and I am going to put in all my effort and I may win.*
- *What about money?*
  Ummm ... money is important. You need money to live comfortably. See, when I started the company, I knew that I would have to survive. I come from a middle class family, and my parents could have only supported me to an extent. Job would have meant more money definitely. *With the kind of effort that I am putting in my company, I was earning much less but I am more satisfied.* I ... wouldn't feel happy, if I were to just win a lottery. I would be happier earning it. You know, it is the way I am living life which is important. *Working hard, having a goal, going for a trek, making a snowman—all of these things is important for me.* People tell me that I must grow the company big and all. But at the end of the day, the company is not so important. What is important is this snowman that I built with my friends on this recent trek. We got together as a team. One of us located a bucket to collect snow. Some of us were building it, putting all the snow together so that it doesn't fall apart. Got some carrots from the camp kitchen

and put its nose. Borrowed someone's hat for snowman. Then everyone came to take pictures with us and snowman. Two little girls posed with it. So that was a lot of fun. The next day, we moved onto the next camp site. So, that was just momentary. When I talk to my friends or other people, I never talk about how much money I have, how much clients I have. I talk about this snowman I built. I guess, people just remember or talk about things which they think is important for them.

- *Any regrets because of your work. Something that you feel has been cut off from your life?*
  The only thing is . . . I never used to sit in one place. I found it very difficult to sit in one place. So, I disliked sitting in the classroom. *Now, I have to sit in one place for a long time.* I have to sit in the same chair in front of a laptop which is something that I had to make myself do if I had to focus on this idea. *Otherwise, at the personal level, the way I am, I would just roam around, play around and meet people.*

The phase of college represented an *academic moratorium* in Samrat's life. One did not sense grave identity diffusion in his narration. He showed signs of effective workmanship whenever he wanted to perform. Thus, there appeared to be a temporary and sporadic, thus, also partially wilful depression of efforts. He seemed to be *playing with nothingness to reach an inner rock bottom on which he could stand firm.* He found it futile to move ahead until he got a worthwhile work goal. He was optimistic enough about the possibility of making contact with his inner resources as and when a meaningful opportunity presented itself. *As his academic moratorium began to reach an end, he evaluated and negated all the future options considered normal and valuable by the society on the grounds of not being appealing enough.* The technical education as well as the future courses of action that it was offering was sensible and modern but *not magical enough to provide that superlative shudder which alone touches on the mystery of experience—something for which Samrat hungered.* What he needed was creative work that could bring together his intellect and industry. Entrepreneurship was just that.

Samrat impressed upon me as someone who was *fiercely independent* in his thinking and actions. What emerged from the conversations was that he could remain with his self, access his needs and fantasies and then set out to create his own world in the form of the business ventures. *He yearned for a free range to display his initiative and enterprising independence.* He would side step the words I used like 'difficult' and 'taking chances' and used his own vocabulary of 'challenge' and 'taking decisions' to bring a personal connotation of *daring and determination* to his endeavours. Even while talking about his company, he saw himself as a separate being who could move out of it and begin afresh.

Samrat was entrepreneurial. *He had identity resources of conviction in his own potential, courage to envisage and pursue valued goals and competence to apply his intelligence, skill and efforts to the chosen undertaking.* There were times when one felt that he was taking a wild risk, but he seemed to be evaluating odds differently. He seemed to relish instability—not so much as a virtue but as pleasure. Thus, the heightened contingency of such a life was no longer experienced as anxiety provoking; doubt was turned into suspense. Then waiting did not become a useless passion. There were also instances when one felt in his sharing about his aspirations, *an unrealistic insistence on settling for nothing short than omnipotence.* However, he showed signs of being prudent enough to assess his inadequacies and know his limitations by listening, considering and accepting the suggestions of people who could 'tone down [his] optimism'. He also believed in working collectively to build strengths by forging solidarity with able and talented fellow mates. Success was wished for by him and worked towards but not demanded. There wasn't a foiling fear of defeat/failure. *Explorations around how he dealt with the risks of failure and probable narcissistic self-injuries would evoke either humour or forceful assertion of wilfulness.* When he would talk about the challenges of his work, he would make the condition appear humorous and make them light by smiling about them. He did not see any situation as a 'do or die', convinced that whatever the outcome, he would survive and could begin afresh. Once, he joined the stubbornness of his one-way will and imagination to the task, he applied himself vigorously and flirted with failure to test whether he would be crushed or whether he would be able to make a place of his own.

While listening to him, I almost felt the joy of witnessing a child play. His metaphors to describe his endeavours—climber and painter—gave an impression that it was important for Samrat to *feel work as play*, to enjoy what he was doing and to discover new horizons. *He abhorred routinisation, regimentation of time and repetition on a regular basis.* While apparently 'marking time' during engineering, a space was being created in which aims or ends could be worked out. He might have been playing for time, for deferral makes room for less familiar possibilities which are more attuned to one's inner proclivities and true gifts; it allows to wonder which ways of knowing, or being known, sustain our interest, our excitement in people, in activities. At that point of time, beginning a company of one's own was such a possibility. The shiftiness one sensed in him, in the form of different business ideas he entertained, was perhaps his way of keeping the future open, an enlivening torture of not knowing whether the beginning of a story will be the end. *He was comfortable in 'setting out' without knowing exactly how he was going to get there—an entrepreneurial ability to leave options open and flexible.* His 'roaming' had the quality of flirtation, a saboteur of fidelity.

True to his playful spirit, Samrat had begun to imagine scenarios afresh which would help him get over the unease of having to 'sit in one place' and give him the leeway to 'roam around, play around and meet people'—all tied by semi-serious vision of creating an 'army of entrepreneurial Davids'. This vision was based on his comprehension of the reality that many people were in need of mentoring to pursue their entrepreneurial dreams and foreseeing a better future for the world. It brought together the lesson ingrained in him by his mother to help people, his proven talent to influence people by smiles and inspirational talk, his experience of having bootstrapped his own start-up and his inner fantasy to rule the world by leading an army of 'one million entrepreneurs' across different commercial sectors. His grandiose fantasy of ruling the world was fuelled by his fascination for the aggrandised figure of King Asoka. In one of his informal conversations, he shared that had he not been born in this era, he would have been a king. He would not be a born king but would become one. He would be Asoka! He was inspired by the fact that 'he built the largest empire in Indian subcontinent and ruled over it; he was not corrupt and his citizens lived a good life; his emblem continued to be a surviving symbol even after centuries.'

II

Every person grows into one's adult role. Here it is important to sketch the nature of growth contexts—family, school and peers and the influence of these on Samrat.

Samrat came from a middle class, nuclear family originally belonging to Rajasthan. He spent the first half of his life in Durgapur where his father was working as a mechanical engineer in a public sector engineering consultancy company. Thereafter, they shifted to Delhi. He recalled his days in Durgapur with fondness. What emerged was an *activity-filled childhood with a balanced emphasis on academics and extra-curricular activities.* He was an eager participant of many productive situations that were either offered by his school context or created by his own ingenuity. He could freely exercise his dexterity and intelligence on tasks as is evident from this:

In my school in Durgapur, I used to participate in a lot of quizzes. So I used to pick up trivia from everywhere, whatever I would come across. I learnt the longest English word. Then once I wanted to find out how to predict the next prime number because I learnt that it cannot be predicted. I could make various kinds of paper planes. When I was in 6th or 7th, I made a solar cooker. I would do many things to see whether they happen because I would have read about them. *I was always like let's see how it is for an experience. I learnt to skate all by myself. I took my elder sister's cycle to a ground and learnt to cycle by trying over and over again.* In Durgapur, I would be into drawing, painting and plays. In classes 11th and 12th, I used to program well. So for long periods of time I used to write computer programs for video games. Academically, the environment was always competitive. There was a lot of emphasis on academics and you had to be good in it otherwise you don't count for much. I would be in top 5 but not topping all the time. But that was okay. *I never got tense because of the competition.* Even in Delhi, I was in the ability section in my school which had high merit students. *Competition was like a game for me. I enjoyed it. Sometimes you win, sometimes you don't. Try harder the next time.*

Samrat's parents gave him a free space 'to be'. They did not demand excellence in studies from him. *He did not feel controlled or pressurised for achievement from their side.* There were no restrictions placed on his play or participation in extra-curricular activities. His mother was more involved in his life and would give him ideas and suggestions. But his father would remark, 'Let him do whatever he wants to do.' Hence, he grew up doing what he wanted to do, that is, exercising his guilt-free initiative. *Work became a self-chosen goal for him.* He gives numerous examples for this:

> In class 12th, I didn't study for my preboard exams because I thought that if I finish learning my entire syllabus in these exams, then I would not feel like studying during my board exams. So, I used to watch TV. My mother didn't ask me why you want to do it. My aunt was visiting us then. She commented on what I was doing. But my mother was fine. Then I studied a lot for my IIT exam. I wouldn't move from my place. I wouldn't look at the TV. The cable connection was never cut off in my house because of my studies. *Even, when I decided to start a company, I initially told them that I am taking a job in a Professor's company since I don't have any other job. At that time they would have just got very upset had I told them that I am starting a company. Then gradually, I told them the complete truth. My father was O.K. with it. My mother would keep telling me for long to do M.B.A.*

> *or take up a job in Infosys. But it would be an immediate communication. I would just say I am not going to do any of this and the matter would end. There would not be any further discussion.*

What came across from his sharing about his parents was that they were concerned about his well-being but not imposing on his life space, affectionate but not smothering in their love for him. *Samrat said laughingly that his mother had reconciled to the fact that he would do what he wanted to do and had asked him to tell her about his 'adventures' after he was through with them so that she could avoid getting anxious.* He was trusted and appreciated by his teachers and parents alike for his good conduct and accomplishments. Samrat shared with a chuckle that whenever anyone would feel angry with him, he would begin to smile and the anger of the other would just disappear.

Of particular interest was his *relationship with his mother. It was a strong, positive bonding from which he derived his inner strength and stability.* His mother was an artistic, sociable and enterprising person. He 'naturally learnt' to sketch and paint by watching her. He described her as someone who always developed a friend circle wherever she went with her friendly, communicative mannerisms, which were similar to his own companionable nature. In our conversations, he had an easy going style of conversation in which the other was duly acknowledged and provided for. She would mobilise and encourage children in the colony to collect funds, clothes etc. for charity. She helped them organise events for various festivals. About his relationship with his mother, Samrat said:

> *My mother would make rice for me if I want to have rice. I would not be a bad son in sense of asking her to do something for me if it is too difficult for her. But she would do it if it was convenient for her.* Now, also when I get back home, she sits with me while I have my dinner and tells me about the day's happenings, asks me about my day. She also inculcated the importance of being a good person in me. She always stress upon good behaviour, how one should not cheat, lie or harm others, be helpful, be nice to others. When I was young, I used to lose my temper easily. She taught me that this is not good. I now don't show my anger. I deal with it within myself. Then I come and deal with the situation. *My mother has taught us [me and my sister] to have faith in God, but not to be superstitious.* So, like I keep a fast on Tuesday but if someday I eat something, it is O.K. I pray daily. *When I leave home, I touch my parents' feet and seek their blessings. I have a lot of faith in her prayers. So whenever I have an important meeting, I tell her to pray for me also. I feel her prayers are answered.*

It is within the matrix of such intersubjective world of mother–child that hope ascends for the child and provides an enduring belief in the attainability of fervent wishes. His mother's religiosity gave him the strength to believe in his visions and efforts and helped in the affirmation of his faith in supreme power. He felt protected by the numinous presence and thus could trust himself and obviate the fear of making all too foolish commitments. Next to the recognition bestowed by the gracious face of the maternal person, the affirmation of the paternal guiding voice is a prime element of man's sense of identity.

While the mother would be spontaneously spoken about, the father was not mentioned much. So when I brought it up for his observation, *Samrat said that he was closer to his mother and resembled her more than his father.* As a person, he described his father as a simple, systematic, straightforward man who would always do his work methodically and on time, not able to understand the motivations and intentions of people well and not go out of his way to please his boss because of which he had to suffer losses at job front. All of these were points on which he differed from him. He did not want to be a mechanical engineer because he did not like the kind of work his father did. The objection was that it was an outdated branch of engineering, while his interest was more in the 'newer' fields of software, Internet etc. He was sure that he did not want to work in public sector because of an environment of low growth potential, sycophancy and inflexible hierarchy that he saw in his father's job. His imagination and chosen field of initiative were much larger—the entire economy. Randomness and diversification were his key ideational elements rather than order and specialisation. He also saw himself as someone who would 'manage' work rather than 'do' it oneself like his father. Networking and social adroitness were seen as important ingredients for success by him. This provided an impression of a young man learning the 'ways of the world' and participating in the 'spirit of times' as a means of consolidating his identity. It was interesting to note that he had been able to create a work role for himself where he would not be subservient to any 'boss' who could control the rewards of work, and in which time, was not strictly regimented, like in the case of his father. *Samrat had clearly chosen a different space for himself—of global player rather than pedantic worker.*

His father emerged as a cautious provider who would ensure that the family was well taken care of [he took voluntary retirement and used the money to buy a house]. Thus, Samrat had a secure base to take off towards new horizons. According to Samrat, his father was not very communicative of what he thought or felt about issues with his children. For example, during admission in college, he did not advise him to fill up any particular option. He did not interact much with his children with an intention of knowing their thought process and then evolving it further to help them make better decisions. He also did not share much of his experiences and learning of life with them. *It seemed that his father was not someone he looked towards for guidance. It was his mother who was more proactively involved in helping her children make their decisions.* It was she who advised her daughter to pursue fashion designing and searched for an institute for her. The mother emerged in his narrations as someone whom he idealised and conferred perfection to. *The father's attitude of 'let him do what he wants to do' possibly played an important role of the countervailing force, helping the son individuate from an intense emotional relationship with the mother and enabled him to have his independent ambitions.* Even though, Samrat wished to be seen as different from his father, there was a certain raw simplicity in his demeanour and appearance and valuing of honesty and integrity which looked like the commonality between the father and son. There was trust and pride in the relationship between father and son.

Peers had played an important role in Samrat's life. They had been constructively utilised to compete with and to test out oneself as well as cooperate with for joint action. He had relied on their advice to take vital decisions such as which coaching institute to join, which engineering college to come to and what branch of engineering to opt for. His close friends had all been academically equal or better than him in whose company he was not misled. His relationship with his friends was based on mutual trust and give and take. As a part of the group, he had not felt swamped by pressure or rejected by his peers if he wanted to something differently. In IIT, he emerged as a leader who could influence people and organise them for activities. It was this experience that gave him the confidence in his ability to form links with people and join them with his innovative vision.

Samrat's individuality was marked by a private self that could contain his tensions, frustrations, rages as well as accomplishments. His needs to develop ideas and verify them were fulfilled by self-reading as well as socialising with diverse people. He could be with himself and at the same time sought people for different ends. The familial environment gave him enough freedom and did not impinge on his evolving self. *Within the secure atmosphere created by the interlinked contexts of home, school and peers, Samrat was able to explore his creativity, experiment with ideas and execute his imagination, in short, play.* His identity resources of trust in himself and his chosen goals, skilled workmanship, optimism and faith in men synthesised to form a uniquely self-directed course of life.

Reflections on Corporate Youth

The unfolding of human life takes place in the psychosocial context in which the individual is located. Thus, any attempt to reflect on the psychodynamic aspects of identity of corporate youth must begin with an understanding of the ethos of interlinked growth contexts of family, education and work in neo-liberal high-tech global economy that shape and organise their experiential reality and developmental potential in contemporary times. Following which, the data gleaned from the case material in the foregoing section is reshaped into formulations capturing the subtleties and complexities of the inner psychological make-up of these youth.

Psychological Characteristics of Social Contexts

A typical feature of family environment of most participants was *high emphasis on academic achievement*. From an early age, both familial environment and educational milieu impressed on them that intellectual competence, professional expertise and a high degree of specialisation were prerequisites for getting ahead in life. While many youth also had opportunities of playing, of participating in extracurricular activities and of enjoying with peers and adults, these were subsidiary to studies, at least in school phase when they were regulated more by parental norms. In the case of Deepak and Krishna, pressure of achievement was so high that it afforded them little scope to associate with peers, explore their interests and experiment with their imagination.

In most cases, the focus was on *treading the well-worn paths* of entering the economic system. Engineering and management were on the top of the pecking order of educational qualifications because they provide smooth access into the world of well-paid work. In the case of Deepak, one could see an acute example of how failure in getting admission in a top-ranking engineering college was felt as a terrible disappointment by him and his parents. *Higher education was viewed in vocational terms*, as passports for upward mobility in the expanding service sector of liberalising India.

P. Bansal, *Youth in Contemporary India: Images of Identity and Social Change*,

DOI 10.1007/978-81-322-0715-3_10,

Competition was a ubiquitous phenomenon in the lives of corporate youth whether in situations of academic performance, admission to institutions of higher education, job placements and performance appraisal at work. They were constantly compared in their intelligence and performance with their contemporaries at school/college as well as work. Since the participants belonged to elite educational institutions, they had gone through aggressively competitive academic environments, thereafter making a beeline for lucrative job profiles which were also highly limited.

Rapid technological changes in a globally interlinked work sphere require *continuous professional upgrading*. The young were required to constantly upgrade their skill and knowledge base and differentiate themselves from their competitors in order to make themselves worthy of better rewards. Alongwith or sometimes even more than specialised expertise, an important skill in any professional/social situation was perceived to be self-presentation and make oneself attractive. In fact, in the market economy, the skill orientation is sliding in importance in comparison to *marketing orientation*. Fromm (1947) speaks of the marketing orientation as growing alongside modern capitalism. In the modern market, both commodities and humans are dependent on their material success on a personal acceptance by those who need them or their services. In the job market, in order to have success, it is not sufficient to have the skill and equipment for performing a given task, but one must be able to put oneself across as 'saleable' in competition with many others.

The new *economic dispensation of liberalisation* in India threw open the gates to new technologies, business ventures, foreign media and consumption goods. The new ideological messages were of imagination-backed initiative and guiltless indulgence. The participants had grown up with access to opportunities—educational/professional/consumption—their parental generation never had since they lived in the shadows of the socialist polity which was characterised by ideology of restraint, scarcity and simplicity. The general mood of consumerist buoyancy and optimism about the emergence of Indian as a global giant was adding to their confidence and ambitions for material betterment. Economic liberalisation has led to an era of multinational companies and outsourcing units of foreign companies and emergence of newer Indian companies in the areas of software, telecommunication, finance, etc. They brought with them an enterprise culture which demands ever-increasing productivity, competitiveness and efficiency through a constant stream of fads and initiatives from its employees but also compensates handsomely with huge pay packets, foreign assignments, performance-linked promotions and café culture. Their expressed values are that of creativity and innovation, and they reward merit and performance. Their thinking and management practices have been different from the ones prevailing in the public sector/government organisations and the fledgling private sector of the pre-liberalised India which had more inflexible and rigid hierarchies, where meritocracy was secondary to caste and regional loyalties and conformity to established codes was valued over innovation. They have business presence across globe and thus give many opportunities to its employees to learn and work abroad. It requires lessons in global employee skills such as sensitivity to nuances of different cultural norms and etiquettes, world knowledge and international lifestyle to fit in the global economic order.

Psychodynamic Dimensions of Identity

Linked to socio-economic environment described above, following psychodynamic aspects of identity constellation amongst corporate youth emerged.

Constriction of Self

A dominant trend noticed in the research is that in Indian urban middle class households of the participants, the male child was rather precociously taken to be something of a worker and potential provider, thus, to be instructed systematically. With the increasing trend of working women, girls were also encouraged to study hard so that they could be economically independent. The culturally sanctioned *high premium on education set as the passport for getting better things in life* makes the growing child internalise the demand for achievement and competition often at the cost of *constriction of other domains of existence such as relationality, play and citizenship.* Parents raise anxious doubts when involvement in other activities takes precedence over studies. The worker identity often becomes a prime criterion of worthwhileness, estranging imagination and creative living. This is most starkly demonstrated in the case of *Deepak* in whose life the parental insistence on competitive achievement was inexorably high and was inextricably linked up with his sense of self-worth. The isolation demanded by exclusive focus on academics prevented him from accessing his liveliness and participating in the fun and gaiety of sportive competition, peer interaction and experimentation with roles. He saw feelings of love and romantic yearnings as distractions from his prime responsibility of 'doing well'. It, thereby, led to his depressive sense of self, brooding over its failures. In the case of *Aanchal*, it became apparent how in a young woman certain potentials were overdeveloped at the cost of certain others in a bid to enter the productive world of work privileging masculine initiative and competitiveness. She too found it difficult to access her relational self which got overshadowed by her single-minded pursuit of success. The budding identity got prematurely fixed on being nothing but a good worker. The selection of academic streams was guided less by inclination, talent and interest and more by pragmatic calculation of whether it would lead to a lucrative career. There was a strict sense of duty in doing what one was told to do and little exploration and experimentation. It does not allow for the natural tendency in childhood to find out by playing, to learn what one must do by doing what one likes to do. Hence, for young people, studies became a ritual to be 'performed' devoid of any intrinsic beauty and vitalising meaning.

The early demands of performance and narrowly defined futuristic goals led to a way of dealing with experience in which diversity of selfhood was sacrificed to favour a limited and standardised range of functioning. In this regard, Erikson (1968) makes a useful distinction between *wholeness and totalism.* Wholeness connotes a gestalt which emphasises a sound, progressive mutuality between diversified impressions and memories, wishes and demands, private self and public existence within self-boundaries which are open and fluid. Totalism, on the contrary, evokes a gestalt in which constituent parts may not have an affinity with each other and may be irreconcilable and are held within a tight boundary which is fixed and impervious. Bereft of the freedom to let oneself loose to deeply and meaningfully relate with oneself, others, society and nature, there is a loss of essential wholeness, one that can fruitfully assemble self-interest and social awareness, career and relationships, focus and fun.

In contrast, *Samrat*, the imaginative technopreneur and *Prashant,* the engineer integrating the concerns of technology, profit and social good within a corporate model, are examples of how free, secure and approving familial environment can help youth live up to their inner capacities and powers of one's imagination and feelings and thus, experience a sense of wholesome existence.

Conformity in Exchange of Privilege

Precocious compliance is a term used by Winnicott (1971) to describe the efforts of young children to conform to their depressed mother's need for them to be cheerful, well behaved, and attentive to mother's emotional needs. The usage of the term can be opened to include processes of adapting to cultural expectations. *The societal demands of self-discipline, competitive achievement, performance and pragmatism were found to be internalised by the youth in a bid to attain economic and educational privileges, to profit from current arrangements of power. Krishna* exemplified this attitude:

> Children are conditioned to satisfy their parents. When my friends were partying, I used to think let them party. I'm going to get more marks than them or I'll get a better rank than them in the engineering entrance exam. Ultimately, I'll be the winner. Let them play their cricket. Instead of wasting 3 hours there I will spend 3 hours in solving more maths problems. That's the attitude I developed. And that helped. None of my school/college mates have reached the level where I have reached now.

Also, assimilation into the dominant trend of the kind of workmanship in demand provides the youth with the optimum combination of free choice, peer solidarity and compliance. Successful performance became a basis of their self-esteem in the eyes of their parents as well as other significant persons—peers, relatives and neighbourhood. *Disha* opined:

> If you do very well in academics, you get a lot of leeway with parents. Like no one can say that this time your party is cancelled because you didn't get good marks. Or you can't do this because your performance was not up to the mark. So the best is to study hard and get marks and get your way. Then the parents are always ready.

In many of their articulations, one constantly heard their tedious struggles of living up to the expectations of their parents, to reflect well on them through their own success and sadness over suppressed longings to feel free from the constant pressure to 'perform' in order to feel light and joyful. Their needs to explore the world in its multidimensionality and test themselves in the various options that it offers to them, take risks and make mistakes were made subordinate to the highly structured vision of life offered to them.

Competition and Comparison

The self-worth of an individual in a competitive world is dependent on *how well he/she compares with the contemporaries*. There were repeated instances of how comparative evaluations of the youths' ability in terms of their ranks in the class, position in entrance examinations, rating of the institution of higher education in which they had been selected, relative salaries were all symbols of their self-worth, affirming/disaffirming their status as 'achieving child'. The constant exposure to comparisons with age-mates and judgments by superiors gave rise to occasional obliteration of self-esteem, self-conscious doubt about 'how good one is' and a sense of shame over one's inadequacies and failures, as was seen in the case of Aasheesh and Deepak. *Deepak* makes a point:

> My parents were spending a lot of money on my education and stay in Delhi. So I was under a lot of stress. For me it was a situation of 'Perform or Perish'. The FIIT-JEE classes that I joined just exposed me to the kind of competition I was up against. It worsened my condition. I felt that everyone else knew everything.

In such situations, one is continuously *assessing oneself in relation to others along the axes of perceived superiority and inferiority*. It becomes psychologically mandatory to project a self-image of being 'better than the rest'. Such a self which is repeatedly defined in relation to the other selfhoods often hides behind its achieving, invincible demeanour the conflicts arising from one's vulnerabilities, feelings of inadequacies and anxieties of 'slipping down'. Such self parts are shame-evoking and are often not allowed space of expression in interpersonal relationships with parents, friends and even with loved partner because of the fear of rejection and ridicule. *A false self thus gets created which is divided, insecure and in need of continuous reassurance of its self-worth.*

Competition also leads to creation and scaling of hierarchy, separating the self from others in a vertical fashion. Just as it is important to keep up with the competitors in appearances, it is also important to distinguish oneself from them in domains of skills, tastes and opinions in order to be ahead of them. The preoccupation with bettering one's own lot, the clamour to get the 'best' which is limited and frantic attempts to consolidate one's own position vis-à-vis the competitors leaves little scope for an ethic of cooperation and collectivity for common good to develop. In *Krishna's* life, one noticed how such competitive urges took on hostile turn in which the other is always someone to be outdone. *Aasheesh* noted almost with a tinge of sorrow that it 'often doesn't feel quite as bad when one's own best friend too misses a promotion or is denied a pay hike'.

Security gained by fighting one's way to an elevated position vis-à-vis the other is paid for by isolation and loneliness, which was the experience of many of the participants.

On the other end, there was *Samrat* who represented a 'game-like' position on competition:

> I would be in top 5 [in school] but not topping all the time. But that was okay. I never got tense because of the competition. Even in Delhi, I was in the ability section in my school which had high merit students. Competition was like a game for me. I enjoyed it. Sometimes you win, sometimes you don't. Try harder the next time.

Peers had been constructively utilised by him to playfully compete with and to test out himself as well as cooperate with for joint action. His relationship with them was of mutual respect, unambivalent acknowledgment of their superior talents and sharing. He also created avenues of being a productive participant in many self-chosen activities where he would not be required to prove himself in relation to others.

Sense of Exclusivity

As I immersed myself in the lifeworlds of many of them, I observed that having made into elite institutions of higher education bred pride and a sense of exclusivity in the corporate youth. Sandipan Deb, author of the book *The IITians* (2004), states that IITians look upon themselves as *special people* capable of competing in their field with the best in the world. He attributed it chiefly to a highly competitive entrance procedure by which only one in every hundred applicant gets admitted. Harvard in comparison takes on in eight. *Deepak* idealised IIT as an institution that made its students 'destiny free'. *Krishna* boasted about how much in demand he was by virtue of having made it to a top business school. *Aasheesh* noted the special charm of the double 'I' institutes (implying the premier educational institutions of Indian Institute of Technology and Indian Institute of Management). The self-importance of being a part of the prestigious institutions is akin to the narcissistic configuration in which the omnipotence and perfection are attributed to the idealised parental figure who is experienced as a part of the self (Kohut 1971). The idealised parental imago (the institutional brand in this case) is based on the conviction 'You are perfect, but I am a part of you'. Students of prestigious institutions have a *self-image of 'being the best' which aid their dream of abundant life of success and recognition without end.* One management institute which was the site of data collection for the research had the job placement tag line as 'Connecting great minds to greater opportunities'. Its placement news read that out of 81 companies confirming presence to recruit, only 26 were able to recruit, indicating the surplus demand of trained professionals from elite institutions.

The danger of exclusive identity fed by such narcissistic self-absorption is that it allows affiliations with those with whom it is similar. It is truncated when encountering those from whom it sees itself as different. *Collecting within itself all what is perceived as superior, the best, the successful within an absolute boundary, it disowns the inferior parts.* What is designated as inferior and vulnerable is projected onto others—seen as belonging to others—if one is identified with the superior position. It is also seen as a possibility within the self that threatens it from inside and against which one is always at guard. Thus, underachievement, for instance, becomes a sin.

Privatism

As individuals trained to be concerned primarily with personal success, acts of extending oneself towards alleviation of human suffering and social responsibility were rare. Urges to do something for the society and the deprived were experienced by them, but they were overcome by more pressing concerns of one's personal life. *The dissociation of the personal from the political and deep-seated pragmatism helps build a sense of private interiority that is disconnected from cultural-- historical context.* The culture of individualism makes it difficult to formulate ideas about the way one's own social environment and those of others affect one's well-being because within an individualistic paradigm of selfhood, success and failure are seen as stemming from personal factors of ambition, intelligence and effort. There is less understanding of socio-economic inequality and political disadvantages faced by large sections of society and an even lesser knowledge of ways and means to engage in social dialogue and action. In such culture, the young are also ingrained with the thinking that protest is ineffective, that authorities know better and that getting to the roots of unjust power is impossible. *Thus, there is a turn away from the broader social scene towards more manageable and controllable private experience and personal commitment. Prashant* was a notable exception to the above trend. An intellectually curious and socially aware person, he could creatively utilise idealisation of his parents and his role model, a corporate leader, to develop a perspective which could align his socially responsible orientation with capitalist principles.

While the public life of corporate youth was found to be characterised by drive, ambition and sharp eye for opportunity in order to continuously better one's station in life, *their private life was an effort to discover/create compensation and justification for their public strivings.* College marked a watershed in their lives. *Most of them moved away from their homes to live in hostels in different cities to pursue their higher education. For many of them, it was hatching out of a certain existence in which parental norms regulated their life space, especially in terms of emphasis on selective academic tasks and performance and controlled fun.* Discipline and hardwork were values that were upheld in the homes of these young people. As they moved away from family homes after school, they were in an environment which was unstructured, heterogeneous and liberal where there was much more choice of activities. When in college, the regulative hold of the home declined, and the casual environment provided the much needed respite from the oppressive demands of academic work. *The student youth culture which characterises college campuses is a world insulated from academic culture and from adult society with its own rites, rituals and traditions.* Its outlooks are distinguishable from the outlooks of adulthood. It emphasises immediacy, excitement, intense feeling, popularity, attractiveness, adventure, daring, consumption and intellectual indifference. The youth recollected moments of light-hearted gaiety, relaxed frivolity and serious deliberations about self and world with friends fondly. *Aanchal* spoke excitedly about her college days:

> Then, I went to law school and it was a whole new world. For the first time I was staying away from my family in a different city. The 5 years there were complete blast. Had the best time there!

Being in love, cutting classes, watching films, going out for trips, mocking defiance of authority, conniving at rules, cracking sex jokes, etc. were the new sources of self-esteem and fulfilment. These were occasions when they formed bonds of friendship, lived up to their desires and fantasies of freedom came alive. Within the insulation of this private world of peers and informality, from the adult world of parents and work, they searched to find themselves. *This was the underside of the conforming youth.*

There were few youth notably, Disha and Samrat, who made use of the free space to enjoy life and broaden their own possibilities. *Disha* could make use of her learning from the peer group to gather courage and support of her parents to pursue her ambitions of working in a different city and marrying her boyfriend who belonged to a different region. *Samrat* seemed to be playing with nothingness while in college, to reach an inner rock bottom on which he could stand firm. He found it futile to move ahead until he got a worthwhile work goal. However, not everyone could utilise it as a positive chance for self-growth and expand one's sense of self. Coming from highly structured home environments, the freer environment of college created conflicts with more conservative parental and home values. It presented the conflict of continuing to be an academically oriented student the way one's parents wished or indulge in the temptations of new free life.

As a future goal, 'the rich full life' consisting of challenging, rewarding work; exciting leisure; recognition from all; and loving interpersonal relations exploits the narcissistic lure of imaginary completion. It holds the promise that one would not lack anything.

Money and Its Symbolic Significance

Corporate youth are branded in media as materialistic and consumerist. It is true that the *new ethos of acquisition, competition and vigorous initiative puts no ceiling on aspirations of good life* defined largely by material success. Besides offering more opportunities for earning through free economic activities, it also helped liberate material needs from any notion of self-restraint and guilt. The thrust is on acquiring the visible signs of success—gizmos, cars, foreign vacations, etc. The exhibitionist display of one's money and status has become a major source of self-esteem. In a rigidly stratified society like India, the pressure for upward social mobility is immense, and money is one of the best ways of climbing the social ladder of status. As children of liberalising–globalising India, the *youth were living the middle class dream of liberation from limitation and want.* They desire more and demand immediate gratification. In a consumerist society, one's autonomous status is recognised in relation to the fantasy of omnipotent 'right to consume' objects of choice. Since there are many upwardly mobile flaunting their plush lifestyles, money inevitably becomes tied with the grandiose fantasies of happiness, freedom and power. *Large quantities of money provide enough omnipotence, and it becomes possible to imagine a more absolute form of invulnerability with only a little more money.* The irredeemability of consumerist promise exploited by the multipronged advertising strategy of selling the lifestyle of rich and the famous, of encouraging all to believe that anyone can make it here and of linking consumption with utopian images of happy and secure life keeps people chasing money.

In research, as one listened to the young men talk about the money they were making, one could sense a pride in them of earning at a young age what their fathers were earning when they were 50 years old. Thus, *in the intrapsychic space, material success was felt as construed by the son as a triumph over the rival father*. However, many times, it was a victory which the paternal figure exulted in, even if secretly, seeing it as personal success and validation of one's own efforts as a parent.

In the inner world of many participants, *their monetarised success was also their gift to their parents* to make them feel proud of them and gain their love and approval. While it may not be wrong to say that all children are motivated to buy comforts for their parents as a token of their love and gratitude towards them, an unchecked materialistic attitude begins to view money as love. In lives of Kapil and Deepak, one finds an effort to not let material enrichment of life override enrichment of emotionally intimate bonds. Kapil stated:

> What I really look forward to in my life is never in terms of career, money, but in terms of family. My life ambition is to keep my wife happy, keep my parents happy. That's how my life is. Probably because I have been loved and cared so much that I look at brighter side of life.

In the market-oriented society, the relative grading of one's worth in terms of the money that one is making also gives *money the power of cultural insignia of victory over peers*. There were also references of how money is essential for gaining love of a girl implying that *love too had become a commodity to buy and consume*. Monetary status secures a favourable position vis-à-vis a loved partner. Thus, economic insecurities also threaten romantic relationships. In the case of women youth, it was found that the economic activity was more of a means of independence and application of their education.

While the young harboured desires of possession and consumption, one found instances which showed their ability to give such impulses a limited space in their lives. One articulation that stands out in this regard is that of *Aasheesh* who noted:

> Money is not *that* important for me. Because materialistic requirements are there till the age of 35–40 years. After that, you don't have a craze for all these cars and gadgets. It is recognition, status and respect for my work, skill and talent that is more important for me.

Another attitude that reflects the youth's *striving to go beyond the lure of money to engage in authentic acts* is found in the narrative of *Samrat*. He shared:

> Money is important. You need money to live comfortably.... Job would have meant more money definitely. With the kind of effort that I am putting in my company, I am earning much less but I am more satisfied. It is the way I am living life which is important.... Working hard, having a goal, going for a trek, making a snowman—all of these things is important for me.... When I talk to my friends or other people, I never talk about how much money I have, how much clients I have. I talk about this snowman I built. I guess, people just remember or talk about things which they think are important for them.

Ideologically, *Prashant* stood for an ethics of responsible capitalism that creates wealth and allows it to percolate down to the lesser fortunate. In the personhood of a role model like Narayana Murthy, an Indian entrepreneur whose guiding philosophy of 'Compassionate Capitalism' blends socialist values of equity with capitalist orientation of free economic activity and wealth creation, he found an ethical framework that could *reconcile usually conflicting objectives of private profit and common good.*

Tireless Initiative and Corporate Dream

Post liberalisation, there is a mindset of 'new possibilities', 'risk taking' and 'can do attitude'. The young are far more demanding of excitement and want to have more, reach higher and faster. Their ambitions are high which are nurtured by the rhetoric of economic boom and global living. They are constantly striving, competing with peers in self-presentation and professional skills, and investing themselves more and more in the professional sphere of life. One noticed in them during the course of research a *quality of 'go-at-itiveness'* at any cost. With an eye on the future, their worth sort of seemed to be in what they were 'going at' in the future and not in what they were in the present. The strain could be seen in their bodies, with many young men suffering from premature greyness, problems of overweight, spondylitis, blood pressure, etc. Women youth, though ambitious, were found to be relatively less pressurised and more relaxed vis-à-vis their career growth.

The absorption of the young in the corporate dream of abundance was of a high level. In their inner worlds, the spirit of confidence sometimes appeared to be bordering on boastfulness, vigour tended towards manic energy and imagination skirted illusion. Inherent in the dream was omnipotence and grandiosity, both of which are necessary ingredients in the will to want and work. However, there was also *alive awareness of the precariousness of the dream*, that it is like a sand castle which is built with enthusiasm and perseverance but which is also endangered by the rough waves. In the narrations of the youth participants, one saw that they could see through the dream and cut it down to size as per the reality demands. They understood that their desires had to be moderated. The actualities that they have to accept is that one may not get the dream job, peers will do better, career progression can be slower than expected, economic slump may be around the corner, job security is a memory of the past and there will be unlimited work-related demands on their time. This acceptance was not, however, without a sense of resentment, frustration, aggression and envy. The disquiet led them to search for fulfilment and significance in family, friendship and leisure. Uneasy jokes about the 'death' that lies beyond the last professional degree, *Krishna's* mockery of the corporate world provides hints that the narcissistically invested object—corporate dream—was not believed to be perfect and could be contemplated with amusement and scorn—an expression of freedom from rigid grandiose fantasies and self-harming strivings.

Part III
Narratives, Conversations and Life Stories of Humanist Youth

Introductory Note

It is often questioned whether altruism, concern for the disadvantaged and idealism could animate the imagination and action of the young in times when the crack between the two Indias, one aspiring to be globalised and the other hopelessly, despairingly marginalised, has deepened. In the context of the research work, my search for such youth led me in diverse directions. I explored the NGO sector and spoke with young people associated with social movements and working with organisations/forums with core emphasis ranging from service provision, advocacy, grass-root action, community organisation, social research and consultancy. It also led me in the unexpected direction of spiritual forms of socially transformative action.

Media often profiles the do-gooders who are happy doing their bit for society. Along with juggling studies and mainstream jobs, many young people in cities do engage in voluntary activities like campaigning for environment preservation, teaching street children, educating and spreading awareness amongst slum dwellers and collecting relief material for victims of natural calamities. Few of them opt for these challenging issues as careers and life work. Within the civil society, there are many organisations that work for the welfare and empowerment of socially disadvantaged sections like AIDS patients, urban and rural poor, victims of sexual abuse and violence, physically and mentally challenged persons, tribals and homeless and displaced people through advocacy and lobbying as well as provision of education, livelihood, medical facilities and legal aid. Along with social movements, these organisations variously termed as non-profit organisations, non-government organisations and civil society organisations constitute the third sector (distinct from state and market). In principle, the citizen/social sector is committed to the project of democracy deepening and is a forerunner in challenging and contesting the hegemonic ideas in society about 'how things should be'. As watchdogs, the social movements and NGOs are dedicated to the task of engaging in public debates, research and action to offer innovative alternatives to neo-liberal ideas and practices of development which increase poverty, inequality and marginalisation in society. While a large number of the non-governmental organisations (NGO) are directing their efforts towards providing relief and delivery of services, there are many others which are struggling to create more radical and systemic alternatives that will bring about broader transformations in the way economy, politics and social relationships are organised.

Besides these political actors, there are other social approaches which are imagining a different world order outside the institutional structure and power dynamics amongst state, market and civil society. This new paradigm which is varied and vast is being termed as spiritual activism or liberation spirituality (Shikshantar, 2007).[1] As the name itself indicates, the movement shares a deep commitment to spiritual life and practice to bring about a fundamental change in the world based on equity and justice. As a basic feature, it advocates reducing one's dependence on large institutions and relegitimising and reconnecting to the local knowledge and wisdom that exist within communities. The emphasis is on forming and strengthening communities where there is space for creativity and imagination to reframe solutions to issues of livelihood, ecological imbalance, sustainable development etc.; for listening and learning to act with love and discernment; and for moving beyond tendencies to divide the world into heroes and villains, good guys and enemies. Spiritual practice provides a way of leaving behind the construct of us vs. them (the grist of sociopolitical activism) and living in a web of relationships that links all. It builds a reservoir of spaciousness and equanimity that can provide access to one's deepest capacities of faith, wisdom and gratitude in the midst of great turmoil and difficulty.[2] The key is in the ability to deeply and compassionately connect with one's own experience and with each other without clinging or rejecting. Spiritual activism promotes libratory forms which lean towards freedom. Examples include experiential and direct education that values students as experts of their own experience, communal and intentional living experiments in which self and nature are more harmoniously blended, artistic ventures that capture reality in compelling and uncharted ways, community-supported organic farming models, religious and spiritual communities that call forth ecstatic expression, nurture contemplative refuge and build strong community. Spiritual activism is a way of being and acting that believes that the fundamental purpose of connecting around a common experience of humanity is to be able to engage, explore and celebrate our very real differences as people.[3]

A total of 15 young persons (men and women) were spoken with for the purpose of research in this section. In the age range of 23–29 years, they were engaged with building environmental awareness and advocacy, innovative educational programs, community organisation and empowerment, human rights' work, politically active action groups, left-wing politics and spiritual activism. These were individuals who were concerned with various ethical, social, ecological and political issues, taking a

---

[1] Shikshantar. (2007). Now Activism. Retrieved November 10, 2007, from http://www.swaraj.org/shikshantar/nowact_toc.htm

[2] Ibid., p.30.

[3] Ibid., p.38.

stand for a just, humane and ecologically balanced world and were acting together with others in a group and were termed as humanist youth.

For the purpose of presentation, an attempt was made to select those participants who had some work experience (at least 1–2 years) in their field in order to provide clearer dynamics of identity formation in a specific direction. A total of eight lives are represented (four men and four women), six in more detail in the form of life stories, narrations and conversations while two in a briefer manner. The more detailed life stories provide deeper insights in the intrapsychic dynamics of individuation and ideology of youth. In spite of their brevity, two shorter cases have been presented as they bring to light certain novel aspects of psychic functioning amongst the young.

Nirmal

I came to know about Nirmal through a feature article done by a news magazine on 'do gooders'. It profiled young persons who were contributing to society and trying to change it for the better. Nirmal, 27 years, was a social entrepreneur working towards promoting environmental education, life skills and active citizenship amongst civil society, state, media and corporates. The first sight of him in person had me baffled because he looked different from his photograph in the featured article. While in person, he looked chic and urbane; in the photograph against the background of the river, his social cause, he appeared a simple countryman. Sitting on the floor of his office terrace or room, we would begin the task of 'doing' interview. The interactions remained quite formal with the time being called up by him at the end of an hour or so. In the midst of cigarette smoke, often out of contact eyes and structured time frame, we both struggled to achieve that mutual recognition in which both of us could come to identify each other. Being the early days of my research and given my own inexperience, probably, I also could not provide the continuity of warmth and stimulation he required for his soul searching. *With him, I often felt confused and frustrated. Often, the meetings would leave me with a sense of 'him not being there' and 'not quite getting' a feel of his deeper self.* During the interactions, while I would sit facing him, he would sit in a position so that his office/desk was in his sight. He could just get up from his work and begin his interactions with me and then after an appointed time would revert back to his work. *Gradually, I realised that my needs were to see continuities in his life, sustained directions and ideological anchors of his identity. Probably, these were not the realities of his life. As I began to become more mindful of these emotions within me, I was able to more clearly understand the inward splits and outward disjunctures in his life.* Through repeated interactions, readings and thinking about his life, I was able to reach some semblance of substratum of his life. *The research work with him spanned over a year and a half generating over 12 hours of interview material. During this time, we remained resolutely on the track of creating meanings, through what he called his 'analysis' sessions, of and for a life which began its journey from a city in Bihar.* The city was a district headquarter and of historical

P. Bansal, *Youth in Contemporary India: Images of Identity and Social Change*,
DOI 10.1007/978-81-322-0715-3_11, © Springer India 2013

and mythical importance. It had been an influential centre of trade and commerce and finds mention in the ancient Hindu texts of Ramayana, Mahabharat and Vedas. Nirmal's narrated his story like this:

> My father is a high school teacher of Sanskrit in Bihar. I was born in a family which had three bachchas ... three of us ... I had a younger brother and an elder sister. We are a very middle class family. *My parents belong to the first generation that has come out of our village in the interiors of Bihar.* My father is the only one who is educated. My mother is not educated. *We are Maithil Brahmins and this is a very big cultural identity for us.* We brought our cultural roots from the village, so in a way we were living our village ways in the city. *It is a very very conservative and orthodox set up. Nothing modern about it. There was always some pooja taking place in the house. There is no democracy in our house ... no discussions, nothing of this sort.* What else?? There is a concept of neighbourhood. One was the neighbourhood of people who live around you and the other was that of the family. We played village games ... gulli danda [smiles]. *My parents had high aspirations from us. Because of their own ambitions, we were given the best education ever. I went to the city's best convent school. So I lived in that cultural context and my aspirations and dreams were the aspirations and dreams of my parents. They wanted me to become an IIT engineer or a 'lal batti' ... i.e. IAS/IPS. That is what is the worth of a man there. When I reflect on it now, I never wanted to become any of this.* As a child, I was very introvert and not much talking. I was sent to do 11th and 12th in a bigger city. I was still fulfilling my parents' dreams. I was doing IIT coaching and studying science. I didn't like science but my mistake was that I was a good student and got good marks in class 10th. I didn't have the courage to speak out that I don't want to do this. I was doing all this for my parents but at the same time, I wasn't sure of what is it that I want to do ... What else can I do. I was traveling all along with them.
>
> Then I was sent to Delhi for my graduation. *I was doing my graduation in Sanskrit because my father thought that it was a good IAS subject. This again was not my choice. I was also preparing again for IIT.* I used to feel depressed ... I had also stopped going for IIT coaching classes and it was only after few months could I tell my parents' about it over the phone. They were disappointed but thought that I would try for civil services. But I didn't want to. *I wanted to disagree with them. To disagree was my point. I felt suffocated by the control they had over my life and its decisions.* I was in a state of fix because I didn't know what else to do. Because, again while I didn't want to do IIT/IAS, I didn't know what else to do.
>
> The first year was very difficult. I knew I was suppressing something ... I don't know what. *I was operating out of anger and frustration.* Then one senior suggested reading for the visually challenged. I did that. I remember sitting on the library stairs and doing that ... for time pass. Just to get my mind off from the distress. In the first break, I didn't want to go back home because that would mean thousand questions of what? why? It was strange because everyone wanted to go back home. Then someone told me about this organization which takes students for exposure trips to hills and does workshop and all. So I went for it because I didn't want to go back home and answer the uncomfortable questions. This was in a way my initiation into social development sector. *I don't see my entry into this sector as a choice but as an escape from an undesirable despairing state. At times, I thought I was taking things upfront, but I wasn't.* I was running away from one situation and creating another. From there, I gradually got involved with N.G.O sector. Became a part of Anti Nuclear Campaign, NBA. *In college, I became an active member of various societies like environment society, debating society. All this exposed me to a new world of ideas, opportunities, people and activities. I was born again. I discovered that I could speak well, was good at networking with people, could do theatre. I was not such a waste* [*emphatically*]. It gave me enormous pleasure to create a space for myself among people through my skills that I never knew existed. Here was a realization of my potential. I met

people who had opinions about social issues. *The energy of working with other young people greatly enthused me.* I remember that we used to just meet, make a play in an hour's time and do it and it would have such an impact [speaks excitedly]. *I realized that young people can bring about a change ... we do matter and our work can bring about a difference. I had begun to get a direction of my life but I was not sure. I was caught up in ambitions and worldly desires. People around me were aiming big – settled jobs, fat pay cheques. I would think what am I making of myself? By doing this, I will just become 'Khaadi and Hawai Chappal' and nothing else.* But again, I wasn't sure of what else. There were these 'career dilemmas' and alongside there were also 'to be loved' dilemmas. *Are you ever to be loved? Because of the kind of profession that you get into, which girl will fall for you? There is nothing that is there.* Who will love a Sanskrit studying, slogan shouting activist? It was all very challenging. On the one hand, my parents' were still expecting me to sit for civil services' examination. They didn't know anything about my engagement with social sector.

After graduation, I wasn't sure of what next to do. I had all these questions in my mind. *Then I thought that I will take a year off, decide what next to do and take up the cause of the river Yamuna, which was close to my heart. Also my past experience of work in the social development sector gave me the motivation to begin the awareness campaign on the degenerated state of Yamuna.* In college, all the work that I was doing in this field had given me some direction and strength to work on this course. When I began this campaign, it hit a chord. Within a month, 500 young people had joined up. It generated a lot of interest and youth response which was a big boost for me. People didn't trust us in the beginning. They saw us as bachchas. But the buzz that the campaign created made me realize that young people can bring about a change. *During this time, I would send my parents news clippings of the campaign in order to satisfy them, to get appreciation from them. They would ... [makes a gesture of tearing] ... well I don't know. They would get angry and ask me "Do you want to become a neta? Get back to work." That really hurt me because while I was deriving so much satisfaction from this work, they were rejecting it all.* My relationship with them was very strained during graduation and the campaign days. They had dreams for me which I was not fulfilling. I had left their plane. The gap between them and me had widened. I disconnected from them. I wouldn't communicate with them.

After a year, the campaign wrapped up because I was to go to Bombay to pursue a postgraduate degree in social work. I came back to Delhi after the completion of the course and began work with a NGO on environmental issues. I was doing well there, heading their environment program. But after 1 year, I realized that No! I need to do something else. *Somewhere I used to dream more than this. I didn't want to end my life doing a 9-5 job and earning x amount of money. Also the success of the Yamuna campaign egged me on. That's when I thought I would start my own NGO. So it started in 2004 and since then I have been with it. It is a space that gives me a lot of pleasure and respectability.*

In terms of my relationship with my parents, it's O.K ... still strained. They want me to marry a Maithil Brahmin girl. It is quite frustrating. They know what work I do. But I share only my successes with them – I am working with so many schools, making this much money etc. ... not the process. I don't ... I am very very aggressively vocal about my opinions on religion and caste but I don't talk to them about my causes, what I think about caste/religion. I can't convince them about it. I don't argue with them. In front of them, I fail [speaks slowly] ... *Though a lot of my work is about awareness building, but I have not been able to bring about change in my own home. I feel a big void. There is no one to share my successes, pleasures, victories. They don't appreciate it much.*

Many times, Nirmal would enthusiastically show me newspaper clippings or write-ups about him, his work and achievements. He would feel happy at my appreciation of him. Success of various projects of his NGO was a great source of pleasure for him. I attended and enjoyed his musical performances where he along with a few others would sing songs of change, protest and vagrancy. Usually, such performances would involve minimum orchestra, and they would not be much rehearsed. But the spirit would be evocative and earthy. During one of the early meetings, which took place after his recent success of musical performance and another project of organic products, he was felt as particularly relaxed. He looked settled and spoke spontaneously, freely and happily. He spoke softly that maybe it was someone's blessings that all was going on so well. In response to my liking for his music, he said smilingly that whenever he felt that he was losing himself, such performances brought him back to the original 'sadak chhap'. He said, "One should not grow so big that one felt disconnected with Bihar."

This life story was deepened and extended over the various interactions that we had. Following the emotional significances and seizing pivotal moments in the narrative, subsequent queries were formulated:

- *You saw your parents' hopes being pinned on you specifically?*
  Yeah ... Because my sister was married. So in Indian cultural settings, once married is not yours. My younger brother ... was not so good in studies. So, because I was bright, I was seen as someone who would become IIT/IAS because that is what is the worth of a man/son there.
- *What brought your father to Bhagalpur?*
  Ummm ... what I know of ... my dadi died when he was 3 years old. My dada was a farmer. He was very ... he never cared for my dad. So he was not taken care of by anyone. So he came to the city, lived with his distant uncle, worked and studied.
- *What is your father's sense of belonging to his native place?*
  I don't think I would ever go back to village. We have a house there. He wants to go and settle there. I don't understand why? *It's so completely underdeveloped!* [Speaks in a irritated tone] There is no electricity ever, no road ever. There is nothing that is there. Even the nearest doctor is 100 kms away. Every year it gets flooded. There are no educated people left there. *But my father after retirement wants to go there. And right now, given the fact that I am going places because of the work that I do, he wants me to come back at some point of time or he wants me to get married to a Maithil Brahmin girl. I don't understand this. At one level, he gave me modern education, had modern aspirations for me ... now he wants me to follow the traditions.* I don't see myself going out of Delhi. The place makes me comfortable. I have a network here. I know people here. My professional aspirations are nurtured here. *Back home, I don't see what I will do there. 'I' gets lost there.* [After a brief silence] But I can't say that I am not a Bihari. I just can't disconnect myself from that identity. *I may be born in 1997 vis-à-vis the new identity that I am talking of, when I began to think about myself on my own, but the years I spent in Bihar have their place.... Though, I don't know what it means to be a Bihari.* Somewhere, I like to believe that my hatred towards communalism began after I witnessed the communal riots in childhood. Probably if I have to identify myself with a community, I'll say I am a Bihari ... But I don't know what is Biharism. *I have tried to minimise the negative aspects of Biharism like understanding of religion, marriage, etc. I think exposure plays an important role. I have been exposed to a variety of things, places, events, opinions in the past 10 years.* My engagement with the elite to the poor, to a variety of issues, to the left politics to the right politics, from social movements to business houses. All of that has also impacted on me. *We take isms from all over and then try to constitute one's own ism. I don't fall into any category. Any opinion is based on circumstance and situation, one is in. I work with NBA also, I work with corporates also. It's conflicting. But I have to take decisions keeping in mind the organisation's needs. It needs money. So you have to make compromises with your*

values. I don't know where is this actually leading towards. In the sense, do I actually have an identity. Of course, that confused identity or that dilapidated identity is in itself an identity....

While listening to Nirmal, I could understand the *suffocation that he felt because of a constrictive and choiceless life* and his rebellion against it. However, I didn't quite grasp clearly *what was it that he found suffocating in the casteist form of religious practice?* What was he trying to repudiate and what was he trying to renew from his cultural heritage in his personal life and work? So, I asked further:

- *You refer to cultural identity of Maithil Brahmin. What does it entail?*
  Like at the moment, it means that I should marry a Maithil Brahmin girl. I don't have any choice or freedom in deciding my life partner. That's what ... I don't have anyone in my life whom I want to marry but *I don't like the idea that I don't have that freedom. I am fearful of quaid. The idea of freedom and choice is important for me. My family is governed by the dictates of caste and religion.* There were always religious rituals being performed in my house. I hated it ... I was made to wear a janeyu. It is such a natak. Even now when I go back home, I wear a janeyu. In Delhi, I don't. The caste system was so deeply ingrained in my parents that in our house there were separate set of cups for serving tea to low caste people and Muslims. Recently, there was a janeyu ceremony for my cousin's son. It was done in the village. It involved animal sacrifice. I had to go because my parents forced me but I couldn't take it. I was disgusted. I couldn't do anything to stop it but the second day when the sacrifice had to happen, I refused to go.
- *What did you find so hateful and disgusting in these practices?*
  Imposition ... the fact that they were imposed on me. *My parents have been very pushy about religion.* Wear janeyu ... fast for 4 days. That's the thing ... a lot of things I was against was not because they were literally bad but because it was imposed on me. *And I felt impositions everywhere ... on what should I study, when should I return home, why I shouldn't play cricket with friends? There was a boundary for everything.* Even today, I have to be back home ... in Bihar ... by sunset. That's my limit. While, in Delhi, I can be out all night.
- *So Delhi allowed you the space to live freely, on your own terms, without the interference of your parents?*
  Yes ... All through they were deciding for me. And well! Not with an intention of harming me, of course. They love me. But I was too much of a bachcha. I was not thought capable of, and I also didn't think I was able to make decisions for myself. *But my parenting has been too forceful, too strong. I was always being filled up. More than school, I was influenced by the environment at home. I felt suffocated.* Besides, I had not seen the other side of the world. I was travelling with them. *Delhi gave me the space to explore and be myself.* Initially here also, I was operating out of frustration. All the dilemmas of work and love would depress me. I would push myself to work so that I didn't have to think about it.
- *What does the Bihari identity mean to you?*
  [Reflects] I don't know.... See when we talk of Bihari, Delhite, Mumbaiite, it's about dressing, language, food, relationships. Most of the times, when we talk of culture, these are 4–5 things which actually come up. But in terms of my food habit, dressing style – I don't really know whether I am dressed like a Bihari [looks at himself].
- *You don't have a Bihari accent also, even when you speak Hindi?*
  Yes ... I don't know what it is? Probably, when in a group, I will identify myself as a Bihari. But, somewhere, I feel, I have tried to minimise the negative parts of Biharism such as the understanding of marriage and religion. I have tried to say No ... that is not what I would like to be.

- *What are some of your reworked understandings on the institutions of religion and marriage?*
  [Thoughtfully] My relationship with God . . . no God, one god or many gods . . . I used to hate going to a temple earlier, but now I go to temples. And suddenly from there, it's turned out that I go to every religious institution now. I go to Gurudwara. There I listen to gurbani. I enjoy langar. Whenever I get time, I go to Nizamuddin Dargah. *I look at the religious institution as a cultural space.* In our yamuna yatra, in which we travel with the river from its source to Delhi, we go to different religious places. *I respect religion.* It is perhaps one of the best things that culture has to offer. *I see beauty in religion. But my anger or hatred towards religion in my early days was because it was so much forced on me.* Then I couldn't see the diversity and beauty in religion. It was that you are a Hindu and you are born in a Brahmin family, so you need to do certain things. Similarly, the marriage thing is also tied up with my being a certain caste and religion.
- *For instance, can you elaborate how do you weave the diversity and beauty of religion in your work?*
  Like Yamuna is linked to all religions: Hinduism [Yamunotri, Mathura, Vrindavan], Islam [Agra], Sikhism [Paonta Sahib] and Buddhism [Kalsi Rock]. For us, *Yamuna is the metaphor of socio–political–economic damages to things of religious and ecological reverence, in today's world.* When we travel with the river, we learn about the communities that depend and survive on the river. We hear their folk tales and stories . . . *the many indias that live within the India.* We witness the transformation of river, from being pure and pristine to sewage as it flows through the cities. The Yamuna is 1370 km in length and caters to the needs of approximately 60 million people along its course. Delhi constitutes less than 2% of the river's total length yet it contributes 70% of the Yamuna's total pollution load. We bring people's attention to the implications of policies and government programs on the river and the consequences of rapid urbanisation and water consumption patterns. The idea is to look at the nexus between culture, development and environment.
- *Why did you choose Yamuna to be your cause?*
  While crossing the river, I had seen its sad state. I felt that something needs to be done about it. *It was a part of my social responsibility towards the surroundings I live in.* I realised that there was a great deal of apathy towards the river. As I was figuring out what I want to do in life, I decided to raise a voice against the apathy that was killing the river, to create a lot of noise and to bring the Yamuna back into the minds of the populace.
- *You come from a culturally rich belt. Do you include cultural elements from there in your work? Do you talk about them?*
  [Silence] Not much . . . Not much. . . .

Nirmal pointed to his *dilapidated identity*. It referred to the fractured outlooks which coexist in a conflictual relationship within him and around him. Much like the river which became his cause, he had *travelled much beyond his origins but couldn't reject, even if he wanted to, his beginnings*; been exposed to much through his journey and was *struggling to assimilate and accommodate the various perspectives* that have influenced him. Much like the gush of the river which makes place for itself to flow, he also made a space for himself in a field which was a new terrain for him through energetic responses to opportunities. Like a river which allows oneself to distribute itself into rivulets, he had also *diversified himself professionally into many roles* like executive director of an organisation, social worker, consultant, activist, teacher, singer, photographer, documentary film maker and personally into traditional Bihari, Brahmin and modern Delhi based, global citizen. *The issues which become central to the understanding of this life from the viewpoint of identity were: What were the various identity fragments that jostled within him? What, if anything, cohered in him? Given the typicality of fragmentation in him, what accounted for this?*

Nirmal was a second generation ex farmer. His father, while retaining nostalgic longing for his native village, never lived the life of a farmer, having come to the city when he was young, and so, he himself had no knowing of what the life of a farmer meant. He was a teacher of Sanskrit, a classic Indian language of great literary–cultural significance but which came to be associated more with narrow forms of religion and priestcraft. Nirmal's parents were simple folks: hard, thrifty and superstitious—but most of all, his father was an ambitious man. *He sent his son to the best convent school and to a prestigious Delhi University college and expected him to become either an engineer or an IAS/IPS—both of them conventional status oriented career choices in Indian society.* While an engineering degree would have allowed an easy access to the modern corporate world with all its attendant glamour, an IAS/IPS job meant enviable power and status. *The parents were orthodox in their cultural–religious ways which was the mainstay of their lifestyle in the traditional setting in which they were living.* However, how the patterned ways of communication of values from the parents to the children determine the sense of authenticity/falseness for the young is a matter of interest here. For Nirmal, it was all a 'natak', implying that *somewhere the translation of customs, traditions and norms by the parents lost out in imparting the vitalizing meanings inherent in them, hence felt as meaningless rituals.* Rather than absorbing the rich secular aesthetic of Sanskrit language, its use was limited for him to religious hymns and verses and seeing it as a driver of one's economic ambition. The restrictive and forceful parenting, in which the mother was eclipsed far more than can be accounted for by the mere pattern of Hindu housewifeliness, was an important catalyst in this generational dynamic. *A rigid, disciplinarian father, status conscious, flaunting his English speaking son in front of his 'lesser' acquaintances, can select a son to justify himself, asking him: What have you accomplished? And what have you done for me?* Nirmal recollected an experience in which his parents were present for a big event hosted by his organisation. He addressed a large, respectable gathering on the issue of environment and active citizenship, following which he sang songs of change. When he enquired from his parents how they liked the event, they replied, 'Good! But you shouldn't sing and jump around on the stage like that. It looks stupid. Also, it would have been so much better had you done the same event back home'. While narrating it, he burst into a vehement bitterness about how they didn't care anything about his satisfaction and pleasure. 'It has always been about their happiness, status, image, pride . . . false pride.' A *depressive detachment from parents* followed for Nirmal when he came to Delhi as was exemplified in his statement:

> I had left their plane. The gap between them and me had widened. I disconnected from them. I wouldn't communicate with them.

During one of the interviews while talking of his relationship with his parents, Nirmal mentioned that after he lost his siblings, his equation with them had changed. I was taken aback on hearing this new piece of information about his life. It took me some time before, I could gather myself and asked him hesitatingly what happened, thinking all the time that it might be too painful for him to speak of death of both his siblings. He replied somewhat vaguely that both of them committed suicides. No one knew what happened to his sister. She seemed happy in her marital home, and one day they got the news. They never found out what went wrong. She had left behind two children. His younger brother was not good in studies. He was studying engineering from a paid institution but not doing well. He was rather notorious and had a girl friend. After speaking this, Nirmal became quiet and I felt disturbed. After some time, he began again:

> *I don't have the energy to actually break away, to make my own choice. I don't want to hurt them.* My equation with them has changed ever since. I have felt my responsibility towards them. I should be there for them, with them in whatever way I can. I make them a few calls now. I visit them twice a year and they come down to Delhi.

Such an intergenerational relationship in which brutal decisiveness of parental judgement led to tortured obediences and resentful feelings created ripe condition for Nirmal to be highly ambivalent about his heritage. *The parental practice of tradition was not felt as naturally persuasive, nor was it experienced as wholesome nutriment to the youthful ideological search of the 'true' values.* This situation arises, especially, in those sectors of society where the cultural institutions of religion and family become heavily ritualised and offer constrictive imageries of superior and inferior, good and bad, masculine and feminine, beautiful and ugly, potent and impotent, free and slave. *The old had to be relinquished to be 'born again': the 'old' was the perspectives intrinsic to the parental traditional lifestyle values and also such parts of one's own self. He could do so because of his physical and psychological separation from his parental set-up.* Living alone in Delhi gave him enough opportunity to start 'living himself'. His younger brother was not so successful. He was the black sheep of the family because he refused the positive goal of working himself up the social ladder by studying well; on the contrary, he followed the negative goal of being intimate with the opposite sex. One may only stretch one's imagination to come close to the utter inner suffocation and dimming of vitality of a young man which would have led him to end his life because it was not his life anyway. *Nirmal's feelings of disgust with the cultural–religious prescriptions stemmed from the fact that they were beaten in him by his parents like many other rules of conduct. At the same time, Sanskrit studying, Maithil Brahmin and Bihari were inalienable parts of his identity. Some of these identities also brought embarrassment to him.* As he stated:

> Studying Sanskrit set me apart from the rest of the crowd. One may be studying any subject; it doesn't raise eyebrows. But the moment others come to know that you are studying Sanskrit, it evokes strange reactions from them. There is a negative surprise.

Hence, there was an urge in him to live down these identity fragments.

Nirmal exemplified the struggle at the frontiers of tradition and modern. The traditional focus of identity privileges interpersonal obligations, familial affiliations over voluntary participation in self-chosen social groups like peers, and rigid role hierarchy in which equality of selves is not achieved. Nirmal's narration was replete with instances when he would bitterly complain about his parents' need to keep him as an 'obedient son', their requirement to retain an image of him as a simple person who didn't even drink tea, their insecurity about him becoming someone else than what they wanted him to become and their ways of pressuring him to do things through emotional appeals rather than rational discussion. *His rebellion was thus a way of breaking loose from these tethers. As he did that, he hurled towards the modern foci of identity which privileges an individualistic, achievement centred stance that allows for carving out a role and space in life for oneself based on attributes and choice rather than on family background or community considerations. At one level, modernity was embraced by him at the plane of lifestyle: conspicuous consumption, technological savviness, eating eggs on Tuesday, wish to choose one's own spouse. One is lesser sure of what had become 'modern' in the inner recesses of his psychic space?* In this regard, only some tentative formulations can be suggested since there was a flux. *He saw himself shifting between modern and traditional values, ideas and lifestyles based on convenience, opportunities, cost-benefit analysis.* He saw his work as a development professional as bearing the stamp of this struggle in his life:

> Activism as a sphere comes out of a life experience kind of thing, than a value based understanding and study. *I have seen caste system. The train of those ill thoughts that my parents have put in my head about caste, class, religion ... If I don't break it, my next generation will have to face similar challenges that I face.* I shouldn't perpetuate the same cycle. *I need to break the cycle and start afresh.* My role as an intermediary is to integrate modern set of values because it means something for my future. I need to break the past in the present so that there is a better future. *So the frustrations of the past are a very very important component and the fear of the future is also important. And also self realized responsibility that you should do something to break the cycle is important.*

In Nirmal's inner world, then ethos of tradition and modernity were co-existent. In his life in city where he felt 'at home', *the ethos of faith was being replaced with ethos of reason; the stance of following the path, living by roles and doing one's duty, was getting substituted for searching and creating the path, living by self-assertion and accepting responsibility voluntarily.* The ethos of closeness, of subordination, of limitations, of replication and of stability had been given way to ethos of loose networks, of interdependency, of aspirations, of change and ambiguities and constant unfolding. *Most importantly, he had embraced the modern ideology of choice and self-determination. He had begun to live and advocate through his work the need to make responsible choices in one's life.*

His work saw him in multiple roles of a teacher imparting value education (notions of freedom, justice, equality), life skills (working in teams, living by one's own initiative, negotiative decision-making), and environmental education (to understand the need of ecological sustainable lifestyle); consultant (training corporates about the need to devise ecological friendly technology); film maker (tracing the journey of waste from source to end and the various stakeholders involved); lobbyist (bargaining with the state machinery on the issues of development); social worker (providing relief, education, etc., to displaced and poor) and singer (singing songs of change). All these roles required him to travel widely, often internationally to meet diverse people and to form alliances with corporate houses, other NGOs, and state departments all of which require the individual to have the ability to be proactive, to respond to emerging realities, not only in actions but also in attitudes and perspectives. *His conscious stances of appreciation of diversity of cultures and secular considerations, commitment to active citizenship and political participation spelt a modern attitude towards social relations.* These positions are underlined by tolerance for differences and intersubjectivity about sharing in one another's fate and responsibility for another's well-being. The political ideology behind it is 'dignity of man': for modernity demands a baseline similarity, in spite of differences that exist among people, so that people can live with dignity and can realistically avail of opportunities to better their conditions of existence.

While in him, one noticed a fight to free himself from the clutches of religious-caste orthodoxy, but one did not find much of a radical rethinking of the institutions of religion/caste/class. To take an example—During a phase of research with him, the topical issue was extension of reservations to OBCs. I tried gauging his attitudes towards the issue but he admitted to not have developed any stance on it. Because of lack of thorough going reflections on many such ideological positions and ideas from Nirmal, he sometimes appeared to be glib and superficial in his articulations, making me feel that he had not engaged with them enough. *There was also an unarticulated sense of how he was continuing the internalised parental way of living. As an inner core, it is most resistant to change. Its hold can be somewhat loosened away from the parental location but not dissolved completely. How were the rigidities of tradition continuing in him? In what forms?—were questions that remained with me.*

His slow admission that he did not want to attend to the personal so much; his almost compulsive concentration on work which is known to often balance the lack of inner direction; his too quick reaction 'I can't be put into any category' whenever any attempt was made during the meetings to deepen a role, value, perspective; his inability to point to factors that might have contributed to the successes in his endeavours because of him not having the time to think about it and almost half wishing that a failure would stop him in his tracks; seeing energy to be the centre of his work rather than issues and debates, led one to sense a dispersion, restlessness in him. *One wondered whether he would be able to see what had he disestablished and what had he established for himself, until a relaxation came into his life vis-à-vis his relationship with parents and their tradition?*

Nirmal's psychological dislocations baffled me. He was a typical participant of my research whose inner world was home to diverse competing identity fragments. Hence, attempts to decipher continuities and directions across his life and work were fraught with difficulties. His experience of dislocations encapsulated in the statement 'I have been exposed to a variety of things, places, events, opinions in the past 10 years' had led him to take 'isms from all over and then try to constitute one's own ism'. *His own 'ism' was vaguely formulated concern of freedom and democracy—enhancing it for all. Of course, one could spot a continuation of his own struggle for choice and self-determination in this formulation.* His lasting environmental concerns about the 'decay' of the river, the 'journey of the waste' from homes to landfills and the struggle of livelihood of ragpickers who 'make a living out of the disposed' hinted towards some *preoccupation with what was dying and desecrated. It probably had some emotional resonance with deathlike feelings of disconnection, of disintegration and stasis, having experienced death from close quarters in his life. His fears about becoming a waste, that is, being unvalued and unloved, dread of being stymied and of falling through his own splits, were few of the discerned inner realities that could be sustaining his drifts as well his manoeuvrability through ideas, values and roles.* Probably, for Nirmal, who had *loosened ties with native family and culture and was creating a new home with new associates*, the self-process would be less a matter of steady and predictable direction and more a manner of flexible adaptation with a talent for coping with widely divergent circumstances.

It is also important to note the *role of ideology of market in the identity dynamic* of this kind. For after all, it was economic pragmatism where son and father could be of one mind. *He joined his father in discarding a slogan shouting social worker identity which would reduce him into nothing but a 'Khaadi and Hawaii Chappal'—identity symbols rooted in mega philosophy of social change, demanding of personal austerity as well as conveying a radical promise of do or die.* In his MSW course, Nirmal wrote a dissertation exploring the phenomena of co-option of social movements by the state and market in the liberalised–globalised world. It helped him *define his own 'marketable' space* within the scenario of sociopolitical action in a more guilt-free way. He acknowledged his work to be *more status quoist than resistive, more mainstream than activistic*. The organisation he had built lent him the much coveted identity of 'someone worthwhile' and pulled him out of the dangers of being a waste. Through it, *he enjoyed social recognition and economic status and fulfilled his own as well as his parents' aspirations, albeit in his own way.*

Debashri

Debashri was a 27-year-old feminist activist working in a feminist NGO. I got to know about her through a research participant. I contacted her, and she responded enthusiastically to the idea of the research. The time around which we started meeting, she was going through problems in her newly married life. In our interactions where both her personal and professional lives were explored, she was eager to share about her personal self wherein she was experiencing her frailties and conflicts. However, she presented a confident and competent side while discussing work and its challenges. Debashri was a well-built, tall woman with hair cropped short. In the photographs of her field work in villages, she seemed completely at ease with the surroundings. She would be nonchalant about late-night travel, living alone in the areas. Her speech, both in English and Hindi, while sophisticated, had the power and roughness required for hard-hitting advocacy in her work arena. Over the five meetings, it was noticed that she had a huge need to make sense of herself and her life experiences. She would often use concepts from theories to explain her own states. She remembered the thrill of coming across *existential philosophy* because it acknowledged choice and loneliness inherent in existence; it spoke of the responsibility that came with choice and the fear of freedom. She faulted Maslow for putting *self-actualization* at the highest level of need because according to her, each individual from the very beginning wanted to become the best that he or she wanted to be. *Feminism*, which she regarded to be her 'religion' and 'political framework', also aided her in positioning herself in the world as a woman, and she used it as a scaffold to understand her needs for choice and freedom. Throughout her conversations, the *ideal of choice* stood out as the major defining principle of her life. *She sought to extend it in her personal life and as well in her work by creating opportunities for it in the lives of lesser-privileged women.*

P. Bansal, *Youth in Contemporary India: Images of Identity and Social Change*,
DOI 10.1007/978-81-322-0715-3_12, © Springer India 2013

I

A part of research explorations with Debashri were directed towards understanding her growth contexts that shaped her convictions in the ideology of self-determination and free will which was at the base of her doing and suffering.

In the first interview, Debashri began her narration of self by stating that she was very very unhappy in school:

> I don't really know why? I felt that at home I had the freedom to do what I want and be what I want. In school, I always felt misunderstood. I was a loner, didn't have many friends. An achiever of sorts, was an all rounder. *But it was always the home which was my comfort zone.* There were lots of transitions in my early life. I was born in Calcutta. Till about I was three years old, we were living with my paternal grandparents in Calcutta. From that joint family living, we shifted to Nigeria. Lived there for 5–6 years and then came back to Calcutta and then to Delhi when I was about 11 years old. I was very close to my paternal grandparents. Till my grandfather died in 2001, I referred to Calcutta as home without realizing that I have spent more years in Delhi. It was like that we may be anywhere but that's home . . . where we have to go back. Looking back, my grandparents were great playmates in my childhood. I used to teach my poor old grandmother Hindi . . . [laughs merrily]. I used to give her big red marks like teachers do . . . very harsh! I was the youngest and extremely pampered. I was always told that you are good and whatever you do is good. Whatever I would write would get framed and put up in the grandparents' living room. It was an open space. All my cousins . . . even the 2nd–3rd cousins would come, eat, live . . . *I have a very closely knit family.*
>
> So moving to Nigeria was a major transition for us. [Speaks in a mildly contemptuous tone] My father just decided to leave his job and said that I want to go for an adventure! He joined a friend's business in Nigeria. He said that we will live there for a few years, see the world and then come back! People thought he was crazy. They told him that leave the family behind. But he was like 'Arre! Kids are young. And my family goes wherever I go.' So for those 5–6 years, we traveled a lot in Africa, Western Europe. He loved driving and travelling, so we would rent a car and go visiting countries. *By the time I was 10 years old, I had been to 11 different countries, seen different cultures. It was also difficult for me. [Pauses] Because we were going from here to there, there to there. New faces, new people, new circumstances. At that point of time, when I was 6–7 years old, I had started bed wetting. For some reason one insecurity has been with me always that I have been left alone. And my way of countering it is to project the opposite of what is inside . . . I just say 'Hell with everyone. I'll live alone.' Because I can't expose this insecurity of mine to everyone, I find a lot of comfort with people who know me well. So I live around people who understand me for what I am all about or at least tolerate me for what I am. That's something that makes it difficult for me to have closer relationality with a lot of people.* That is what I felt initially in my relationship with Siraj [her husband]. He was the first person, other than my family, I was close to. Never had a serious intimate relationship before that. In school also, I always felt that no one understands me. I was an achiever in academics, extracurricular activities. I had these all round interests. But I always felt alone, at least in the friends' sphere. *It was more just my family which was my support system and mainly my sister. My parents, of course, and mainly my sister.* Besides, I also feel low in terms of self confidence. I can't forget this incident when in a new school in Delhi, in a Maths class . . . I always thought that I was very good in studies. In that class, we were supposed to write the predecessors and successors for the numbers written on the board. But I couldn't understand the question because I was not used to reading numbers with commas. I spent the whole maths period feeling so worried. I was like shit! I will never be able to get ahead in life. At the end of the class I went and asked the teacher and she very lovingly

explained it to me. Then I felt that Oh! It was so simple [smiles]. This memory stays with me. I still think that I am not particularly smart. But I am very hardworking and a quick learner. I don't think that I have any particular talents. I think I am rather stupid. My G.K. is poor. I am just hardworking.

In this self-effacing moment, I saw her face full of sadness and her eyes looking lost and unfocussed. After a brief silence, I said 'You sing well, I remember'. Her face broke into a smile, and she drawled that it was an inherited talent from her grandmother. I asked her further:

- *Your family has been a big influence on you ...*
Yes. Very big. *I am a lot like my father. Even to look at!* People say only the moustache is missing, otherwise you are Rajat only. Siraj says that I have that also ... [smiles] *My mother says that he survived, in spite of his thick head, because he was a man. You will not because you are a woman. He took life very seriously and lived by his principles.* He would just refuse to go to someone's place because according to him, he was a cheat! My mother would be like, how does it matter? But he wouldn't go. He believed in Gandhigiri ... born on 2nd October that he was. Just live by your values, don't bother about what the others are saying and continue doing what you believe in. *This is a very salient principle for me ... integrity.*
My parents never stopped us from doing what we wanted to do. My father wanted to study law but because of his parents he had to study engineering. *So he always believed that people should not make choices by force. He wanted me to become an IAS/IFS officer. He himself also always enjoyed advocacy, policy formulation kind of work.* But when it actually came to taking decisions, there was never any pressure from him. *I made my own independent choices for my career and all other things of my life.* It felt as if life is in my hand. It's just a way of life that I have developed ... to have life in my hands. Though, I have also begun to recognize that it's not always the case ... and I am not very comfortable with it.
My mother was also conscious of the fact that we don't lose out on anything. *Both of them said that you do whatever you want to do: dance, sing, theatre, study.* Don't bother about household. That can be managed. One very good thing about my parents was they spoke in one voice. We, as children, never had to face any conflict in terms of what is right and what is wrong. *They both fiercely believed in being independent, being self reliant, and stand on your feet. These were things which were taught to us from the time we were in crib. This is repeated many times in our house.* My father bought a house of his own in Calcutta, even though, he was living with his parents. Similarly my mother also says that just because we bought a house in our lifetime doesn't mean that you would stay with us only. You make your own. When we are not there, it's yours only. And that's one thing I admire about Siraj also. He is a completely *self made* man. Having lost his father rather early, he has struggled financially, emotionally. But it's not easy. *Let me tell you this. I have not liked it always ... to be independent and all. Why should I be independent? I also want support. I am constantly battling the urge to have attachments and being independent.* Even as a feminist activist, you say these nice things about being independent but you also want certain relationships, emotional attachments ... [After a brief silence] When I was having problems with Siraj, my father told me that you have to be independent, stand on your own two feet and do what you want. Don't think about 10 other people. He would accompany me while I was looking out for a PG/rented accommodation after I decided to move out of Siraj's house.
- *You would have liked to live with your parents after moving out of Siraj's house?*
Yes. I was feeling very lost. But I did rent out a flat close to my office. I remember, even when I got married, and had to shift to Siraj's house in Delhi, I was very anxious. Too anxious. This whole thing that now that is going to be my home was just too anxiety

> provoking for me. And it's strange because, I have lived in the interiors of Gujarat, Rajasthan, and now I go and live in rural areas of U.P. – all as a part of my work. *I am independent in that sense but I want care . . . I want to be taken care of.*

In Debashri's internal world, her family loomed large. *Her deep psychological needs were of security and stability which were fulfilled at home, within the warm comforting environment of the family.* She had few trusting friendships outside the family. Her fantastical 'Planet O' inhabited by her trusted people was the outcome of the pact 'I love you and you love me and the rest of the world be damned'. This provided a highly gratifying source of narcissistic supplies of emotional support for her and obviated the need to seek other relationships and experiences.

Her relationship with her father was particularly vital to her self-identity. As a younger son, his upbringing had been a 'crowded one'. Debashri recounted, 'My father used to say that his mother was the mother of the entire family. It was never like she was his mother only. Sometimes I feel, he resented it'. In comparison to his elder brother who was extroverted and flashy, her father was quiet and reserved and worked behind the scene. When his brother got married and moved out of the parents' house, he was compelled to forgo his admission in a law college in order to be near his parents. The regret of not being able to pursue law degree which was his 'dream' stayed with him. While he pursued engineering and lived with his parents in deference with their wishes, *he harboured a core of almost 'militant' individuality* which was reflected in his 'adventurous' decision to leave his job and country for a new, untried work assignment, in buying a house for himself to underline his separateness from the parental set-up, in his self-righteous ways of living life. Probably frustrated in his own emotional needs because of the felt lack of exclusive mothering, her father had developed defensive manoeuvres by which he suppressed his needs for nurturance and *formulated the ideal of 'being on one's own'*. It was used by him to chart his own independence from parents (while at the same time willingly fulfilling his responsibilities towards them) and society in general. *In Debashri's accounts of him, one also found instances of his emotional/relational self.* He was someone who easily cried while watching a movie, something which was always joked about as sissy behaviour by his wife. When her mother went for theatre and dance performances, he would baby sit them. He and her mother had created an open house in which her cousins and friends used to often drop in. *Though Debashri experienced both sides of her father's personality, she had grown up by identifying with, ever more completely, the stubborn selfhood of her father.* This was aided by the repeated talk in the family by both the parents about the importance of being independent and self-reliant. The father's definition of independent selfhood was perhaps not his most adjusted attribute, but it was overvalued by her and identified with strongly because of the immediate way it affected her, in reality and/or fantasy.

The father's voice reverberated through Debashri. *She would make sense of her life in conjunction with the life of her father, often drawing parallels with him and making his attitudes the basis of her own ideals and goals.* She had an idealising relationship with her father. The internalised idealised image of father as a self-directed man made her feel powerful and in control. Helpful in the formation of such a father image was her mother's attitude towards her husband which was that of basic respect and concurrence. In her own words, *'My father's ideas and attitudes were implemented by my mother'*. Her mother also believed in and had created spaces for her own individualised functioning, but she did it within the fold of her family, by continuously negotiating with the pressures of relationships and tasks of the household. While going along with her husband's ways of living life, she felt, as a wife, the heat of and recognised, as a mother, the dangers of too much of wilfulness and stubbornness. *The mother who appeared as an earthy, practical and fluid person was sidetracked in her own being.* A tight system of ideas developed around her understanding of an 'individual' as a 'lone frontiersman' who is agentic, self-governing and emotionally independent. This was in conflict with her own desire to be taken care of. *She said 'I have been taught and have internalised that you don't need anybody to live a happy life. But my own needs are that I want people around me to live a happy life. That's the basic contradiction'. Because of too literal identification with the paternal dictum, she was struggling to embrace all the diversities and dissonances of the most private and public aspects of existence, her needs and stances.* Since her own emotional needs of relationality were of dependence (to be taken care of) rather than mature interdependence (to be responsive to each other's needs), she viewed similar needs of care of others fearfully, lest they became burdensome and interfered with her autonomous existence. An absolute boundary separated individuality and relationality for her, both seen as mutually exclusive to each other, not to be admitted within each other's ambit.

Within the familial milieu, she experienced a lot of freedom to be and do what she wanted. Never up against any boundaries, she had felt self driven and autonomous. However, it was a freedom that had been granted to her and not negotiated with her. She never had conflicts on matters of lifestyle and values with her parents. *The world which had been prestructured for her, in which limits had not been tested to check for their pliability, had given rise to an identity which was self-insistent, which wanted to be in control and felt any blockage of self-directed activity as acute frustration.* She admitted to her own rigidity and inflexibility by stating that making decisions of her life on her own was most important for her. She shared, 'As long as no one is forcing me to take certain paths, making choices ... as long as I am the one taking the call, it works for me. I should be able to prioritize on the basis of my needs'. For her, such sense of freedom was critically important. *She returned again and again to the idea of her lifestyle as the most valued part of her life, the feeling that she was free to do what she wanted when she wanted to.* Talking of her experience of living with her mother-in-law for 8 months after marriage, Debashri said 'It was very suffocating for me. Just very very suffocating. Then I took a call and I told Siraj that this is what is happening to me and I am not able to live my normal life. I am not able to work, not able to enjoy. Things that I like doing, I am not able to do that staying here. I need my own space'. Spoken in a childishly insistent voice, one heard in this complaint her inability to create her space within the ambit of the marital home. She admitted to have tried but not too hard.

Her situation in her marital home was complicated by a domineering and controlling widowed mother-in-law. After the husband's demise, she had to struggle to maintain the standard of living and had hoped that the son's earnings would help restore their previous lifestyle. According to Debashri, her husband was constantly belittled by his mother for choosing an NGO job which did not pay too well and was made to feel guilty about not taking care of her well enough. He was not able to satisfy his mother, and this kept him perpetually in a state of tension and guilt. He expected Debashri to understand his predicament and help him deal with it. For her, the solution was that the couple should live independently and he could continue to take care of his mother while living separately. This was perceived by him as an act of abandonment of his mother by him and thus not an emotionally viable solution. Debashri, on the other hand, found it difficult to adjust in an environment where there were restrictions on her movements and activities, the familial rituals and norms were more conservative than her own modern upbringing and in which the dynamics between the son and the mother were far from congenial and resolved. The deadlock in the relationship continued for about a year during which Debashri shifted briefly in her parents' house and later in her own rented accommodation. Her husband would often pay her visits and come to live with her for short periods of time. They attempted to forge a sense of togetherness while maintaining their separate spaces but finally decided to opt for divorce.

II

Professionally, Debashri had been adventurous and competent. She had been working with a feminist grassroots organisation in the field of adult women education. Below are excerpts of interviews explicating her *work-related interests and motivations, guiding principles and goals.*

- *How did you enter the field of social work and feminist politics, in particular?*
  I think I have been *much influenced by the women in my life*. They have been strong women. *They are strong headed, opinionated, confident women: my mother, my sister, many of my cousins, my aunt. All of them carved out a space for themselves, wherever they were, in their family, at workplace.* Even my dadi [paternal grandmother] and her mother were very interesting women. My dadi's mother was one of those culturally accomplished upper caste/class woman. She was also very energetic, in the sense of keeping the family together. My grandmother was the eldest child and liked to be powerful like her mother. She could really get her way ... [smiles fondly]. My mother got married when she was only 19. She was in the second year of her graduation. My father and my grandfather were very interested that she finishes her education. But she didn't want to. She was like that now I am married. I'll sit at home and do my own thing. And she did that. *She was always in control of her mobility. In Calcutta, she was a part of these theatre and dance groups.* So there have been times when she was gone for the practices and my father would baby sit us. Even though she didn't work, she had control over the finances. *Her biggest thing is her attitude towards life.* She is unfazed by the difficulties. She maintains her cool and is so spirited and can make the best of every situation. *She is my role model when it comes to embracing newness. I am not good with it.* But she has an appetite for it. There are times when she tells me that I should give up my set ways and be more adjusting and I tell her that I can't be like her. Even at 58 years, she is full of life. She wants to visit new places, check out new

cuisines, new trends. *She has truly been a pillar of strength for all 3 of us in the family.* My sister is also a big influence on me. She is five and a half years older to me. *She is very emotionally stable and strong person, very different from me. She also works in the social sector and I got introduced to this kind of work via her.*

When I was in college, I was exploring this sector through college society. *There was certainly a value base that was guiding me that I wanted to do something that will make a difference to people's life.* That was pretty much clear to me. So while in college, I was working with children with autism, went for rural camps. The first time, I began to take active interest in feminism was in Political Science class. That was the first time, I heard of governance and power hierarchy in family. Before that governance was something happening in Panchayati system and Parliament. *To know that family is a site of governance too was a revelation. Then I realized that my own home is rather gender defined ... as in terms of gender based division of labour and I excitedly told my mother that.* She just laughed and said that it's nice that you are learning all of this but life is to be lived practically. There are a lot of subtleties. I understand that now when I go to field.

I did my Bachelor's dissertation on self image of rural women subjected to violence. After my graduation, I worked on a research project with a NGO for a year. It was a NGO working on the issue of empowerment of women from various dimensions – economic, social, cultural, psychological.... I looked at the *issue of self esteem and how women are building their own confidence through decision making, mobility, financial independence through personal and pooled savings, having an account in the bank, being a part of women's self help group.* It was a good exposure. I got to do my data collection in Rajasthan and Jharkhand. But by the end of the day, I was questioning the work of the organization, especially its policy of micro credit. You can't build women solidarity around money. You have to touch the main issues of exploitation and subjugation which is the lot of the women. So around that time, I began thinking what about land for women? All the documents are still in man's name. Do we bother who is actually doing the farming? After a year's break from studies, I wanted to get back to studies. *I had applied for management courses as well. But then just decided to not take the exams. I joined MSW instead.* I chose to go to a feminist organization in the tribal belt of East Gujarat for my internship and also later for my final placement. During this time my politics was becoming more and more clear. *I was getting convinced that unless you address the issue of power, there is little that you are doing. While my readings about the history of women's movement in India and feminist frameworks were convincing me of the value of more politicized work, they were also creating a need in me to see the reality at grassroots level. My question was always, what's happening with the rural poor?* Because if I, with urban upper middle class educated background with certain privileges, get so distressed when I experience any kind of violation, then what is the fate of someone who doesn't even have the backing of education, class, caste etc. *I thought there was a huge divide and I didn't want to limit myself to the urban reality.* That's why I chose to work with this organization in Gujarat because it worked with rural, poor, Dalit women with a feminist orientation. Even when I was moving jobs and looking for a Delhi based organization, I knew that I wanted to be in a feminist space. Also, I was very keen on continuing with field based work. So my current job also fulfils the three categories of poverty, rural, women.

- *So feminism convinces you?*

Yes absolutely. *The feminist lens helps to look at the structural imbalances in power. Class, caste, religion, gender – all are structures of power. And a person is placed in these structures ... a woman is placed in all these structures.* The analysis of power is also very interesting in feminism. I believe that power is a limited resource. *To empower someone, you have to give some of your own power. A mother-in-law has to give some of her own power to the daughter-in-law to empower her.* Both the organizations that

I have worked with have been grounded in the realities of women's lives. Not like one kind of generalization that – All women in burqa are oppressed! We understand that wearing burqa is a different cultural expression that helps many women access many spaces which would be otherwise out of their reach, helps their mobility. Not to say that burqa is desirable but if she is able to strategically use it to do her own thing in a man's world, then I think she is being empowered. So like these issues, we discuss a lot from various perspectives. One keeps going round and round. There is no one final answer. You keep thinking and formulating your stand. That is the challenge of a work like this. *Besides, the work culture of a feminist organization is great. There is so much of reflection, personal sharing, self critique, learning laterally and in an organization like ours which is field based, trying to negotiate continuously with the ground realities and theoretical frameworks.* There aren't much of hierarchies. I don't think I will have this kind of freedom anywhere else.

- *What has been the nature of your work like?*
  The first organization that I was working with in Gujarat was engaged in *mobilizing the women through self help groups and other livelihood based interventions.* After bringing the women together, train them for leadership, strengthen their political identity of being tribal women, tribal sangathan [organization] so that they could act as a pressure group in the region to demand their rights. It is one of its kind organization because they had a *bottom up approach to issues.* The founders lived in the villages, understood life there, the issues and concerns – political, economic, and cultural and then began work. My work was to do gender training with the tribal women, help them reflect on their experiences as tribal women, write proposals. Another large part of my work was to link up with the larger Right to Food network. In the current job, I am primarily involved in training the women's leadership, grassroot workers and teachers.
- *Can you elaborate what are the elements of gender training?*
  Basically, you first begin with experience – *when did you first realize that you are woman? A tribal? Then go on to understanding power.* We have role plays where we ask them to describe a common household situation where there is husband, wife and mother-in-law. Similarly in other contexts with Sarpanch, Block Development Officer etc. Then through these role plays help them *understand the structures of power which govern their lives: caste, class, religion, age, gender . . . what is the structural nature of their oppression.*

  The aim is to *begin a process of questioning: Who is setting the agenda? Who is controlling power in the family, in the panchayat, at the block level and beyond?* Help them recognize the structural imbalance, which in itself is such a huge struggle. To make them understand that it is not ok for someone to hit you. And how patriarchy structures gender relations in such a way that while men beat their wives, wives cannot. It takes much time, sometimes years and of course, a lot of resistance. A large part of gender training is also about breaking gender stereotypes. A woman is beaten up in a village and not in a town – trying to bust such myths. Also, how patriarchy came about? The role of other structures of power like religion and caste and their role in strengthening patriarchy. It's also very important now-a-days to speak of media. We do this kind of *awareness generation through literacy and educational camps with women.* We use educational material to get these kinds of political messages across. We believe that *literacy and education are rights that women and socio-economically disadvantaged communities have been denied.* For literacy to indeed be empowering and transformative the education process should connect with women's lived realities. For this, we embed our literacy work within the contexts and lives of the women we work with, and by exploring ways in which literacy can help women confront the challenges they face in their daily lives. Hence, the *educational process and material also engages with Right to Information, Right to Work, Right to Food, Right to Health, and Right to Violence Free Society.* The actual interventions include basic things like holding a pen, reading, writing, basic maths, asking questions in Panchayat, how to demand rights in the family, at the block/district level. How to say this is what I want and then use a legal way or a jati panchayat or some other cultural forum to get your rights. Another very important intervention is to *help the women become a part of larger movement and collective.* Going to nearby districts, visiting other organizations and collectives, interacting with new people – helps in broadening horizons. Come face to face with diversity and also uniformity. That helps to understand the structural nature of reality.

- *What do you mean by empowerment?*

For me empowerment is not a goal. It's a journey. *It's a journey of first understanding about your condition. How are you placed in the world and why are you placed like that? Recognizing the structural inequalities and power imbalances. Once you do that, then you begin your fight for entitlements, your rights. To have more control over your life, your resources, your sexuality, mobility, finances, property.* To be able to make decisions, have agency in life, to be able to make some choices, if not all. *Empowerment is about reclaiming self dignity and upholding it. From an organizational point of view, it is important to respect the individual.* That people can identify their own needs and fulfill them. You cannot force people to fight for displacement. If a person says that I want to take Rs. 20,000/- and go and live in the house which is being given to me as a resettlement scheme, then you have to respect that. There then your fight is at the larger level – What is the policy of resettlement and rehabilitation? Is it serving the needs of the displaced? What is the notion of such development? Who are the beneficiaries of it? Are there alternatives to it? Another dynamic which I came face to face during my work in Gujarat was the conflicts between the local organization and the mother organization. The process of local sangathan to wean from the mother organization is a painful process because many choices the former may make which are not what the original leadership wants. The original leadership has to have a lot of vision and maturity to deal with these tensions. Like the leader of sangathan in Gujarat wanted to contest Zila Parishad elections which didn't go well with the organizational leadership. They also develop their aspirations which you can't deny them. There are many of these subtleties.

For need of empowerment to be recognized, you have to recognize the *value of equity.* Equity is recognizing that people are not equal and you have to have special conditions for people to be equal. *Empowerment is about creating enabling conditions for people to become equal.* The politics has to be right for any real empowerment to take place. For any kind of sustainable solution, we have to *ensure the participation of the poor and create spaces of negotiation and dialogue between organized poor communities and state.* Also spreading awareness in the larger civil society and with other NGOs is also very important. It's not only the state but the larger civil society which also need to be educated.

- *How as an urban educated feminist activist do you negotiate your relationship with the poor rural women? Aren't the differences in the context a limiting factor?*

That's an interesting question. [Reflects] For one, *if I look closely at my own life and of women around me, we also face similar problems.* Like domestic violence is almost as much in cities as in rural India. Similarly issues like mobility in night, threat of bodily harm, consensual sex are as much relevant to us as they are to women in the villages. So there are many shared experiences. In fact, we do talk about our urban struggles as women during gender trainings. I mean, how many of us are able to negotiate condom use in our sexual relationships? I might think that I am liberated. But when you look closely, you realize how in subtle and obvious ways you are being affected by the same social and psychological forces. Then you pitch your struggle for relative autonomy, freedom. *We don't go there as experts, in that sense. I see myself as placed in similar power structures as them. Feminism helps me to do that.* It's just that because we have something going for us, whether it is education, financial independence that we can make spaces for ourselves. We have opportunities. *So the larger framework of equity and justice takes over and justifies the work that we do.... Besides, there have been moments when I have felt such a weakling in front of these strong, resilient dalit women. They have amazing strength in spite of the adverse circumstances that they live in. They also create opportunities to laugh, play and have fun.*

> Listening to their tales of oppression and coping with it is an enormous amount of learning for us as well. That is why I was personally so keen to have a work profile where I am in touch with field realities. *Just going to villages, living with people, chatting with them gives a lot of strength to any movement.* You realize that there are dualities. I am wearing my Hush puppies and going to Bundelkhand and working. There is a divide that cannot be overlooked. *But as long as you are self reflective, open in your stance, democratic in your working and political in your understanding of the reality, your work as a social change agent is worthwhile. Being a part of the larger women's movement also helps.* You see what are the other issues besides the ones that you are working on. The openness to discuss the challenges of the work like this in the organizational space is also a great way of learning how to make these continuous negotiations. I have been inspired by strong women leaders I have worked with. Some of them are urban, many of them are actually rural . . . these sangathan leaders. They are quick in their decisions and their mobilization ability is marvelous. Coming from the same background as others, their courage to just break away is awe inspiring.

It appeared that the feminist world view allowed Debashri to feel strong and make sense of her strivings for independence. According to her, *'Feminist is not only who I am but also who I choose to be'*. It explained and fuelled her need to be *self-governing, choosing and in control.* These personal values were also inherent in the empowering educational work that she was doing with the poor, rural women. The basic aim of such work was to *protect and enhance women's autonomy within the internal logic of a given system, use culturally situated approaches to help women negotiate and bargain within the constraints of different patriarchal arrangements.* A democratic and inclusive approach was adopted for such work. The *solidarity of conviction about the feminist ideas and ideals shared in conversations and actions with other like-minded women* provided her the invigorating affiliations—sisterhood—in productive and political life.

Individualism and equalitarianism inherent in the 'rights' strain of feminism are important ideals to be striven for, especially, in contexts where women have been oppressively tied down with the domestic/procreative tasks and denied the equivalence of individuality and citizenship. The 'relational' discourse in the feminist framework has attempted to study the feminine identity and define it in its own right. This discourse reflects without apology the potentialities and needs of the feminine psyche shaped by her somatic existence as well as social position. From this lens, true emancipation for women lies not in equalling the model of 'self-made' granted by the self-made man but in being uniquely creative just when it has become quite clear that she can match man's performance and competence in most spheres of achievement. This kind of feminist politics identifies the uniquely feminine potentialities of relating, receptivity and replenishing. *Debashri could align herself with the 'rights' framework more than with the 'relational' framework. However, within the chosen ideological agenda, she was making use of the psychological resources of love and support received at her home to listen, empower, enable and strengthen the disadvantaged women in their life struggles. She was making connections with their psychosocial difficulties through the emotional insecurities and vulnerabilities that were a part of her otherwise competent self-image. It is instructive to note that she began her journey of work with disadvantaged women through research explorations of their self-image, self-esteem, confidence level and decision-making power—concerns that were as much political as were personal for her.*

If the importance of feminist movement can be seen as collective elaboration of the struggles of women forging their identities amidst the *mutual complementation and contradictions of freedom and responsibility, agency and care*, then for women like Debashri, the challenge is *how to make decisions as individuals that would render their lives most continuous and meaningful as carers, workers and citizens?* Also as a feminist, *how to enable all women to make use of the technologically and politically given opportunities to act responsively towards self and others and have an ethic of individuality which is inclusive of relationality in personal and public life?* Debashri had been able to make her autonomous decisions in the areas of production and politics but couldn't sustain (for which the husband's anxieties were equally responsible) the mutuality in affiliations of love and procreation needed for the identities to fit sufficiently to make a pair out of two persons. However, through her work which required her to get into 'many grey areas of life' and her marital problems because of which she was seeking counselling and 'learning to become more flexible and open', *she was struggling to move beyond her psychological need for totalistic image of autonomy as self-contained individual which brooked no further choice towards wholesome notion of autonomy as inclusive of relationality which permits greater tolerance of tension and alternation.*

Sujata

'I am stumped whenever someone asks me what am I doing', said Sujata in a mortified tone. A 27-year-old, frail Sujata was a lawyer by training and was working in the field of human rights' activism. In our two interactions, she shared her past history and her present scatter, alternating between doubts and clarity, idealism and practicality, hurt and humiliation and healing. Her confusions were stemming from not knowing 'where she was going' both in work as well as in her relationships. *She was simultaneously beset with value conflicts over her work, parental pressures to marry and uncertainty about a love relationship.*

Her growing up years were marked by *powerful experiences of feeling small, unregarded and unrecognised at home as well as with peers.* She began by saying that she could now talk about that phase with a lot more detachment, but it still hurts. Unsure of what it was, she spoke hesitatingly about how in a new school girls in her class would suddenly stop talking with her and would disregard her completely. Another friend ridiculed her failure to get into medicine and her subsequent decision to get into law. These memories also brought forth memories of *being treated inferior to her brother* by the maternal grandmother and parents. As the eldest male child, he was considered smarter than her, and his achievements were spoken of in glowing terms. He also was critical of her abilities, once telling her that she would not be able to even pass her 10th class which made her feel extremely anxious. All of this made her diffident, someone who would not open her mouth in the presence of people, not knowing whether she was right in what she was saying and whether she was being understood. At home, she perceived *her father to be a 'conservative dirty Brahmin middle-class male'*, a tyrant, very ritualistic and a blind follower of his parents. He would punish his children by not allowing them to enter the house if they didn't adhere to the deadline to be back home by 6.30 in the evening. For a couple of hours they would just stand out, and only after her mother would plead with him and promise on their behalf that they would not repeat the mistake again were they allowed in. He insisted on her wearing a bindi and lehenga (traditional South Indian attire for young, unmarried girls) as markers of decency and was furious at his daughter-in-law's behaviour of calling her husband (his son) by name. She saw her *mother as dependent on her husband,*

P. Bansal, *Youth in Contemporary India: Images of Identity and Social Change*,
DOI 10.1007/978-81-322-0715-3_13,

but at the same time someone who was much less ritualistic and open minded than her father. She could negotiate her way in the household matters 'making things more relaxed for us, children'. Her mother was a well-educated woman who left her home in her youth to take up a teaching assignment in a different city much against the wishes of her parents. She was also the source of emotional support and strength for her daughter, an ally against patriarchal discrimination.

Sujata's parents had begun to mount pressure on her to consider marriage, but she had been evading going back home to meet the prospective matches. When she talked about her reasons for the same, one sensed a *mix of reactive rebelliousness predicated on fears of being crushed in a role as well as ideology-backed attempts to question the gendered norms of marriage.* She spoke:

> I think I have this huge mental block in my mind about rituals. *I don't consider myself to be one of those who would subscribe to the common notions of what is done and not done.* Like giving the guest tikka, putting a flower in your hair. All of these customs don't come naturally to me. Or if it is a festival, you have to wear a sari and participate in a pooja. May be, I am sounding too stupid, completely stupid in taking up these things too seriously. But what I am saying is that these things don't make any sense to me. And my fear is that once I'll get married, this is what will ensue because the people that I meet are the religious, conservative lot. When I look at my father, I get stunned. He says things like cooking come naturally to women. I don't understand how he can say such things! And I wouldn't be able to handle it. So I am protecting myself. [This fear was linked with her depressive breakdown when she felt herself to be very inadequate in a job and could not find a space for free functioning because of an over controlling supervisor] My mother has also been an influence on me. She has got a very different take on marriage after 30 years. She says that you need a man in the home to change the bulb, and I find it very funny. But I know that she is worried. She asks me, what will you do? You will be lonely.... *But it's also like if you are asking me to do this, I am not going to, how much ever you may want. I am not going to subscribe to your views of living life. I am an adult and I can take my own decisions.* I am not saying that you are wrong. But what I am saying is that there are lots of options in the world, and I should be able to choose the ones that appeal to me. *The other thing is that I am a certain sort. A lot of things that I do are something I don't talk to my parents about. They don't know that I smoke or that I have a sexual life. They know that I drink.* I don't want to shock them. They will not understand or probably they will ... I don't know. But I can't be hiding these things and getting into relationship. I don't know whether I will be marrying this guy I am seeing. We have not explored that. [Silence] *Besides, the whole thing is also very patriarchal. This whole thing of women are expected to do certain things and be a certain way is very patriarchal. For me it's also very personal. It's very difficult to fight it at home but that's where it's most visible.* I can't take it lightly. Probably people don't take these things so seriously. Once you are married, these issues don't matter. I don't know ... Sometimes I think, am I sort of ... am I pretending to be somebody I am not? Then I think it can't be. *But that confusion is there—where are you in terms of your politics? Where do you lie? Are you really the radical or are you actually the conservative? I don't know but I hope not. Because if that's so then I will get to know in a few years' time.*

As I listened to Sujata, I felt that she was struggling to establish her separate identity as an 'adult'. She would repeatedly assert that *she was an adult which according to her meant being independent, living by one self and having the freedom to make decisions about one's lifestyle and 'what is right and wrong'. Battles of autonomy were being fought by her on the identity defining issues ranging from personal dressing and grooming (she had got her hair cut short which she knew would create furore in the house) to observances of religious practices, sexuality-related attitudes, performance of gender role and selection of marital partner*. By choosing to live away from home, Sujata was escaping the oppressive environment at home and rebuilding a sense of worthwhile and autonomous existence. In her words:

> When I left India [for higher education], I had made up my mind that I am not coming back to India. *Living abroad, you see a world which is completely different and liberal. Socially, there are no bounds. People get out of their homes when they are 16. Of course, they don't know what to do? But they are happily on their own.* Here, even when we are 30 and married, we are staying with our folks. These are two different worlds. And for some reason, I am unable to live upto the thing that people here want me to do. *For me, the whole idea is to be independent, just be on my own. I don't want to live with my parents as an adult.* It's very important for me because that's how I identify myself. And that's how I think adults should be. When I go back home, the honeymoon period is for 10 days. It's great fun. But after that you are back to your own lifestyle, your own values. *I don't believe that I am breaking rules or things like that. It's a kind of understanding you develop over a period of time.* A lot of things contribute to that. When I was 18, there was this orientation program that I went to with my friends. *An organisation used to run these programs for young people with an objective of introducing them to different worlds from what one knows. It was a huge influencing factor. You are looking at Dalits, power relationships, property less and issues of sexuality.* At that stage, you can understand that but you can't articulate them in that way. It left a very big impact on me. *Then when I joined Law College, I would just run away from classes and attend lectures and talks at different places.* I was very hesitant and wouldn't open my mouth but was taking it all in. *Then college abroad was a very interesting phase. Not only are you living alone and studying interesting stuff but also meeting interesting people.* I also got good grades there which helped boost my self confidence enormously. It helped me leave behind my past experience of feeling "not upto the mark". *I got interested in the whole issue of political conflicts and governance, meaning how does the state deal with challenge to its authority? What is the relationship between state and individual? It sort of gave me a direction in life.* I am still learning about it more and gaining confidence in this field. Now, I work with refugees. They don't have citizenship and are trying to navigate a completely different system in a different country. So their rights, protection against deportment, helping them relocate to a country of their choice are issues on which I work. I have to deal with state institutions like bureaucracy, police, hospitals, UN agency. They are intimidating. They are opaque. They refuse to look at real concerns and are most resistant to change. But you got to be at it! I have slowly begun to get better at negotiating with them, to get my way with them.

In dealing with institutions and persons (familial and extrafamilial) invested with authority and power, she was in the process of clarifying an inner sense of right and wrong—an ideological sense. However, the deep entrenchment of the established thought frameworks and practices within and without makes it much more difficult to question their legitimacy. *While opening them out for ruthless inquiry, one is often left with lingering doubts about what deal is one making unknowingly or quite knowingly with the 'establishment' for the sake of one's own advancement, and with what profit? This confusion is what at the base of Sujata's struggle to define her politics—radical or conservative*. Her ideological struggles were receiving emotional impetus from her strivings to wrest self-esteem, agency and autonomy as an individual and as a woman from the heavy scaffolding of tradition and convention.

The confusion of values also percolated into her work. *Her conviction about the human rights' activism that she was engaging with kept waxing and waning.*

While she was learning to deal with its challenges and issues more competently, she was struggling to position herself in it. The meaninglessness of her functioning was aggravated by her inability to see any personal growth in the work that she was doing and also by low salary which made a decent existence in a metropolis very difficult. *Her work-related conflicts were emerging around the same time when her boyfriend was going through his own work paralysis.* While he was considering deregistering from his Ph.D., she was thinking of resigning from her job. Her current boyfriend, whom she had for long known as a friend, had undergone a disillusionment of aims. Defying his father, he charted his own occupational path but was now beginning to feel at a loss in terms of where his career was heading. He had begun to talk about making money. She signed off by saying:

> Yeah! So I don't know where am I going. I am rambling and rambling and I don't know what am I thinking about. *I can't explain where am I am going with my career.* I get defensive when people ask me about my work. You don't want to get married because you want to lead a certain lifestyle. Here in Delhi, I have the freedom. But it no longer feels liberating because it's so difficult to make the ends meet with the money I make. But still this is what I always wanted to do—living independently, making your own choices about the way you want to live. So it's like I am where I wanted to be but I am now not feeling good about it. I don't know where this relationship is headed. So yeah. . ..

Manoj

A lanky fellow, Manoj, 23 years old, introduced himself as an engineer in 'yinpharmason technaaljee (a satirical reference to information technology peppered by a Malayalam accent) looking for other things to do'. *With engineering being a time filler, his real love was music.* Trained in Carnatic music, he had learnt violin, but his proficiency was as a pianist and he was an aficionado of Western classical music. He was born and brought up in a South Indian town which is well known for its missionary hospital/medical college and a private engineering college. His parents were doctors in the hospital, and he had lived all his life in the hospital campus and studied in the schools managed by the Christian missionaries.

Manoj's family consisted of his parents, his elder sister and both sets of grandparents. Talking about his life, he shared one of his earliest memories as that of being taken to a nursery school by his paternal grandfather, a gentle school teacher, to whom he was very close. As a young child, he was not as good as other children in reading and writing. The teachers tried to force him, and his grandfather said, 'No! He will start writing in his own time'. He remembered being taught his first alphabets and numbers by him. He passed away when he was 5 years old, but Manoj retained his fondness for him. His parents described him as a kind and simple man, fair in his conduct and atheist in his religious beliefs. He would let Manoj scribble all over the floor with a chalk. *Manoj did want to take his own time at every major decision-making step.* After 12th class, he wanted to take a year off or do a social science course and in the meanwhile figure out a way of doing music professionally. However, following the trend, he wrote the medical exam for the missionary hospital. *But he felt rushed into making a decision which would affect his whole life. Besides, he also had the urge to experience the outside world—'Before one realises, you are a doctor, married to someone you know from the hospital, and your children are studying in the same schools as you did, and you are giving them the same lectures as your parents gave you!' Thus, he withdrew his application from the medical college.* He was, however, unable to resist the pressure to do something 'worthwhile' and *ended up studying engineering.* Though, it didn't really hold his interest much, it gave him the freedom to interact with people from rest of India, to see life beyond the confines of the campus. *In college, he began to*

DOI 10.1007/978-81-322-0715-3_14, © Springer India 2013

read a range of books on alternative discourses of development. All of this greatly stimulated him and contributed in a large part to his perspective towards how a just world should be. During the college days, he had a lot of disagreements with his parents on their lifestyle. He objected to their possessing two cars, seeing it as personal greed which helps in sustenance of capitalist economy that is exploitative of environment. He refused to buy a bike to commute to college. Rather, he would cycle to college. *After finishing college, he turned down a job he had got in a software company, feeling that he was being sucked in a system where he didn't really belong.* Instead, he lapped up an *opportunity to work on a community health project in a remote district of Orissa.* Enriched by the experience and strengthened in his beliefs of the importance of grassroot democracy, he returned home after 6 months amidst anxious parents who were just not able to understand what their son was upto. *While feeling more drawn to work in the field of either music or this 'whole thing of social justice', he eventually had to settle to try out civil services.* It was a 'respectable' choice he made with the consent of his parents. During the time I met him, he was preparing in Delhi for the civil services' examination with sociology and psychology as his main papers. While enjoying the new ideas and theories he was learning, he was aware of the 'potential soul-numbing nature of huge edifice of bureaucracy'. *He would become pensive whenever conversations veered around to whether civil services would allow him the space to express his deeply held values of social justice and development.* Unsure of where he would be eventually land up, Manoj often remarked with a relish that he was '*muddling*'.

The campus life loomed large in his consciousness. Remembered affectionately as a stable and secure life with fond memories of pot lunches, gully cricket and sharing books and films with neighbourhood friends, it was also viewed dispassionately as an overprotected privileged existence. The residential campus was perceived as an island with a culture quite different from the rest of the township in which it was located. In terms of the spoken language, music preferences and reading habits amongst the young, it was much more Westernised than the other part of the town. Citing instances of politics between Christians and Hindus, and even amongst different sects of Christians on the campus, he asserted the *need to accept plurality and coexist.* An early exposure to Christian teachings in school and Hindu traditions at home helped him see the convergences between religions.

Interactions with him spanned over seven long discussions. They were held during winters in a park. He would carry a school bag and used to be dressed simply and rather unfashionably. In the focused research inquiry and informal conversations, he came across as someone with an intelligent mind, curiosity to know, learn and question and who had passion to build logically sound arguments in service of his cherished *ideals which were a unique combination of scientificity, humaneness and spirituality.* He thought actively about the possible solutions to the systemic problems in human development and happiness. *If debates on development brought forth his remarkable intellectual capacities, talk about music underlined his artistic side.* I involved myself in his lifeworld by reading many of his books and discussing their ideas. I also listened to his favourite music, much of which was new to me. We had a couple of interesting discussions on *how doing music was quite similar to doing the kind of qualitative research which I was doing because both involved attunement, deep listening and intuitive knowing.* He would come alive while sharing about his musical interests and pursuits. His voice would brighten up, and his mood would lighten. Conversations with him led me to isolate *three aspects of his identity—muddling, music and ideas of social transformation.* Below, I am presenting fragments of our exchanges on the foci of music and 'muddling', all of which gave glimpses of his individualised functioning.

I

- *You are happiest when you talk of music.*
  Yes. It's great fun. *After 8th class, it was music. . .music. . .music. . . all the way.* I was never much of a socialiser. I used to sit and practise for hours. Hardly noticing the time going by. It's so interesting. Studies had also become secondary to music. I used to play in the school assembly for the choir. Also took part in the inter-house activities. College was good. Playing alone is one thing, but playing with a group is another kick all together. We revived the college music society when I was there. I was its secretary. We had a small group going. The other guys in the band were phenomenal, very passionate about music and not doing it just for image but really digging in music. We had gone to a couple of college fests and won all of them. *With a little more courage, we could have gone professional. But then everyone has concerns of parents, career, settlement.* Then in hospital campus, there used to be Easter/Christmas celebrations wherein I was active. One of my most cherished memories is of a play that was done on the graduation day. (Smiles broadly) It was a musical, and I kind of took the entire charge of music for that. Sat up all night and transcribed every note of the music. We didn't have sheet music for this play, so I had to really listen and write down the notes for each instrument. The music was quite complex, and it was extremely challenging and just a lot of fun. . ..
- *Without the sheet music, it would have been tough, indeed.*
  Yeah. . .. Actually, I play by ear. *I kinda have a good ear, so I listen and figure out the notes. In fact, when I was learning music, I wasn't having so much fun because I was poor at sight reading, that is, reading from the score. It's ironic that my sight reading improved after I stopped learning.* Because then I used to hear a lot of classical music. When you listen to a piece, you have an idea in your head about how it sounds like. You also have a feel of the composer's work. Then I used to get its sheet music and play. It was then that I began to figure out the relationship between what was written and what I was listening.
- *Would you consider making music your career?*
  I would love to. It is something that is very important to me. . . and people think that it cannot be done, but it is quite possible. *I would like to teach mainly.* Because this whole recording thing. . . there is no way of knowing what to do because there are fads coming and going. *I feel one has to do what makes one tick, feel alive. I would like to play what I want to play, not what someone else wants me to play.* You kinda have to figure out what you like. *The music has to play within you.* When you feel the sounds, play with them, you improvise. Without your knowing, you have altered what you had heard. Also, there are so many things that you can do with music, for example, in your college (referring to my workplace), if they have a day in a week when people can just come and sing/perform. No competition. *You encourage that side of people; help them value in them their musical side which is there in all. I find this whole notion of*

professionalism very problematic. Why does everything have to be of that terribly high standards and specialisation? You know, just be. There is merit in doing small things. In college, there used to be these conferences. So we would organise performances during dinner. They were these small, more informal occasions rather than these large, great musical nights. The interconnection with audience in itself was such a good feeling. These are the kinds of things that I would like to do in music.

- *(Feeling excited) Interesting! Why don't you do music only then? You have the talent, interest, qualifications and ideas.*
  I would love to do it... but... but I don't know. I know that it pays decently. I mean I can earn as much as I would have earned in my initial years as a software guy. (Silence) My music teacher used to teach English literature in a local college. Then he left it to join his brother in Sivakasi to do community health work. You can do other things as well. But my parents... you can't expect any parent in India to understand this. I am not sure. Let's see...

Manoj's musicality, as an inner core, had managed to remain autonomous of the demands of popular music industry and the faddish compulsions of peer group. He had his own standards in opposition to standardisation. His inclinations—Western classical music rather than rock/pop which are much more marketable, preference for small scale events, penchant for improvisation, interest in innovative teaching, dislike of excessive professionalism—created a unique pattern of musical 'play' which could be personally enjoyed and socially shared. *His unhindered musical activity allowed him enjoyment of solitude and use of his distinctive abilities—creative living. It permitted him to dwell in a space in which he could 'muddle about' and 'figure out' the synthesis between his inner proclivities and outer opportunities in avocational, vocational and ideological spheres of experience.* By looking around at people who were doing music, he had found opportunities to make a living through music. *Through the research interactions, one could also see a continuity of his ideas across the domains of music and social action.*

Manoj's insistence on *being, aliveness, feeling—kernels of his individuality*—was reflected in the kind of lifestyle he favoured as well as in his ideal image of the world. In terms of lifestyle, Manoj favoured a *low-cost, family-oriented living. According to him, 'Life is about being alive... a state of being rather than an actual thing. Career is one aspect of it.* Family is a big part of it and not just one's immediate family but also a group of friends who are like family. And of course, music'. In an ideal world, he would have liked to be a musician. But at that moment, he wasn't sure of what form his life would take. In terms of his career, it could be civil services. It could also be some interesting/innovative NGO work like promoting open-source software and natural forms of farming. *He would like to explore what appealed to him. He acknowledged the importance of money but didn't want his life to revolve around it.* Instead he preferred to live simply.

While he had to negotiate his career decisions with his parents who weren't happy with his 'too out of the way' preferences, he wasn't made to feel estranged from what he liked to do spontaneously and joyfully. Within the familial matrix of emotional attachments, maternal expectations of high academic functioning and anxieties around respectable settlement of the only son, *he was able to avail a sense of rightfully delimited autonomy,* which is used in the service of affirmative action whenever human dignity and independence is infringed. *Not wanting an encore of his parents' life, he explored options, vocational and ideological, different from them.* Though not mutinous, Manoj always had challenging questions. When his mother would scold him for not coming first, he would gently ask her, 'Why can't you be happy with someone else's child coming first?' He would protest when they would tell their maid's children that they should 'come up' in life by asking them, 'Would coming up mean becoming like you? Isn't cleanliness an index of good health? And if it is, how the work they do is intrinsically less worthy than what you do?' He would wonder, 'If everyone in the world were to become doctors, from where would we get food?' *The hospital campus environment where he had spent his formative years was instrumental in shaping his perceptions and personality.* The passion and prevalence of Western music due to strong Christian presence and the ongoing debates on the increasing commercialisation of the medical profession, the chipping away of vision of decentralisation, and the need for exemplary leadership in the hospital and its subsidiary branches were important influences on him. *He was also deriving inspiration and courage from associating with people (like his music teacher, his college senior) who were taking the road less travelled. The intense phase of questioning and rejection of his parents' materialistic values gradually led to an acceptance of their positions stemming out of their own life histories.* He began to realise that his parents had studied on scholarships and struggled to be where they were. They had neither the access to the critical debates nor the luxury to rebel.

Manoj's *mother* was described as a religious-minded lady who had high expectations of academic performance from him. He would often question her ritualistic ways and also her ambitions for him. *But she was the one whom he turned to for care and emotional support, which by his own admission he needed a lot.* He immensely respected his *father as a humane doctor* who believed in spending time listening to his patients for making a diagnosis rather than relying on diagnostic tests which were often quite expensive and beyond the means of many patients who came to the missionary hospital. He also took pride in him being a much sought-after teacher who was loved by his students. He was reserved and philosophical like him and *identified closely with his humane, yet rational approach to issues and debates.* In his own being, he sought to *integrate loving, symbiotic modes of living with rational views.*

II

A large part of research engagement was geared towards understanding Manoj's framework of sociopolitical–spiritual transformation combining what was newest and oldest in ideas and ideals. For this, I read through many of the books that he had found useful to formulate his ideas, his blog entries, and followed his participation in social action movements. Below are certain fragments of conversations providing a formulation of his stances:

- *How did the ideas of social justice and development begin to take shape for you?*
  I entered this journey with a book called '*The Way: An Ecological Worldview*' by Goldsmith. It's an awesome book that demonstrates logically point by point how most of the fundamental principles taken for granted by our modern society are fundamentally flawed and are leading us in the opposite direction of the healthy and happy life they promise. So he *critiques the paradigm of science and economics which rationalise and legitimise the kind of development and progress that we are seeing now.* It is basically saying that the problems that we are facing are not because economic development has not progressed far or fast enough, as leaders in scientific and economic establishments would have us believe, but because human activity has disrupted the natural world—its biological organisms, families, communities, ecosystems. It is a very rational book which provides the *underlying principles of a truly ecological world view in terms of recognising our real wealth—that on which we really depend for our welfare—as natural wealth, that is, our favourable and stable climate, our fertile soil, our free-flowing rivers, as well as the traditional families and communities.* Then '*Small is Beautiful*' by Schumacher was another very powerful book. It basically talks of *sustainable development, issue of scale and 'enoughness' as in what humans need and the appropriate use of technology.* Then 'Grapes of Wrath', George Orwell, P. Sainath, God's Debris... all of these were revelatory. Also, there is a *group of young people in Chennai who used to meet and discuss politics, activism* an all. I used to go for those meetings. Then there is *my friend, a senior in school and college,* who left his good, well-paying job to do environment education in schools. He had been a big, big influence. You know, his father is not alive, and his mother works in a government department. He is the kind who really needs to hang on to his job... but he chose to live differently... live his questions. Then there is *my music teacher* who went to Sivakasi. Another very big inspiration for me was *Dr. John with whom I worked in Orissa.* He is a hospital staff child. He chose to go and live in a missionary hospital in a remote place in Orissa, and he has been there for now over a decade. He is very good, and he is doing fabulous work with the local people there.
- *What is your politics?*
  My politics... I think in the current state of affairs, some kind of socialism makes sense. A *democratic socialism* is what we need. I think that state has a big role to play in ensuring welfare and all the enlightenment ideas. The problem with free market capitalism is that politics is totally neglected. One doesn't understand that politics is integral to economics and environment. It is everywhere. *Democracy has to be made really egalitarian.* It has to ensure that everyone's voice is heard... all stakeholders are listened to. Like, if you take the example of NBA. The politics and asymmetry of power is in the clash of worldviews. Those who are pro-dam are thinking that there is money, progress and other things linked to it. But, the fact of the matter is that big dams don't work. Even for electricity, it is not as good as microhydel projects. Even for irrigation, it is destructive because it creates greenhouse gases, methane, etc. because of stagnation of water. So, on every count, it is worthless. The other side is the people who are being displaced. There is a deficiency in understanding that what you are destroying is a way of life... not to make it monolithic/exotic concept but to understand that this way of life has an intrinsic value. Forest has a qualitative value of its own. Not only as something which has utility for humans but as something which has its own system and rhythm.

- *Do you think we shouldn't have private sector then?*
  See, if you look at Cuba, Castro is not entirely opposed to having a private sector. But it has to be strongly regulated. What I have read of Cuban economy is that they have become food self-sufficient. They have managed to become really really self-sustainable—invested in renewable energies, organic farming. Become independent of pesticide lobbies. And their health system is known to be one of the best. Its literacy rate is very high. Main thing is that they took into account the cultural context of each place, and they mobilised a huge amount of youth for literacy and also politicisation. *Have a private sector but make your democracy strong so that competing interests are given their place. For that probably, the existing structures have to change.* I think the existing countries of the world are too big. I don't think at this scale, it is possible to have a really good system in place. Like, 'Small is Beautiful' talks of this concept of scale. *There is a critical size beyond which production, technology, political structures would lose vibrancy.* Anything beyond that would involve some sort of large scale organisation and generalisation which would not be valid and will lead to asymmetry of power. *This is also what Gandhi was saying. In India, Panchayati Raj was supposed to do this. But unfortunately, the system didn't become effective.* There is no flow of information upwards; it has been reduced to an implementing authority. Like the place in Orissa where I was working, the elected representatives of people were good. But the bureaucrat who is the Panchayat secretary was the problem. So this how the system gets blocked.
- *But India has always had a mixed economy?*
  Yeah.. But in the current scenario, it doesn't seem to be working. We are following the American model which is dangerous. Inequalities have drastically increased after liberalisation. There is another caricature that people have in their mind which is that state would destroy creativity, spirit of innovation and free enterprise. Unfortunately, Russia and China have confirmed these fears, but if the polity is decentralised, flexible and transparent, then there is no reason why this would happen. Also, like in India, after liberalisation, especially, in the public sector, we have confused profitability for efficiency. Some things are not meant to be profitable. *You are meant to do what is right which is not necessarily profitable. This whole monetisation of economy is very problematic,* because money puts everything in one dimension. *But in life, everything is qualitative.* There is an ancient saying which I find very wise: Only when the last river has dried, when the last tree has felled, when all the fish has died, will you realise that you cannot eat money. Compensation or another piece of land to the displaced population of farmers whether because of dams or SEZs is not a solution because you are destroying a way of living. It is a civilisational issue. The agricultural labourer is the most ruined person in this country... why? When he is the one who gives us food on which we survive.

  What I have come to believe strongly is that economic models of both America and Russia with their levels of centralised and capital intensive industrialisation are unsustainable. *Anything which is environmentally unsustainable will lead to economic and political asymmetry. The environment has to be considered as the first thing.* Take what you need and not as per your greed. See, even Gandhi was not against industrialisation. He said that if we feel the need of machines, we certainly will have them. Every machine that helps every individual has a place. But the problem arises when scientific or technological solutions poison the environment or degrade the social structure, when it concentrates economic power in the hands of few people. But because we look at efficiency in a purely monetary sense, we use a lot of machines and methods which are unnecessary. For example, tractor will not increase the productivity of land in a given span of time. The ground will take its own time to throw up food. The only thing is that you can reap faster at a much lower cost because it removes labour. Also, there is a lot of new research that is saying that you don't need to use pesticides for rice after years of people using it. *We need to really break a lot of our mindsets about what is good and efficient.*

- *The push is towards becoming larger, bigger whereas you are advocating smaller, non-exploitative, harmonious ways of existence.*
  I know it doesn't fit in the present scheme of things, but *we are going to face the brunt of our expansionist zeal very soon. So, we need to examine what we are doing logically. Where are we going? What technology are we using? Is it desirable and giving us the desired effects?* See, after all what is science? It is basically a way of coming out with all the logical practical possibilities. The possibility that we choose to work with depends on the purpose. *If the purpose is maximisation of profit, the way we use science will be different. If our purpose is sustainability, then it will be geared differently.* In India, in Andhra, there are a couple of NGOs who work with local populace in growing their own food, fully organic, based on whatever can be grown, in that climate, using rainwater harvesting. They have also set up their own PDS because they have surplus. They are rotating food crops with cash crops like organic cotton. This is an alternative, provided you accept that bajra, ragi, millets are as nutritious as wheat and rice which is what the government PDS pushes. That's the kind of change you want to see.
- *What was the project in Orissa about?*
  It was with the community health department of a missionary hospital. The department has health centres in villages under its jurisdiction. The project I was working on was to collect information about the number of deaths, the reasons of death and ways of preventing it. The purpose was not just to have a document of it but to have this *information as a part of people's thinking.* So we would organise meetings with local people in the villages and through a dialogue would ask information and also tell them what to do to prevent illnesses. What is very striking there is the relationship between people in the department and the villages. It is very intimate. *The health department works on the terms of the people there. They listen to them, and I think it is very important to listen. By listening, you become an agent of democracy yourself.* Dr. John, who heads the department, would ensure that the money is used for the purpose for which it has been sanctioned. He maintains close relations with individual donors, because he accepts money only from individuals and not from funding agencies. He has this philosophy that if something has to be done, one should begin work on it. The money will come. There is a primary school in the area. So they spread the word around whenever they need teachers for the school. There will be a brief interview, and even those who are not selected are kept in touch with. I learnt a lot there. *One could see how you can make systems come alive.* The community health department had such appeal there. There were committed people who were doing good work. *It was my first-hand experience at seeing how people can be empowered to become self-governing.* Like, every village which wants to work with the department will have one lady who would stock medicines. She would be given basic health training. In fact, most of the social workers there are not professionally trained. They are the more educated people of the neighbouring areas who have been trained. Similarly the teachers. So there is a sense of working for your community's welfare. It was there that idea of civil services also began to take shape because *Dr. John said that bureaucracy can make a lot of difference, and I was myself seeing how systems are there, but you need leadership.*
- *You think civil services will give you a chance to play out some of these ideas that you have?*
  Hmmm... yeah. I hope so. I realised in Orissa that a dynamic IAS officer can do much. You can make the systems alive. Like this team that I was working in. They were not working mechanically. They were working with purpose and faith, in close association with the locals. In the initial years, even in IAS, you work closely with people, and if you have a vision, you can accomplish something... I mean, I know that the structure is also suffocating and very hierarchical... I hope I can be different. One of the coaching institutes for civils has a tagline that says, 'Training steel pillars for the country'. (Laughs) I hope I would be something different than a steel pillar.

- *Different in what sense?*
  Different in the sense of … being vulnerable. *To be able to really listen to others without judgment. To be open to others, accepting of differences and creating spaces for joint action… that is what I think vulnerability means.* It enables you to include people. *I would like to build an environment which is meaningful, emotional, spiritual and energetic.* There are some things which have to be done in groups. Like one person can't suddenly get up and say that I will cycle to work now. *You have to have groups of people evolving strategic modes of action… like groups of people doing organic farming or small scale handicrafts. It is from these spaces that our understanding and critique of larger political, social and economic structures can grow.* From such spaces can emerge new and more caring ways of living: creating, adopting and enlivening technologies and institutions that are sustainable and democratic. The quality of space is at least as important as any action or result that may emerge from it. It has to be a loving, enabling space.
- *Being vulnerable rather than invincible??*
  Yes. That's most important. *We have to first give ourselves the space to just be, like a child in play (smiles). Open and receptive to our own selves.* Only then can we create spaces where others can just be. I know that I used to be very fanatical about my ideas of social justice and all during college. Things became very bad between my parents and me because of this. I was becoming very critical of their lifestyle. Also, this group in Chennai whose meetings I used to attend, I used to see people becoming extremely argumentative and sticking to their point of view. Then there is no coming together. *It shouldn't be an exercise of line drawing rather it needs to be an attempt at centre defining. There has to be constant willingness to expand and transform our perceptions, to see common threads between our own ways of being and those of others, even when there are apparent external differences.* Now, I have chilled out. I *think the spiritual part of existence is necessary…* to understand that genuine, mutual and loving relationships with people and nature are at the base of any constructive change.
- *How do you think such loving, democratic spaces can be build?*
  I think listening is crucial in this. You remember I was telling you how I find difficult to listen to other because my mind is constantly talking and I have a tendency to try to convince others of what I am saying. And you had said that listening to music can be a prototype of listening to people. It is from there that this idea of vulnerability and listening crystallised. Because, I know that you can listen to music in an analytical way, analysing the sounds and frequencies or you can feel it in an intuitive way. Just because you know the notes doesn't mean that you know. You have to let go of your biases and tendency to hold onto what you already know to listen. That's when there is deep understanding.

In Manoj's ideas, one noticed the *infusion of spiritual and moral values in economics, science and technology*. He stood for a new orientation of science and technology towards *the organic, the gentle and the non-violent*. Championing the need for participatory democracy and just economic system, he advocated the *need for spaces of love where people could heal from the alienation from their true selves and hence forge communion with others and nature*. The inner transformation was felt as important as the changes to be brought about at the systemic level. Through the research interaction, he was able to see parallels between listening to music and listening to people as means of knowing and doing. *In the realms of music and social action, he emphasised on values of small scale, emotional sensitivity, community and energy*. An important emerging identity element of Manoj was *to 'be' before to 'do'*. By going on being, which forms the basis for self-discovery, he was allowing himself doubt and delay so that his aspirations and visions could secure a style of individuality for him. He intuitively grasped *inwardness, that is, responsiveness to self, and sensitive indwelling with fellow humans in natural order, that is, responsiveness to others*, as the basis for egalitarian and sustainable polity and society. In his anticipated role as a civil servant, he saw himself to be an agent of change. Expecting conflicts between his sense of self and the institutional function, he hoped of finding ways of working that transcend ordinary institutional practice. His self-definitional attempts of formulating *ideologically coherent universe represented efforts at synthesising diverse frameworks of change—social, political and spiritual and of thinking systemically about nature, man and polity.* He envisaged creation of institutional spaces which care and tolerate, include and preserve and offer democratic leadership to the same.

Shalini

I met Shalini in the course of my search of youth activists. She was a 25-year-old bright-faced and charming young woman. During the discussion about my research work, she showed much interest in the theme of autonomy and individuation that I was exploring. She enthusiastically agreed with the premise of the work that youth is a stage of psychosocial moratorium in which people often experiment/explore to find their 'space' and 'niche'. On getting to know about her work, I felt that she was on a spiritual–experiential journey rather than a sociopolitical activist path, as I had imagined. Intrigued by *her preoccupations with 'love and harmony'*, I wished to know and understand her better. She was soon *leaving for a shivir (retreat) to learn about the precepts of the 'darshan' (philosophy) named Jeevan Vidya that she was exploring*. We decided to begin our interactions after she came back from the shivir.

When we met next, Shalini was excited about her experiences of shivir and spoke glowingly about them. She described it as 'new phase' of her life in which she was getting the answers to her life questions. She remarked that it was difficult to believe that so many young people had come for it and they all had the same question of *how to live life in a peaceful, happy manner? This she put down to a general unease in urban youth with modern living that is so cluttered with things, yet none of them give satisfaction, a life which is stressful and self-defeating in the end.* The shivir and the darshan, she asserted, provided a basis for an understanding of a life that is meaningful and a society that is just, humane and ecologically sustainable. It made one hope and see that *another world is possible*. Caught by her conviction, I asked her to elaborate on what the darshan was all about. She hesitated on this and said that she would like to first share her life context and her journey to this 'destination' before she can meaningfully talk about it. Through the four interactions, she spoke extensively about her school, college and work experiences. The last two meetings were devoted to understanding her engagement with Jeevan Vidya and explore its precepts.

P. Bansal, *Youth in Contemporary India: Images of Identity and Social Change*,
DOI 10.1007/978-81-322-0715-3_15, © Springer India 2013

I

Shalini completed her schooling from an elite public school of Delhi. In school, she was a *willing part of numerous social service projects* that involved interacting with and teaching slum and mentally challenged children. She saw that as an early initiation in the social development sector. After school, following her brother's footsteps, she applied to the American universities for her graduation in economics. She acknowledged good humouredly that she was never much interested in studies and could not care less where she would pursue higher education. She secured admission in a few colleges, and her father left the decision to choose one on her. This she remembered as the first major personal decision she had to make. Before that, she and her brother had lived a sheltered and protected life. Everything was always done for them, provided to them. She described her college experience abroad as thus:

> *On reaching the college, I was in for a culture shock.* The first week was the orientation week, and what a long week it was! Every day was a culture shock! The ice-breaking games had innuendoes to sex which I didn't understand much. I also got exposed to the drinking, dancing, partying scene on the campus—all of which I was not comfortable with. So, the first year was tough. Thankfully, I didn't have a phone connection at that point of time. So I couldn't convey my general sense of loss and being lost to my parents. I dealt with it myself. Gradually, I came to know the international students in my college, and I started to get along really well with them. I was friendly with the American students also, but I was never close to any of them. *What I saw there in terms of stress on appearances, smoking, drinking and dressing up being essential to one's acceptance, sex being the ultimate thing, disturbed me but I could also not escape it. So I dabbled a bit in smoking and drinking, not in a big way. I remember picking up some dresses to see whether I look better in them because some of my acquaintances thought that I had a rather conventional dressing sense. I began reading books on love and sex that were given to me by my friends [laughs]. All of this really impacted me. In fact, I think I continued in this 'crazy' mould even after returning to India. Now people tell me that at that time I looked and behaved like an American.*
>
> In the course of time, I got more and more *involved with the International Association—a cultural–social body of international students.* That is my most enriching experience there. The people who were already a part of it were such genuine, loving people. *They treated me like a family.* Even the office was like a home with something or the other being baked in the kitchen, everyone comfortable on the couches and chatting up. The environment was very relaxed and warm. We used to organise cultural activities like musical evenings, food melas, etc., for international students. Once, we did a sheesha-hukka afternoon because we had a lot of mid-eastern students. Then many American students came. Otherwise they would just find our events boring [laughs]. Another major highlight for me was to know the community where my college was. I used to take long walks in the city adjoining the college and it was a pleasure. I interacted with city people also through the workshops on disaster management, first aid, etc. I was taking voice training classes from a cute old lady who lived there. Once, I went to a wrong house and chatted with a Spanish person for over half an hour. It was so much fun!! Later when I was narrating this to my friend, she told me that the city is unsafe; it is full of poor Spanish and black people. But, I never felt scared because I never had any of these preconceived notions. Then when I was in the third year, we started inviting speakers to talk on issues of international politics. There was a keen interest amongst students on this. *Through documentaries, talks, I also got educated about the various international conflicts. I remember watching a documentary on Israel–Palestine issue which was very powerful. It opened my eyes to the fact that people are at war everywhere.* Till then I used to feel very passionately about the Kashmir issue

because my mother is a Kashmiri, and my maternal grandparents were forced to leave Srinagar because of the terrorist insurgency. They had come to Delhi to meet us and when they returned back, their belongings had been thrown out of their house, and it was occupied. So they picked up whatever they could and came back to Delhi. Some of their best friends betrayed their trust. *My mother is very anti-Muslim. Coincidentally, my best friends in school and college have always been Pakistani Muslims.* While in school, I would often go to my friends' house, her parents used to love me so much and take me around the Pakistani embassy. Similarly, in college... my mother never liked my strong friendships with them but I bonded very well with them. Because of what I had seen in and heard from my family about the conflict in Kashmir, it was an important issue for me. *I used to get confused about my liking for my Muslim friends and my mother's hatred for the community. I wanted to know more about what happened? Why were people fighting?* Because based on my interactions, I felt that Muslims were good people. So, in college, I found a professor specialising in S. Asian politics and I read up considerably on Indo-Pak relations, Kashmir issue. With my roommate who was also a Muslim, there used to be heated debates on Kashmir issue with both of us privileging our own viewpoints gleaned from what we have been told and heard. We had numerous discussions on Shariat, Islam, Hinduism, etc. I remember once she told me harshly that it is ridiculous that we, Hindus, bow our heads in front of stone idols. I was quite taken aback by it. But we always found so much of warmth and care and similarities in views/outlook about life in general with each other that we never fell apart. Besides, some significant shifts in thinking on the Kashmir issue happened for both of us. We came to understand and respect the reality from both sides.

Then, Gujarat riots happened. When I saw reports of it in America, I was very disturbed. When you are away from home, anything going wrong at home always hits you badly. *I guess, by that time violence and wars had begun to dominate my consciousness.* [Here, she paused and reflected]. *During my stay in America, I had come to know about the crisis in my family. My parents' relationship was at its ebb.* My father had started practising Transcendental Meditation and had become more reclusive than ever. He would spend long periods of time meditating and became quieter than before. My mother frustrated by his withdrawal had begun to confide in me, during my vacations, about her problems with him. These problems had always existed between them because of my father's uncommunicative stance, but I could never see them. This made me change, mature by a couple of years. I became a much serious person.

On my return to Delhi during the college vacation, *I started attending the meetings of an association of NGOs who were working on the Gujarat issue.* Soon the word spread, and many young people joined us. *We called our group 'work for harmony'*. We decided to launch an awareness campaign directed towards youth to bring to light the right facts about the riot and also to get people talking and thinking about their prejudices about different communities. The crux of our work was that people fear differences, and in situations of conflict and threat these get heightened which lead people to react in unimaginably cruel ways. In our workshops with students in schools and colleges, we tried to get them to *discuss the stereotypes towards the 'other' they held and then help them to overcome them.*

In the last year of college, I witnessed September 11 and the fallout of it on the Asian community in America. I was so very upset with the mistrust, hatred and hostility directed towards Asians and Muslims in particular. I was shocked with how my friend circle began to disintegrate. The environment had become negatively charged. It really depressed me. By the end of the fourth year of my graduation, I was itching to get back to home.

From Shalini's sharing, what came across strongly was that *to have loving, warm human relations was of utmost significance to her.* During all our interactions, she would be very hospitable, placing tea in front of me, offering food. She was always polite and friendly with the employees of her mother's hospital where we were meeting. To see her family being ridden by conflicts was a big set back to her. *Disharmony in human existence at familial/global level became an omnipresent reality for her.* This was in contrast to the image of her family environment as comfortable and secure. At a point, I asked her to share something about *her family*. She said:

> Family for me always meant more than my immediate family when I was young. As a child, there were many cousins who would be staying with us for varying periods of time. My uncles and aunts would keep dropping in. And, of course, my grandparents lived with us. I have never felt a lack of love in my life. I used to like sitting with my dadi [paternal grandmother] for her prayers. When my nana–nani [maternal grandparents] were in Srinagar, I used to go there for my vacations. It used to be very beautiful. Even when they came to Delhi, I used to love getting the tikka from my nani who is a big Sai Baba devotee. So, I had a peaceful sort of childhood. I had a good equation with our old maid and her daughter. When her daughter had a baby, I was so excited. I really liked being with the child and taking care of the child. *I always received good vibes from people, never felt lonely or that didn't have people to turn to in case of need.*

So, this idyllic cocoon was experienced by her as disintegrating, creating insecurities and a drive to repair, to heal. Her work with students in schools and colleges during Gujarat riots brought to light another facet of her personality that she strove to engage with the *essential humanity of other individual beings which is common to all.* According to her, the man-made stereotypes created divisions and conflicts; otherwise, there were enough similarities in people that could draw them closer. This was clear in the strong relationship she shared with her Pakistani-Muslim friends.

Once home, she *tried out small assignments in corporate sector* because her parents wanted her to give it a try. But instinctively she *did not like the work and the corporate culture of competition, impersonal relationships, etc.* She wanted to work in the social sector with youth on the issue of education. From her own experience, she realised that young people have questions and their search requires direction and expression. She also felt that education was an arena from where solutions can come. *Because she felt so disconnected with her own formal educational process, she sought to have a framework of knowledge which was personally relevant and meaningful. Her search was for a system of education which provided more than literacy and a job; it was about helping an individual acquire knowledge about self, society and environment and also to lead a happy life.*

In her first job in the educational sector, she was a student mentor in a school program on life skills' training. The emphasis was to know oneself—aspirations, needs, nature; understand each other interpersonally so as to build trust, communicate and work as a team and grasp the importance of sustainable development. Students were taken to rural sites to explore an ecologically balanced way of life. This had an immense effect on her. She found the *simple and natural way of rural living fascinating*. She strongly felt that this was the way of living happily and meaningfully. But the question was how to give up one's city life? In the meanwhile, *her perspectives on issues of 'development', 'progress' and 'modernity' had also begun to evolve.* While quizzed about what was her significant learning on these issues, she began passionately:

> There was a big shift in my thinking. *While studying economics in college, ideas of freedom, individualism, free trade, capitalism and competition, all were leaving impressions on me. I was exposed to such discourses and was convinced about their rightness. But with this exposure, I began to question them. My teammates helped me immensely to look at the mainstream notions of development and opened alternative viewpoints for me.* I think development and progress can scarcely be seen merely in terms of rise in GNP or industrialisation, or technological advancement. While these are important accomplishments, their value must depend on what they do to the lives of people. Are these really improving the quality of life of people? While we have more and better flyovers, there is a corresponding increase in automobiles as well. So in terms of ease of driving, there is a marginal improvement. These automobiles contribute to pollution which adversely affect health and also cause global warming. Besides, having so many segments of cars, each with its own branding strategy, creates artificial needs in people. A person wants a particular car to maintain his/her status and image and thinks that it will give happiness but it doesn't. The moment someone buys a better car, he/she will again begin to feel unhappy. So the cycle continues. *Such development doesn't provide lasting well-being and also comes at a huge expense of resources.* Development should be sustainable which uses natural resources to the point where they can be replenished. But it is not happening. In agriculture, we are using seeds, fertilisers and pesticides which are ruining the soil quality and its productivity. Dams are flooding villages, upsetting waterways and destroying fisheries. *Development is also destroying traditional life patterns, native knowledge and local wisdom, in the name of science and modernity.* When I went to villages, I was enthralled by how much those people knew about nature, soil, life without really being taught those things. But now village youth idolise city life. So many of them are migrating to cities, leaving their traditional occupations and feeling miserable here because it is an alien culture and life. City people are unhappy because in spite of everything, they are feeling a void. In the process of amassing wealth and conveniences, they are sacrificing their health, mental peace and relationships. The problems are abounding. So what is the solution?

The solution presented itself to her in the form of a chance encounter with Sawantji, the person running a voluntary organisation in Nainital and his exploration of a darshan called Jeevan Vidya based on Saha-Astitvavaad (broadly translated as co-existentialism). She interacted with him during a youth camp that she had organised for a group of students at his campus. She narrated her journey from that point with deep sentiments:

> *During our discussion, I felt a new clarity dawning upon me.* It reformulated my questions as: Will relationships in the family and other interpersonal relationships always be about differences of opinion, inequality, conflict, emotional distress and unhappy compromises? Or is it possible for everyone to have mutually fulfilling and meaningful interpersonal relationships? Is unhappiness, meaninglessness and discontent an inevitable part of human life? Or is it possible for human beings to live a purposeful and meaningful life? Would human beings always be divided by nationality, religion, race and gender? Or is there a universal human identity that subsumes these superficial differences? Is exploitation, poverty, injustice, discrimination, violence and war an inevitable part of human existence? Or is it possible to have a just, equitable and undivided society? *I was completely spellbound by his clear articulation of my most important concerns and the possibility of a meaningful way of life and a humane, just and sustainable society.* He suggested me to attend a week-long retreat [shivir], in which rudiments of the Jeevan Vidya philosophy are communicated. When I attended the first shivir, I was astounded... so emotional. *I felt my*

> *search has finally come to an end. This is it. I wouldn't have to wander any more. It was like you are searching for some answers that nobody is able to give. But here I could see a harmonious interconnection amongst personal, interpersonal, social and ecological facets of life.* I could feel that the stithi [state] within me is changing. I was feeling at rest, at peace with myself, assured that there will be no reaction from me.

As she paused here, probably to relive that moment, I wondered what she meant by 'reaction'. A brief moment later, I asked it to her. She laughed merrily and explained:

> I have had many phases in my life. *College was one phase where I was volatile. I felt extremely agitated about the wars and violence taking place everywhere. So, I was like we have to fight this.* We had discussions, debates, screened poignant documentaries, organised marches. All of this generated enough emotion, stirred people, but beyond it no constructive movement happened. It didn't lead to acceptance of each other, as people, as human beings. *Then when I came back and started working in the social sector, I became very critical of modern life and the form of development that was sustaining it. I would incessantly argue with my parents about its ills.* I mocked the kind of affluence that I had, the meaninglessness and hollowness of it, the ever spiralling needs that it creates, the stresses it induces and the toll it takes on our lives. Besides, the stark divide it creates between the rich and the poor. I would tell them go and look at the slums, how pathetic is the condition there. The ecological costs that this form of development also greatly disturbed me, the plastic waste, landfills... all of that. So, I had become very argumentative and aggressive. In those days I would eat up anyone on these issues. My mother called it 'reverse snobbery'. She said that just because you are from the NGO sector, you look down upon people who enjoy a prosperous life. I felt disturbed by their discomfort with me and my attitude towards them. Also, besides critiquing, I wasn't doing anything. I didn't have a positive plan of action. I was stuck. I couldn't have possibly gone and lived in a village. I had begun to understand that I am displacing my emotional unease with my life situation and am actually feeling frustrated in not being able to do much in altering it. I have seen that this kind of reactionary energy doesn't take you much ahead. *You can shout slogans, do dharnas, fight the system. But at the end, what helps is being responsive... it's important to stand up but also stand in the centre of one's deeper knowing that there is no 'them', there is only 'us', and that us is everyone.* Then, my father introduced me to Transcendental Meditation [TM]. I also dabbled with 10-day silent retreat of Vipassana. TM did calm me down considerably. That was a distinct advantage because I had become very aggressive and that used to disturb me no end. But I didn't find authenticity there. The people who were doing it like my father's teacher and the founder of TM, I met him in his centre in Holland... I somehow was not satisfied. It's difficult to put a finger on what is it but, I was quite disappointed with the whole system—the institution, pundits. *I think I wanted to meet someone who was genuine to the core, who didn't have contradictions. My benchmarks were on living.* I saw it with my father. He is heavily into TM and he meditates for long periods of time. He is also very calm, never gets ruffled. He is knowledgeable about Gita and can really hold his own on existential questions like why are we born? What is the purpose of life? But I don't think he has found ways of living with his family. So what is the point? *In Jeevan Vidya, I found depth of understanding, very genuine, caring people and a program of living which flows from understanding.*

It is evident that Shalini has had a series of absorbing, passionate experiments which is distinctive of youth. *One could also see in Shalini an intense questioning of the parental, more specifically, the paternal way of living and a striving for more authentic and meaningful system of life.* The effort was to map out the continuities and changes from the parental way of living and the place of Jeevan Vidya darshan in her individuation.

II

Shalini belonged to a *modern upper-class family*. The place where we would meet was a hospital, located in a posh South Delhi colony, owned by her mother. The room was tastefully and expensively furnished. Her father was a businessman. They lived in a farmhouse on the outskirts of Delhi. Hence, material prosperity was assured for her. Economic affluence also accorded her the opportunities to gain exposure to set-ups/situations/experiences that moulded her. Whether it was the kind of elite schooling experience which gave her a chance to contribute positively to the lives of others and an option to play hockey that set her apart and made her deal early enough with her 'difference', American liberal college life that accorded her a space to deal with her own life and seek new experiences or as simple as money providing her the much needed mobility required to visit the various sites to gain conviction in the philosophy that she is engaging with, abundance provided her liberation. *Shalini was conscious of this fact that she had an affluent background, but she was quick to point out that she never got spoilt by it.* She gave the credit for this to her *mother who belonged to a middle-class family of professionals and who had to strive for everything—education, house, etc.* She maintained that *she had been a lot under the influence of her mother* who made her value what she had and instilled self-discipline in her which she sees missing in her *brother who according to her has been under their father's influence.* Her mother was experienced by her as a strong woman who stood up for her convictions and took proactive steps for the larger good of the family. When she got married, she had to face opposition because it was a love marriage and that too inter caste. Besides, she did not fit into the conventional orthodox daughter-in-law role because she was working as a doctor and came from a more progressive nuclear family environment. She had to struggle to make her space in the joint family and she did it in her own caring, honest way. *Identification with such a mother created in Shalini psychological capacities of relating, of directing one's life and also to have the strength to live down in one's own life what was not acceptable to self, in her case the trappings of the extravagant life that her father privileged.* Shalini's description of her father was often in contradistinction to her mother. Her *mother was perceived as 'militant'*, while her *father was very calm. Her mother was communicative* and gave practical suggestions and advice, while her *father was reclusive* and his advice never realistic. However, it was *in identification with her father that she got drawn to the spiritual traditions.*

In order to get a clearer sense of how she was staking out an autonomous path, a specific question was asked of her—*How do your parents respond to her involvements in social development work and the philosophy of Jeevan Vidya?* She responded that her father had some very strong opinions. *He felt that all her work on social issues was rubbish.* He did not think anything needed to be changed. During college days and subsequent to that also, she would get very hurt by such comments. She used to feel that he was so insensitive, so caught up with money. Both she and her mother agreed that he was happiest while spending. *He was fond of everything high end.* So even while talking of his retreat spot for meditation, he never looked at frugality. This did not agree with her. She said categorically:

I don't champion 'tyaag', but I also don't approve of excessive cluttering of life with material possessions. It is not about suppression of needs but gradually realising the chief purpose of life. Once that becomes clear, these possessions become irrelevant. Like, now I don't smoke because I realised that I was doing it to live up to a certain image, to gain acceptability. I don't feel the need to hang out with friends all the time. I am now more relaxed because I know that these are not important for me any longer.

She understood that they would never be able to agree on many things ideologically because they had two extreme ways of thinking about life. While he thought that humans are continuously in a situation of war, she believed that existence is inherently harmonious and we disrupt it with our lack of knowledge. She valued meditation but she did not agree with its aim to help make a person be by himself. She believed that it was as important to know how to live with people as to be alone. Crucially, she felt that it was no longer important for her to get her father's approval on what she was doing. *This, however, did not any longer generate any anger or resentment in her. Rather, she was renewing her relationship with him wherein she accepted him lovingly as a person with his own life history and perspective. This was a major leap in her life* because earlier she used to feel extremely influenced by his criticism of her work and would develop self-doubt. *But now, she believed in herself. She attributed this conviction to her experience of seeing her own evolution in a constructive direction and also to reaffirming 'idealising' presence of many teachers and living examples of the darshan whom she was very close to and whom she regarded as utmost genuine people.*

Shalini's present direction in life seemed to be borrowing from her understanding of what was amiss in her family which she also saw playing out in the world at large. She also viewed it as the culmination of all the learning that she gained from her previous experiences in life. Alongside the marital problems that had developed in her parents' life, her elder brother had not been able to find a suitable course of life for himself. From Shalini's description, he emerged as a person who had grown up in his father's shadow and hence could not take a hold on his life. He was caught up with aspirations of earning big money because that was the sign of a successful man. Too much pampering and provision had disabled him from regulating his own life. He was vague about his own needs and skills. The father would not ask him to get his act together and take on adult responsibilities. Whenever pressurised by his wife to speak to the son, his constant response would be that he would grow out of it. Shalini attributed these problems to her brother not knowing what he wanted from life, getting caught up in images and not having proper understanding of how to live. She saw the solutions to all of these problems in Jeevan Vidya. She described it as:

> A philosophy which provides a basis for alternative solutions in all facets of human life—for personal problems, interpersonal relationships, education, social and economic structures, means of production and an ecologically sustainable way of life. It is a proposal that needs to be examined and analysed by each individual, that is, it has to be free from any

sectarianism, mysticism or spiritual leaders. *This is a basic difference between my father and me in the sense that his allegiance is to the Gita and he sees its words as the apostle of truth while I always check the veracity of this proposal by applying it to my own self, whether it satisfies my needs and requirements. The base of it, all of it, is internal evolution and exploration.* There is no organisation, no money involved and no steps to be followed. It is all very decentralised. There is a Babaji whom one can go to if anyone lacks conviction about the understanding, but in terms of the program of living, everyone can have their own. *Through personal exploration, it draws one's attention to the fact that one's true aspiration is to be continuously happy/content/at peace. To achieve this one has to realise the coexistence inherent in the universe amongst nonliving matter, plants and animals.* For it is only on realising the harmonious order inherent in the universe that human beings understand their role/purpose in it and their relationship with all other entities. *To be in harmony within oneself is a natural corollary of living in harmonious coexistence with all other entities. The philosophy talks of harmony at many levels—at the level of I, body, family, society, nature and existence.* The distinction between 'I' and 'body' is important. *'I' has different needs than the body. 'I' requires love, peace, respect, affection in order to be happy. Body requires food, clothes, house, car, etc., as physical facilities.* The problem arises when we confuse both, when we begin to think that we will get happiness from amassing physical facilities. So we spend considerable part of our lives working at jobs which are not meaningful because that gives us purchasing power to consume but we are unhappy. We earn in the anxiety of having enough in case of an illness, not knowing that our current lifestyle is the biggest threat to our health. Also, there is no end to getting something bigger, better. So it is an unending cycle which provides no satisfaction. *So, the crux is that there are different yojanas [programs] for meeting the needs of I and body. For my 'I', I need to live in a relationship, realise it, fulfil it. For my body, I need to do some production/work that can manage my lifestyle.* It is important that your work involves some physical labour and enriches your relationship with nature, or at least not work against nature. *Jeevan Vidya outlines the knowledge/content and the mechanisms/systems [e.g. in education, production, healthcare, social organisation, etc.] required to create a world order in which it is possible to have mutually fulfilling relationships and prosperity in families as well as a sustainable and ever-enriching relationship with nature.* The understanding remains the same for all and I have seen it with my own eyes that different people with different life journeys have come to strongly accept these ideas. This along with my own inner movement gives me the conviction that it has truth. The programs/activities to execute these ideas will vary according to the context [rural/urban], skills and opportunity of a person. *There is a lot of flexibility in it... it is not prescriptive. It just clears your vision and focusses it on the reality. I think for me the biggest pull of this darshan is that it tells me how to live relationships, how to be in a family arrangement where one is happy.*

On being asked what she meant by knowing how to live, she replied:

I mean living in a family consisting of blood relatives, friends, etc. It would be ideal if 3–4 generations can live together. I think family of 10–15 people is the best economic unit to operate out of. Some people can earn money by utilising their skills. Some people can do farming. *There all are in mutually beneficial relationship with each other, contributing positively to each other, shouldering their responsibilities towards each other, basically fulfilling their relationships which is what brings happiness, contentment.* I have seen an experimental set-up in a small town where six couples live together. These people have different skill sets; someone is a baker, few are engineers. They bought a piece of barren land and turned it into a complete green area. They also helped the neighbouring village farmers to build small waterways to irrigate their land. In due course of time, they have garnered so much of goodwill in the area. So some of them do farming and use the produce for personal consumption or sell it to earn. The others have started holding workshops and training programs on various issues in the surrounding educational

> institutions. There is one child in the family who goes to the school and is taken care of by everyone. There was so much of trust in that set-up because people were secure in their relationships with each other. It is an ecologically harmonious arrangement. I think this form of living together sustains happiness. I understand some things cannot be avoided in a big city. But even here we can better our lives if we follow its basic precepts of not confusing needs of 'I' and 'body', relating with people for who they are rather than on the basis of their appearances. Also like car cannot be given up in the city. But we can always use something like biogas which is replenishable and cleaner form of fuel. I see my cousins' children in US. They are all born with allergies because there is so much of processed food going in the mother's body. Eating organically produced food reduces health problems manifold.

It was felt that the *relevance of darshan* in her life was manifold: *Firstly,* darshan as a 'vision' restored authority in her life. *She could see in it clear articulation and solution of problems: personal and global.* Her capacity for faith then emerged as a more focussed hope attuned to an ideologically coherent universe in which the *personal change and social transformation, spiritual strivings and material needs could be seen in one frame.* She learnt the precepts of the philosophy by taking into herself the thoughts and voices of Sawantji and his wife, Babaji and others who were embodiments of the framework. *As the loved gurus, their very presence and knowledge restored intimacy and was instrumental in bringing about transformations in her inner states (stithi).* Her former feelings of conflict and violence dissipated. As she saw her deeply held concerns being responded to, she experienced her inner world transforming from state of disintegration to one of feeling integrated, from dreaded intimations of fragmentations to blissful experiences of wholeness. As we reached the end of our interactions, Shalini was moving to Nainital to 'absorb' the philosophy more deeply and to develop her skills in non-alienating forms of learning and natural healthcare, in order to prepare herself for setting up a place of her own like that. Her new life was a community set up, isolated in the mountains, of a markedly trusting, benevolent and spiritual spirit, in the company of gracious gurus. *Secondly, it helped her recover her personal core freer of artificial appearances and compulsions of modern life.* She was increasingly turning towards indigenous systems of ayurveda and naturopathy (in contrast to allopathy which her mother subscribed to), yoga and simple living which helped her overcome her uneasy habits of smoking, drinking, partying (picked up through her exposure to western education abroad) and reconnect with native knowledge and local wisdom. *Thirdly, the decentralised, non dogmatic and context-sensitive nature of the framework dumbed down her fears of non participation, exploitation and righteousness.* It also enabled her to form meaningful human relationships in which individuals dealt with each other without masks, pretences and games and from which all participants would grow. In her engagement with this darshan, she found people who were inclusive and authentic whom she could lovingly make a part of her extended 'family' and got a direction in her life about how to build a 'home', a sign of psychosocial fittedness for a young woman wanting an identity in which personal relationships could be harmoniously blended with social engagement. *For her, spirituality meant a continuing involvement with and bettering the familial--social relationships as well as efforts directed towards bringing about constructive changes in the patterns of living of people at large. Finding this amiss in her father's way of spiritual practice, she found her own balance in Jeevan Vidya.*

She was looking forward to her new abode and wanted her parents to feel assured of her. Her partner, whom she was marrying soon, had also decided to move to Nainital. He was from media background, was exploring Jeevan Vidya and was using it to clarify his own vision in life. He still had aspirations of city life but was largely convinced of the 'rightness' of the understanding. She was preparing herself for a life in which her intimate relationships with her partner as well as family could be blended harmoniously with her spiritual–aesthetic strivings.

Praveen

I met Praveen through a common friend when he was in Delhi for a short stop-over while returning back from Mussorie where he had gone to attend a workshop on self-knowledge. As three of us basked in the sun in a park, we had some interesting exchanges on spirituality, psychology and social action. A soft-spoken, articulate person in his mid-20s, he spoke about the ideas of J. Krishnamurthy, Gandhi's Swaraj and shared his travel experiences of meeting friends and visiting set-ups where people were experimenting with community living in harmony with nature. He joked about his nonworking status as I vented my exhaustion of managing several jobs together. He showed curiosity in the research and my observations about young people, and so I asked him if he would be interested in sharing his personal journey. Since he was returning a day after, we met the subsequent day for a research interaction, and I developed few themes over emails.

Praveen was a mechanical engineer by qualification and had worked as an environmental engineer for almost 2 years in an automobile company. During engineering itself, he had *begun to think and learn about issues of environmental damage, development paradigm, globalisation, poverty* etc. So he had a critique of corporations before he entered his job, but he still wanted to get a first-hand look for himself, and also he had to earn for his family. He belonged to a lower middle-class family. His father had expired and his mother was a clerk in a government department. Praveen *resigned from his job as his dissatisfaction with profit model of the corporate world increased, deciding to see if life could be organised around a different set of values rather than that of limitless expansion*. Research inquiry with Praveen focused on mapping his motivations, values and struggles inherent in his endeavours to 'live his questions'. The interview went as below:

- *What do you do for a living?*
  Right now, I am not 'working' for the last year or so. *I have a lot of questions on what is right action and what it means to live responsibly in today's times. I have been volunteering for many 'social change' activities since college days, like 'educating' poor children, spending time at old age homes, being a part of youth collectives, spreading awareness and information dissemination, corporate environmentalism etc.*

P. Bansal, *Youth in Contemporary India: Images of Identity and Social Change*,
DOI 10.1007/978-81-322-0715-3_16, © Springer India 2013

Apart from these direct involvements, I have also had the opportunity to interact closely with many activist friends from diverse backgrounds, philosophies and approaches to social change. However, I am now losing the inner meaning these activities had held for me and am revisiting some of the root questions again. *What is my understanding of social change? Why change at all? How is it interrelated with the individual? What is 'right action' in an increasingly reactionary society? Have not been able to work wholeheartedly until the answers for these questions are found.* So over the last one year I have just been staying at home, thinking, reading, slowing down and let the answers emerge from within.

- *What was your job profile as an environmental engineer? And what were your dissatisfactions with the work?*
Theoretically, environmental engineering involved taking care of the company's compliance with environmental laws, improving its performance standards, reducing resource consumption like water, energy, reducing hazardous waste generation etc. But I realised that companies were primarily preoccupied with profits and growth and if they didn't keep up to this, then they wouldn't be able to survive in the current market. Even if a corporation was willing to take these seriously, there are limits to how much of the above work can be done within the growth economy. So a lot of my work involved writing fancy reports on sustainability and corporate social responsibility creating an image for the company it didn't fully deserve. Of course, we were also allowed to tweak a few things here and there on the ground to make things better as long as it didn't cost the management too much money. So from such experiences, *I had begun to feel that it was futile to work for the creation of a just and sustainable society from within a corporation, within the framework of their current design, vision and core values of competition, limitless growth and preoccupation with profits. So I decided to step out to work on things I find more meaningful and closer to heart like working with children, strengthening local food systems, community media etc.*
Just before quitting, I had spent a month in Ladakh attending a conference on globalisation which brought together proponents of counter development from across the planet to question the basic assumptions behind economic globalisation and to articulate *alternatives in defence and renewal of local economy, knowledge and peace.* After that, to come back and sit in a cubicle and continue to do what I was doing seemed absurd. So I resigned right after coming back from trip.
- *Any anxieties, conflicts that the decision brought?*
There was anxiety, fear etc. of stepping into the unknown. Didn't know what to expect. But I had some savings as backup and friends who had taken such choices in the past. But it was a *blind leap of faith* as well a bit. But it just didn't feel right anymore to continue, so I left. *As for conflicts, there was always the question of money, how will I take care of the family, what will I do for a living etc. These are still there even now.*
- *What have you been doing thereafter?*
After that, I volunteered at a school and tried testing out few of my ideas in *environmental education.* This was my own school and gave me a huge opportunity to know myself because the kids in that school resembled my own tendencies largely. Dealing with them closely gave me an opportunity to understand some of the influences that have shaped my own life and choices. As far as environmental education is concerned, I felt that all forms of curriculum should be avoided at first. The need is to first *create spaces where children can connect to nature without any predefined plans, agendas or expectations where they establish a relationship with it by their own free will and in their own ways.* While information, curriculums and intellectual understanding are all important, what's paramount is a *coming alive of the heart for inspired action* to emerge. I realised it for myself as well as for students that our kind of schooling gives us knowledge which is textual and passive. We lack the living knowledge of how real world functions. Apart from sound knowledge of the subject, the teacher has to be

grounded and connected to life oneself and not interfere or micromanage the children much [teachers usually do the exact opposite]. I realised that only towards the end and there is a lot to unlearn in this respect. Besides, I also did a few interviews with people who were engaged with wholistic social change. Over the last one year, I have just been *trying to understand myself and things happening around me.*

- *What is the nature of this process of understanding oneself and things around oneself?*
  The process is to *be completely alive to each moment*, keeping all of oneself open and observing all that happens within and without in the field of consciousness in that moment. Some call this meditation. It's not easy to get it right straightway and requires patience. I guess that is what I have been doing—practice. Living each moment is not dogmatic. It's also not about external actions. *Inner clarity and peace decides whether the moment has been lived or not. And the inner voice and conscience knows where our actions are coming from. Just that it speaks in a feeble voice, and most of us are too noisy within to hear it.* I am trying to understand—who am I?; what should I do in life [i.e. what is the purpose of my life?]; how to live in alignment with one's *values of living and loving well, being genuine at all times and reducing the violence in our lives*; gathering courage to walk away from the comfort zone path, face insecurities that come with it, non-acceptance of the family and society.
  I guess the insight into these questions and the strength to stand secure in them comes from the inner self. There is no one formula. Sincere contemplation beyond intellect holds the key, I feel.
- *How does attention to the dynamics of inner being interrelate with social change?*
  I have come to realise that this is a split that has to be healed. As I dabbled more with philosophy and spirituality to deal with some unpleasant happenings in life, *I recognised that environmental degradation, economic globalisation, business corporations, schools, George Bush [and Dick Cheney], limitless growth, farmer suicides, riots and wars, corruption, the oil crash, loss of biodiversity, development etc. are not disconnected issues but are the manifestations of the growing chaos and fragmentation inside us - individuals and communities. And these external manifestations cannot be genuinely dealt with, without an inward pilgrimage towards spontaneous order and wholeness.* I also feel it's very vital to understand how deeply entrenched we are inside the 'machine', as much as it is rooted inside us. We have embraced the systems and structures, and we feel happy because we are given physical security, economic security, comfort, leisure and entertainment. *Today, as much as we need a revolution in our states of being, we also need to evolve fresh ways of organising human activity [economic, social and political] to facilitate the flowering of life.* I see no way out of our individual and collective crises until this dichotomy is bridged, the split between *radical critique and radical spirituality*. I feel the 'activism' we need today is the living of our lives as embodiments of both of these at the same time—*lives of resistance and regeneration* as two sides of the same coin. Inner freedom from the past, from the thought structure, from the organised, standardised collective mind is absolutely necessary if we are to meet one another without mistrust or distrust, without fear, to look at each other spontaneously, to listen to one another without any inhibition.
- *How do you negotiate with the concern of money to manage a lifestyle and take care of family?*
  The concern is there especially now with growing inflation and dwindling savings. So far I could manage with what I had in the bank, but soon I will have to start earning again. *Hope to find a job that I resonate with and doesn't conflict with my values like jobs with certain NGOs I like or freelance writing.*
- *How does your family take to your decisions and endeavour?*
  I am coming to accept that unpredictability and flux would be a large part of my life and it might never be settled. This sometimes does cause insecurity, but so far I have managed to not let it direct the course of action. But will have to see how things turn

out as life becomes more challenging. *Dealing with family and world has been difficult. Their ideas of success and security don't match with mine. They feel let down regarding the expectations they had from me and are scared for my future.* This has been a constant point of stress and tussle between us, close relatives and some friends included.

I don't have much of a strategy dealing with this. I try to be as honest as possible and engage with them from the heart. It doesn't always happen this way though. At such times it causes emotional stress and non-acceptance of the circumstances. But of late it doesn't feel as bad. Maybe I have come to enjoy loneliness and solitude more. And being on the path to discover truth for oneself unlocks its own source of energy, and this makes it possible to deal with external challenge.

- *But how radical/unconventional can one be?*
  There are no limits. Fear is the only barrier. But it's not radical living for the sake of it, but it's about listening to inner voice, the conscience, the voice of the heart. How 'radical' we turn out depends on how much we listen to it. How much responsibility we take for living in alignment with it. Fear places a lot of roadblocks to this but that's the challenge... to break through that.
- *What are your personalised meanings of work, success, security, settlement? According to you should these terms be replaced by other terms to map life?*
  Work is an activity that is truly inspired by the goodness of the heart. It doesn't matter what I do, but where the motivation comes from defines work. *The work that I want to do is the life that I want to live. Success is a sense of fulfilment that accompanies a job well done and for the right reasons.* How it 'feels' after the work is done is success in my opinion. If there is contentment and fulfilment after... as far as security and settlement is concerned, I don't understand them well yet so wouldn't be able to say much about them. Doesn't mean I don't think they are important. A certain amount of security [not just material] for a rainy day, unexpected emergencies, a sense of well-being etc. is certainly important. But where does one draw the line is the question. Many times we let fear dominate and keep accumulating [possessions, relationships] and then too much of it becomes a burden. I feel if settlement means rootedness to a place and culture, then it's a good thing but if it means stagnation as it conventionally does, then it's not very healthy.
  Motivation, inspiration, vision, energy, purity, simplicity, beauty, love, peace, community, inner meaning etc. are some of the words life should be mapped by.
- *Is there a community of people you interact with for guidance or discussions on 'right action'?*
  There are no friends whom I am in active dialogue with over such guidance. Most of them are dead and speak through books and their life stories [smiles]. *Vivekanand, Jesus Christ, Gandhi, Krishnamurthi etc. are some people whom I have found a lot of guidance from. Otherwise there are a lot of friends I have met and in touch with who are trying to live soulfully.* The sincerity of their effort is quite an inspiration and a source of strength. I also volunteer for a few days in a month in a reforestation project in Auroville near Pondicherry. The people who run it are of similar intent and it's great to meet them.
- *Is this search best done alone?*
  The search need not be done alone but truth can only be arrived at alone. This might sound a bit paradoxical because there are Buddhist sanghas, the Christian fellowships, the ashrams in ancient India. While salvation and nirvana happen to individuals, the pilgrimage can be done collectively in a spirit of brotherhood and community. However, there are no hard and fast rules really that all this is a complete necessity for awakening. Awakening has its own momentum and things unfold accordingly.
- *How has been the journey this far and how does the future look like?*
  The process of searching for new meanings has been one filled with chaos, where the going is not always smooth. There are times when everything loses meaning. Existence

> becomes a bore and a pain. One feels lonely, disappointed and dejected. At times I am way too radical and at other times way too arrogant. Words feel hollow and one doesn't care. But one survives all of that, comes out battling with help. *So the future looks challenging, but there is a sense of excitement to meet life at its edge. I guess it will be both difficult and fulfilling at the same time.*

The significance of a life like Praveen's in the current research on youth's identity lies in his efforts *to 'live his questions' in contrast to preoccupation with 'making a living'*. In spite of coming from somewhat impoverished environment, he sought enrichment of soul and human relationships and not simply material enhancement. *While the worldly, material reality kept encroaching his consciousness in the form of fears and temptations, he was resolutely going about deepening his inner world.* While life historical details are not available, he did mention that he was much influenced by the goodness of his father and teachings of his missionary school which stressed on compassion and humanity. He was striving to find answers to how to be and what to do through a withdrawal from the world around as is reflected in his 'staying at home, thinking, reading, slowing down and letting the answers emerge from within'. His exploration was not so much in the form of seeking psychosocial fittedness in which one's own cultivated potentialities are sought to be expressed in a creative niche for the purpose of impacting the society. Rather, his search was for a form of jointness of existence in which a state of harmonious balance between self and surround is reached through inner transformations. *Within the spiritual world image realising a state of profound consciousness and attaining more illumined qualities of being through disciplining of mind and soma helps transcend and thus individuate from the intense emotional involvements of family and other significant social groupings. Praveen experienced these struggles of individuation in his own life while dealing with the expectations from the family to have a 'conventional' settlement, handling one's own fears and dejections and learning to live and coming to enjoy the solitude that comes with such strivings.*

He saw reaching a sense of wholeness in his own being on the same continuum as restoring wholeness to social order. Inner chaos was seen in a reciprocal relationship with outer disarray. *He thus strove to make an 'inward pilgrimage' for meaning to connect more deeply with activity directed outwards for necessary social change.* The lives of Gandhi, Vivekananda, Krishnamurthy and Jesus, he was devotedly reading and drawing inspiration from, had combined elements of activism with those of emotional and religious mysticism. The historical endeavours of Gandhi and Jesus were directed towards regeneration of religious vitality as a tool of sociopolitical transformation. Vivekananda's vision of modern Indian identity was to integrate a rational, scientific model of inquiry and the aims of technological modernization with the essentials of the traditional Hindu world image. Krishnamurthy is one of the most 'intellectual' of modern gurus, with a following chiefly among the most modern and highly educated sections of Indian society. Praveen's experience of teaching students of his school was reflective of his own rational, intellectualising tendencies. *Thus, within his own psychic space, he was struggling to activate a synchronicity of fragments of rationality and spirituality, scientific temper and religious spirit and action and reflection.*

Saumya

Saumya, 25 years, was working with a People's Rights Movements in India. On getting to know about her from a common friend, I called her up and spoke to her about the research idea. She responded that she might not be with the movement for long but would be interested in participating in the research work. We first met after her return from a national convention on the issue of special economic zones. Following a brief introduction to my work, Saumya spoke at length about the issues central to the movement with which she was working. Her powerful and nuanced presentation made amply clear her understanding about the facts of the matter and her involvement with the struggle that had a 24-year-long history. Listening to her made me realise with all my senses and intellectual faculty the severity of the various social/economic/medical as well as the livelihood concerns that face the survivor community over the generations. She also effectively explained the grave challenges that people's struggle faces in the form of state apathy and its unstinting support to the expansionist attempts of the big corporates who care little about the dignity and welfare of the people. *As a seasoned spokesperson of her campaign, she showed links between her own cause and the various other movements in India, terming them all at the core as struggles for a life of dignity, preservation of livelihood.* Her convincing arguments created a charged emotional context in which I felt as a 'victim' of the tragedy that I had not directly experienced but to which I was unwittingly joined by becoming 'somatically aware' of the poisonous substances which are flowing through my blood because of the chemicals I intake through food, water and air. She optimistically hinted at the power of youth if they decide to become anti-corporate and refuse to use their products, services and shun employment opportunities with them. She added gleefully that it would give the state a big cause of worry.

Saumya's primary work responsibility was to create awareness about the movement amongst the student community in India and to develop a reactionary support base for the same. As the first person to hold the job of youth mobiliser for the campaign, she had designed her work profile and style to include various elements of political advocacy, community organising and lobbying. She visited different campuses and shared stories of sufferings of generations of people affected by

P. Bansal, *Youth in Contemporary India: Images of Identity and Social Change*,
DOI 10.1007/978-81-322-0715-3_17, © Springer India 2013

toxic waste and contamination and showed them documentaries on the struggle, corporate accountability, environment and allied concerns. She said that according to her:

> Youth campaign is very important. It is necessary to build a force that can support any movement from below by offering human labour, skills and above all energy. By believing in the sociopolitical values of the struggle, young people can do much to stall the insidious erosion of ideals like justice, human rights, accountability of corporates and government and people friendly development. An aware and conscious community will respond to the situation whether it is Bhopal, Vietnam or NBA. As we say, there will be a 'culture of questioning' rather than a 'culture of silence'. You can be an activist teacher, an activist doctor. It's not necessary that you become an activist by profession. But whatever you do, you are aware. It is what Ella Wheeler Wilcox says in this poem:
>
> *To Sin by silence, when we should protest, make cowards out of men.*
> *Had no voice been raised against injustice, ignorance and lust,*
> *The inquisition yet would serve the law*
> *And guillotines would decide our least disputes,*
> *The few who dare must speak and speak again*
> *To right the wrongs of many.*
>
> So to respond and react in defence of what is right is important.

Her conviction about the legitimacy of the concerns of the people's movement which she was joined with was unflinching and it showed up repeatedly in her myriad interactions with me and other people and her fieldwork which I had many opportunities to observe both in Delhi as well as with the survivor community outside Delhi. She called herself a 'campaigner', a designation she choose over 'development professional' which was far too corporate according to her and 'activist' which was far too hard for her. *Over one and a half years of association with her as a researcher and later as a sympathiser of the campaign, I witnessed her growth in the sphere of social action. Saumya's life story always had two sides: One, which described her difficulties, disappointments and dilemmas about being a young person in the sphere of social activism and second, which reflected her conviction and commitment to resistance politics. The latter received a vitalising boost during protest actions by the survivors spanning over 3 months in Delhi at Jantar Mantar during which she was closely involved with the planning and staging of actions and which also brought her into face to face confrontations with the establishment in the form of police, politicians and bureaucracy. During that time, she would often recount the successes of the actions at shaming the government with much glee and showed forbearance at the wait and failures. She experienced herself getting more 'radicalised' and capable of maintaining an equanimity in the face of challenges, which was also affirmed by the leaders of the campaign, much to her satisfaction.*

Conversations with her usually began with her talking about the latest update in her life, which would be either a new development on her work front or a housing problem that she would be facing or some chat that she had about life generally. All of it would be shared with alacrity which marked her speech in a characteristic way. She was effusive in her talk, quick in her thinking and self-analytical in her stance. *My interactions with her led in two directions: Her educational and work-related experiences and her familial milieu. All of these are woven together to lay out what were the boundaries negotiated in her thought and living to adapt herself to an 'activistic' life, a struggle of identity for herself. An attempt was also made to get an insight into the psychological roots and development of her political consciousness and belief in social action.* Below are excerpts of interviews as well as her narrations.

I

- *Tell me something about your educational career.*
  In school, we were 3 friends, very close. We were called 'the trinity'. [Excitedly] We would bunk our classes to have our own discussions. *I find that phase of my life very important because we were reflective and thoughtful.* We used to wonder about things like this teacher wears a different saree every day, that teacher repeats her sarees often. So how would this teacher feel in comparison with the first one? In fact, we actually got so much concerned by this that we went and asked the teacher. So she told us about her family and how she feels about the situation. So, like this we used to ponder about a lot of things. *It wasn't just studies for me. We used to keep an eye on all the going-ons in our school. From an early stage, I wanted to become an advertising person.* I had a passion, a dream of being in the ad world. Trust me, nobody could have composed so many Oscar acceptance speeches while sitting on the toilet pot as I have [Laughs out aloud]. Every day, I would make a new speech. Since, I didn't know any other prize in advertising, I thought Oscar would be the one. I would be the Saumya Sharma—the copywriter types. I would see on TV: the red carpet, flowing victorian gowns, speeches, acknowledging people who have contributed to one's life. It was all fascinating to me. But then it all got lost. Now, I try to think a lot when I stopped fantasising about this and composing creative speeches. I don't know whether I really had an obsession with the award and the speech. Whether it was a way of making an identity for myself through all of this, reaching out to people, telling them that this is what I am? I don't know.

  Then I came for my graduation in mass communication to Delhi. College was.... I was not a person whom people knew in college. I wouldn't speak much and hence was quite inconsequential. It was a different world from home. There I also experienced some injustice from the teachers' side in the form of partiality towards someone less meritorious. *Why should influence and contact be the criteria and not merit especially when you always professed that merit is the criteria. It disillusioned me.* Then during college, we had to do an internship. So I applied to a leading news channel and was so pissed off with them when after waiting for a couple of hours, the receptionist just told us that we couldn't meet the person that day. I was enraged at their high-handedness and their lack of sensitivity. Then, I applied to another NGO and had a very good experience of working with people there. I had fractured my foot, but they made space for me and gave me work which I could do. It was a very nice, sensitive environment. *So, I had begun to question the media, its role and its culture. Those were conflicting times for me because I always wanted a corporate high profile advertising job for myself. But, I had increasingly begun to feel that deepest of my values would not be respected in the media culture.* I didn't find the lifestyle there compatible with my own.
- *Values and lifestyle, in what sense?*
  Like, I have never been loose with words. I don't... can't use swear words which I saw being very freely used by everyone. It is one of the most violent forms of behaviour, I think, to use gaalis [swear words]. Then, the bad experience with the news channel office put me off. *I was, like, if after rising up in life if you can't be*

sensitive to people and if you think that you are defining people's life, then in a way you are deluding yourself. Also, all this page 3 journalism and the state of media reporting, all of it made me disconnect from the media scene. Basically, I didn't find it as humane as I wanted it to be, as sensitive to people as I wanted it to be. But I was in a big dilemma. My good experience of the NGO had attracted me to the social sector. Also, the idea of working with people was interesting in itself. I had applied to both Indian Institute of Mass Communication [IIMC] and Delhi School of Social Work [DSSW]. I got through both. Everyone counselled me that I shouldn't leave IIMC. It means assured job, good salary, up market lifestyle. *My father also wanted me to join IIMC. He had almost lived the ad world dream with me.* But I was not feeling like it at all. So then, he said that if your heart is not in that, then you do what you want to do. *So I joined Masters in Social Work [MSW].* There I was very active. I was doing many things. One was, of course, studies; second, work with an organisation as a student mobiliser for colleges; third, general secretary of union; and fourth, community work. It was satisfying and creative. After I finished my post graduation, I got an internship with another NGO. There also the experience was very good. They took me to World Social Forum, treated me with dignity and as an equal. Made me feel included. That reinforced my belief to be in this sector. *I was becoming more convinced that this is certainly where I want to be.* At the same time, I also started realising that the two set-ups were not as different as I had made them out to be. There is politics, use of swear words, open relationships, abuse, broken marriages, in both the set-ups. Even in my present work, I see how power is used by the leaders. There is politics over who will be included in the inner circle of influential people and who will be excluded. The decisions, sometimes, are not democratically taken and opposition is not tolerated. *But the only thing which was and is a major differential for me is the kind of satisfaction in work that I have in the social sector. In advertising world, you would not refuse a client, even if you know that its product is harmful.* For example, look at Pepsi. Your company would not give you the freedom to not do an ad campaign for this company. In fact, you would be required to highlight the positive aspects of the product and hide the glaring negative attributes. *This is the price you pay for the money, fame and comfortable life. For me, the issue was whether I want to make such a compromise with my work. The creative satisfaction of designing an ad campaign is present in this current work also. Because we are also designing a campaign for justice.* Just as through advertisement you mobilise people, we are also garnering the support of people. In fact, in my IIMC interview, I had said that I want to do public service advertising campaigns. My thinking, by then, had begun to shift in this direction. In my present work, I am creating a support group of young people through a campaign for the survivors' cause. So the work is very satisfying. *The compromise here is that you have to cut down on living expenses, minimise your needs, if you are into genuine work with people.* Because if you are a consultant, then you lose contact with the ground realities. You become a document making machine in which one document is based on other documents. For me, my personal choice was this kind of work because I don't think I was in a rush of making money anyways. *Whatever money I am making, 10–15 thousand is good enough for me to survive in Delhi.* And, also I realise that the way other people look at you change. They feel you are different. You get a different kind of respect.

One another thing that had happened, and it was a big influence, almost a milestone in my life was the visit to Narmada Valley. After my graduation when I was working with this organisation as a student mobiliser, I went for a field trip to Narmada Valley. It was... what you say, when you start searching your soul. Till that time, I was like a princess, at the high end deciding that I would not go to corporate sector because they used bad words. In Narmada, I realised that I was deciding not to come back here because of all selfish reasons. I don't know whether it was the right thing or the wrong thing but certainly even now I would say that I would not go back to Narmada because there is no coming back from there. You would stay there for the entire life. I am still scared of this.

- *Why do you feel like that?*
  Because it was just so much. *It will give you the highest sense of working with people. You see so much. People demolishing their houses with their own hands.* The house that they had build with their own hands 2 months back. Why? Because government authorities would not come to raze your house but you have to give a sample of your house as a proof that it doesn't exist now. Only then you would get compensation. *I found it really unnerving.* I think, to build home in itself is such an investment, not just money wise, physically, emotionally, culturally. It is a double torture to break it with your own hands and be uprooted. Then, there was another incident; we had gone to see a panchayat meeting. There was this old lady sitting next to me. So as we got up to leave, she held my feet and begged me to stay on. She implored, 'Oh! Please don't go. We will do whatever you want us do. We don't have anything to give you. But take whatever we are left with, but please, please save our land. Don't let it be taken from us'. This was when I knew we were returning the next day. I did not know what to say to that woman.... *In MSW, we had studied a principle of work which said that don't get emotionally attached. It is something, I have found very hard. I am still struggling with it. How can you be emotionally detached and yet work?* Either it is a utopia but I don't find it a positive utopia. Somehow, I feel that you would not feel that rage unless you emotionally connect with people. Unless that happens, their pain is never yours. You will be able to only think about issues. Economic effects, environmental influence, social ramifications... is all what you would be concerned with. *I had never seen so much of poverty ever before. One scene after the other... I would be exposed to and slapped by so many different kinds of things which would challenge me and my perception of life and work.* One family was telling me that their daughter-in-law had to deliver her child on the rocky land. People are going through hell there. I feel even a road would be more comfortable. How would that girl have withstood the pain in such inhuman conditions? Fertile land is taken and people are thrown in some rocky area where they can neither have a decent living nor livelihood. *One thing was clear that there was no going back from here. But I couldn't free myself from my barriers.* I could not muster the courage to stay back where I knew that campaign needs people. Where I knew that there was so much of acceptance for me. That introspection is still going on. Why did I not decide to be there?
- *What were the barriers that constrained you?*
  I felt very emotionally triggered. I knew that there is so much magnetism here that you would not be able to break the force and come out. See, it is also the truth that whosoever has worked in Narmada, has worked there for 10–15 years. Even when they moved away, they remained strong supporters of the movement. When you live and work with the displaced people there, you learn it by feeling it once. There are different things which give people this experience of being in a cyclone, being pulled, being sucked. For me it was this. *It was about losing oneself completely. No one knows the many leaders in the movement, all middle class that have given up their lives to make a life in the valley. Someone who is an engineer, only son, only child in fact. He decides to leave his family and settle in the valley. There the utmost responsibility is Narmada. Your parents might be sick, but at that point if you are on a hunger strike, what will you do? Will you leave the strike to visit your parents? These are things that affected me. I don't think I could give up my family, my core of papa, mummy and all.* Once, on Raksha Bandhan, I couldn't go back home and even talk to my brother. He was so upset that he cried the whole day.
- *The core is also about a particular vision of life that one builds up, like to have a stable career, marriage, children. That also begins to get dismantled when one goes into such way of life.*
  That's also because we don't have role models of this kind in this work. I haven't come across anyone who is happily married and is an activist. There are relationships... but

they are either open or broken. Rosy Didi, one of the woman activist in Narmada whom I am very fond of, told me that Saumya don't expect much from marriage. It comes with conditions and an expiry date of 10 years. She has a broken marriage. One problem is also that we are so aware of our rights and ourselves that this awareness in itself becomes a problem sometimes. Like other women would be okay, if husbands were to take decision. But this will not happen in the case of women in our kind of work. Isn't it a violation of this right and that right? Isn't it male chauvinism? It becomes difficult to then manage relationships. I have seen with other activist friends, that their arguments have no basis. I have never been into relationship, so I don't know where my awareness will lead to conflict in it. *But, yes it is scary to not see family life in this work space. And, I do want to have a family. One has needs of love and care.*

- *What about the actual hardships of a life like this?*
  I didn't feel living there would be difficult. To walk for miles from one village to another, to make do with very little things, were not really the issue for me. The reality was stark and it hit me. . .the old woman, the man breaking his own house. *It made me believe the urgent need to commit oneself to the movement. But I was not prepared to give a lifelong commitment to the issue where I knew it was required and appropriate.*
- *How do you deal with the issue of money which is not much in this work? It means one has to live a frugal life which doesn't afford much comfort.*
  Yeah. . .it's not much. But it is enough for me to survive. I mean, I joke about it by saying that see my life has so much of variety. I am comfortable in AC also, in fan also and without fan also. Where else would you get such diverse experience? Actually, it's also not only a joke. *It really frees you from so many unnecessary hassles.* I don't bother about where would I stay? What would happen if I go to villages? What would I eat? I have grown over these things now. Besides, I don't think I was ever in a rush to make money. *If I had to make money, I would have just opened a shop.* And also, I took up earning fairly early in my life, from graduation days. So, I could always save money. Even now, I manage within whatever I earn and also save a little. So, that's not an issue for me. *I know that I can earn my living.* I don't compromise on the quality of clothes I wear. If I have to eat a chocolate doughnut in Café Coffee Day, I will go ahead and have it. *I don't compromise on the quality of fun I have. For me, fun is not about hanging out at expensive restaurants. You can have fun in a modest place also if you have good company.* I also have a very good support system of friends and family on whom I can always rely for help, if need be. I am also not opposed to comfort. Like sometimes I travel by AC because I get rashes due to sunlight. So, the fare for one way journey is paid by the campaign and the other half is paid by me.
- *This is certainly a good way of looking at it. But, you would agree that life can certainly do with more money.*
  See, it's like this. I am happy with the work I am doing. So, the compromise that I am making is for this satisfying work. *I will not deny that one has to minimise one's needs.* Like housing is a big problem here. I have lived in dingy rooms because they were cheap. That's why Kamini's house is such a haven for us.[1] I often stay up here. This is one of my favourite hangouts. I keep looking out for opportunities to come here. It gives me a sense of space and peace. Both of us have stayed in rooms which are so dingy that

[1] One of our meetings took place at her friend Kamini's house located in one of the many winding lanes of a nondescript Delhi locality. The house was furnished with bare minimum essentials; a bed sheet spread over a mat, a noisy cooler, cotton curtains and a mobile charger were the objects of one room. Kitchen had the resources to cook up a simple, nourishing meal which we had made use of to make rice pulao after a long conversation. The other room was strewn with many half open cartons and bags, some of which she informed me belonged to her friend and some of them to her friend's friends who were on a look out for a house.

it gives us enormous pleasure that now we have a terrace. We take all our friends to the terrace to show them around. It doesn't bother us that we don't have much stuff. It's happiness in its own right. So, you manage like that. In fact, because of the frequent changes of house, I have begun to think why to have so many possessions. [Winks] Just have a bag full of clothes which you can carry with yourself and spend the night in any friend's house. Just keep rotating in different friends' house. Even in my current job, I spent my training days living in a survivor's house which was far from comfortable. But, I understand that it's a part and parcel of the kind of work I do. My parents say that at the moment you are single and young so you can live like this. I agree with them also. . ...*I don't deny that I have economic insecurities. But, I don't think too much about it. As long as I am having fun in work and life, I am okay with it.*

- *How did you overcome these usual concerns of where will I live, eat and all?*
  By doing it. How else? See, once, I was travelling in a train and I didn't have a confirmed ticket. So, I just spread my sleeping bag in between the seats and slept off. I had never done it before, and once I had done it I was comfortable with it. The hesitation was gone. Because, actually, it is only hesitation and nothing else. *This hesitation stops us. Just try it and see. Also, this backup plan thing. Why do we have to play so safe? What will happen if I don't succeed here? What will happen if I fail there? What will happen... you will come back to from where you started? You will always survive. I know I will survive. And above all, you have your parents and friends.* They haven't divorced you. I know that I can borrow money from my friends in case of dire need or stay over at their place. One has to extend oneself to different things. Only then will we know what we really want to do and can do. She pointed to a poster on her office wall which read:

  Your life is your life
  Don't let it be clubbed into dank submission.
  Be on the watch, there are ways out.
  There is light somewhere.
  It may not be much light but it beats the darkness.
  Be on the watch, the gods will offer you chances.
  Know them, take them.
  You can't beat death but you can beat death in life.
  And the more often you learn to do it, the more light there will be.
  Your life is your life.
  Know it while you have it.
  You are marvelous, the god's way to delight in you.

- *Why are you so wary of calling yourself an activist?*
  Well! When I joined this sector I was told I don't look like a 'movement girl'. So when I asked them what you mean by that, they said, 'No! You see you could have well been in development, creative work. Open a school for children and all'. Because my personality comes across like that. *I am generally not aggressive. Only when a boundary would be crossed would I get aggressive. And this is a requirement in this kind of activist work.* Even when provoked, I would pursue a process in which I would be firm yet polite. *I don't outrightly discard other. And in this work, it becomes important to discard the other.* [Indignantly] That set me thinking whether I am really suited for activism or not. Is this the only way? *Labels are tricky. Many times they are just words and used in a very limited sense.* It appears to be becoming a big thing to call oneself fearless. It adds a certain amount of stature. Why? I mean, why I should be less important because I am scared of certain things. *Why it is that someone who obeys society is never taken as a leader?* Also, labels set boundaries for the person himself. Once, you gain them you have to live up to them. I remember an incident when a group of students had questioned the integrity of one of our ace campaigners, just because she had dinner in a slightly

> plush restaurant. *Why should such asceticism be expected of activists? Do doctors think of their patients all the time?* If I don't do a thing in line with my labelling, my credibility would be at stake. *Another thing which is my biggest fear is that my personal exploration shouldn't be at stake. The most selfish guiding principle for me is that whatever happens, I am not compromising on my quality of life, the way I want to live it.* Just because people have expectations from me, I am not going to restrain myself and lose out on my experiences, my life, my individuality. I would like to sometimes obey simple structures. Why should I always create complexities in an already complex life? *The objective is not to further one specific political ideology always. It is about what are your core values as human being....*

The above excerpts shed light on the meaning and relevance of activism for her budding identity. It was clear that she was invested in and excited about her work. Her belief in the work and the learning opportunities it offered kept her satisfaction level high. *It received a vitalising boost during protest actions by the survivors spanning over 3 months in Delhi at Jantar Mantar during which she was closely involved with the planning and staging of actions and which also brought her into face to face confrontations with the establishment in the form of police, politicians and bureaucracy.* During that time, she would often recount the successes of the actions at shaming the government with much glee and showed forbearance in the face of wait and failures. She experienced herself *getting more 'radicalised' and capable of maintaining an equanimity when confronted with challenges, which was also affirmed by the leaders of the campaign, much to her satisfaction.*

Crucially for her, activism was a way of feeling more like a human being. She sought to experience the humanity of the wronged and the poor, to the point of imagining herself in their situation and speaking up for them, with them. By upholding the ideal of *'justice as inner conscience'*, she immersed herself in a collectivity (the community's songs and jokes had become her own), a movement to struggle on behalf of a better 'toxic-free' future. It buttressed those inner structures that reaffirmed her ability as a human being to matter, to make a difference. *During our interactions, Saumya spoke indignantly about the various disturbing visuals and stories of suffering that she had seen in and heard from the affected communities in Narmada Valley and her present site of work. It helped her gain conviction about the rightness of the people's struggles as well as gave her the imagery of ever impending death and disaster which was infused in me during the first meeting with her.* Sensitivity to the continuing dangers of violence, exploitation, repression, annihilation—all of which at the ultimate level makes one feel divested of larger connectedness to the various modes of symbolic immortality—might be contributed to her holding onto death saturated images. They served to anchor her in profound and dangerous truths of disintegration—even those obtained second hand. Many of the protest actions of which she was a part like 'death in' wherein one lies as dead bodies in front of the entry are meant both to confront onlookers with the spectre of doom in relation to certain policies and to provide demonstrators with a semblance of a 'survivor mission'.

The conditions and circumstances in which she lived were of a very different kind in which she was raised. *Whether it was a menacing rape threat issued by a policeman, living in a shanty room where a survivor had committed suicide and which still bore the imprints of his painful life, separation from nurturing family and friends while making a place for oneself amongst the survivors' community and leadership, economic insecurities or phases of depression, Saumya was learning to survive through it all.* Her faith in God and support of family and friends kept her morale high throughout. She felt a deep affinity to Camus' statement: 'In the depth of winter I finally learned that there was in me an invincible summer'. *Such experiences often lend the basic satisfaction, even joy, in being alive, in not having died or done to, along with a sense of having undergone an experience that is illuminating in its hardships and pain.*

Saumya derived her *strength and conviction from a loose flowing group of people spread across the country and a network of friends who shared sociopolitical commitments.* They would go to meetings, do mailings, organise actions as well as go to parties and have fun together. She had also forged *strong links with the community leaders of the movement.* She looked up for *professional and personal mentoring from a senior activist–journalist whose personal living was an example of activist life for her.* An engineer by qualification, he had been a travelling journalist specialising in investigating and reporting on the environmental and human rights track record of corporations. *Felt as warm and inclusive, she idealised him for having an activist vision along with a stable home base of wife and adopted daughter. She was also guided by the resolute political vision of the leadership of her own campaign, whose integrity and radicalism were felt to be inspiring by her.* Besides, she had friends and associates in the mainstream culture which provided her flexibility to venture out in the larger space as well as reflected her need for balancing multiple levels of partial belonging.

The movement work had clearly led her to *become more politically informed, gain competence of mobilisation, understand campaigning tactics and strategies and make use of these for political activity and manoeuvring.* No longer apolitical, she was learning the *art of political articulation* in civil space. She was also a *political optimist* which is integral for any change agent. Saumya knew that the trend of corporatisation could not be reversed but believed that every such struggle would ensure that the threat of another industrial disaster could be averted or at least postponed. *Capacity for play* which can tolerate frustration and even defeat was as much present in her as capacity for work. She had a *gentle self-mocking style and a sense of humour* which made her an entertaining story teller. Her need to keep the fun element high in her life served to lubricate her experiences.

Living in an atmosphere of relaxed social and sexual mores, poetry and music and continuous talk about personal and political, *Saumya was insistently reworking the established sectors of her personality like habits, comforts, propriety, and social norms.* She had become conscious of her Brahmin identity and had been grappling with concerns of how to decastecize herself. *Crossing boundaries in her mind, Saumya strove to deal with fear and threat of bodily assault.* A self-confessed romantic, deeply sensual and prone to fantasising, she retained an open awareness that dream of intimacy could verge on a nightmare and the sexual union of man and woman could become a zone of genital combat even in the much desired marital relationship. Thus, rape did not appear as the 'ultimate transgression' to her.

Her own intense longing for a couplehood which was the site of affirmation of her feminine identity, in body and soul, paradoxically also kept alive a darker sense of feelings of anger and disappointment vis-à-vis the relationship to man. Her work activities also required her to address her own fears. She had to sometimes share living space with men as in a dharna, where men and women sleep alongside. While living with the community, she shared a house with a male survivor. Whether it was the issue of being out in the city late in the night or travelling in the general compartment of a train, she was convinced that the fears were in one's mind. She believed unless, one let oneself go, took chances and experiment, one would not be able to release oneself from the bondage of one's assumed limitations.

However, there were *personal dilemmas that faced her about a lifelong commitment to the activist way of living*. Such a commitment was perceived by her as demanding giving up her core of 'parents and siblings', which was a painful thought for her. Hoping for a more fun-filled and romantic life than her parents, she yearned for marriage. *The 'infamy' of activism sector, especially in the context of women, made her doubt 'her chances of ever getting married if I were to enter the mass movement activism'. She once jokingly remarked, 'One day, I would come back home from an action and my husband would tell me, "It's all over"'*. The *imagery of 'home'* was significant to her and came up recurrently in her accounts of her parents' struggle to build a house, the man in Narmada Valley who was breaking his own house to get the compensation, her own housing problem in Delhi and her wish to have a house of her own. It appeared that 'home' as an object of her imagination had multiple psychological significances for her. As a young person, to have a house was a sign for her to achieve 'economic independence'. It could well be a site for 'homing' that offered the gratifications of a stable, familiar existence. It might also be a fantasy of a desired two-person universe with the husband. All of these desires were felt as quashed if she decided to throw her lot with the mass struggles. It was this hard reality of an activist's life which made her doubt whether she had the 'steel' to become an activist and whether she would like to be one. *However, home was also that edifice which irrespective of whether it was of straw and mud or bricks and mortar was recognised by her as sheltering souls and bodies and this connected her empathically to the struggles of people, whose worlds were destroyed because of state and corporate apathy.*

Getting into the *role of activist was also seen as an antithesis of her youthful need to 'move' and 'explore'*. She saw her life 'as a project, maximise it and fill with various colours within the framework of certain values and principles'. *She was not an ideologue* and preferred ideas and ideals to large belief systems, favoured continuous improvisation in occupational arrangements and in expressions of conciliation and protest. In line with such thinking, Saumya had begun to think of pursuing a Ph.D. utilising her work experience in activism and educational qualification in mass communication. She was envisaging a research work to study how public and media communication was fashioned by key sociopolitical movements, in times when 'media' was increasingly becoming pro-corporate, to communicate its vision to the different stakeholders, to attain various political goals and influence corporate behaviour and government policy. She was actively thinking of *developing herself in the field of political and rhetoric communication to build effective propaganda against the state–corporate nexus.* This field was aptly suited to her talent of articulate speech and desire to be in media. This integrative act was a telling proof of her ability to create direction of life in which various aspects of the identity could be reconciled.

II

In order to get an insight into the *psychological roots and development of her political consciousness and belief in social action*, one had to grasp her need to 'demonstrate' her convictions and to 'speak up' in defence of what is right. *Intrinsic to activism is the motive to make public one's private convictions, and her impulse to express herself in all situations joined her to the activist domain.* This came across most vividly in her recounting of a dramatic childhood memory which was a 'landmark' memory for her:

> My father's best friends used to come to our home on Diwali. So I had taken on the responsibility of preparing the dinner for them. They all were very fond of me and would appreciate my efforts and give me Rs. 101/- as a loving gesture. But what I didn't like was that everytime they came, they would bring this bottle of alcohol. They wouldn't get drunk or anything like that...but I began to greatly resent it. I began to doubt whether I was important, the food that I and my mother had planned so meticulously and prepared so lovingly was of any consequence to them. Because no one drinks in my family. That meant that we were anyways not a part of that entire scene. We were not important. If drinks are more important then meet up anywhere and have them. Why involve a family who can't share that? Why should I look forward to preparing the meal when it means nothing? So it was very hurtful to me. I told my father about my feelings and I told him that if it is bothering me then it should bother you as well. You should tell your friends about this. But my father just wouldn't bring this up. A couple of Diwalis went past in the same fashion. I felt more and more alienated from their circle. So on one such Diwali night, I was sitting quietly and thinking. My quietness is also like... the silence before the storm. The drinks appeared. I looked at my father but he didn't say anything. So, I said that I want to say something. My father immediately tried to quiet me down but my uncle encouraged me. So I said 'How would you feel if all of us are together but these drinks are not here?' So they grasped it. One of them got up, picked up the bottle, went out and threw it, came back and said that it would be like this. My uncle said that he really appreciated the fact that I had the courage to speak my mind.

Another pivotal self-element of her was the *desire to be 'recognised'*. As the eldest daughter and a bright student, Saumya enjoyed a special status. She has been acknowledged by the authorities: parental/institutional. *As someone who likes to be in the 'thick of things', she wished to count for something.* Her tepid affinity for her graduation days when she was 'rather inconsequential', her fantasies of winning the supreme award for her work, her gratitude for being made to feel worthwhile in the NGOs she worked in—all reflected her wish to be recognised, thought of, as someone in one's own right, an independent selfhood. The 'power struggle' of recognition originally played out in the early parent–child relations is an enduring struggle of constant tension: At the very moment of realising our own independence, we are dependent upon another to recognise it. For the other to truly recognise and confirm the self's existence, the other must also be recognised as a self. And each self must renounce its claim to be all there is.

A heightened awareness of this dynamic interplay of self and other in Saumya could be gleaned from numerous instances strewn in her conversations. In her own words, 'I have been acknowledged by others for small, small things. At the same time, I have also been cast aside on many occasions. In fact, I think I can now write a paper on "social inclusion and exclusion" [bursts out laughing] given the fact that I have an especially keen sense to experience this feeling'. The transgression of one's selfhood, denial of one's subjecthood is the psychological bedrock from where rage emerges. It is this rage which when meets the language of ethics takes the form of moral outrage against the paternalistic state in the political space. *Saumya's own internal struggle of negotiating between her subjectivity with that of others, of reaching a subject–subject relationship is also the struggle, in a certain sense, of people's movement. Here, the war cry is for a life of dignity, protection of one's native pattern of livelihood.* This power struggle is enacted in the larger political space of confrontation between people and state. The state with all its force has to contend with people who with all their might strive to set more symmetrical relations of power, to achieve recognition of their subjecthoods. *Saumya's indignation often took the form of asking the question: 'Why can't we acknowledge each other?', 'Can there be a form of relatedness beyond the dynamics of domination and submission?'* As someone who did not easily subscribe to the fashionable banalities, she protested rather than remaining indifferent or submit. Her struggle of autonomy was to arrive at a form of self–other relationship wherein both are affirmed.

It is also important to understand the contribution of her parents in her psychological development. Her family consisted of her parents and her two younger siblings, a sister and a kid brother. Her father was a gynaecologist by training but practised as a general physician in the state government. Her mother was a housewife. She was the first child in her larger family to come to Delhi to study. She found the alliance between her parents an unusual one because her father came from a family with very limited means. Her mother, on the other hand, was from an affluent family. Wondering why her maternal grandfather chose all eldest sons as his sons-in-law and that too who came from families much below his own station, Saumya speculated that it could be because he had the confidence that they would be able to build their lives from the scratch, independent of any family support. *She admired the amazing sense of initiative, responsibility, enterprise and survival instincts which her father had shown not only in educating himself but in settling his siblings, getting the family debts paid off and building a house for his family. She questioned herself that would she be able to so as much as her father?* Probably not. But she derived confidence from his life. *She saw her father as principled and strong.* Saumya recounted an incident of conflict between her grandmother and father on the occasion of naming her kid brother. The family later discovered that the priest who performed the holy ceremony was a Valmiki (converted Brahmin and not a Brahmin by birth). Her grandmother insisted on repeating the ceremony terming it as a bad omen. Her father not only refused to repeat the ceremony but also logically argued that if the qualities of such a priest who was not born a Brahmin but became one by self-realisation and learning were to be passed on to the child, it was the biggest blessing for the newborn, rather than a bad omen. She saw her mother as struggling alongside and assisting her father. She also saw her evolving in her own self through her negotiations with and observations of life. *While coming from conservative strata of society, she found her parents flexible and open to discussion and learning.* She had always shared her thoughts, views and experiences of all kinds with her parents and found them thinking, reflecting along with her and expanding their horizons. Her parents were supportive and proud of her work; however, they did harbour anxieties about such an active pursuit of the values that they themselves believed in. While mindful of their anxieties, she was not guided in her actions to immediately placate them.

Saumya's evolving identity was linking together *diverse self-elements—zest for newness and adventure with longing for home and stability; passion for action and excitement with introspective deepening through poetry, music and talk; fashioning communal links with collectives outside with forming communion with the supreme power and oneself; and principled social action with personal experimentation.* Her poetry (to which I had access through her blog) and religious observance of meditation gave glimpses of her ability to contain her fragments and hope for illumination at the end of the tunnel. *One of the key challenges for her feminine identity was: How to combine family commitments with activist convictions? It was a matter of grave concern for her which she often dealt with uneasy laughter combining pain and humour, but the combinatory possibility of which she always kept open in the recesses of her imagination.*

Jayant

Jayant, 29 years, was a sociopolitical activist, writer and coordinator of a political organisation which represented the concerns of the social action groups and peoples' movements in Delhi. Since the four decades post emergency, the organisation had been active against state oppression of democratic dissent. It believed in making immediate and relevant responses to several ongoing issues, concerns and needs like the struggles of the marginalised communities against displacement, the struggle of fish workers, violation of human rights and the rights of dalits and tribal/indigenous people. Following the initial contact over email and telephone, I reached his office to meet him. After introduction, he led me to a room in which four people were sitting watching a video of a badly burnt man, close to his death, being rushed to the hospital. The voice accompanying the disturbing visuals explained that he was a tribal from Jharkhand and had self-immolated himself over the non-payment of funds under NREGA (National Rural Employment Guarantee Act). The office was simply furnished and had a lot of political magazines and journals on display and few bunk beds offering rest and refuge to struggling people who come to Delhi from different parts of the country to voice their concerns to the state.

The interactions with Jayant spawned seven lengthy meetings over a period of 4 months. An energetic and warm person, he took avid interest in the research process. While sharing about his life and work, he was lucid and reflective. He guided me through his political stances and personal life with ease, openness, clarity and detail. Often, I would send a brief research note to him ahead of the interview explicating some salient understandings of life themes that I had generated as well as further concerns. The research concerns were well understood by him, and in fact, much of the research proceeded in the absence of active probing since many of them were brought up and responded by him in the flow of the narrations. His writings also contributed to nuanced understandings of his political work, attitudes and emotions.

P. Bansal, *Youth in Contemporary India: Images of Identity and Social Change*,
DOI 10.1007/978-81-322-0715-3_18, © Springer India 2013

I

One major focus of research with Jayant was to understand his political socialisation, that is, to chart out the influences and events in his journey and development as a resistance activist. From the beginning of the interactions, one found Jayant having *radical political opinions* on wide-ranging issues. His passionate stand was '*Politics is life. If we are having two meals a day to eat, it is a political act. I am political because I see it as the only way to be*'. A Syrian Christian from Kerala, he had a *highly politicised parentage*: His father was a protestant priest who spearheaded the Dalit Christian struggle for equality of rights within the Church, and his mother was a party worker of CPI (M) in Kerala. *He saw his parents' lives as serving the cause of social equality, social justice and social transformation.* His earliest political school was his own home and among his teachers, his parents. Being a son of a radical priest father and communist leader mother contributed immensely to the shaping of his political identity. He saw real strong convictions for social justice and social transformation on both sides. *He closely observed and imbibed his parents' political behaviours and styles.* Talking of his parents' journey, Jayant recounted:

> *As a 6–7 year-old child, I witnessed the first struggle when my father was arrested inside the Church during the Holy Communion by the state police for supporting the Dalit Christian struggle of equal voting rights in the Church.* It was alleged that he was instigating the Dalits for caste violence against the upper castes. The family also witnessed violence. My father was jailed, my mother and sisters were attacked and I got hurt in it. My father was expelled as a priest from the Church which amounted to social ostracisation. But, rather than tendering an apology to the Church, he filed a court case challenging the expulsion which he won and was reinstated. But he was sent off to a Dalit Church which was like a punishment transfer. That sunk the family into financial crisis. His engagement with the Dalit rights' movement and the backlash he received led him to lose faith in Church and religious framework of Christianity. He began to ask—How is it that the body of Christ [Church] is actually strengthening forms of discrimination against people? He also began to find links between religion–politics and religion–state. Why did Church support Indira Gandhi during emergency? He became more and more critical of institutionalised Christianity which downplayed the reformist spirit of Jesus and glorified him as a magician. Through his extensive readings, he developed a theological point that Jesus was crucified for being radical but his followers converted him into a magician. *He then used this point to argue that Church and the state benefit each other by maintaining status quo. Following his understanding, he immediately began to align himself with people's struggles irrespective of whether they were Christians or not.* He found peers across the country—leaders of oppressed communities. He joined forces with comrades from all over—Chhattisgarh, Jharkhand, Uttarakhand, tribal movements, Dravidian movement. He also developed himself as a liberation theologist, a rare kind in Asia at that time. He got a lot of invitations from S.E. Asia, Europe and found a lot of partners in the anti-establishment church group. Our house was the home for many radicals during their underground times.
>
> *My mother, on the other hand, entered politics through the women's movement.* She was encouraged by a senior communist leader's wife to get into women's rights movement. As a party worker in CPI (M), she grew to the level of party leadership because of her sheer intellectual calibre and also because she brought Christian women within the Communist party fold. As a churchy Christian in a Communist party which is staunchly atheist, she was

constantly pushed to think about what it means to be a 'Christian Marxist'? *By virtue of being the wife of a radical priest who was reformulating the message of Jesus in the language of emancipation and liberation which is the language of Marxism, and by her own political influence, she pushed the party to accept practising Christians in the party and also discuss how religion and politics can coexist.*

Speaking of his childhood and college years, Jayant shared:

I started reading 'The Hindu' newspaper at the age of 8 years, very very early in the life of any Kerala kid. *Because you are always eager to know what is happening nationally, internationally because you never felt distanced by it. It was almost like a compulsion on me that you cannot but take notice of whatever is happening in not just your immediate neighbourhood but in communities across country, in other nations.* What is the political change that is happening in the post emergency era? I used to *adore characters like Sparatus* about whom I happened to read some fiction and see a play. His life completely impresses me. [Excitedly] A slave leader of his times, a trade unionist by today's definition, influenced me a lot. In class 4th, I had written an essay on what are the similarities and differences between Jesus and Sparatus after seeing the play on Sparatus's life. *In class 10th, I wanted to write about Hinduism.* I had read a lot of Hindu religious stories like Ramayana and Mahabharata written by Mali. After that, I read their adult versions also, but the children's version connected deeply. But the editor once refused hinting that he would not be able to publish my writing because I was a Christian. That's the pact of secularism... don't allow people of a religion comment on other's religion. *There was a joke in my family when I was younger that I would turn into a Shivaite. For I wondered after all what is the place of a dark god amidst the fair ones? He looks like a Dravidian.* And I believed that Shiva has died. Shiva has died to save the people... he couldn't have survived after consuming the poison.

I used to read a lot. I took up humanities in +2 because I wanted to study history. *I am convinced that if you want to understand yourself and the world around you in the present from past, then history is the tool for it.* In 11th and 12th, I had read Gramsci, Lenin and even the right-wing political writers because I wanted to understand their arguments. It was also the time of globalisation, and a lot of material was available on this phenomena. So I had read a lot on WTO, North–South debate etc. So after my school, my father's friends advised my parents to send me to Delhi for college education. I joined History (Hons.). It was an elite institution, and I had never been a part of elite educational institutions before that. I have studied in government-aided schools. In 7th, I was shifted to an English medium school from a Malayalam medium school because my elder sisters found it difficult to cope with studies in English medium in college after having studied in malayalam medium. Some of my thought process is still in Malayalam. *In college, I couldn't be but part of every issue that was important.* Like, I used to rag. I had no problems in ragging. *But I have gone and assaulted people who ragged with caste bias. It didn't take me more than a year, probably because of natural instincts of leadership, to establish my identity as a strong radical inside college. I was a dada in school as well.* And I was always vocal. I remember when I was in 5th class, two archbishops had come home for a truce negotiation with my dad. My dad had challenged his expulsion from the Church in the court. They didn't want the church matters to be taken out to a civil court. So they had come for a dialogue with my dad. They went out of the house because of me, a 5th class student. My father didn't even ask uncomfortable questions. I was the one who asked all sorts of silly, uncomfortable questions. Started with joke—there were a lot of mosquitoes. So the bishops were kind of getting troubled by them. I said sarcastically—we grow them here. Because even if you would kill them, the 3rd day they would resurrect. They are all Jesus' followers. They are all Christian mosquitoes. The 3rd day, they will resurrect... Sheer sarcasm! A blasphemy in front of archbishops of typical orthodox orientation. *But I was extremely sharp and sarcastic at that age because of my circumstances!*

> In college, I was kind of setting myself up and was also being set up by others as a rebel. *At one point of time, I thought I would be out of college because of my radicalism.* For me, anyone who sells Christianity like soap powder is unacceptable. So whenever I got a chance, I would hit at them. I got a campus evangelical group thrown out of college. *Besides space for radicalism, college also offered me intellectual stimulation.* Because of my extensive readings, I was opinionated. This arrogance was thrashed by a renowned history professor in our college. He played the devil's advocate in my life. He would ask me such uncomfortable questions. *He pushed me against the wall and said that you have not developed any independent thinking of your own. This was the first time, I had heard this.* That hurt a lot. But that made me to really sit down and start formulating on my own. Not that I think I have developed it even now, but it's a search.

Hearing about the growing up experiences of Jayant, one felt that *religion and politics were his toys.* As was obvious from his childhood memories, he played around intensively with religious images and symbols and discovered their political significances, whether it was of Jesus as a social reformer, Sparatus as a trade unionist or Shiva as the protector of the masses. *Much of this make-belief play continued to animate his present convictions in the theatre of politics and war. Radical theological understanding of Christianity* was the guiding force behind his energy and initiatives. According to him, Jesus was not a magician or a miracle man. He was a radical who was intent on bringing justice to the oppressed. He narrated a tale in the Bible which he had heard when he was a child about a yatra Jesus did sitting on an ass:

> In the whole journey, there were people chanting slogans. Then someone asked him, 'Why don't you ask them to keep quiet?' He said that if these people would not express rebellion they feel in their bones, then these stones would start shouting.

He was convinced that Jesus was crucified because he dared to challenge the religious system of his time and energised and enthused people to participate in the larger process of change. *This imagery of Jesus as a reformer informed his own political proclivities to support people's fight against injustice.* In his article spelling out the dilemmas and hopes of activists, he wrote:

> *I am increasingly convinced of the importance of these battles on the streets.* Whether in Delhi, Kalinga Nagar or in Sonbhadra, *people's struggles have always been fought and won on the streets,* against powers that have tried to curtail people's rights and take away natural resources. I try to find new meanings to the slogans, to the negotiations, the press releases and most importantly to my own role as a supporter. I see the new dawn of people's politics that proclaims the celebration of life...

The radical education he received just by observing his parents deal with all kinds of situations, be it physical violence, allegations, mud-slinging and negotiations, helped him understand in no uncertain terms the necessity to approach 'real' politics. Perhaps Jayant's early *sense of specialness contributed by his intellectual excellence, precocious political consciousness and oppositional leadership qualities made it possible for him to also nurture the psychological need to 'be extraordinary'*. Not wanting to be one of the 'normal kinds', he wanted to live by his convictions to challenge structures of oppression, wanted to be central in his sphere of living rather than peripheral and ignored and wanted to exercise his intelligence to formulate political views and visions effective in engineering social transformation in line with the principles of equality and justice for all. *His impassioned political stances were to be in opposition, to put one's neck on the line and to support people's politics.* Playful imagination leads to informed and inspiring vision—a vision which takes into account facts of history and geography, ready social actualities and the inner lives of the people. Only that can be a basis for action and help overcome an ever-ready sense of vulnerability, impotence and irreality. *Jayant had begun to engage with a political vision of unifying the struggles of diverse social actors behind a common goal. He believed that for political action to be effective and for protests, resistances and insurrections to be really able to change things, they need to come together in an act of mutual solidarity and orient their actions according to a thorough analysis of the political situation.* He understood the new politics to be an art of constructing a social and political force capable of changing the balance of power in favour of popular movements.

Jayant evoked the *imagery of 'genetic transmission'* while speaking of his proclivities towards social–political action. He had been a witness of and fellow traveller with his parents. He had seen a *jointness of vision in his parents* where his father's revolutionary sermons were converted into political actions in his mother's work. *He kept his parents close to each other and as ever-present images within himself fuelling his radical political understandings and emotions.* The parental ideology was not only felt as naturally persuasive by him but also experienced as wholesome nutriment to the ideological search of the 'true' values. References to genes, blood and circumstances often came up when he talked of the formation of his political character, his orientation to judge the dangers and traps of sociopolitical work and his precocious ability to comment on political issues and events which he had not dealt with as an adult activist but had learnt about while growing up. He, in fact, did impress me as someone who was way ahead of his age in his political acumen. *He was a self-confessed 'Abhimanyu' and believed that like him had learnt the art and science of breaking into the political game from his parents' experience but had to rely on his own intelligence to evolve the strategies of finding a way out.* He *spoke of his father with a touching tender affection*, almost incapable of being disillusioned or critical of him. He *spoke of his mother empathically*, mindful of her struggles as a wife of a radical priest and as a mother of two back to back children (her sisters). *However, there have been moments when he used harsher tone for her and also referred to her as 'the patronising parent'*. When this was pointed to him, he reflected:

> *I have actually gone much more on my mother. Reactions, repulsions, anger, temperament-wise.* I look at her as myself. So when she does something, I immediately jump on her and question her. But when my dad does something, even if I have to be critical, I'll say it in exactly the same way my mother says. She would smile and go in the other room and say, 'Why are you getting into this? You shouldn't be bothered about it'. I just completely adore him like my mother. I am a fan of his. That's what I have inherited from her. *She sees him as someone who has made her who she is. She thinks that if not for an equality respecting person like him, she would have been another retired college principal.* But because of a partner like my father, she could take the best out of her life. For me also, it's a hero worship for the only man in my life whom I have had chance to observe closely. *He is like a mentor*

> *to me. I have always seen him at a slightly higher pedestal... I will not count on him for any organisational matters. He doesn't have the capacity to do that. My mother is an organisation person.* She was one of the pioneers of the women's collective in Kerala. I am one too in my own small way. He is much better at writing his stuff and giving intellectual speeches. And he is a great one to go for case studies, examples, stories, narratives. (Jayant is a writer too and in his interactions, he would often use a lot of examples to explain his point.) He is a detached person, and that's probably one of the reasons for him not being able to take the movement forward to the rightful conclusion. It's a failure if you look at it. But I will not say it [laughs]. *He had never been a personalised, attached guru for anyone. My mother was someone who was attached to the ground.* She was in women's movement, and a lot of women think that she brought them to public life. *I would also like to be a consultant, friend, guide to people. That's my political role. I see myself as an extension of my mother. The bond between her and me is very close.* I feel that she has moulded me and made me who I am. If I am a great cook, it's because of her insistence that her son should be able to manage his life better. It was she who made me realise that I don't want to be another patriarchal man. *But I am not her photocopy. I am her part 2 [forcefully]. I don't want to replicate what she did. In fact, I want to avoid making the mistakes that she made. I want to be a new experiment.*

Adherence to a way of life cannot remain a reliable factor in one's inner sense of continuity unless one is involved in the common hardships, hopes and hates of that life. These keep an ideology relevant. As a growing child, he had seen many scenes of turmoil at home. Jayant traced his beginnings of political consciousness to the violence experienced by him at the age of 7 years. He indignantly asked, 'What I haven't understood till now is why someone has to take violence for talking social justice? Why is Church which is the propagator of social equality denying the very notion of social justice? Why the Indian state which is supposed to be founded on the ideals of social justice, equality and sovereignty is behaving as if it doesn't know what equality means?' He narrated many *instances of hardships (financial, emotional) that the family faced because of its political work.* One such was missing church:

> *Missing church is a big bleeding factor in our family. We were not given church membership. It's like a social ostracisation.* My mother went against my father's wishes and applied for a church membership in a Dalit Church. Probably her framework was if I were to die today, where would I be buried? Where will my children get married because the Church is not giving membership? But she was humiliated, and her request was turned down. She was told you are an upper caste Syrian Christian, you should apply for membership in one such Church. My father was extremely upset with my mother for this weak act. He didn't talk to her for weeks. *I have seen that on Sunday mornings at 9; it was very difficult for them to sit at home. They would sorely miss Sunday Mass.* We, children, started watching Ramayana and Mahabharata on our neighbours' TV. We never had one. When I would come back, I would see both of them with full eyes and heavy faces. My father was so used to taking the Sunday Mass, but suddenly, he was deprived of his right as a priest to give the Holy Communion. It pained him a lot because it wasn't just a right given by the Church. It was his orientation, his parents' blessings and his siblings' blessings which got him to a situation where he was ordained by the Church to give Holy Communion. When it is taken back from you, your whole self is as if negated.

But Jayant also saw affirmative actions being taken by the parents to keep the hopes and meanings of their existence alive. Like his father, within a year, he established a parallel tradition of holding Holy Communion in public spaces. It was a big act of defiance and also affirmation. He would buy the normal bread and not the sacred sacramental bread because he would say you don't have to follow rituals. Some of these were non-Christian masses where he talked about people's rights and people's movements. Once a more meaningful alternative came in, he stopped missing church. Jayant did not find his parents ever repenting their ideological views.

II

Another focus of the research with Jayant was to understand, within the intergenerational framework, what changes in political emotions, stances and contexts were taking place which were affecting his identity formation. *One of the things that he remained unconvinced about in his parents' living was economics:*

> *One thing that never left me in the midst of all of this is the desire for money. Both my parents are against property.* Both of them wrote off their ancestral property. But, there were times, when my mother would get very upset. These were times when she wouldn't be able to give gifts in gold to her siblings' children. This is a Syrian Christian tradition. For two days, she would just cry and say that am not able to do my basics as an aunt. She had also left her job to marry my father. So she complaint bitterly that I lost my economic identity and for everything I have to ask you for money. And he never had money, so there was no question of any financial gifts to anyone. *So my mother would come down from the pedestal that we had kept her at many times and talk as a very materialist person.* She would be sad about the fact that she couldn't make gold ornaments for her daughters, couldn't get a life insurance policy for her son's education and had to plead in front of others for his education. *But that was her real self. Her emotional reactions were visible. She would be put back by setbacks. My father had something very gaudy about him. He always lived at that pedestal up there. He is detached from the material world.* He always had this confidence that things will go on. But that agitated my mother a lot of times because she knew that things were not good on the ground. But at the end of the day, she developed that resigned acceptance that if he says things will go on, then probably things will go on. Let's wait and watch what happens. [After a reflective pause, he continued to speak slowly] I never had my parents gifting me any clothes. It was when I got admission in Delhi College that for the first time in my memory my father bought me a shirt. Not because of any reasons for my not liking a foot cover that the first shoe I wore was when I came to Delhi. *That's the only thing in my personal life that I am not out of the clutches of—personal greed and ambitions.*

Jayant's 'greed' also reflected in the sphere of influence that he sought for himself. The only time he spoke with mild critique about his father was when he was asked in what ways he thought his political career and standing differed from that of his parents? He made a rather aggressive beginning by saying that he was finding himself very different terrain-wise, positioning-wise from them:

> For example, why is it that my father didn't join politics during the Dalit Christian struggle? Had he done that he would have surely become MP, MLA, minister. But *he opted to do something which was extremely unromantic, extremely nonexciting which is to continue within the Church and lead the fight from within the Church.* Especially, looking back now, it is clear that he was not strategic enough to grow into another sphere from the church space.

He would find himself in a constant state of turbulence, battling out the temptations that surrounded him. After college, he had worked with a media house. There he had climbed to the position of being a reporter. Then he was offered the post of a newsreader which he realised to be a much more powerful post than that of a reporter because of the visibility and fame aspect of it. He was also being paid handsomely. That is the time when according to him his aspirations and ambitions began to get formed and soared. He had a lot of opportunities to grow there. But when one of his stories was not aired because it was not viable at that point of time, he decided to quit. He labelled it as an instinctive decision which later made him realise that it was the political actor in him which was hurt by the business mentality of that media house. It was then that he realised that he gave far too much importance to his political sensibilities. But presently, he had been offered two anchoring roles. He phrased the conflict as thus:

> One wants to *go back to mainstream media* to aspire to be a Karan Thapar, Vir Sanghvi, Prannoy Roy twenty years down the line. *I must admit that these offers are very tempting not just because of finances but also because of reach, fame which affects your ego.* Do you still want to be shunted out in some corner, just working with some limited people? Then you are making a choice to limit your own reach, you are actually making a choice to limit your own openness. It is a very nasty conflict one is in which involves money, social prestige, reach. *Once in a while, an ear opens, and you hear the Eden snake's voice saying that what the hell are you doing? Why don't you just eat the apple and get settled into reality?*

The conflict represented the crack in the intergenerational continuity that was felt as central to his political existence. It pushed him to appraise his parents' stances and have his own doubts and opinions about them. It also impelled him to formulate his own directions in line with his personal aspirations and understandings of changed historical context of social action. *The process had been ridden with shame about his 'greed' for money and visibility, guilt over the felt infidelity to the internalised values and doubts about the truthfulness and reliability of the newer turf being created by him.* There were times when he seemed to be giving up because of lack of meaning, direction and appreciation. There had been phases in his life when he wanted to return home. For long, every year he would fall seriously ill. Depression surrounded him when within a year or so of working with a media-based NGO, he started finding himself stagnating. The stagnation was both economic and intellectual. However, he combated his stagnation, much like his parents, by recovering his energy and emerging as the unofficial fundraiser, innovative intellectual and good coordinator in the organisation. *One of the ways he had tried to balance his principles of life and temptations of money and social prestige was by resisting the inducement of 'the Eden apple' (the lure of a well-paying media job) and by resolving to look at other fruits on offer in the garden of political activism.* Realising that since much like Abhimanyu he had already lived twenty years in aggressive political activism, why should he waste this strength in another stream? He, however, decided that he would prioritise his economic needs equally with his political and intellectual needs. Thus, he 'shamelessly' bargained for his salary in the current organisation that he worked in. It's interesting to hear how he argued for *his position on money*:

If I have to be a full-time activist, I have to be a paid activist. I don't have the luxury of a house or parentage that will take care of my livelihood. If I am giving 18–20 hours of my day for this choice of life, then I have to earn from this. And this is not only for my own survival but all those who can't earn right now. Now, I put a cheque for my parents who are not earning. I also send money for a cultural group in Kerala which is practically defunct because of paucity of funds. I am happy I am doing it. I was much more miserable when I couldn't do that. When I joined this place, I raised everyone's salary. It was necessary. People were working for peanuts here.

Work-wise, he was finding himself on a different territory than his parents. As a coordinator of a social action organisation in urban setting, *he defined his identity as a supporter of people's struggle rather than the leader.* As a *paid activist*, while he mulled over the politics of funding and paid activism, he also agonised over the temptations and trappings of urban life and his own hunger for money and power. But much like his father's positive framework, he had been renewing the meanings of his work during the crisis. *Knowing that there weren't any final settlements to conflicts like these, Jayant appeared to be struggling to have his 'greed' well in hand which would ensure that he would not be impelled to act against his values. He was learning to contain it by employing it in ways that took care of the needs of other.*

III

While defining his own role in sociopolitical activism, *Jayant found himself responding to the post globalisation scenario which according to him had a different politics from the parental generation.* In such an era, he found *anchorage of his political role as a supporter of struggle of masses in the image of a Biblical character Simon of Kurena.* An intense moment was forged when he spoke about him, and I listened to it with ever-increasing fascination:

I would like to believe that what I am doing is what Simon of Kurena did. He finds a small mention in the Bible. He was not a disciple of Jesus neither a follower. When Jesus was walking with the cross on his shoulder, he fell down 14 times. So there are 14 fall points that are commemorated on Good Friday. After his 14th fall, this man came forward and said I'll carry the cross. *He himself fell down several times. But this is not something which you find in Bible as a ritual. No one commemorates his falling down.* So he carried the cross to the place of Christ's crucification. That's the way I have begun to define my role and my organisation's role. This is my conviction. *I am fully aware that I will not be crucified. I, as a middle-class citizen of this country, will not bear the brunt of globalisation and liberalisation.* It is the adivasi, Dalit, fish worker, agricultural labourer, factory worker who will be most adversely affected by it. *I am only looking at ways of easing the walk from the time he can't carry the cross of oppression alone.* Probably he needs help! Pick up the cross from him from there and walk him till the end of the path. Ultimately, you know that the state has decided to crucify him. There is no way he can escape. At the end, he will be crucified. So, I am not giving any false hopes to that man that by taking your cross, I am taking your crucification. No! I am only easing your agony. *I am very convinced that I should be there to pick up the cross. And this is what I will try and do my entire life. I have not come across this interpretation of Simon of Kurena from anybody else. It is just my own*

> *fascination with him, reading and analysis. I would personally like to have more Simons of Kurenas around.* I would like to find my own Barnabas, the son of encouragement. Through my writings and forums where I get to speak my mind, I want to politicise people, processes more and more. *In my personal capacity, I like to discuss, share, laugh about the personal and political challenges facing young activists today.* We even have such a group going. I want to share my enthusiasm for people's struggles, of the big and small victories that they achieve.

Firmly of the belief that *there was no substitute for people fighting their own battles*, he saw the role of the middle-class activists as supporters rather than leaders of these struggles. He saw it as a natural course of events that struggling people were taking decisions for themselves and finding mechanisms to do that within democratic processes. *He labelled this politics of self-determination of various people's movements with indigenous leadership as 'Healthy Anarchism'*. He was defining *his own identity as a solidarity activist* who believed in opposing oppressive structures of state–corporate–NGO nexus and *encouraged democratic politics outside formal representative structures.* He would be much happier empowering, supporting and protecting the interests of people who wanted to fight for their own justice. He understood separate and supportive identities of solidarity activists and mutual respect between struggling communities and activists to be a key element in this form of social action.

He was candid in acknowledging and accepting that the ground of middle-class intelligentsia/activists was not the same as that of the struggling masses. He spoke at length about the *challenges and dilemmas of middle-class activists* in today's world. He was convinced that middle-class activists were not the route of social change because of their own interests of property and moralisms. He added in a sarcastic tone:

> At one level, they served as *convenient buffers for the state* because of their polite language and sophisticated tactics. But the affected people are not bothered about the image, what the media would carry to the masses. It is people like us who are worried about whether we will be branded as an armed movement. They don't care! They are fed up of us and our moralisms. They have realised that the perceptions of the media, of the middle class contribute nothing to their struggles. They talk of violence in absolute self defence. After all, when you see rocket launchers on the other side of the river, you need at least country-made guns. You have to have bullets to shoot down the person sitting on the other side firing rockets at your house. You can't counter them with kitchen knives. *Another issue about middle-class leadership is, because at the end of the day, howsoever, convinced you are about the cause, your first instinct will stem from your middle-class self and upbringing. Also, it takes a life-giving commitment to be trusted by people, especially when your own community is the part of the perpetrators.* Till the time Medha declared Jal Samadhi, major pockets of Narmada Valley were not with her. If anything goes wrong in Narmada, the criticism would undeservingly go to Medha. If people die in police firing, the first accusing finger would point towards her. She will die of her own guilt, I am sure. *That's not the case with new social movements. Here, everyone is an equal stakeholder. So the decisions on what tactics to pursue in protest actions must be made by those in whose name the action takes place, the decisions whether or how to impose sanctions or boycotts on governments and companies must be made by the communities directly affected, and the decisions over critical interventions in the internal politics of struggling communities are made by their own leaders.* Supporters can advise and argue, where there is a relationship of trust, but we cannot have an equal voice and should not make leading decisions.

Jayant's political vision was to overcome the dispersion and fragmentation of the exploited and the oppressed and to cohere the many expressions of resistance and struggle. Experimentation with this vision led him to be a vital part of an initiative—*Sangharsh 2007*. He explained:

> It was a collective struggle to defend the right to life, livelihood, habitat with dignity and sovereignty of the nation and its peoples. The people's movements, voluntary organisations and concerned citizens across the country came together to continue the resistance against the neo-imperialist designs, 'development terrorism', militarisation of society, corporate-driven globalisation, onslaught on peoples' resources and the deprivation and atrocities against adivasis, Dalits, women and minorities. The aim of this endeavour was to *build an alliance of different struggles, movements, resistance groups working on different issues to come together in a mutual act of solidarity and support and endorse each other's demands.* The purpose was to bring the social movements out of their pigeonholes and have them interact with struggles taking place in other parts of the country, learn from each other's experience. Another very important idea behind this initiative was to put forth a people's charter. This was a big step towards redefining social movements. Because social movements, by definition, addressed certain issues that affect them. *The attempt here was to formulate people's vision of alternate India, an alternative development paradigm which would affect different sectors like foreign trade, agriculture, nuclear deal, land rights.* So the people's charter had sections called 'We Assert' 'We Demand' 'We Denounce' 'We Support' speaking of 'We assert the right to life with dignity, freedom from fear of violence, and peaceful coexistence, the rights of ethnic nationalities to determine their collective political future. We demand the acceptance of principles of peoples' sovereignty over natural resources like water, land etc. We denounce all kinds of caste and gender discrimination, communal prejudice and caste injustice. We support the people's will in Jammu and Kashmir etc.'

Reflecting on the possibility of lasting and effective alliances of people's struggles in the present point of history, Jayant spoke with a hint of disappointment. He opined:

> *Each movement is fighting its own battle. But if they all had one common goal, things would have been very different.* Today, social movements in India don't have a common goal. If you say, defeat Imperialist Globalisation... what does it mean? You have to relate it to people's immediate concerns to align them with the larger resistance. *After all, resisting Imperialist Globalisation is about resisting coastal zone management (CZM); it's about fighting against TATA Motors, Mittal Steel, Reliance Mafia etc.* Why can't Mehndiganj people come together with others such as fish workers, handloom weavers, Singur and Nandigram and launch a large-level struggle action across country in a united fashion? If they do it, whatever the Government of India or the army may do, the whole life of Coca-Cola in this country will be 7 days... I can give it in writing. *But there are several factors that are operating which are preventing such alliances.* For one, it has become very difficult to identify the common enemy. Like in the times of Independence struggle, the common enemy was British. But now, the number of actors have become so many that it becomes increasingly difficult to pin down an enemy. Who represents Imperialist Globalisation... is it the state, is it the NGO working in the area? Secondly, if we take the example of Narmada movement, it could have easily become a movement against development paradigm promoted by the World Bank. It didn't. Why? Because the Gujarat Government took the task of engaging the movement by crushing their networks, human resources on an everyday basis. So in that process, it got engaged in fighting with the Gujarat state. So the state has this capacity to disengage you from larger politics by engaging you in smaller, more immediate ways. The same problem is with NGOs. They

> are getting so specialised that if one is working on reproductive health, it will not even look at education. It will not join any street demonstration against globalisation, war, state terrorism. Many of them are busy implementing The Millenium Development Goals of UN which is the agenda of same forces that are perpetuating poverty, war and violence on poor people across the world. If we look at the workers' movement... it is so splintered. There are agricultural workers, industrial workers, fish workers, handloom workers. Besides, there are categories of state and non-state employees. Ideologically, what's the division between them? Nothing. It's the state that segregates different sections of workers. The state effectively ensures the non-alliance of the various sections of workers. The worker's unity is gone. The struggles are becoming much more reactionary and responsive to the diverse ways in which the state is doing the offensive, and they have no option but to become like that. Within movements, it is very tough to bring together a very patriarchal caste chauvinist movement like BKU with Dalit agricultural workers.

Listening to Jayant's polemics was like being a witness to *his 'internal parliament'*. Diverse movements, voices, stakes and agendas were represented therein jostling, conflicting, allying and betraying in this scene of activity. *His incisive analysis kept alive the tension between interests of middle class and that of struggling people, the stakes of factory workers and agricultural workers in SEZ, the agendas of NGOs and people's struggles, the grounds of political parties and social movements and the politics of funding and resistance activism.* His affiliation with several different stakeholders of the political process, movements, political parties, NGOs and activists allowed him to forge a debate amongst them within himself and with others, hence encouraging a sort of internal democracy of voices. He also strongly advocated the *continuous interpretation of and experimentation with thought frameworks and forms of struggle: be it Gandhism, Marxism, Maoism, Anarchism etc. in the light of the contemporary historical–social reality*, not just within the established organised ideological units but also outside of it. Along with championing the need for visible, disruptive displays of power, he *strongly supported a more democratic approach to the life of the mind and creating spaces for ideas, analysis and visions* in activistic work and life. He was vehemently *against dictated ideologies* and leadership by intelligentsia. Instead, he *stood for organic intellectuals* (a term borrowed from Gramsci), emerging from the ranks, capable of stimulating the knowledge that exists within people—derived from their cultural traditions, as well as acquired in their daily struggles for survival. He believed that grassroot leaders along with distinguished public figures could help in the construction of political and social forces necessary to push the process of deep social transformations.

His personal struggle was to accommodate his own internal contradictions, dilemmas and conflicts between resistance activism and mainstream temptations. In Jayant's upbringing, the *desire for money was a negative identity fragment,* that is, an identity a family wishes to live down—even though his mother was aggrieved by economic hardships at times—and the mere hint of which it tries to suppress in its children. But by acknowledging the negative image, he came closer to enjoy the freedom that comes to one who knows and accepts the self even in its darker aspects.

Reflections on Humanist Youth

In order to understand the development of sociopolitical consciousness and belief in social action amongst humanist youth, it is required to take a stock of the psychosocial context in which they were located. Following that, shared psychodynamic aspects of identity constellation amongst youth are presented.

Psychological Characteristics of Social Contexts

Contrary to the popular opinion, the humanist youth were academically sound and intellectually capable. They all had access to elite education and received good grades in their courses. Most narratives converged on an image of *family which emphasised on academic attainment but also gave them considerable freedom and support to explore their talents, engage with social issues and express their thoughts and convictions, even the unconventional ones.* Key instances include Manoj who received a lot of encouragement from his parents for his musical talent and no conditions were placed on him for achieving certain standards of excellence and following popular trends and Saumya who recalled being thoughtful and aware about the happenings in school and having the space to confront her father's friends for an act that she thought was improper. *Many of them recounted being witness to and/or participating in open discussions, debates and conversations on values, ideas and social concerns at home which impacted their minds.* As they grew older and developed their critical perspectives, many of them *confronted their parents' middle-class materialist values.* While challenging the conscience of the parental figures to test their inner authority, they also showed *strong identifications with a principled parent* who was felt as spokesperson as well as embodiment of the 'worthwhile values'. They drew their intellectual strength and support for their ideas of social change from one parent in the family. In life stories of *Saumya, Debashri, Manoj and Vijayan,* their fathers emerged as intellectually strong, principled and honest. For *Shalini,* while a nurturant identification with the mother brought out the

P. Bansal, *Youth in Contemporary India: Images of Identity and Social Change*,
DOI 10.1007/978-81-322-0715-3_19,

strength to critique the excessive materialist life that her father privileged, it was in identification with her father that she was drawn to the spiritual traditions.

Families of Nirmal and Sujata constitute an exception to the democratic familial milieu of other participants. The daunting presence of conservative and domineering authority figures that set pedantic limits on their life space and refused to reflect on their own moralisms and orthodoxies set off these young people in desperate search for liberal discourses which affirm choice, freedom and dignity for all.

The phase of college education marked a critical juncture in their lives. It was during these years or sometimes after that they seemed to have reached a point where *'the establishment options' became uninteresting to them and they turned towards increasing commitment to the project of social change.* While the reasons for the same differed, a big role was played by the social scientific discourses they came across, the nonacademic voluntary activities they participated in and the affiliations they forged with people and institutions engaged in sociopolitical debates and action. *Their goal of academics was not specifically vocational or professional preparation.* Their educational backgrounds of human rights law, history and social work exposed them to social and political theory which gave them the analytic tools to investigate and understand the practices, institutions, characters and ideals of the society, its consistencies and contradictions, what it has been and is becoming and the solutions and alternatives in line with what it should best become. *Manoj and Praveen*, in spite of their engineering backgrounds, felt a deep sense of *affinity with critical debates and concerns in realms of society, politics and economics.* While working with participants such as Manoj, Jayant and Naveen, I read a range of books and thinkers from where they derived their passion and vision of transformative action. They also created *opportunities of self-learning by engaging in various kinds of voluntary activities. Shalini*'s engagement with social work during school and International Association—a cultural-social body of international students—during college was experienced as enriching by her. It educated her on various international conflicts and deepened her search for frameworks and ways of living which oppose domination and violence and promote harmony, justice and love. *Nirmal*'s chance involvement with the NGO sector gave him a reprieve from the depressive state and also a direction in life. For both *Saumya and Jayant*, the leadership position that they occupied was a training ground for their future roles. *Sujata* strengthened her position in human rights law by absorbing the conversations and discussions at alternative law forum. Thus, the picture that emerged is that rather than treating the phase of higher education solely as a period of apprenticeship for preparation for entry in professional market, they used it for building critical perspectives, learning to commit to a position and ways of acting in support of it and exploring causes and collectives that they could offer their loyalties and energies to.

The *development of a critical and creative consciousness requires spaces where individuals and groups can engage in private and public dialogue* with themselves and others, hear into differences and disagreements and claim a greater sense of agency and empowerment with which to engage with their worlds effectively and creatively. *The social sector provided that opportunity for them.* Many of them explored this sector through voluntary work and field exposures during their educational phase, and later, they entered this field as professionals and activists. It embodies the universalist critique of modern society in which many sections of people are still struggling to gain access to basic amenities of life and to whom the constitutional guarantees of equality, justice and freedom are still denied. *Hence, the agenda of this sector is to extend the principles, privileges and benefits of the society to all.* NGOs, as prominent actors of this field, have been known to act as catalysts of radical and transformative social change, through their association with grassroot struggle in various forms. In the Indian context, the action groups that appeared during the late 1960s were committed to the people, the country's democratic principles and values, civil liberties, justice to victims and above all a commitment to equality and liberty. They were formed by a range of educated people who were dissatisfied with the impact of the development on poverty alleviation and responded to the community issues such as violation of human rights, ownership over natural resources, social justice and class/caste/gender oppression (Sen 1993). *The last two decades have seen a proliferation and change of role of civil society organisations within the neoliberal project of international development.* NGOs have increasingly become partners of state and donor agencies in implementing development programs. Thus, the state is shrinking its social responsibilities and transferring them to civil society organisations. However, in most of such spaces, state actors are in practice unwilling to share their decision-making power with respect to the formulation of public policies, and functions and responsibilities of organisations are restricted to the implementation and execution of these policies (Dagnino 2008). The reliance of NGOs on national and international governmental organisations for funding has led to compromise in self-determination, semi-detachment from social movements that are more embedded in the political processes and adoption of apolitical state centric development agendas while claiming to operate according to distinctive, autonomous logic. There are also growing pressures on NGOs to compete for development funds, formalise their organisational structures and 'scale up' their work. *The NGO space is also becoming like a market with a lot of new entrants making NGOs pay more attention to the whole area of branding and competitive positioning. All this compromises the inclination and ability of such organisations devoted to development to engage in acts that are radically transformative.*

The participants chosen to be represented in this work were aware youth who understood the political–economic environments in which these organisations were placed. *Many of those who were placed in the citizen sector were engaging with ideological issues of power and structural inequality and alternatives to them.* While acknowledging the various constraints that affect the functioning of this sector, they still saw it as a *socially sanctioned professional space which grants the possibility of becoming a part of the process of doing some 'good work'*. By offering an inducement to collective experimentation with alternatives, an institutionalised space helps overcome a sense of inhibition and guilt. There were few others who turned towards *spiritual forms of activism* which encourage reducing one's dependence on large institutions and established thought frameworks and champions the power of individual people and communities to make a difference through wisdom, imagination, faith and love.

Psychodynamic Dimensions of Identity

The following formulations aim to capture the subtleties and complexities of the inner psychological makeup of humanist youth.

Narrative of Self-Exploration and Social Participation

Most humanist youth came from families where they had enough *autonomy to explore the world beyond home*. Using this freedom of choice and action, they searched for institutions, people and discourses commensurate with their native temperaments, idiosyncratic needs and fantasies and favoured capacities. *Engagement with issues and sociopolitical work had a radicalising effect on the values of the participants.* It opened up for inquiry how the everyday world we live in is created and sustained, its historical roots and dynamics of power. Through radical readings, reflective conversations, self-analysis and transformative exposure to strange and unfamiliar realities, the *youth had begun to question the sedimented ways of understanding the world.* As I immersed myself in the lifeworlds of many of them, I observed that they were seeking and surrounding themselves with opportunities of dialogue, participation and innovation. *They were part of groups, collectives, online communities and mailing lists which served as open spaces for reflection on self and world, deconstruction of old ways of thinking, questioning the exclusionary discourses of class and caste and trial and error with newer ideas and practices of social participation.* While deepening one's own relationship with oneself, solidarities and alliances for joint dissent and action were also being built up.

I felt that our research conversations also often became open yet contained contexts in which they could take a stand to validate their own affects and doubts while at the same time interrogate them. *They welcomed and used the intersubjective encounter to expand the area of consciousness, to hold contradictory impulses and to pre-empt formation of new sentiments.* The research interactions with many of these participants spanned over six to seven meetings, usually lasting for two to three hours each occasion, in which one felt gripped by their intensified elaboration and deepening of self-narrative. *Their language ceaselessly tried to capture their convictions and doubts, ebbs and flow of meaning and despair about their commitments to social action, fledgling visions of personal and historical future.* They were attuned to the ambiguities of their belief systems, uncertainties of the direction of life course they had chosen and potential loss of their activistic energies—self-elements which they were carrying within themselves in their journeys of self-discovery and sociopolitical work. *As compared to their peers who had joined their selfhoods to more conventional and circumscribed tasks, they had more protracted moratoriums.*

Orientation Towards Alternatives

When dominant social modes and ideologies are challenged through spiritual and political means, an interior sense of self that finds alternative orientations becomes possible. A strikingly common feature in the lives of all those interviewed was a refusal of the 'establishment options'. These options were clearly open to all of these young people who had gone through competitive academic scenarios as successful, intelligent and capable students. During college years or sometimes after, they seemed to have reached a point where the mainstream vocational options became non-meaningful for them and they began to explore alternative courses of action. *The reasons for this change in direction towards increasing commitment to project of social change were varied.* For Jayant and Saumya, it was precipitated by a sense of ethical inadequacy of the conventional options. *Jayant* left his lucrative media job because of his resentment with the business mentality of the media house. He opted for unpaid employment during which he did coordination work for National Alliance of People's Movement which gave him more satisfaction. *Saumya* had nurtured the high profile dream of becoming a copywriter. But after having experienced the indignation with the high-handed attitude of the corporate media coupled with discomfort with money spinning, but morally impoverished work available in the sector, she decided to opt for social work rather than a degree in mass communication which would have been certainly more lucrative. After her social work degree, she decided to work for a people's movement rather than take a more conventional NGO job. *Shalini* instinctively disliked the corporate culture of competition and impersonal relationships and thus moved to the NGO sector. There, she began to revise her ideas of rightness of free trade and capitalism in the light of alternative notions of development. But it was the philosophy of Jeevan Vidya that stilled her emotional search for an authentic framework for a meaningful way of life and a humane, just and sustainable society. *Debashri* skipped entrance examinations of MBA as she became more convinced of her place in feminist social work. *Manoj* refused a job with a reputed software company after he finished engineering feeling that 'he was being sucked in a system where he didn't really belong'. *Nirmal* rebelled against his parental wishes to make him into an IITian or an IAS officer by drifting into social sector. *Praveen* gave up his job as his dissatisfaction with profit model of the corporate world increased, deciding to see if life could be organised around a different set of values rather than that of limitless expansion. *Sujata*, escaping from the tortured obediences of paternal authority, felt an affinity with the rights' orientation of feminism and human rights' law.

Whether the moving away from conventional careers was motivated by intuitive dislikes or by articulate principles, the decision was always spoken of as an act of authenticity. The ensuing activities had contributed to a growing sense of rightness for them, in both meanings of this ambiguous term. On the one hand, they reflected a growing feeling that what they were doing was psychologically 'right' for them—in accordance with their needs, liking and responsive to their talents. At the same time, 'rightness' meant a growing sense of moral rightness—a conviction that what they were doing (though frustrating, difficult and filled with hardship and triviality) was for them in accord with their principled purpose. Saumya described her work as a 'campaigner' for the people's movement as being immensely fulfilling. She could absorb her childhood fantasy of being a copywriter in the current work where also she was devising campaigns for public awareness and mobilising their support. She spoke with glee about the headline that she had thought of for the youth campaign 'A Life with Dignity and Justice in a Toxic free world'. Her deep need to 'speak up' in defence of what is right and her indignation at her experiences of denial of her selfhood which when met the language of ethics took the form of moral outrage against the paternalistic state oppressing the common people. *Nirmal* discovered his own potential through his engagement with social sector. Being made to feel worthless by his parents because he was not trying for engineering or civil services—options that were hallmarks of being a 'success'—he had begun to 'feel like a waste'. But as he got more involved with issues of social–environmental importance, he recovered his talents and could feel validated by the impact he was able to make. Having thus found his niche, he also found his issue, namely, active citizenship and democracy. Both of these concepts spell a modern attitude towards social relations, something that he had been trying to forge in his personal life. Fearful of 'quaid' (confinement), he strove to be free, active, live life by his own initiative—all of which were in uneasy tension with the traditional-orthodox ethos reflected in the stance of living by the role, doing one's duty, of limitations and of stability that characterised his parentage. For *Jayant*, dissatisfaction of the 'political actor' in him had led him to depressions and physical illnesses (a fact to which he attributed psychological meaning) which cleared off once he entered his current job which satisfied his political, intellectual as well as economic necessities far more adequately. Because *Shalini* felt so disconnected with her own formal educational process, she sought to use the precepts of the philosophy to develop a system of education which provided more than literacy and a job, which could help an individual acquire knowledge about self, society and environment and also to lead a happy life. In advocating the need to break free from the organised structure of thought and institutional frameworks of state and market, *Naveen* was offering a challenge both to the established order and an alternative to the form of sociopolitical activism that resists against it. In spite of coming from somewhat impoverished environment, he sought enrichment of soul and human relationships and not simply material enhancement. While the worldly, material reality kept encroaching his consciousness in the form of fears and temptations, he was resolutely going about deepening his inner world. Welding close connections between inner life and vocation, they were gathering intellect, affects, principles and action into one related whole.

Democratisation of Self

Whether the idiom was that of political fight for human rights or of spiritual coexistence with nature and fellowmen, the struggle of all these young people was to *move beyond a form of relatedness characterised by the dynamics of domination and submission*. It is a search for an all inclusive identity where the *relations of power between selfsame and others are symmetrical* and where both sides can come to identify that they are constitutive of each other. This ethic of human inclusiveness also extends to embrace an identification of self with the natural world (to be human is to be part of nature) and a tendency to value all things in nature equally.

This project of expanding freedom for everyone involves schooling in opening out to encounter and dialogue with differences, deeper listening, widening of sensibilities, and of holding conflictual and plural subjectivities. This constitutes the intrapsychic dimension of democracy. The young participants of this work were found to be grappling with the challenges of nourishing such intrasubjective and intersubjective sensitivities and sensibilities that are critical to the making and sustaining of democracy and peace. *Manoj* expressed his struggle pithily:

> We have to first give ourselves the space to just be, like a child in play. Open and receptive to our own selves. Only then can we create spaces where others can just be. I know that I used to be very fanatical about my ideas of social justice and all during college. Things became very bad between my parents and me because of this. I was becoming very critical of their lifestyle. Also, this group in Chennai whose meetings I used to attend, I used to see people becoming extremely argumentative and sticking to their point of view. Then there is no coming together. It shouldn't be an exercise of line drawing rather it needs to be an attempt at centre defining. There has to be constant willingness to expand and transform our perceptions, to see common threads between our own ways of being and those of others, even when there are apparent external differences. I think listening is crucial in this. You have to let go of your biases and tendency to hold onto what you already know to listen. That's when there is deep understanding.

Witnessing and participating in the struggles and sufferings of fellow beings, the youth felt a deepening of their own sense of humanity. Whether it was *Jayant* witnessing violence against his family for standing up for Dalits' rights, *Saumya*'s moving account of a man breaking his own house in Narmada Valley or *Debashri*'s crusade against violence against poor, Dalit women, they were dealing with situations that rupture the way one normally thinks about the world. In turning to orient oneself to unexpected experiences and unfamiliar departures, one begins to take up a *transgressive relationship to those norms that have implications for one's very experience of self. In acknowledging the right of disadvantaged to live a life of dignity, these young people were forging an involvement with, identification with and collaboration with those who were superficially alien: the peasant, the Dalit, the poor and the survivor*. They shared a general sense that injustice was being done to certain sections of society and it needed to be redressed. Their inner movements were in the direction of complex and heterogeneous identity in which otherness and difference can be articulated and the conflicts inherent in pluralism can begin to be encountered, tolerated and symbolised within the subject.

In *Nirmal*'s life, one could spot a continuation of his own struggle for choice and self-determination in his formulated social concern of 'enhancing freedom and democracy for all'. What had truly become democratic within him is a question that cannot be attempted to be answered within the scope of a research work with any sense of certainty; however, *one could spot an expansion of self in which ethos of tradition and modernity could dialogue*. In his own words, he defined his activist challenge as:

> If I don't break it [caste system], my next generation will have to face similar challenges that I face. I shouldn't perpetuate the same cycle. I need to break the cycle and start afresh. My role as an intermediary is to integrate modern set of values because it means something for my future. I need to break the past in the present so that there is a better future.

Being amidst a network of friends with shared socio-political commitments, living in an atmosphere of relaxed social and sexual mores, poetry and music and continuous talk about personal and political, *Saumya was insistently reworking the established sectors of her personality like habits, comforts, propriety and social norms*. Through an engagement with spiritual traditions and forms of social action, *Shalini, Manoj and Naveen were opposing the exclusive privileging of the materialist side of human beings and stood for bringing back into the centre of political, cultural and economic reality, a deeper engagement with the spiritual aspects of human beings' role on this planet*. In spite of coming from difficult economic environment, Praveen sought enrichment of soul and human relationships and not simply material enhancement. They were *seeking out collective spaces where people could self-organise themselves outside the purview of state, market and social organisations*. In frames of spiritual activism, true freedom is not in demanding 'one's right to have rights' from the authority regimes; rather, it is realised when one develops the internal capacity to not be the victim or captive of any form, experience and condition. This means deeper understandings of who one is and this is based on realities beyond the conceptual, the intellectual and the known. Such understandings will surge forth when people can compassionately connect with one's own experience and with each other without fears of denial, rejection and righteousness. It also advocates regeneration of local cultures, wisdom ecologies, interconnections with nature and champions the power of individual people and communities to make a difference through wisdom, faith and love.

Participants like *Saumya, Jayant and Debashri* saw *grassroots involvement with the communities* as a key value of their work. They saw the link with populace with which they were working as the source of energy, enthusiasm and hope. The resilience of the community gave them the strength to struggle with them. It helped them to maintain their values internally and at the same time provided credibility and downward accountability as well as evidence of detailed examples to assist their advocacy and lobbying efforts. Besides, they favoured *participative decision-making* in which everyone counts. As middle-class change agents, they wished not to be seen as experts and de-emphasised hierarchies. *They worked with the awareness that the community needs empowerment as per their needs, pace and social context*. Their attitudes were of privileging local wisdom, helping them speak in their voice and respecting the needs of the community to take their own decisions that affect their fate. *In seeking to experience the humanity of the socially disadvantaged, they also acknowledged sometimes with guilt their own privilege in a world dominated by suffering, a wanting sense of the communal grounding, fledgling moral clarity and limits to capacity for effective action that could bring an end to this suffering*. Jayant's life narrative and conversations brought alive the various tensions that afflict the activism space between conservative interests of middle classes and justice needs of struggling people, the reformist agenda of NGOs and politically transformative vision of people's struggles, the corrupting politics of funding and resistance potential of activism.

Cooperation and Solidarity for Common Good

Any movement of social change relies on collectivity of people acting together in concert for a better society, better future. Hence, the 'I' joins the community of change makers to form a 'We'. *The humanist youth expressed the need to unite to experiment, create and execute shared visions of social transformation.* They sought to create alliances across a range of issues and agendas. *Jayant*'s experiment with Sangharsh 2007 (an attempt at forming coalitions of different struggles, movements, resistance groups working on different issues to come together in a mutual act of solidarity and support and endorse each other's demands), *Saumya*'s passionate stand that she was in support of all such struggles that are aimed at enhancing the dignity and right of livelihood of people, *Shalini*'s endeavours to bring people from different nationalities to 'unite for peace' are illustrations of their attempts at forging solidarity to pursue collective goals. *Debashri* drew her strength from the larger women's movement. *The new ethic that results is that of cooperation and collectivity in which everyone grows together rather than at the cost of one another.* The effort in such endeavours is to create fora/mediums/mechanisms that can lead to sharing of ideas, views and agendas, to honest debate and discussion of differences and pursuit of collective programs, to sharing of insights and merging of human support, to an enlargement of and sharing of resources, to fostering and benefiting from both solidarity and autonomy. But Jayant noted with disappointment that this vision is beset by lack of trust, competitiveness and intolerance for difference.

Play of Combinatory Possibilities

The convictions and commitments of humanist youth were felt to be like rolling configurations, evolving and fluid. *Their selves were moving in a moral space of questions directed towards investigating the motivations and meanings of their actions, their impact, the value basis of their identities and their doubts, dreads and dilemmas over activist way of living.* Conversations of this kind with like-minded peers in which they could entertain the chaos, the compromises with the ideologies and the contradictions within themselves and each other were found to be a major part of their self-definitional attempts.

Their narratives were reflective of their *identities maturing to find the nature of that which must be cared for—people, environment and values.* They were seeking a common denominator in human life—some kind of *worldwide identity bridging affluence and underdevelopment, a cosmic wholesomeness embracing ecology and humankind.* They stood for expansion of human rights to all, alleviation of poverty, political inclusion of marginalised sections, protection of environment, empowerment of vulnerable groups and awareness building amongst middle classes. Many amongst them engaged with a *range of ideological frameworks like Marxism, democratic socialism, Gandhism, anarchism, feminism and deep ecology and philosophical discourses like Jeevan Vidya and those of Krishnamurthy.* They looked for personal inspiration towards the lives of great men such as *Jesus, Gandhi and Vivekananda.* For *Jayant,* his father as well as other radical comrades associated with social movements and action groups; for *Saumya,* the leadership of the people's movement she was working with; and for *Shalini,* Babaji who has formulated the framework of Jeevan Vidya and other learned people who had engaged with the philosophy deeply were the *idealised figures in their personal lives* from whom they gained courage and conviction to stay on the track. The *presence of contemporaries* who shared radical doubts about the state of things helped them in providing the much needed camaraderie and play through which they can not only see what is before them but also the power to foresee what might prove to be true in the future.

A critical feature of humanist youth was their wariness in calling themselves as activists. When asked what he thought being an activist meant, *Jayant* hedged and said:

> I don't know what is the meaning of a 'full-fledged' identity of an activist. I think everyone is active about certain issues in one's life. A political activist, probably, is one who has a radical sociopolitical understanding vis-a-vis issues. Someone who is ready to put one's neck on the line. Someone who is in opposition.

His narrative goes on to show how his own intellectual and political identity needs would suffer from dissatisfaction with the state of activism, loss of meaning and direction as well as temptations of money and power. *Saumya*'s distaste of mega-political discourses reflected in her remark 'debates about Marxism and Socialism look good as drawing room discussions. These are just intellectual opinions. Ultimately the issues in reality are much more complex.... What you need is concrete political action which will have an impact' as well as her personal dilemmas about a lifelong commitment to the activist way of living which would restrain her 'personal exploration', need to 'sometimes obey simple structures of life' and preclude 'her chances of ever getting married if I were to enter the mass movement activism' led her to define her role as a campaigner. It was a designation she chose over 'development professional' which was far too corporate according to her and 'activist' which was far too hard for her. *Vimal* acknowledged his work to be more status quoist than resistive, more mainstream than activistic and that institutional imperatives often override the development imperatives. He feared becoming a 'Khaadi and Hawaii Chappal'—identity symbols rooted in mega philosophy of social change, demanding of personal austerity as well as reminiscent of a radical promise of do or die. Seeing energy rather than issues and debates at the centre of his work, social work for him probably buttressed those inner structures that reaffirmed his ability as a human being to matter, to make a difference. In sharing about her struggle to position herself in the field of human rights' activism, *Sujata* brought forth certain critical critiques of the functioning of NGOs as well as the state of thinking and interventions that prevail in the sector. She pointed out that there was 'little thought given to understanding deep structures', too much emphasis on 'fancy report writing, practical action and implementation'. She added that there were 'too many questions that are up for grabs' and 'utter confusion over which project is one supporting' (implying whose side is one taking—the resisting community or the state). Entertaining doubts about the relevance and rightness of the debates of state vs. people, development vs. livelihood and communism vs. capitalism, *Naveen and Shalini* had begun to turn towards spirituality which emphasises knowing of oneself and initiating change from oneself, one's home and communities.

Given their young age and changing experiences, the highly plastic and pervasive nature of the ideological regime of neoliberalism which can co-opt any resistive effort and the lack of a concise and coherent narrative of its alternative, one can understand the struggles of humanist youth in positioning themselves in the debates of and interventions for 'another world'. There is a mix of technocratic interventions in the form of service provision which do have an effect—fragmented, momentary, provisory and limited, but positive—on the reduction of inequality and the improvement of living conditions of the social segments involved and experimentation with new forms of politics and social living. *Besides, they were mindful of their own complicity in the established structures as well as the needs to avail the privileges and the ease that come from abiding by the dominant models. In this regard, the issue of money emerged as the major stumbling block in their lives.* All of them had an ambivalent relationship with money. Ideologically, the participants were opposed to the homo economicus model of man. They were critical of the ethics of market-led development. While few saw it as widening the gap between the rich and poor, the others critiqued monetarisation and quantification as values that were leading to spiritual–aesthetic depravity of human lives. *In either case, money was seen as corrupting one's political as well as spiritual essences. It represented the negative element which they would like to live down but which, to use Jayant's metaphor, was like the 'Eden apple' which offers irresistible temptation.* However, *at personal level, many of them suffered from economic insecurities that came with low payments for the work that they were doing.* One heard worried concerns about the difficulties of managing a decent lifestyle in a city which 'moves on wheels of money'. They sought not to self-marginalise themselves too much. *But at the same time, they were resisting getting wrapped up in the modish malaise of the world. Thus, they were trying to search/create in between spaces wherein imaginative and authentic living was possible.* The equipoise of their budding identities required a balancing act of multiple levels of belongingness to the collective of their privileged ideals and resistive energies and to the mainstream community offering experiences of being regular and comfortable. The continuous forays and retreats into divergent circumstances can disintegrate into a sense of self which is totally pragmatic, opportunistic and generally ad hoc. Critically aware of this propensity, *the humanist youth were activating internal forms that would endure as a perspective in moral space*. *Jayant*'s anchorage of his political role as a supporter of struggle of masses in the image of a biblical character Simon of Kurena, *Saumya*'s project to have a colourful life within the framework of certain closely held values and principles, *Manoj*'s hope of being able to become an agent of social change even in bureaucratic set-ups and *Shalini*'s strivings to blend familial belongingness with her spiritual–aesthetic endeavours are few examples of youth-seeking flexible living bound up with ethical commitments.

Part IV
Summing Up

Youth in India: Identity and Social Change

In the cycle of generations, youth is recognised as a bearer of fresh energy, and he/she tests the vulnerability, strength, integrity and possibilities of the adult society to assess what the society would make of, ask of and allow himself or herself. The mutual sizing up is also accompanied by mutual plea (by both youth and adult representatives) for being recognised as individuals whose potentials are needed by the order that is or will be. Within the setting of psychosocial evolution, youth's endeavours in the existing system have the power to confirm what is worthwhile and reform the rotten in the image of a new reality. No longer is it the task of only the old to teach the young the meaning of life. The young, too, by their actions and responses tell the old whether life as represented by the old and presented to them has meaning. In the human youth, fidelity is expressed in the alternation of affirmation and repudiation of social institutions and cultural traditions which reflect aspects of parental attitudes and interests.

Social change and identity should be thought in terms of the interplay between inertia and flux. In cultures as well as in individual people, inertia (maintained by traditional psychological patterns) and flux (stimulated by pressures towards change) are strong—change is at the same time perpetual and perpetually resisted. Young people are central to this process of socio-historical change, not because they make great historical decisions or discover great truths, but because they feel most intensely the inner urge towards exploration and change. At an age when self must be created and identity defined, their strong response to ideals and ideologies produces pressures towards change—sometimes constant, sometimes explosive—in all societies. In India, the focus on the young generation has led to polar opposite generalisations about the nature of young people's contemporary historical experience. There is first the claim that nothing is really changing, that although things may look different on the surface, deep down everything is as it always have been. And then there is an opposite assertion that young people in India have changed beyond recognition. The truth of youth's experience lies somewhere in between.

The following chapter focuses on the theme of intergenerational change and continuities in sampled urban middle-class Indian youth. In the process, the work attempts to bring alive the urges towards change and the inclination to hold onto

P. Bansal, *Youth in Contemporary India: Images of Identity and Social Change*,
DOI 10.1007/978-81-322-0715-3_20, © Springer India 2013

conservative patterns present in the liberalising Indian society. The discussion is divided into following sub-parts:

I. In a traditional and collectivist society like India, family occupies a pivotal space in the inner world of the people. Focusing on the urban middle-class family milieu which is in the midst of the pull and push of tradition and modernity, the work attempts to capture a few patterns of intergenerational relationships between parents and children. It presents the images of motherhood and fatherhood as well as changing notions of being a son and daughter in contemporary Indian society.

II. In this section, the attempt is to understand whether the Indian family is waning in importance in today's times because of modernising socio-historical forces.

III. The endeavour in this section is to present the psychodynamics of youth stage in contemporary urban India unveiling images, dreams and desires of autonomous living of the young men and women.

IV. This section reflects on the interplay between the identity of the Indian youth and the larger sociopolitical order. It attempts to address the questions—Is urban Indian youth a monolithic category? Is young India conformist and sold onto the consumerist dream? Does it have the spirit of experimentation and rebelliousness that takes it towards directions not charted in traditional maps of stable career progression? Are a few of them willing to look beyond the security of a regular pay cheque and take chances with their creative urges and be socially responsible?

V. In the end, few thoughts are gathered about certain psychological attitudes, ideals and ethics that should be encouraged so as to build a constructive society and create a wholesome identity for the coming generations in India.

I

The Child in the Relational Matrix of Indian Family

In order to understand how the task of individuation is negotiated within the fold of family by the urban middle-class Indian youth, it is instructive to look more closely at the images of intergenerational relationships emerging from the narratives of participants. *The attempt is to answer—How is identification and differentiation vis-à-vis the parental introjects balanced within the intrapsychic realm of the youth?* The four dyads—son–mother, son–father, daughter–mother and daughter–father—have been explored, and dynamics of intergenerational change and continuity have been reflected upon towards the end.

The Case of the Male Child: Sons and Mother

The psychoanalytic observations on the bond between son and mother in the Indian context reveal that the early childhood of the Indian male is enveloped in and often overpowered by his mother's lavish protective nurturing and love (Kakar 1981).

There is an intensely affective and gratifying cocoon of mother–son, especially in the initial 4–5 years of the young boy before his world of childhood widens into the man's world. The anthropological and psychological literature emphasises the contrast between an earlier, more or less unchecked, benevolent indulgence and admiration of the society of women and a relatively stern and unfeeling male world full of rules and standards of conduct and responsibility. Because of cultural expectations and actual social patterns, a profound inner connectedness in the Indian man to his mother lasts throughout life. Given the prolonged symbiotic mode of relating with the mother which is highly emotionally and physically gratifying for the child, the Indian male develops a strong identification with his mother and a maternal–feminine stance towards the worldly world (Kakar 1981). The inner world of Indian men is thus decisively influenced by both the 'good' and the 'bad' versions of the maternal–feminine. Taken into child's ego, the 'good mother's' maternal tolerance, protectiveness and nurturing becomes the core of his positive identity. Alongside this positive identity, however, and normally repressed, is its counterpart: the negative identity that originates in experiences with the demanding, sometimes stifling, all too present 'bad mother'. This split maternal image symbolises the Indian boy's critical psychosocial dilemma: *how to enjoy his mother's love and support without crippling his own budding individuality?* For any attempt to separate himself from her arouses guilt that not only dims the benevolent mother imago but also threatens the sense of one's own uniqueness of which she was the original guarantor. This universal developmental dilemma is aggravated in the Indian setting because of the profound, often unconscious reluctance of the Indian mother to 'release' the male child, to let him go in an emotional sense, for he is the psychosocial guarantor of her own identity as a woman in a traditional patriarchal set-up.

The research found that in the inner worlds of the male participants, the mother was overwhelmingly preserved as an affectionate and protective presence ensuring a core of well-being. The mother was the benign teacher of the son. Many shared strong emotional bonds with their mothers and were taught lessons of propriety by them. Samrat's mother emphasised the importance of being 'good and helpful', while Aasheesh's mother would implore him to give up the habits of smoking (of which his father was unaware) and eating non-vegetarian food and cite examples of successful elders in the family who had become 'big' without having to resort to them. Jayant learnt his lessons of sharing household responsibilities and be a non-patriarchal man from his feminist mother. As compared to the father, there was lesser privacy from the mother who was aware of most of the going-ons in the son's life. Aasheesh's mother knew everything that he did and where he was during every part of the day—information that he voluntarily shared with her. For Krishna, his mother was the only one with whom he could freely share his feelings. He divulged his feelings of love for a girl to his mother, something that he dared not do it with his father. As an immediate and responsive figure, she was involved in the daily caretaking functions as well as supervision of the sons. Thus, often it was the mother who would pull up the son for not studying and sliding in his performance, wake up early in the morning to send him for tuitions, wait for him to came back from work and serve him hot food. *In times of stress and narcissistic injuries from the external world, it was the soothing, consoling, reassuring presence of the mother who restored a sense of intactness and self-regard.* This was revealed in Aasheesh's turning to his mothers (both his biological mother and his aunt) in distress and checking with them that would they accept him back if he failed and wanted to come back home. Yet another instance of the strong desire for the comforting presence of the nurturing mother was glimpsed in Krishna's fantasy of coming back home from office and lying down with his head in his wife's lap, like he did with his mother, and she would place her hand on his head and soothe him.

From their sharing, it was felt that the mother was often empathically sensed by the sons and they wished to take care of her needs. For instance, Krishna saw his mother to be a co-victim of his father's dominating presence and did not want her to feel anxious about him. Aasheesh joked that he did not want to take away his mother's right to select a bride for him, a matter of anxious concern for her.

While the mother was a largely positive inner presence in the lives of most male participants interviewed, one also fleetingly glimpsed traces of ambivalence in them vis-à-vis her. *In many instances, the mother was highly expectant of academic achievement and competitive success.* It would be her emotional communications about living up to the family's name and making parents proud that had a more immediate effect on the boy's psyche. Manoj once broke down recalling the enormous pressure he felt from his mother's side to come first in the class:

> It was my mother who would scold me if I wouldn't top the class. She has always been more ambitious for me....

Whenever she became unfeeling, it deeply depressed the inner world of the son. This was found to be the case with Deepak who could not forget a painfully caustic remark of his mother doubting his good intentions to take care of the parents, 'At the moment, your father is earning and you are at the receiving end. Things will be different when you will earn and we will be at the receiving end'. Such a hard-hearted attitude coming from the mother who is expected to be someone most attuned to one's sentiments can create deep feelings of hurt and anger towards her. Yet another facet of Deepak's relationship with his mother was an openly romantic conjugal relationship shared by his parents. His father was his rival in enjoying the mother's affection and devotion. Also, his mother's evident admiration of the 'man' in her life had created a superior image of the father in his mind which he could not surpass. Thus, whether it was educational success, heterosexual love, peer acceptance, physical appearance and drive, or his resolve to 'take care of the family', he found himself falling short of the achievements of the father—all of which lent a depressive quality to his personality.

In Nirmal's life, one found that his mother was eclipsed far more than can be accounted for by the mere pattern of Hindu housewifeliness. In his narrations, rarely ever she emerged as a separate individual. Rather she merged within the image of a rigid, authoritarian father to create a conjoint parental imago demanding the son to justify them, bring them referred success.

Amongst the research participants, two lives—Samrat and Jayant—serve as useful illustrations of identity dynamics of sons balancing close maternal identification with individualised functioning. Both of them felt very emotionally close and similar to their mothers in their native temperaments and capacities. Samrat 'naturally learnt' to sketch and paint by watching his artistic mother. Jayant felt that he had inherited his mother's abilities to organise and mobilise people for political action. In comparison with the father, the mother emerged as a more real person available for personalised interaction. In both these young men, one noticed a sense of primacy, of specialness which originates in the earliest relationship with devoted mother. As the only son of their mothers, they had an unconscious conviction of their superiority which was being expressed in their work-related fantasies and imageries. They did not want to be 'normal types' or pursue 'regular jobs'. Their sense of superior mission was, of course, reinforced by their environment in which they emerged as leader of peers and won praise and admiration from teachers. As much loved sons, they idealised and nurtured their mothers in return. An emotionally close bond between mother and son, however, was not felt as imposing on their life space. They appeared as quite free in choosing the directions of their lives, even the ones that did not find the mother's approval. Samrat spoke:

> My mother would keep telling me for long to do MBA or take up a job in Infosys. But it would be an immediate communication. I would just say I am not going to do any of this and the matter would end. There would not be any further discussion.

He laughingly shared that his mother had reconciled to the fact that he would do as it pleased him and had asked him to tell her about his 'adventures' after he was through with them so that she could avoid getting anxious. Jayant was staking out differently from his mother who was a church-going Christian in matters of religious faith. Also, in spite of a strong emotional pull to go back to his hometown in Kerala to be with his old and ailing parents, he was holding himself back in Delhi because that is where he saw his future. As he noted perceptively:

> I feel that she has moulded me and made me who I am. If I am a great cook it's because of her insistence that her son should be able to manage his life better. It was she who made me realise that I don't want to be another patriarchal man. But I am not her photocopy. I am her part 2 (speaks forcefully). I don't want to replicate what she did. In fact, I want to avoid making the mistakes that she made. I want to be a new experiment.

Jayant's insistence that he was not her 'photocopy' also revealed his irritation with her patronising attitude. He referred to her as the 'patronising parent', who would sometimes try to direct him and limit his display of independence and initiative in political matters.

The Case of the Male Child: Sons and Father

Erikson said that next only to the recognition bestowed by the gracious face of the mother, the affirmation of the guiding voice of the father is a prime element of an individual's sense of identity (Erikson 1958). The father–son bond is crucial to the adult identity consolidation of Indian men as male identity is based not only on early feminine identifications but also later masculine ones. It has been noted by psychoanalytic writers (Bose 1956; Ramanujam 1983; Courtright 1985; Kakar 1981) that the Oedipal situation in India and its modal resolution are a variation of the classic Western myth of Oedipus which Freud found to embody the dramatic expression of the repressed childhood desires to bond with the mother and exclude the father. Given the intensity and ambivalence of the mother–son connection in the Indian setting, the need for the father's authority and guidance becomes even more pressing, the necessity of Oedipal alliance often outweighing the hostility of the Oedipus complex. The father must take the boy out of the domestic world of women and introduce him to the world of men, the public realm of work and politics, the way his father did with him. The son needs the father as the ego ideal, a tangible, solid presence to lean on, learn from and measure oneself against in order to stabilise and strengthen one's own psychic structure and masculine identity. The strong pre-Oedipal feminine identification of the young boy accompanied by a growing awareness of the undisputed authority of male elders in the family leads him to adopt a position of feminine submission towards all elder men (father, grandfather, paternal uncles) in the family. Thus, identification through submission is the dominant Hindu form of Oedipal resolution, rather than identification through the dethronement (metaphorically 'killing') of the father (Obeyesekere 1990). The son exchanges the active phallic initiative for an 'apprentice complex', as Fenichel called it, in which he takes a passive–receptive stance towards male authority that one day will enable him to become a man in his own turn. Obtaining such deference, respect and loyalty from the younger person creates a reciprocal obligation on the male authority to be benevolent, nurturant and supportive of the former's advancement.[1] The son is also vitally important in the patriarchal set-up for various ritual and economic purpose.

A.K. Ramanujam (1983) shows in the light of Indian cultural tales, folklore and myths that the direction of aggression in the Indian father–son relationship is reversed. It is not the son wishing to supplant the father but the father suppressing the son. Whether it is the Ganesha myth or the story of Bhishma, both sons win

[1] Notwithstanding the individual variations, the Father (as a symbolic figure) introduces the son to the productive and economic ethos of the social order. By guiding the son through the tasks and goals of becoming an adult member of the society, the father derives the emotional satisfaction of seeing his way of life being continued. The stronghold of the ideal of generational solidarity in Indian culture is borne out by the popular Hindu belief that the father can be reborn as the son's son and the son might once have been the father. Thus, the son through identification with the father's roles, habits, interests and skills comes to duplicate rather than replace the father.

power, honour and titles as rewards for submission to the father figure.[2] In both the legends, the power of the father figure is never overthrown. After a fight or willingly, the son submits and identifies with the father. This creates the psychosocial dilemma for the son: *how to win his father's benevolent patronage without emasculating himself?* For disobedience and transgression of paternal authority results not only in guilt but also the fear of being at the receiving end of frightening wrath of the father. The Oedipal situation erupts when the preoccupied/intensely jealous father figures do not fulfil their generative responsibility to lend direction, structure and organisation for the son's life and satisfy his self-esteem needs to be recognised and appreciated by them. Rather, they try to do him in.

From the research narratives of male participants, the image of the father that emerged was that of the provider. *As the head of the family and the primary bread earner, the father looked after its material needs. The fathers were instrumental in providing a context in which the sons could fulfil their parents' as well as their own aims and aspirations.* So whether it was the financial support to their educational careers in the best possible manner (sometimes within limited means as in the case of Deepak, Nirmal and Kapil who came from modest families) or in few cases encouragement to the sons' initiatives and avocational interests (like Samrat whose father lent money in the beginning of his entrepreneurial venture, thereby supporting his fantasies and endeavours and like Manoj whose father bought expensive musical equipment for him to enable him to pursue his love for music), the father came across as the benevolent sponsor of the son's advancement. This in turn created strong deferential attitude towards the father and his authority in many male participants. *The son wished to receive nurturance and approval in return of respect and loyalty to the father figures (which often include an assembly of male*

---

[2] In the story of Ganesha, the elephant-headed god, the mother Parvati goes for bath and stationed Ganesha, her son, at the door, telling him not to let anyone in. When her husband Shiva wants to enter, Ganesha, unaware of Shiva's true identity, tries to stop him. Angered by Ganesha's impudence, Shiva cuts off his head. Later on coming to know about the identity of Ganesha from Parvati, Shiva repents and replaces his head with an elephant head. He also confers on Ganesha various powers and privileges. Thus, the Ganesha story ends not with Oedipus fate of tragic acceptance of the exile from the mother and submission to the superego demands represented by the fathers, gods and fate. Rather his story ends with his restoration and a new beginning in which relations between parents and child are reconciled. Iconographically, he is more often represented with his father, or father and mother together, and seldom with his mother alone (Courtright 1985). In the myth, when Ganesha comes to understand that Shiva is his father—a recognition he acquires only after receiving a new head from the father—he is given the primacy of place before all the gods and accepts his role as the Lord of Obstacles, become a yogi and a dancer (like his father). In the epic Mahabharata, Bhishma, the first son of Shantanu, renounces both kingdom and his reproductive sexual life so that his father may marry a fishergirl and continue his sexual/reproductive life. Bhishma, lifelong celibate, lives on to become the most revered old man of the epic, warrior and wise man. In the Ganesha's myth, the father's aggression is directed to the son because of the father's jealousy of the intense mother–son bond which excludes the father. In the tale of Bhishma, the father needs the son to renounce his sexual prowess and vigour so that he could prolong his life of pleasure.

elders such as grandfather, father's elder brother, father, teachers and superiors at work).

Tales of the father's struggles to come up in life, his superior achievements and his commanding position in the social/professional circles, often shared by the mother or the father as well as whatever is sensed by the son himself, aid in the creation of an idealised image of a father figure whose perfection and omnipotence he can adopt himself. Such reverential attitude towards the idealised authority figures restores intimacy and the narcissistic perfection of infancy, 'You are perfect but I am a part of you', for the son. *There were strong strivings for emulation of the paternal figure(s) and taking in their qualities.* Typical example of such intergenerational relationship was found in the life stories of Aasheesh and Deepak.

An interesting cultural dynamic of the father–son relationship found was that the father's authority was almost never directly challenged. *There was no open, verbal expression of differences in values and attitudes and resentment against the paternal domination by the son in front of the father.* The son found his way to be himself through covert means. For instance, while Kannan's father kept the pressure on him to pursue his Ph.D. rather than take up a lucrative job, he maintained a meek stance in front of him while continuing to do what he thought was the sensible thing to do. Similarly, while Nirmal saw himself as being 'aggressively vocal' about his opinions on caste and religion, he didn't argue about it in front of the parents. As he said dejectedly: 'In front of them, I fail'. On being shot down so quickly when he began to broach the subject of starting a company, Samrat avoided a direct confrontation by initially lying to his father that he was working with a company started by his professor. After being made to feel very small by his father's severe scolding in front of everyone during a marriage for his naughty act, Deepak became watchful of his conduct in front of him and other elders, but away from them, he could be open and expressive. A passive–aggressive stance to deal with authority figures has been found to be quite common amongst Indian males.

However, amongst the male participants, coexisting alongside the strong psychological need of acceptance of the dominance of those in power and the wish to incorporate some of their power into oneself were various kinds of ambivalent emotions. *One noticed a subtle trend of private defiance in which the young men tried to free themselves from needs of continuing a way of living upheld by the paternal figures.* Often indulgences and irreverence could be enjoyed while being away from home. The lack of physical proximity provided the much needed freedom from the excessive ideals of perfection set by/ascribed to the father figures. For instance, both Krishna and Aasheesh enjoyed the hostel life as offering them many avenues for youthful escapades and adventures with peers. They confessed that their academic performance was not matching the standards that they had earlier, but it was a trade-off that they were happy making.

Whenever sons, like Deepak, were unable to live up to the achievement standards set by parents, it created traumatising feelings of being a disappointing son to an 'all giving' father. Driven by an acute need to offer restitution to the father whose self-regard was found to be inextricably intertwined with that of the son, Deepak strove to be a dutiful son often at the cost of his own desires and wishes. *In such cases, 'identification by submission' is tainted by conscious feelings of resentment, pain and hurt towards the father who is acknowledged to be responsibly concerned but also overcontrolling and overdemanding.*

The budding sense of masculinity of the son can also be overburdened by the demand to be 'like the father'. An omnipresent image of the paternal figure which is variously experienced as grandiose, perfect and all giving makes it ever more difficult to 'duplicate' the father. In the sons, it leads to emotions of continuously feeling small and be restrained and meekly compliant in front of the father. In Deepak's case, his father emerged as a big personality who was popular in his friend circle, handsome and active, kind enough to take care of his mother-in-law when her own sons mistreated her and his wife's object of love and admiration. As a son, becoming like the emulated father on various counts was a feat made ever more difficult for him to achieve because of lack of opportunities supportive of his own efforts to grow up. As discussed earlier, the son needs the earthy and tangible presence of father to strengthen his own psychic structure and consolidate his masculine identity. So when the father is of little help in his boyish struggles to prove his manly worth, the son can have the damning experience of finding himself failing. *Manifesting itself as depressive outbursts or simmering rage and rivalry against father and fatherlike 'authority' figures, an anti-authoritarian stance can take shape in such instances in which the young hold the authority figures guilty for their shortcomings and for limiting the area of exercise of independent enterprise of the young and subordinates.* As an act of revenge for being 'done to', the youth take great pleasure in outdoing the father figures, a culmination of secret hope of the young boy that one day he would be big enough to defeat the father. In the present inquiry, it was found that in their intrapsychic space, material success was construed by the sons as a triumph over the rival father.

Yet another intergenerational pattern that has been found amongst young men is that of attempting to repudiate the 'old', that is, the perspectives intrinsic to the parental traditional values and also such parts of one's own self, and introjecting a new value system. This situation has a high probability of arising in those sections of society where the parental practice of tradition is not felt as naturally persuasive nor is it experienced as wholesome nutriment to the youthful ideological search of the 'true' values. Evidenced in Nirmal's case were feelings of disgust with the heavily ritualised cultural–religious prescriptions that were beaten in him by his parents like many other rules of conduct. A rigid and authoritarian father imposed contradictory demands on his lifeworld—wanting his son to leave behind the impoverished surrounds of his upbringing and climb the economic ladder of success by becoming 'either an IIT engineer or an IAS/IPS', but at the same time needing him to be an obedient son who remains true to the dogmatic cultural–religious identity. Such intergenerational transmission of constrictive imageries of what it means to be good or bad, superior or inferior, masculine or feminine by the paternal voice can be experienced by the younger generation as imposing pedantic limitations on one's imagination and initiative to carve one's self-chosen identity.

Then, there were others in whom one discerned more conflict-free relationship with the father. Rather than being burdened by the emotional need of paternity to see its way of life continued by the son, these young men had the space to find a world of their own. *While the fathers were involved in their sons' lives, there was not much conscious pressure on them to either justify them or revolt against their injunctions. Through a mix of tendencies of forging close identification with and emphasising difference from the father, these young men felt themselves as masters of their own fate, living life by their own initiative.* Both Prashant and Manoj had absorbed the principled morality of their fathers but were trying to formulate their own idiom of ethical action. Various role models encountered in real life or in books and through media were enabling them to rework their borrowed understandings of social change. These role models were also 'fathering' their attitudes and guiding their deeds. Jayant's life presents a telling example of a father who, by allowing his son an emotional access to his inner world, let him detect his limitations as a father and as a man so that the son's masculine identification is with a realistic rather than a perfect image of his father. He had been a fellow traveller and a close observer of his father's life in which he had many opportunities to see, listen, absorb and learn from his sharing of his experiences and knowledge, all of which contributed immensely to the shaping of Jayant's personal and political identity. Even though a self-confessed fan of his father, he was subtly critical of his father's political vision and monetary attitudes. He was finding himself on a different turf politically and personally, given the changed sociopolitical climate and his own ambitions and aspirations. Similarly, Samrat had chosen a different space for himself than his father—that of global player rather than pedantic worker. His identity was based on his perceived difference in personality, outlook and interests from his father whom he humorously regarded as fairly artless and outmoded and also somewhat ineffectual. From an early age, he saw himself as good as and even better than his father. The grandiose self 'at large' in the psyche led him to create a work role of an entrepreneur for himself in which he would not be subservient to any 'boss'.

Kapil's narrative reveals yet another facet of the relationship between the son and the father in which the son felt immensely protected, unconditionally accepted and yet free. *It was a father–son relationship in which the maternal ambit of protective love and permissive instruction was recreated.* A teacher and a friend, Kapil's father was a dependable constant to learn from, be loved by and emulate. However, because of having been protected far too much and sheltered from taking on adult tasks and responsibilities by the father, Kapil felt himself to be 'very kiddish' and needed to discover and consolidate his masculine identification with the father in order to attain maturity.

The Case of Female Child: Daughters and Mother

Though, anthropological accounts indicate the marked preference for sons all over India, there is also somewhat paradoxically, abundant allusion to the warmth, intimacy and affection of the mother–daughter bond. When a woman gives birth to a daughter, there is no comparable reversal of her position in the familial–cultural space. Thus, her rearing of the daughter as an infant does not result in an equivalent degree of idealisation as is the case with the son towards whom she is portrayed as being devoted and ever ready for practically unlimited emotional investment. As Kakar (1981) notes, 'For daughters, the mother is not an adoring figure on the pedestal: she is a more earthy presence, not always benign but always there'. A mother's unconscious identification with the daughter is normally stronger than with her son because in her daughter, the mother can re-experience herself as a cared-for girl (Chodorow 1978). In the Indian society, the girl's guest status in her natal family as someone who will marry and leave her mother for good also leads the mother to re-experience her own past conflicts around separation due to marriage. This tends to increase her indulgence and attention towards her daughter. Emotional closeness and access to an earthy mother and via her to attributes of femininity and female role activities characterise her daily world. The mother is the daughter's confidante, counsellor, teacher and model who helps her envision and secure a clear sense of herself as a woman. A continuous and ongoing attachment and identification between the mother and daughter creates the danger of dependency. In such a situation, if a mother does not encourage separation from and lessening of infantile dependence of the daughter on herself, it creates the emotional conflict in the daughter about *how to maintain a positive personal and role identification with her mother without feeling fraught about being different from her.* The daughter wanting to individuate may experience rageful confusion of boundaries with the mother, and any attempt to become different from her is felt as bringing disapproval and loss of love (Kanter 1993).

In the present research, the female participants described their mothers as capable women, growing and evolving with changing times and their circumstances. Not many were in paid employment, but even domesticity seemed to give them a tangible opportunity to be productive, to experience autonomy and to exercise power. *Many participants found their mothers as open-minded, spirited and strong women. They were in charge of running the household and made many of the vital decisions in the family's interests.* Even with a highly orthodox husband, Sujata's mother was a countervailing force, who was able to create spaces at home which were not rigidly traditional. The daughters also found their mothers evolving in their own selves through their negotiations with and observations of life—their own and those around them. Thus, the daughters could identify with their mothers not only for qualities of nurturance, family orientation and home management but also for their proactive behaviours, decision-making abilities and practical wisdom.

They were also encouraging their daughters to study, work and make a life of their own. This was in contrast with their own lives of stay-at-home mothers. They supported the daughter's career decisions and were proud of their achievements. Also in these middle-class homes, there were no deliberate training in and conscious inculcation of culturally designated feminine roles of childbearing and homemaking in the daughter by the mother. *Crucially, in her own roles as the wife and the mother of a daughter, she seemed to be setting a model of feminine identity which emphasises a woman's connections to others but not exhort the 'virtues' of self-effacement and self-sacrifice in social relationships.* An anecdote shared by Saumya served to underline how her conservative mother also did not any longer regard docility and submission as qualities that defined womanhood. The incident took place soon after Saumya's cousin sister got married and came for the customary visit to the parents' house the day after the wedding. Her sister narrated the unfolding of the events during her first night with her husband to eager women including her own mother, Saumya's mother and Saumya herself. She described that as her husband approached her, she began to laugh and draped herself tightly in a sheet. Her husband, good naturedly, tried pulling the sheet but she resisted. They both treated it as a joke, talked for some time and then went off to sleep. The girl's mother on hearing this got very worried and scolded her daughter for repelling the advances of her husband. She told her that this was a mistake on her part which she must never repeat in future. She must defer to the wishes of her husband. On hearing this, Saumya's mother intervened and asserted that after all the years of training to not let any man come near her, let alone touch her, the young bride could not be expected to let her guard down immediately with a stranger, even if he was her husband. She added that the man has to understand the young wife's reservations and fears and work to dispel them.

All the young women were professionally educated and had career aspirations, and they sought self-expression and success in their work-related activities. Importantly, all of them wished to balance their work life with marital relationship. In fact, difficulty in achieving this balance, like in the case of Saumya who was heavily doubtful about the possibility of combining family commitments with her activist convictions, was experienced as a grave challenge to the feminine self. While working status was felt to be an inalienable part of their individuality, they were aware of the need to coordinate their career growth along with the domestic and maternal responsibilities. They looked forward to the continuing emotional and logistical support of their own mothers in fulfilling them. Disha, for example, in envisaging her mother as also the caretaker of her own children, seemed to be expressing the desire of recreating the home that her mother provided her. This was found to be the case with many other female participants as well. This underlines the emotional and generational continuity between the mother and daughter. Chodorow (1974) states that women's mothering produces socially gendered daughters with particular psychological capacities and object relational stances that are central and definitional to the women's location and responsibility in the domestic sphere. Mothering for women, thus, represents an intricate weave of personal desire and social demand. There is ample evidence to suggest that marriage and maternity represent inert needs of female subjectivity, quite unshattered by the fact that so many women today are not at all content with just being a 'wife' or a 'mother'. This is a potential source of stress for the contemporary young woman who is going beyond the roles performed by her mother in trying to find her place both in home and in society at large. *Striving to realise some essence of her mother who either has been a full-time homemaker or for whom career has been secondary to the family responsibilities, the daughter is likely to experience much conflict and ambivalence in reconciling her desires for individual fulfilment through work (towards which all her education has been directed) and caretaking responsibility in the womanly roles of wife and mother (which are dictated as much by personal desire as by social demand).* Because no longer can a young woman devoted to hardwork and study which has expanded her horizons intellectually, socially and emotionally come to find fulfilment only in children, kitchen and religion.

Looking at instances of young women like Debashri and Aanchal, one also infers how single-minded career orientation in women, often encouraged by the father figure, proves to be disharmonious with the demands and traits required in intimate love relationship. Placed in a highly demanding professional space requiring high levels of competence and initiative in work, these young women displayed a strong stance of privileging an autonomous existence in which they were in control. A high degree of commitment to such a professional identity was conflicting with the demands and responsibilities of relationship and making it difficult for them to access their relational capacities which were sidetracked by the individualistic pursuit of work endeavours.[3] As the earthy, fluid, nurturant maternal presence was relegated to the margins of their identity, these daughters experienced conflicts in making their lives more continuous as carers and workers.

Sujata's life provided a different facet of this conflict. Subjected to gender discrimination in an orthodox patriarchal family set-up dimmed her sense of self-worth as a girl. Away from home, she was living an active, emancipated femininity (buttressed by the feminist ideology) which, given her history of cultural devaluation and self-deprecation of girlhood, was constantly prey to shame and doubt. The mother was experienced as someone who within the conventional womanly role was negotiating with the orthodox patriarchal structure and creating few spaces of autonomy and freedom for herself and her children. The internalised mother while setting her daughter off on a journey of self-discovery also exerts a regressive pull towards tradition, and that creates a schism in one's values. Thus, while challenging the gender roles and opening them for ruthless inquiry, she was also aware of her inner propensities of backsliding and fitting into the conventions as represented by the mother. Stability and certainty that comes with time-worn ways of living are strong psychological needs which conflict with independence and freedom that accompany choice and exploration. Such conflicts were also experienced in the arena of sexual behaviours by Aanchal and Sujata who were experimenting with sexuality within love relationships which may or may not

[3] It is important to note that for both men and women when certain potentials like achievement orientation and competitive motivation etc. are overdeveloped at the cost of others, it might bear fruit in the role of the worker but it creates conflict in the life tasks of intimacy and parenthood. For conjugality and parenthood to loose at least some of its unnecessary forbidding aspects for both sexes, there has an emotional ecology in which there is freer inter-identification between sexes in everyday life. The future of having more whole and complete persons lie in reclaiming and integrating the feminine, the loving-nurturant parts of our psyche with the masculine propensities.

lead to marriage. Battling guilt and anxiety over their sexual activity outside the sanctioned space of matrimony, these women were developing feminine codes which would allow them a freer erotic life without being irresponsible about it.

Thus, one can say that while mothers often encourage their daughters to choose a different way of life from their own (for instance, by insisting on education), they also transmit in an unconscious way the selfsame gender-specific ways of relating to the world and oneself. The daughter's gendered subjectivity becomes a complex experience of negotiating change and constancy, of reconciling the mutual complementation and contradictions of freedom and responsibility, agency and care in her identity as a woman.

The Case of Female Child: Daughters and Father

Psychoanalytic observations have found that the selfsameness between the mother and daughter which creates intense feelings in the mother of the daughter as one with oneself is moderated by the father. The father–daughter bond, as in the case of the son, serves in part to loosen the daughter's primary unity with and dependence on her mother. Thus, the father provides a much needed sense of separateness from the mother to the daughter. He represents to the young girl the abstract world of work and politics, beyond the mother's concrete world of domesticity. In addition to the mother's empathic connection with her, the daughter looks to the father figure(s) for the same confirmation of her specialness that the son receives from his mother (Kakar 1996). The father's solicitous attention and involvement in the girl's activities and her growth are instrumental in securing for her a sense of individual confidence in her unique abilities and talents. The erotic attachment of the girl to her powerful father can be gleaned from the many ways she tries to charm, attract and strive to meet his expectations of a good girl. He is also the one who by his approving look and words can give the growing girl an affirmation of her feminine attractiveness. In the social role of the protector of the girl's chastity, the father guards the daughter against the temptations and opportunities of sexual nature stemming from the world outside the home by monitoring and restricting her activities, attire etc. He himself also tends to withdraw from his daughter at the onset of puberty, feeling that he should no longer exhibit physical closeness lest he himself gets captivated by a sexual desire for her (Nagpal 2000). What follows is disappointment of the girl in her developmental need to receive the acknowledgment of her budding femininity from the opposite sex, the first representative of which is the father and then the boys of her age. For the young girl, it creates the psychosexual difficulty of *how to enjoy intimacy with the father without the undue dread of what the intimacy will lead to.* Only safe psychosexual encounters with the father can save the growing girl from the anguish of being thwarted in her erotic desires either because of a perceived lack of feminine charm or fears of sexual coercion in the intimate relationship with the man.

The image of the father that emerges from the narratives of many female participants is that of an approving and supportive figure who had ambitions for the daughter and affirmed her own aspirations. *The father was often found to be a benevolent sponsor of the girl's education and work, taking personal pride in her achievements and reinforcing her professional identity and their independent thinking.* Rather than distant and aloof, the father–daughter relationship in many instances appeared to be quite involved. From helping the daughter prepare for debating competition, to ferrying her to and fro from dance parties, to engaging in ideological conversations with her, the father was experienced as close and approachable.

The father in few instances was the role model for the daughter. In the lives of Saumya and Debashri, one saw that they learnt from their fathers the lessons of independence, initiative, rationality, living by one's convictions and struggle to build one's life. Shalini's turn towards the spiritual traditions in search of peace and happiness was guided by the presence of her father who had deep philosophical outlook in life. However, his particular spiritual-meditative interests did not satisfy her needs for an ideologically coherent universe in which self-transformation and social change, spiritual strivings and material needs could be reconciled. This forced her to look beyond the identification represented by the father towards the clearer self-definition offered by the philosophy of Jeevan Vidya which was also engaging the enthusiasm of her mother. A different picture seemed to emerge from the life narrative of Sujata. The father along with the other male members of the orthodox family including her elder brother who was the 'son' and thus special, her paternal uncle who was widely known to be a sexual libertine and a vagrant but still accepted by the family and her maternal grandfather whose tales of authoritarianism were narrated by the mother, constituted the oppressive patriarchal force against which she had to contend to protect and preserve some semblance of equality, autonomy and positive self-esteem for herself. Her strong fears of being crushed by the patriarchal norms and institutions were making her evade a conventional marital arrangement. Instead away from home, she was exploring her erotic–sexual side of personality with younger, non-threatening male partner with whom her anxieties about her identity being swamped in heterosexual relationship were taken care of.

Another important facet of the daughter–father relationship that was revealed was the father as the guardian of girl's feminine sexuality. The father expressed disapproval over the girl's dress, behaviour and relationships with boys. The daughter's intermingling with boys was frowned upon. The daughters, through exposure to modern and free environment of education and work where there was constant interaction with males, were going beyond the paternal protectionism and experimenting with freer erotic life. They were forming love attachments but were biding their time to enter marital relationship. The period of doubt and delay can serve to create a psychological awareness in the young woman that the dream of intimacy, both emotional and sexual, with the man verges on violation of one's psychic and bodily boundaries which possibly can ease her difficult struggle of settling into the relatively harsh reality of marital context.

Summation: Images of Mother and Father

In the inner worlds of the male participants, the emotional ties with the mother were found to be deep and close. She was a ubiquitously affectionate and protective presence in their lives, taking care of their daily logistics for as long as they lived with the family. Even when grown up and staying away from home because of education or work, she remained the most reliable source of emotional support and succour, a role that came to be shared by the loved partner in the case of those who had one. In their own turn, the sons knew of their mothers' expectations of success and desirable behaviour from them and strove to meet them in an attempt to keep them happy and satisfied. In the emotional world of the young male participants, coexisting alongside the centrality of the nurturing attachment to the mother were conflictual emotions of being over-regulated, disappointed with maternal love and pressurised for achievement. There were times when they yearned to feel free of the maternal ambit to have their own 'adventures'.

In the case of female participants, the mother's feminine self and family orientation were positively viewed. However, the young women were found to be evolving their own definitions of femininity and womanly role. As well-educated women seeking self-expression and growth in their work-related activities, they were living away from their families, managing independent households and being highly mobile. In their youth phase, these women were showing great degree of individualised functioning in decisions pertaining to matters of educational–-occupational choices, selection of marital partner, nature of social life and experimentation with sexual and erotic intimacy. For them, the psychosocial struggle is about negotiating how gendered they chose to be. Identity of these women sought its enrichment as much from external recognition for their individual efforts in occupational endeavours and meaningfulness about feeling part of a larger group with a sense of shared mission as from relational bonds with primary and new family. The maternal transmission of old-fashioned gender-specific ways of relating with self and world was found to be creating contradictions and conflicts with their active engagement with new aspects of the larger world.

Moving onto the images of father, in the research explorations, the paternal authority was almost never directly found to be challenged by the sons. The father was often an idealised and omnipotent figure for the son, an image supported by the admiration offered by the mother to the father. His felt authority offered direction, structure and organisation to their masculine identity. While wishing to prove worthy in their eyes and reflect well on them, the young men were also subtly differentiating themselves in the realm of work-related attitudes and aspirations and outdoing them in terms of the money they make and consumption needs. They desired greater freedom for and recognition of their individualised way of functioning from the paternal figures.

In the narratives of most female participants, the father appeared to be quite involved in the daughters' lives, encouraging and supporting their decisions and independence. Clinical experience and group discussions with middle-class women suggest that in families where mothers are not career women, a daughter looks up to the father and identifies with him as the representative of the modern, external world. His is the decisive voice that influences her career choice and legitimises her career aspirations.

Daughterhood and Social Change

From the perspective of social change, it can be discerned that the social psychological changes taking place in the daughter's identity are more profound as compared to that of the son. As the middle-class girl grows up, her subjective experience of gender-based discrimination in her family is substantially lesser than her traditional counterpart. They feel themselves to be accepted and cared for by both the parents. In such homes, higher education is welcomed for the daughters so that she can achieve a measure of autonomy. Parents are also supportive of the girls' working status which is seen as contributing to the family's income after marriage and also makes her capable of standing on her own feet if, unfortunately, the marriage breaks down. Professional education for a girl is also seen as standing her in good stead in the marriage market where well-educated men and their families often seek well-qualified girls. More than anything else, education and the social exposure add to her self-esteem and makes her feel more in control of her destiny. Prolonged educational careers and needs of career settlement are leading to late marriages for many women who are career oriented. Middle-class modernity has given young women greater say in the marital decision and made them inclined towards a more companionate marriage, in which her emotional needs and career priorities are taken into account by the husband and she is recognised as a person. *However, modernisation and individualisation in terms of higher education, career orientation and intimacy needs generate considerable conflict with internalised and socially expected traditional attitudes and values around womanhood.* Expectations remain that even when the girl attains higher education and positions of work, she will keep up the traditional familial manners, roles and responsibilities. This brings the assertive and independent identity of the young woman forged over years of education and freedom granted to her in her own house in conflict with the traditional role expectations of deference and subordination from the daughter-in-law and wife.

II

The Changing Complexion of Family in India

It is now a common understanding that 'culture and psyche make each other up' (Shweder 1991). A person's inner make-up, conflicts and aspirations not only reflect the idiosyncrasy of his or her own familial background but also significant aspects of the dominant social and cultural patterns of that society as well as important elements of social change. This section presents aspects of continuity and change in the familial role structure and social interaction patterns in urban India which then also affect the experiential sense of identity of its members.

The Indian family, in its extended form, has been traditionally the source of emotional care, provider of economic support and marker of social position for its members. There is no denying the fact that the institution of family continues to be the social and psychological locus throughout life in the inner landscape of vast majority of Indian people. As the primary agent of socialisation, the psychological importance and power of the familial values, rituals and obligations have been found to cast a long shadow on the emotional lives of the urban youth populace. The research showed that there is a mix of family environments—traditional and orthodox—more demanding of achievement and controlling of sociability, on one hand, and a distinct trend of liberal home atmosphere with greater freedom to children to take decisions in matters that concern them, on the other hand. The majority of young men and women experienced considerable freedom in their families to explore their attributes and capacities and decide on the course of their lives. *The family relationships are stretching to allow for greater consideration of the child's and particularly the adolescents' specific wishes, abilities and inclinations in the educational, occupational and social sphere.* There is a greater recognition amongst the parents that the child may function in a more independent way, thus the personal identity of the growing child is responded to much more. Within the familial matrix of emotional attachments exerting a pull towards maintaining sameness with the internalised parental presence, the youth were able to avail a sense of rightfully delimited autonomy to set individual goals. A few illustrations are in order. Samrat grew up doing what he wanted to do, that is, exercising his guilt-free initiative under the patronage of a liberal father. As the first-generation entrepreneur, he could play for time to arrive at less familiar possibilities which were more attuned to his inner proclivities and true gifts. Jayant kept his parents close to each other and as ever-present images within himself, fuelling his radical activism. However, conflicts over money, social prestige and reach had pushed him to appraise his parents' stances and have his own doubts and opinions about them. He had begun to define his own political space in line with his personal aspirations and understandings of changed historical context of social action. Growing up in a traditional form of family organisation in India, that is, the extended family, Disha used the opportunities of modern education, independent living and being around peers to gain the wider ground available to her outside the home. Whether it was the decision to study engineering or marry a boy of her choice, she selected her own paths and in doing so 'brought her parents up'. They trusted her judgments about her life, and they deferred to her wishes and preferences since she served as their window to the changing social–economic mores. Shalini's spiritual–aesthetic strivings, while borrowing their origins from her father's spiritual leanings and her mother's nurturant capacities, were evolving within the framework of a philosophical darshan of Jeevan Vidya. Her idiom of spirituality as absorbed in the gracious company of much loved and respected gurus meant a continuing involvement with the familial–social relationships as well as efforts directed towards bringing about constructive changes in the patterns of living of people at large. Finding this amiss in her father's way of spiritual practice, she found her own balance in Jeevan Vidya.

Research does indicate that smaller, nuclear families and affluence have permitted Indian middle-class parents to become less authoritarian and more responsive to children (Saraswathi and Pai 1997; Kashyap 1993; Saraswathi and Ganapathy 2002). A study by Kapadia and Miller (2005) of adolescent–parent relationships in nuclear, Hindu, upper middle-class urban families in the context of interpersonal disagreements on scenarios of marriage partner selection and intersex intermingling highlighted the modernising pattern of a family environment that was more conducive to the articulation of individual preferences. The interaction between adolescents and their parents was characterised by responsiveness to the feelings and welfare of all parties involved. In both the scenarios, neither party appeared to want to assert their views on the other. As a result, they tried to mutually accommodate each other's wishes. It was interesting to note that in this study, both parents and adolescents favoured the adolescents' perspective more often in relation to the personally consequential issue of marriage partner selection than in relation to the less serious issue of intersex intermingling. This tendency to defer to the adolescent's wishes reflected the concern that the resolution should bring satisfaction to the children (e.g. 'my children should remain happy, and that is where my happiness lies'), as well as some concern that the children may not accept the parents' view readily so it was better to give in rather than to create unpleasantness. Kapadia and Miller also argue on the basis of their findings that the adolescents welcomed their parents' views on important life decisions and operated from an image of parents' role as that of not only knowing what was best but also as having a responsibility to guide their children. They were trusted to do/advise what was good for the adolescent. Thus accommodation of parents' wishes by adolescents was not indicative of them relinquishing their personal interest in the service of family goals, but a means, through listening to the perceived wisdom and authority of their parents, to promote their own welfare and that of the larger family. Equally, parents' actions were not characterised by an assertion of power over their children but fulfilling their duty as parents to assume the role of active guardians of their children's welfare.

The present research shows that where there were demands of subservience to parental expectations for achievement and conduct beyond personal capacity and preference of the child, little open dialogue, intolerance for difference, control through emotional means and low psychological flexibility in parents to adapt to changing times, the psychological well-being of the young person was compromised. *A heavy emphasis on conformity to parental values and expectations of specific kinds of achievements and conduct often led to reactive rebellion and/or false self-organisation.* Conflicts over initiative found expression in denial or in a self-restriction which kept an individual from living up to one's inner capacities or to powers of one's imagination and feeling. Caught in a matrix of obedience and control, Deepak's life presented an example of how overidentification with the perceived expectations and obligations led to the development of 'false self' in which his imaginative living was heavily compromised at the altar of the narcissistic needs of being regarded well by others. Any act of self-assertion and failure to live up to the standards was perceived as counter to the cultural ideal of a 'good son' and evoked shame and guilt. In the lives of Nirmal and Sujata, one came across rebellion to break free from the tethers of absolute prescriptive role acts imposed on them by family and religion. The cultural institutions of religion and family had become heavily ritualised in which their creative self-impulses were cut off. The parental practice of tradition was not felt as naturally persuasive; rather the harsh decisiveness of paternal judgments led to tortured obediences and resentful feelings. This created ripe conditions for both of them to be highly ambivalent about their heritage. It led to inner fragmentation, feelings of low self-worth and depression.

While the family is still the central institution of Indian society, there have been shifts in the ideologies governing family life and interactions. Nuclear family is increasingly becoming an acceptable and even a desirable form of family structure amongst middle classes. Some form of social and psychological jointness, though, continues to exist in the form of families getting together to celebrate festivals and go on annual vacations. Even amongst joint living conditions, there is greater psychological nuclearisation amongst family units and contraction of obligations towards distant kin. The nuclear family has its disadvantages, but one of its upside is that it has less rigid and flatter hierarchical structures because of the presence of fewer elderly members towards whom deference and loyalty are obligated. This creates greater space for negotiative parent–child relationship to develop in which children can participate more effectively in decision-making process of the family, especially in matters that concern them. Growing up in nuclear households, the youth in research had seen their parents as heads of families, making decisions by themselves and be more self-reliant at least in matters of daily living. It allows a possibility for a more companionate husband–wife relationship where homemaking responsibilities can be more equitably shared and affection can be more openly displayed. The mother in such household is protected from the excesses of the elderly women and restrictions on her behaviours, enlarging her scope of freedom which she may be able to impart to her children. Also, in such set-up, the father's relationship with sons and daughters is also found to be closer, as evidenced in the lives of young participants, than in the joint household where the involvement of the father with his own children is frowned upon since he is supposed to be impartial to all. It is suggested that the early experience of having fathers who are no longer distant and forbidding figures and are emotionally accessible to both sons and daughters will change notions of the desirable power distance in institutions and the expectations that young India will have of its leaders (Kakar and Kakar 2007).

The Indian middle classes have enthusiastically embraced Western style education, the prerequisite of employment and the enterprise culture brought in by the era of multinational companies and the professionally managed Indian companies since the liberalisation in 1991. These have introduced and intensified the structural elements of competition and achievement motivation in the Indian society which run counter to the cultural ideals of cooperation, accommodation and modesty. *So on the one hand, the familial relationships foster needs of interdependency, containment of impulses and effects which can disrupt emotional relatedness and attunement to reciprocal obligations in various hierarchical contexts; on the other hand, the competitively individualistic educational and work environments demand assertiveness, initiative, egalitarianism and autonomous functioning.* These contrasting situations often create psychological conflicts for personal functioning which will then need to find their own resolutions in newer kinds of integrations within identity. Such conflicts have been documented most clearly in the narratives of Deepak and Aasheesh whose familial selves experienced tensions from within because of the unremitting expectations of bringing referred success to their families through their achievements and conduct and from without because of the Western orientation of competitive individualism characterising the work sphere.

The greater availability of global options for leisure, career, consumption and models of intimacy available to the Indian urban elite in today's world has weakened the hold of family-anchored identity. There is much greater psychological freedom available to the youth for upward social mobility and integration in the global consciousness. No longer can they rely only on the customs, traditions, values and lifestyle of their parental figures and caste grouping as the basis of their own lives. This again creates discontinuities between the traditional norms and demands of modern lifestyles. Can a working girl be expected to live up to the same standards of mothering which her stay-at-home mother could fulfil and whether it is even necessary to do so? How can a young man entertaining fantasies of globe-trotting and jet-setting lifestyle deal with restrictions on his aspirations due to the requirements of a dutiful son?

In the current scenario, parental authority is also contending with the power of peer authority. Peer group is emerging as a powerful source of direction for young. The peers are important, not only for keeping up with the external details of clothes, bank balance, food preferences etc. but also in the quality of one's inner experience. They are looked upon for guidance in what experiences to seek and in how to interpret them. They serve as important sources of information, support and companionship to make sense of the world whose signposts are unfamiliar to the parents. Notable examples in this regard are the lives of Disha, Samrat and Nirmal where one sees how the presence of trustworthy peers helped them to reduce reliance on their family for guidance, opened new frontiers of experience and prepared them to face and meet situations that were novel. On the other hand, limited opportunities of social interaction available to Deepak deepened his isolation and feelings of being out of sync with the world. *What is being found is that while the direction of the individual's life is implanted early in life by the family elders, he or she also has to learn to respond to signals from a far wider circle than is constituted by the closely knit unit of family.* The new age value of 'networking' was referred to as important by majority of young people spoken to for research. In today's times, remaining connected to diverse people from different walks of life serves an all-important purpose of remaining informed about the opportunities and developments in the larger world. Also, the relative waning of the power of parents in being the identification model for certain roles and aspects of functioning in today's times has led the young to seek inspiration from people beyond the household—corporate honchos, older colleagues, mythical figures, great personalities of the past and, interestingly, the older peers. The role model of youth in material success was not the older generation. Rather it was their contemporaries or slightly older peers. Students who succeed in getting a good job at a salary their parents could not dream of in turn motivate another batch of youngsters. Many of the participants showed eagerness and involvement in guiding the conduct of the younger members, indicating a trend of subdivision of the stage of young adulthood into older and younger young adults in which the former takes responsibility for the latter. Saumya and Nirmal were seeking to create a more politically informed, self-reflective and socially active youth force, and Samrat wanted to promote entrepreneurship amongst young people and mentor them. This potential of age-specific ethical capacity in older youth, however, needs to be recognised and cultivated by mature adults.

The parents too are in a flux, trying to cope with changing times and dealing with a growing individual who has manifold opportunities of traversing different social groupings and meaning systems, much beyond the home. The older generation understands that times are changing and they need to be changing with times, growing and learning through their own experiences as well as through their children. They are enjoying the many consumerist temptations on offer and acknowledging the importance of technology. In a certain sense, this is a good sign because it means that the parental generation by going under stress of changing times is creating schemas which the children could find relevant and continue in their own time.[4] *Thus, whether the Indian family will be able to continue as a vitalising institution in the inner worlds of the individuals depends on whether it can flexibly give greater scope of freedom to its growing members, support the evolving of inner potentials of all its members beyond the prescriptive roles and responsibilities and, at the same time, 'take care' of what it has created.*

---

[4] The danger lies when confused parenting, unsure of its own inner authority, abdicates too quickly when challenged by the growing individual. The search of youth is not for all permissibility, but rather for new ways of directly facing up to what truly counts. When this search ends, the oscillation between what is right and wrong is stemmed. To clarify the wavering of their own conscience, they must challenge the conscience of the individuals in parental and authoritative positions. This calls for all the firmness that adults can muster; what is at stake is not their professional stature but inner authority. The temper tantrums of the child exemplify the severe test to which the parents' tolerance and disciplining technique are put to. When the response of the confused and impatient parent is to give in—comply—to the demand of the child, it replicates in the personality make-up of the child, a pattern of being unable to tolerate frustration and 'giving in' to his or her impulse. If this pattern of relationship was to extend itself by continuity into the arena of adult living, then the family also becomes a consumption unit where the other becomes an object of manipulation/extraction, for seeking gratification, and not as a counterpart to be cherished in a mutually fulfilling, reciprocal relationship.

III

Conception of the Youth in India: Emerging Trends

It is a dominant belief that adolescence as a distinct phase does not exist in India (Anandlakshmi 1978; Ramanujam 1979). However, this understanding neglects the fact that social adolescence in the form of phase of apprenticeship when the young are trained in the skill and trade of their cultural group exists cross-culturally. Seen in this way, adolescence as a stage of preparation to become full members (economically and sexually active) of the society constitutes part of a longer series of continuous, well-defined stages. The transition from childhood to adulthood is then given full meaning in terms of ultimate cultural values and symbols borne by various adult role models. In agrarian societies, like the traditional India, the ascendancy of youth over old age proceeds smoothly and at the right age because it tallies with the survival needs of the entire family and with the facts of biology. So, it is 'natural' that as the father's vigour declined, a son just reaching the prime of his physical strength and mental abilities should take over. However, in sectors of societies where forces of industrialisation, urbanisation and modernisation hold sway, the age-free criteria of professional skills, political power and economic status begin to dominate and family-kinship groups progressively become less capable of determining individuals' orientations and behaviours by their history and tradition. This brings into light the psychological dimension of the adolescence stage—the normative self-definitional struggle to delineate one's place in the society. Because in such societies, the young person is no longer assured that the dominant position will be its own in a foreseeable and not too distant moment by the logic of natural order of things. Also because the possibilities of lifestyles and action potentials are flexible, diverse and numerous, the youth has to make ever-narrowing selections of vocational, ideological and sexual choices in line with its self-elements cultivated in one's personal history and the ideal prototypes of the day. Youth in urban India is faced with similar psychosocial tasks. Thus, the urban centres of Indian society are witnessing the phenomena of psychological adolescence and its extension into youth which is real and not merely a media artefact.

Both youth and their parents feel that the contemporary world in which the young have to take their place is fast changing and its value orientations and ethos are different from those in the past. Pavan K. Varma in his analysis of Indian middle class (1998) captures the difference between the outlooks of the generations grown up in the socialist times under the policies of 'protectionism' and 'self-reliance' and the current generation growing up in the liberalising India. He opines that a certain placidity of temperament has conventionally been associated with the middle class: the predictable goals, the limited ambitions, the contentment of the humdrum and the routine and the simple certainties of a job, wife and family. The image which the middle class was happy to cultivate about itself was 'We are only middle-class people', conveying a modesty of reach and a resigned acceptance of the parameters of effort and result. Many generations of Indians after independence lived in a world which was congruent with this reality. People were happy with the manageability of their limited wants. There was much less competition, options and choices were fewer, there was an element of continuity even in change, the reference points were fixed and ambitions had a ceiling. However, the new ethos of acquisition, competition and vigorous initiative puts no ceiling on aspirations of good life defined largely by material success. There is a new cultural mindset of 'new possibilities', 'risk taking' and 'can do attitude'. The young have high ambitions of wanting to have more, reach higher and faster. Such attitudes have also been discerned in the research participants, both males and females, more explicitly amongst the corporate youth.

The youth is thrown much more on its own powers to 'make a role' for itself because there is no prescribed role in which it can slip into. A globally linked hi-tech world demands assertiveness, enterprise, independence, creativity and self-renewal and is continuously unfolding, making change and complexity its key features. This has led to individualisation, implying a thrust towards greater consideration of the adolescents' and young adults' wishes and inclinations in a number of areas by the elders, and the imbibing of an ego ideal by youth to be somewhat more independent of familial and community enmeshment (Roland 1988).

As has been noted by other observers of Indian culture and endorsed by the findings of this research, '... a young Indian neither seeks a radical demarcation from the generation of his parents nor feels compelled to overthrow their authority in order to "live life on my own terms".... *In India, it is not the rupture but the stretching of traditional values that becomes a means for the young person to realize his dreams for life' (Kakar and Kakar 2007, p. 15).* Even in the realm of political values, most of the sampled humanist youth, while critiquing the institutions and practices of the society and neoliberal world order, were relatively close to their parents and drew their intellectual strength and support for their ideas of social change from one parent in the family.[5] They were establishing continuity with some aspects of their parental tradition while repudiating, renewing or reforming other aspects of this tradition.

Few Youthful Symbols of Autonomy

While retaining and strengthening emotional connectedness with the family, the Indian youth are found to be seeking out experiences which enhance a sense of 'the individual' who can choose, explore and express freely. *The technological artefacts of capitalist individualism—the iPod, iPhone, iGoogle—are central to the creation of feeling of 'I' self—autonomous, unfettered and self-directed.* Living in a world

[5] This is in line with the findings of Keniston's work (1968) which emphasise the relative solidarity between the political activists and their families and fail to support the popular view that student political activism in general is a form of rebellion against parental values.

full of consumerist temptations, the young have come to cherish a sense of possession: the freedom to purchase and consume without the pretence of any notion of restraint and limitation. Liberalisation, in a certain sense, fostered an exultant and exuberant escape from Gandhi's emphasis on austerity and Nehruvian socialist ideals. It provided the ripe opportunity to make a break from the attitudes and thinking of the past, the moment to bring out into the open desires long held back. Now it was the state policy to 'open' the economy to the objects of desire. Flamboyant consumerism now enjoyed the justification of an ideology. Whether it is a Pulsar bike or a pair of Nike shoes, an MBA degree or a girlfriend, in a consumerist culture, possessions contribute to the individual's definition of identity—not just social but also personal. Individuals use consumption in general and products and brands in particular to define, form and communicate their identities. Through conspicuous consumption, people make some aspects of their own self tangible and more concrete. One's body, clothes, speech, leisure, pastimes, eating and drinking preferences, home and car, choice of holidays etc. are regarded as indications of the individuality of taste and sense of style of the person. Gizmos and gadgets like mobile phone, MP3 player and laptop, of which the young are most enthusiastic users, make it possible for a person to carry his or her world with oneself. Thus, one is 'home' anywhere in the world. The imagery of home as a particular place, physical structure and stable source becomes more fragile. The vast amount of time which Indian adolescents and the youth are spending on internet, blogging, googling and social networking is raising anxieties amongst parents. However, the young who live by the credo of *'I link, therefore I am'* are investing themselves deeply in the online world to escape constraints on their real-life experience, reinvent themselves innovatively in the anonymous virtual world and for sharing self-expression with people across the globe. The home page of a popular social networking site, Facebook, is an instant hit because of its feature of putting up one's status messages 'What's on your mind' for all to see and respond. A sense of being personally adrift is furthered by unparalleled geographical freedom afforded by travel opportunities and access to all kinds of information available at a click of the mouse. Mobility and connectivity are serving as conduit to self-discovery and making the world a global village. Besides, the Indian young are aggressively taking to the world of knowledge. They want to be in step with the spirit of times, learn through exposure to diversity and feel competent, socially and technologically.

The Script of Dream and Desire

The phase of professional education followed by financial independence has been found to be the most individualised phase of functioning for the sample of youth. As they moved away from their homes to study and work in different cities, they could create a psychological distance between self and parents and gain more freedom in thought and action. While someone could 'live one's dreams', for someone else, leaving home meant 'decline of regular study habits'. For many humanist youth, the phase of college was critical in shaping their critique of the social order through their participation in sociopolitical debates and action. Almost everyone concurred that in the casual, stimulating and less structured environment of college, they accessed and gave expression to different aspects of their own personalities which were till now restrained by the demands of academic work on which school and parents stressed. Peer authority replaced parental authority. Far from the watchful eyes of the parents, in their private world of peers and informality, they lived up to their desires and wove their fantasies. *It is this second language of dream and desire where one came across the restive impulses of the youth for excitement, intense feeling, daring adventure, passion—to keep moving—losing and finding oneself anew.*

Deepak's fantasies about being an IITian and his daydreams of becoming an entrepreneur, Nirmal's fears of being a waste and getting stuck in a rut and Krishna's ambitions of 'changing the world through hiring and firing people and [corporate] mergers and acquisitions' spelt their desires for feeling 'moved' and for feeling essential in 'moving' something along an open future. Coming from families in which the restrictive environments created powerful estrangements and divisions within the self, for these young men, such desires offered the exciting challenge of a new reality of choice and initiative and new chance of being reborn as someone with guiltless ambition and competence. Saumya's passionate stance of 'not going to restrain myself and lose out on my experiences, my life, my individuality'; her joy in travelling far and wide, living a life in which she was 'comfortable in A.C. also, in fan also and without fan also'; and her empathic socially responsible actions on behalf of the struggling masses highlight yet another facet of a young woman's sense of active vitality derived from a feeling of inner development and outer momentum. Not only was self the focus of change, but the goal was also to create movement in the outer world, to move others as seen in her efforts of contributing to sociopolitical change. Her youthful restlessness was also harnessed by her passion to travel (a form of geographical dispersion), alternation between lifestyles of upward and downward mobility and a compelling psychological need to identify with the most distant and apparently alien. Shalini's deep sentiments of finding peace and harmony on the discovery of the philosophy of Jeevan Vidya which brought her agitated search for authentic answer to the question of 'how to live' to an end reveal the youth's strenuous and self-conscious efforts at self-transformation, using whatever spiritual, cultural, therapeutic or chemical means are available. Finding inspiration in innovative metaphors describing their endeavours, Jayant and Samrat were applying themselves vigorously to their chosen tasks, courting failures and battling temptations of easier options to test whether they would be crushed or whether they would be able to make a place of their own. When living the life of desire, if the youth experienced estrangement, absurdity and disconnection from the interpersonal and social world, they also secretly harboured the opposite feeling of omnipotentiality—the sensation of absolute freedom, of living in a world of pure possibilities and of being able to achieve or change anything.

The two fascinating images which have been found by the research to be emerging on the horizons of social imagination of corporate and humanist youth are Entrepreneurship and Activism, respectively. These two images held them in ambivalent thraldom, evoking a mix of fear and wish, many of them imagining, testing, questioning and withdrawing themselves vis-à-vis them. Probably these roles exploit the enthusiasm of the young because they hold out the promise of challenging work with a meaningful ideology attached with them. They encompass the invigorating vision of changing the world, of making an impact and of being a part of something vital that is bigger than oneself. While entrepreneurship is projected as the driver of economic growth, activism is needed to bring about the much needed reorganisation of existing society. The anticipated pleasure and satisfaction in taking meaningful action in line with one's core beliefs is behind the fascination that society caught in mundane existence feels towards them. The fact that these choices are not about big money and immediate returns, the normative motivations, but a chance to act on one's own fervour, to be where one is needed and to prove how well one does there, keeps them in the shadowy realm of creative deviancy.

Besides work conquests, love and romance also dominated the conscious and unconscious fantasies of the youth. Urges to experience the freshness and spontaneity of love free of all social restrictions and internal prohibitions were acutely felt by young people. One of the participants, Nikhil (his narrative could not be included due to paucity of space), was particularly evocative about his wish to fall in love. A 24-year-old commerce graduate, studying to become a chartered accountant, Nikhil spoke with a deep sense of longing, betraying a hint of desperation, for a romantic partner. In his words, 'Life needs some pleasure, happiness. You can't be happy by yourself. You need someone to be happy with, enjoy your life with. For how long can you keep studying, following a routine? It's so so boring. You need love to spice it! If I had a girlfriend, I would have had fun. It's a different feeling, you know... just to hold hands with someone while watching a film, go out in the rain, to talk to when low. Then you feel that you are "living" life. ... Even the fights and disagreements are interesting. One of my friends was telling me how he made up with his girlfriend after a fight. He sent her many many smses, she didn't reply. Called her many times, she would just disconnect them. He got really scared! He thought probably it's over. He tried waiting... you know... the usual mind games that people play... thinking that she will contact. When she eventually did after 3 days, he was on cloud 9. You should have seen his face! So they got back together and had their own little party. It was so nice... the fear, panic, wait, relief, happiness, sadness... that's what is living, right! Not these books and exams and job and failures and successes (he signs off sadly)'. Love often serves as a psychic loosener, jarring the soul out of the narcissistic sheath of normal, everyday, self-limiting routines. In India, close proximity between sexes is frowned upon even in urban modern cities. Even in research, one found parental restrictions placed on interaction amongst boys and girls fearing that it would take away their focus from studies and dilute their career orientation. For the girls, greater circumspection about her dress and relationships with boys is advised by the society because this is supposed to affect the girl's and her family's reputation as well as her marriageability. *Thus, dream of love in such context is a subversion of the accepted mores prescribing the relations between the sexes. It is also a way of circumventing the relentless demands of concrete reality requiring separateness which conflicts with the urge to merge and be one with the beloved. In a deeply hierarchical society where class and caste barriers are strong, the desire for love is a challenge to the family obligations and keepers of traditions.*

Sentiments of feeling alive and enthralled with the entry of an erotic feeling towards a girl who in many ways was felt as different and thus attractive were heard from Krishna and Deepak. She represented not merely a source of pleasure but also signified a conglomerate of precious attributes which struck them with awe. For highly introverted young men living thus far restrictive and dull emotional lives focused too exclusively on concrete work goals and ambitions, the talkative, carefree and active girl served as a complement—completing the desired coupling. Both of them indicated a freeing of ambitions and an urge to go beyond what they have been doing so as to impress and take care of the needs of the loved female partner which is suggestive of elaboration of masculinity in them. Falling in love during adolescence brings to fore a remarkable ascendancy in masculine or feminine traits. This shift signifies that sex alien tendencies have been conceded to the other sex and thus can be shared in the mutual belonging of the partners to each other. With the stabilisation of sexual identity, there is elaboration of ego interests and attitudes consonant with sexual identity (Blos 1962). A similar shift taking place towards feminine responsiveness and responsibility in interpersonal relationships due to erotic intimacy with her boyfriend was seen in Aanchal's life history. The direction of emotional development towards the formation of heterosexual, extrafamilial, non-ambivalent object relations during young adulthood is an important step in the individuation of an individual. It may be said that through emotional and physical intimacy with the loved other, the young adult creates an emotional constellation with the help of which he or she can hope to re-establish oneself in a new family.

Co-educational opportunities in school and college allow for freer intermingling between sexes. The choice of love object and the nature of attachments thus formed are influenced by the dynamics of relationship shared with one's parents which over a period of time under benign and favourable conditions become progressively differentiated and, within certain limits, may stabilise reciprocally in partnerships. Another participant, a freelance media activist (his narrative could not be included due to paucity of space) imprinted his first heterosexual relationship with deep yearnings for the protective, pre-Oedipal mother and for the bliss of oneness with her. He recalled: 'I wanted her [the girlfriend] to feel exactly as I do, always; and to be with me, whenever I need her. In fact, in college I wanted to just be with her, roam around with her. I would ask her to miss classes and come for a movie with me. Nothing else mattered except for her. Without her, I used to feel completely lost. When she went to US for her vacations, I completely lost it. I would drink myself to sleep. I would keep asking her to come online and chat with me, call me. She wanted to go abroad and work. I had thought that I would go with her. She would work and I'll do my PhD or something, be with her and have a comfortable life'. In this case, one can discern a passive dependency in the adolescent phase of this young man, wanting to be the object of nurturing care, intolerant of separation and difference. In the case of Sujata, her very first heterosexual relationship lasting for 8 months with an Irish guy whom she mockingly described as a 'conservative bastard' saw her unconsciously repeating the pattern of male dominance and female submission. Given her history of having to contend with the strong patriarchal values at home and being made to feel devalued as a female, it comes as no surprise that the first relationship was a recreation of patriarchal gender relations witnessed in and internalised from home environment. In Sujata, one noticed a tendency to get influenced by her boyfriends. She considered herself rather naïve, and two of her later boyfriends had been younger, but she found them much more worldly wise and admitted to having 'grown' in their company. It is suggested that these types of love relationships were helping her leverage out of the family nexus. The choice of younger, non-threatening male partner, took care of her fears of being crushed by them (impressions of male authority that she carried from her experience of male figures in family) and at the same time offered her the opportunity to explore her erotic–sexual side of personality that had been so severely kept in check by the father through restrictions on dress, conduct and mobility. In many such relationships, the boyfriend comes to acquire the meaning of surrogate parent, and the self-identity of the girl gets centred on what the boyfriend expects and want of her, all within the illusion of choice.

The above discussion indicates that many social changes in India are taking place vis-à-vis the life stage of youth. Prolonged academic lives, late marriages, impetuous and free spirit of youth culture, importance of extrafamilial ties, dream of love and desires of self-expressive and individualised functioning and consumerist supports for the same are the psychosocial aspects of contemporary young India.

IV

Kaleidoscope of Youth Identities

Young India is often spoken of derogatorily as status quoists, furthering the twin objectives of self-interest and material well-being along well-worn career paths and patterns of social living. Not only are the youth seen as apathetic and naïve towards problems of poverty, social injustice and ecological degradation that surround them, but also found to be unexcited about innovative ideas and social change. While they are creating quite a splash as consumers, they do not seem to be generating equivalent optimism in the public and political life of the country. Through an exploration of the orientations of young towards competition, materialism, dissent, democracy, social responsibility and power, the present research has attempted to respond to the popular perception that the Indian youth are conformist, alienated from social realities and living for immediate returns on traditional goals of status and power to the exclusion of the pursuit of knowledge and creativity. It has also reflected on psychodynamic dimensions of identity and psychological characteristics of growth environment of diverse sections of urban Indian youth.

The two sectional discussions on identity patterns of corporate and humanist youth have attempted to provide a differentiated picture of identity potentials within these two groups of young people. The life stories of the *corporate youth* reflected that a large majority of such youth felt sufficiently engaged by the vision of infinite progress projected by the liberalisation–privatisation–globalisation (LPG) model of growth based on ever-increasing cycles of production and consumption. *The LPG model can be understood not only in economic and political terms, but it has deep psychological implications as well.* For the new India, liberalisation has meant release of consumerist and hedonist desires which were kept in check by the scarcity economy of the socialist past. Promotion of private enterprise signifies encouragement of individual initiative and a sense of dissociation of personal from the political. Globalisation has resulted in greater access to diverse lifestyle options available internationally and has weakened the hold of family-anchored identity. By dint of its very practicality (the fact that 'it works'), the dominant world view of free market capitalist model of development provides a sense of inspired activity to those finding their niche within it and helps to bring to ascendance certain psychological qualities, social institutions and cultural values that aid the goal of materialist and technological expansion. The research narratives exemplified that psychological qualities of self-discipline, hardwork, productivity, competitive achievement orientation, rationality, pragmatism and emotional neutrality have been precociously expected of such young persons in the contexts of home, education and work. The early demands of performance and narrowly defined futuristic goals internalised by them led to the limitation of their identity and consolidation of identity needs around their technical and occupational capacities. Many of them were going along with their parents in a kind of fraternal identification, pursuing the age-old motivations of upward mobility, career success, social prestige, money and family togetherness. They were harbouring ambitions along well-worn paths, acquiring skills and credentials which would help them profit from current arrangements of power. Socialisation through family and education to make use of the opportunity structure offered by the globalising–liberalising economy gave them little opportunity to engage in systematic critical analysis of society, economy and politics. To do that would rock the boat and would challenge their normalised perspectives. The expectations of stable career progression as an index of personal success and family pride precluded the possibility of looking beyond the security of a regular pay cheque and taking chances with their creative urges. It was seen that their diversity of selfhood was often sacrificed to favour a standardised range of functioning in which other vital domains of existence such as relationality, play and citizenship were estranged. Identity then lost its essential wholeness which could have fruitfully held together self-interest and social awareness, focus and fun. While assimilation into the in-demand trend of workmanship provided the youth with the optimum combination of free choice, peer solidarity and compliance, it also put on them constant pressure to perform and compete with contemporaries.

In a competitive world, the self-worth of an individual is dependent on how well he or she compares with others which keeps bringing forth self-conscious doubt about 'how good one is' and a sense of shame over one's inadequacies and failures. In many lives studied within the purview of research, it was witnessed that a self-image of an achiever and 'better than the best' projected on the outside hid behind itself insecure, vulnerable, underachieving self-parts. A false self then takes shape with a divided self-image. The ideology of competitive individualism that characterises the business world of profit builds a sense of private interiority that is disconnected from cultural–historical context. Also frantic attempts to consolidate one's own position vis-à-vis the competitors leave little scope for an ethic of cooperation and collectivity for common good to develop. Rather they separate the self from others in a vertical fashion and feed a sense of exclusive identity which collects within itself all what is perceived as the superior, the best and the successful within an absolute boundary. What was found as an identity trend amongst many corporate youth was a turn away from the broader social scene towards more manageable and controllable private experience and personal commitment. While urges to do something for the society and the deprived were experienced by them, they were overcome by more pressing concerns of one's personal life. The lack of inner questioning, critical deliberation and affirmative social action noticed in these youth could be attributed to their low understanding of socio-economic inequality and political disadvantages faced by large sections of society and an even lesser knowledge of ways and means to engage in social dialogue and action. What was also found was that while the public life of corporate youth was characterised by drive, ambition and sharp eye for opportunity in order to continuously better one's station in life, their private lives were marked by an effort to find excitement and fulfilment beyond performance. They searched to find themselves in friendships, love, music, arts, sports, poetry, blogging etc. This was the underside of the conforming youth who were seeking individuality in a prescriptive culture that demands conformity with the middle-class vocational values and outlooks and standardisation of aspirations. As discussed in Section III of this chapter, there is a covert struggle amongst the Indian middle-class youth to wrest freedom and autonomy from the heavy scaffolding of tradition and structuring of futures. *Erikson (1968) notes that such youth tend to manage the identity confusion of free market democracy created by the recognition of narrowness of role, limited status, enforced sacrifices, institutionalised inequalities and built-in contradictions with 'simple trustfulness, playful dissonance, technical virtuosity, "other minded" solidarity – and a distaste for ideological explicitness'* (p. 165).

The *humanist youth* represent a section of young people who maintain a critical, sceptical distance from the system, are disposed towards taking a visible stand against injustice and oppression and hope to change specific sectors of society so that they will no longer be so outrageous. Their identity-seeking outlook leads them towards sociopolitical activism and/or new forms of communal life and collective action outside of the traditional political life. Through sociopolitical work, radical readings, reflective conversations and transformative exposure to strange and unfamiliar realities, these youth had begun to question the sedimented ways of understanding the world. Their life stories revealed that the 'establishment options' were open to all of these people who had been successful, intelligent and capable students. But during college years or sometimes after, they seemed to have reached a point where the mainstream vocational options became non-meaningful for them and they began to explore alternative courses of action: sociopolitical and spiritual. Rather than treating the phase of higher education solely as a period of apprenticeship for preparation for entry in professional market, they used it for building critical perspectives on the existing society and exploring causes and collectives that they could offer their loyalties and energies to. Most narratives of such young persons converged on an image of family which emphasised on academic attainment but also gave them considerable freedom and support to explore their talents, engage with social issues and express their thoughts and convictions, even the unconventional ones. Most of them had not personally experienced poverty, discrimination, exploitation or oppression, but they were participating in the struggles and sufferings of those who were disadvantaged and deprived. They saw the existing society in need for reform and were bringing to light the critical issues facing the life on planet such as alleviation of poverty, political inclusion and empowerment of marginalised sections and ecological destruction which are often sidelined by the power structures because of narrow self-interest and other political, religious and economic considerations. They stood for democracy, deepening aims of public debates, participative decision-making, collective action and securing economic, social, political rights, privileges and opportunities to all the citizens. Most of them were opposed to the exclusive privileging of the materialist side of human beings and stood for bringing back into the centre of political, cultural and economic reality a deeper engagement with those aspects of human beings' role on this planet that further social justice and a recognition that we are an integral part of the natural world. Their engagement was with values of interdependence, of responsibility, of ethical and moral life, as well as a deeper striving for equity and dignity. In them was witnessed a process of democratisation of self which meant nourishing intrasubjective and intersubjective sensitivities and sensibilities such as dialoguing with differences and building symmetrical relations of power between selfsame and others. The identity trend in such youth was not towards building an exclusive identity that allows affiliations only with those with whom it is similar, as in the case of corporate youth, but towards human inclusiveness in which each one 'counts'. In throwing their lot in the movements directed towards helping others gain a voice, name and face, they were breaking out of their own smug middle-class tendencies of 'delineating oneself by declaring the others as basically dangerous and, therefore, to be ignored if distant enough, to be demeaned when too visible, and to be attacked when threatening to encroach' (Erikson 1977, p. 57) Such youth provides the much needed bulwark against a unidimensional description and popular understanding of young India as socially apathetic.

V

Directions for a Wholesome Identity: A Way Ahead

A society like India which upholds tradition-backed stability often stifles imagination-backed initiative and exerts strong pull towards maintaining psychological status quo around prescriptive role acts and hierarchies. When in the name of guidance and protection, the representatives of adult generation impose pedantic constraints on the imagination and initiative of the growing child; he or she learns to constrict himself or herself to the point of over-all inhibition, building deep and lasting resentments against the arbitrary power of the patronising authority. For the creation of a wholesome identity in coming generations, healthy individualism needs to be promoted in youth. A spirit of inventiveness and imagination should be encouraged so that young can learn by playing—what one must do by doing what one likes to do. Also, the intergenerational relationships should be democratic so that a healthy companionship can develop between young and old. This much needed companionship holds out the possibility of keeping the hidden hatreds and envy between generations within limits and setting free the purposeful initiative of the young in the direction of futures which are not only permissible but also possible and tangible. A new ethic needs to be inculcated in the coming generations that will reconcile the efficiency and individualism of free market with fairness and concern for the larger community.

The research suggests that '*play*' is critical to human growth. In order to help the growing individual develop his or her identity in a wholesome manner, its age-specific ability to play has to be released. *Play has the quality of a free activity—self-chosen, absorbing the person intensely and utterly, offering the thrill of creation and discovery that kills monotony and conformism and allowing anxiety-free release of fantasy and fear*. It is indeed in the play stage of human development that the child who now has greatly enhanced locomotor and language skills 'seems to be more activated and activating... approach new areas that seem desirable, even if they also seem dangerous, with undiminished zest and some increased sense of direction' (Erikson 1968, p. 115). It is this stage from which the child must emerge with a sense of purpose as a basis for a realistic sense of ambition and initiative. Each generation has to create its own sense of purposefulness in its way of life. Especially in a modernising society like India, the individual cannot replicate the lifestyles of the previous generation. The young have to deal with the contradictions of 'traditional' and 'modern', 'family culture' and 'peer culture', 'old values' and 'new ideals' throughout their socialisation which often create inner conflicts in them. Thus, the youth are entitled to doubt and delay in order to synthesise their diverse identifications in some coherent whole in their own historical time. In youth, play which takes the form of exploiting the opportunities for doubt and delay, experimenting with activities and subjectivities beyond the established modes of meeting life situations and, taking chances with one's own feelings, thoughts and fantasies must be encouraged. As the age group which is most eager and enthusiastic about experimenting with whatever is 'new and exciting', they are constantly making and remaking futures: personal and socio-historical. The socialisation, thus, has to provide inputs for healthy individualism. For healthy individualism, like devoted deviancy, contains indignation in the service of a wholeness, without which psychosocial evolution will be doomed. As active social agents, the youth should be understood in their own right, in terms of their own needs, desires and capacities. They should be granted opportunities to engage in voluntary and non-obligatory activities which allow the youth to test themselves, to discover their capacities of character and personality which demand testing and definition. Young must be offered opportunities to participate in decision-making in family/collective affairs. Such repeated chances at representative membership which promotes personal responsiveness and responsibility of the individual in choice and action will go a long way in developing an attitude that thinking on one's own is not an act of subversion, an unproductive deviationism, but the beginning of a voyage of creation and discovery. Similarly, the ethos of educational system has to go beyond the culture of ritualistic conformity and obedience. New perspectives, latest trends and infrastructural facilities have to be made accessible to allow the students to explore new options and find their own kind of work interests. For instance, it has been found that technology incubation facilities that have sprung up in many engineering and management institutions across country are nurturing the entrepreneurial proclivities of many young people. Such infrastructural supports are needed to channelise youthful exuberance towards causes that defy the safety of time-worn vocations and secure income. Educational environments should be the breeding ground for development of creative thought and action in research, social critique and nation building rather than reproduction of set ideas and practices.

The intergenerational relationships should be such that young and old alike can open out to encounter and dialogue with differences, widen sensibilities and hold conflictual and plural subjectivities—the prerequisites of becoming a global citizen. In a changing world, the adult authority is under unprecedented challenge. The adults are caught between the urge to become peers of their children, alternatively to wilfully insist on continuation of one's own ways of living through their children. Both are dangerous trends because both prevent the youth from coming into their own. The youth cannot test their own worth, their own strength and vitality, the very things they feel most dubious about, when all they can push against is a vacuum, or an adult society more than ready to give way, to act more youthful than what even befits youth. Similarly, when the older generation refuses to make place for the coming generation and does not allow it the pleasures of transgression and make their own mistakes, the youth feels caught in a matrix of control and obedience and unable to replace the adult authority with one's own. The development of age-specific ethical potential in spheres of sexuality, intimacy, work or pastimes in a new generation is dependent on the generative capability of the representatives of older generation to meet the former's questions and concerns with clarity and conviction gained from the dignity of one's life. The inbuilt ambivalence between generations cannot be wished away and must be borne. The young will always, covertly and overtly, mock and flout the traditions of the previous generation, at the same time, secretly and unwittingly repeat elements of it in their own times. The old in the hidden recesses of their psyche will be aware of the historical relativity of their lifestyle but also wish to offer something more lasting to the coming generations. It is precisely this interplay of generations that ensures companionship between the parent and child and an experience of essential equality in worth, in spite of the inequality of developmental schedule.

Unless a nation and a society produce citizens who care and not merely consumers who want, there cannot be a politically stable or economically resilient basis for progress and prosperity. In a country like India where squalor of poverty coexists with world class affluence, youth should be initiated by inspiring figures in business, politics, academia and social sector in debating ethical issues like: *Can expansion mean only technological and commercial development or also an opening out of the boundaries of one's identity to include within oneself an active concern and action for the superficially alien—the deprived and the deformed? Can emancipation imply not only consumerist salvation but also freedom from irrational hatreds and prejudices that create divisions amongst human beings? Should not a mature democracy offer to its citizens a workable identity in which scientificity and economic progress are balanced alongside humane and ethical virtues? Should consumption be not only about freedom of spending but also include an active concern about the ethics, aesthetics and ecology of consumption?* Young India with such a new psychological and ethical orientation can constructively affect the history of its times.

References

Adams, G. R., & Marshall, S. K. (1996). A developmental social psychology of identity: Understanding the person-in-context. *Journal of Adolescence, 19*, 429–442.
Anandlakshmi. (1978). *Socialization for competence.* Delhi: Indian Council for Social Science Research.
Arnett, J. J. (1997). Young people's conceptions of the transition to adulthood. *Youth and Society, 29*, 1–23.
Arnett, J. J. (1998). Learning to stand alone: The contemporary American transition to adulthood in cultural and historical context. *Human Development, 41*, 295–315.
Arnett, J. J. (2001). *Conceptions of the transition to adulthood from adolescence through midlife.* Manuscript submitted for publication. *Journal of Adult Development, 8*(2), 133–143.
Arnett, J. J., & Taber, S. (1994). Adolescence terminable and interminable: When does adolescence end? *Journal of Youth and Adolescence, 23*, 517–537.
Blos, P. (1962). *On adolescence*. New York: Free Press.
Bose, G. (1956). The genesis and adjustment of the Oedipal wish. In T. G. Vaidyanathan & J. J. Kripal (Eds.), *Vishnu on Freud's desk: A reader in psychoanalysis and Hinduism* (pp. 21–38). Delhi: Oxford University Press, 1999.
Bose, A. (2009, September 24). *Why I became disillusioned with the revolution?* Retrieved October 10, 2009, from http://epaper.mailtoday.in
Cartwright, D. (2004). The psychoanalytic research interview: Preliminary suggestion. *Journal of American Psychoanalytic Association, 52*, 209–242.
Chodorow, N. (1974). Family structure and feminine personality. In M. Z. Rosaldo & L. Lamphere (Eds.), *Woman, culture and society* (pp. 43–66). Stanford: Stanford University Press.
Chodorow, N. (1978). *The reproduction of mothering: Psychoanalysis and the sociology of gender*. Berkeley: University of California Press.
Cote, J. E., & Allahar, A. L. (1994). *Generation on hold: Coming of age in the late twentieth century*. New York: New York University Press.
Courtright, P. B. (1985). Fathers and sons. In T. G. Vaidyanathan & J. J. Kripal (Eds.), *Vishnu on Freud's desk: A reader in psychoanalysis and Hinduism* (pp. 137–146). Delhi: Oxford University Press, 1999.
Dagnino, E. (2008). Challenges to participation, citizenship and democracy: Perverse confluence and displacement of meanings. In A. J. Bebbington, S. Hickey, & D. C. Mitlin (Eds.), *Can NGOs make a difference? The challenge of development alternatives* (pp. 55–70). London: Zed Books.
Deb, S. (2004). *The story of a remarkable Indian institution and how its alumni are reshaping the world.* Delhi: Penguin Books.
Doughlas, J. (1970). *Deviance and respectability*. New York: Basic Books.
Douvan, E., & Adelson, J. (1966). *The adolescent experience*. New York: Wiley.

P. Bansal, *Youth in Contemporary India: Images of Identity and Social Change*,
DOI 10.1007/978-81-322-0715-3, © Springer India 2013

Erikson, E. H. (1950). *Childhood and society*. New York: W.W. Norton.
Erikson, E. H. (1958). *Young man Luther*. New York: W.W. Norton.
Erikson, E. H. (1964). *Insight and responsibility: Lectures on the ethical implications of psychoanalytic insight*. London: Faber and Faber.
Erikson, E. H. (1968). *Identity: Youth and crisis*. New York: W.W. Norton.
Erikson, E. H. (1969). *Gandhi's truth: The origins of militant non-violence*. New York: W.W. Norton.
Erikson, E. H. (1974). *Dimensions of a new identity*. New York: Norton.
Erikson, E. H. (1975). *Life history and the historical moment*. New York: W.W. Norton.
Erikson, E. H. (1977). *Toys and Reason. Stages in the Ritualization of Experience*. New York: W.W. Norton & Co., Inc.
Erikson, E. H. (1979). Report to Vikram: Further perspectives on the life cycle. In S. Kakar (Ed.), *Identity and adulthood* (pp. 13–36). Delhi: Oxford University Press.
Fountain, G. (1961). Adolescent into adult: An inquiry. *Journal of the American Psychoanalytic Association, 9*, 417–433.
Freud, S. (1927). The future of an illusion. In *Standard edition of complete psychological works of Sigmund Freud* (J. Stratchey, Trans., Vol. 21, pp.1–58). London: Hogarth Press (1968).
Freud, A. (1958). Adolescence. *Psychoanalytic study of the child, 16*, 225–278.
Fromm, E. (1947). *Man for himself: An inquiry into the psychology of ethics*. New York: Rinehart and Company.
Josselson, R. (1980). Ego development in adolescence. In J. Adelson (Ed.), *Handbook of adolescent psychology* (pp. 188–210). New York: Wiley.
Josselson, R. (1987). *Identity diffusions: A long term follow up. Adolescent psychiatry* (Vol. XIV). Chicago: University of Chicago Press.
Josselson, R. (1988). *Finding herself: Pathways of identity development in women*. New York: Jossey-Bass.
Josselson, R. (1996). *Revising herself: The story of women's identity from college to midlife*. New York: Oxford University Press.
Kagitcibasi, C. (1996). The autonomous-relational self: A new synthesis. *European Psychologists, 1*(3), 180–186.
Kakar, S. (1981). *The inner world: A psychoanalytic study of childhood and society in India*. Delhi: Oxford University Press.
Kakar, S. (1982). *Shamans, mystics and doctors*. Delhi: Oxford University Press.
Kakar, S. (1990). *Intimate relations: Exploring Indian sexuality*. Harmondsworth: Penguin Books.
Kakar, S. (1996). Modernity and female childhood. In S. Kakar (Ed.), *Culture and Psyche: Selected essays* (pp. 24–28). Delhi: Oxford University Press.
Kakar, S., & Kakar, K. (2007). *The Indians: Portrait of a people*. Delhi: Penguin-Viking.
Kanter, R. (1993). Becoming a situated daughter. In J. Mens-Verhulst, K. Scheurs, & L. Woertman (Eds.), *Daughtering and mothering* (pp. 26–35). London: Routledge.
Kapadia, S., & Miller, J. (2005). Parent-adolescent relationships in the context of interpersonal disagreements: View from a collectivist culture. *Psychology in Developing Societies, 17*(1), 33–50.
Kashyap, L. D. (1993). Adolescent/youth family dynamics and development programmes. *Indian Journal of Social Work, 54*, 94–107.
Keniston, K. (1968). Why students become radicals? *Journal of American College Health Association, 17*(2), 107–118.
Keniston, K. (1971). *Youth and dissent: The rise of a new opposition*. New York: Harcourt Brace Jovanovich, Inc.
Kohut, H. (1971). *The analysis of self*. New York: International Universities Press.
Lifton, R. J. (1993). *The protean self: Human resilience in an age of fragmentation*. New York: Basic Books.
Mahler, M. S., Pine, F., & Bergman, A. (1975). *The psychological birth of the human infant: Symbiosis and individuation*. New York: Basic Books.

Marcia, J. E. (1966). Development and validation of ego identity status. *Journal of Personality and Social Psychology, 3*, 551–558.

Moller, H. (1968). Youth as a force in the modern world. *Comparative Studies of Society and History, X*, 237–260.

Nagpal, A. (2000). Cultural continuity and change in Kakar's works: Some reflections. *International Journal of Group Tension, 29*(3/4), 285–322.

Nandy, A. (1995). *Alternative sciences: Creativity and authenticity in two Indian scientists*. Delhi: Oxford University Press.

Nandy, A. (1998). *Exiled at home*. New York: Oxford University Press.

Nandy, A., Trivedi, S., Mayaram, S., & Yagnik, A. (1997). *Creating a nationality: The Ramjanmabhumi movement and fear of the self.* Delhi: Oxford University Press.

Obeyesekere, G. (1990). Further steps in relativization: The Indian Oedipus revisited. In T. G. Vaidyanathan & J. J. Kripal (Eds.), *Vishnu on Freud's desk: A reader in psychoanalysis and Hinduism* (pp. 147–162). Delhi: Oxford University Press, 1999.

Offer, D., Ostrov, E., & Howard, K. I. (1981). *The adolescent: A psychological self portrait*. New York: Basic Books.

Phillips, A. (1994). *On flirtation*. Cambridge: Harvard University Press.

Ramanujam, B. K. (1979). Towards maturity: Problems of identity seen in the Indian clinical setting. In S. Kakar (Ed.), *Identity and adulthood* (pp. 37–55). Delhi: Oxford University Press.

Ramanujam, A. K. (1983). The Indian Oedipus. In T. G. Vaidyanathan & J. J. Kripal (Eds.), *Vishnu on Freud's desk: A reader in psychoanalysis and Hinduism* (pp. 109–136). Delhi: Oxford University Press, 1999.

Rindfuss, R. R. (1991). The young adult years: Diversity, structural change and fertility. *Demography, 28*, 493–512.

Roland, A. (1988). *In search of self in India and Japan: Towards a cross-cultural psychology*. Princeton: Princeton University Press.

Roland, A. (1996). *Cultural pluralism and psychoanalysis: The Asian and North American experience*. New York: Routledge.

Ryan, R. M. (1993). Agency and organization: Intrinsic motivation, autonomy and the self in psychological development. In R. Diestbier & J. E. Jacobs (Eds.), *Nebraska symposium on motivation: Developmental perspectives on motivation* (Vol. 40, pp. 1–56). Lincoln: University of Nebraska Press.

Ryan, R. M., & Deci, E. L. (2000). Self determination theory and the facilitation of intrinsic motivation, social development, and well being. *American Psychologist, 55*, 68–78.

Saraswathi, T. S., & Ganapathy, H. (2002). The Hindu worldview of child and human development: Reflections in contemporary parental ethnotheories. In H. Keller, Y. Poortinga, & A. Scholmerich (Eds.), *Between biology and culture: Perspectives on ontogenetic development* (pp. 80–88). London: Cambridge University Press.

Saraswathi, T. S., & Pai, S. (1997). Socialization in Indian context. In H. Rao & D. Sinha (Eds.), *Asian perspectives in psychology* (pp. 74–92). Delhi: Sage.

Sartre, J. P. (1965). *Nausea*. Harmondsworth: Penguin.

Sen, S. (1993). Defining the nonprofit sector: India. In L. M. Salamon & H. K. Anheier (Eds.), *Working papers of the John Hopkins comparative nonprofit sector project, No. 12*. The John Hopkins Institute for Policy Studies: Baltimore.

Shweder, R. (1991). *Thinking through cultures: Expeditions in cultural psychology*. Cambridge, MA: Harvard University Press.

Spence, D. P. (1982). *Narrative truth and historical truth: Meaning and interpretation in psychoanalysis*. New York: Norton.

Varma, P. K. (1998). *The great Indian middle class*. Delhi: Penguin-Viking.

Winnicott, D. W. (1971). *Playing and reality*. London: Routledge.

Index

P. Bansal, *Youth in Contemporary India: Images of Identity and Social Change*,
DOI 10.1007/978-81-322-0715-3, © Springer India 2013

MIX
Papier aus verantwortungsvollen Quellen
Paper from responsible sources
FSC® C105338

If you have any concerns about our products,
you can contact us on
ProductSafety@springernature.com

In case Publisher is established outside the EU,
the EU authorized representative is:
Springer Nature Customer Service Center GmbH
Europaplatz 3, 69115 Heidelberg, Germany

Printed by Libri Plureos GmbH
in Hamburg, Germany